A HISTORY
OF THE
JEWISH
EXPERIENCE

A
JEWISH

HISTORY OF THE EXPERIENCE

BOOK ONE
Torah and History

BOOK TWO
*Torah, Mitzvot, and
Jewish Thought*

LEO TREPP

BEHRMAN HOUSE, INC.

Copyright © 2001 by Behrman House, Inc.
Springfield, New Jersey
www.behrmanhouse.com

Manufactured in the United States of America

Project editor, Jeannette Morgenroth, Ph.D.
Editorial assistant, Clifford Green
Design and composition by Juanita Dix

Library of Congress Cataloging-in-Publication Data

Trepp, Leo.
  A history of the Jewish experience : book 1, Torah and history;
  book 2, Torah, mitzvot and Jewish thought / Leo Trepp.—
  [Rev. and updated ed.].
      p. cm.
  Includes bibliographical references.
    ISBN 0-87441-672-8
    1. Judaism—History. 2. Judaism—Customs and practices.
I. Title.

BM155.2.T7 2000
296—dc21   00-028933

This work is dedicated as a loving memorial to

Miriam Trepp

(1916 – 1999)

by her husband, the author,

her daughter, Susan Lachman,

with husband Mark,

her grandchildren, David Greenberg,

Amy Greenberg, and David Lachman.

———————

May her soul be bound up in the bond of life,

Her memory be an abiding blessing.

CONTENTS

BOOK TWO
Torah, Mitzvot, and Jewish Thought

PREFACE

This "old" book is also a new book. Its previous editions have been a guide, teaching text, and reference to Jews and Christians. I have been encouraged by the widespread opinion that it is a good, simply written introduction to Judaism that requires no previous acquaintance with Jewish history and life, giving a full picture of both. My aim is to take account of recent Jewish scholarship and yet keep the book accessible.

Much has happened in the Jewish world since the last edition of the book in 1972. The intervening years have seen the growth of Israel, conflicts with its neighbors, and glimpses of peace. After the collapse of the former Soviet Union, Russian Jewry was liberated from intolerable persecution; its contact with the rest of world Jewry has released new energies. The women's movement, striving for the religious equality of Jewish women, has made progress and offers challenges and promises for the future. Wider acquaintance with Jewish tradition and new interest in some of its aspects have called for an expanded treatment of subjects only briefly sketched in the previous edition, such as Jewish mysticism and Kabbalah. Denominations in Judaism have undergone changes in policy and practice. I have learned much during these years, especially as a teacher of university students. The text of the book has been reshaped, much has been changed, and new material has been added.

This book began in response to a request by Jewish friends

in search of a concise general outline of their history and faith. The work was also suggested to me by non-Jewish friends asking for an explanation of Judaism addressed to non-Jews. Judaism can be fully understood, however, only as it is lived, for it is more than a set of dogmas and principles, more than the sum total of its laws and commandments. Judaism started as the faith of a people. The faith has formed the people, and the people have fashioned their faith in a process of never-ending evolution. Judaism is eternal faith and eternal people, a living dialogue between God and the Jew, between the Jew and God, between Jew and fellow Jew, and between Jews and the non-Jewish world. Judaism is a conversation not only between the members of any living generation but among all generations as well. All Jews speak to their past, as the past speaks to them; they address the future, and the future responds. Judaism also speaks to the world, wishing to share the ideals for which Jews have lived, suffered, and died. In turn, Judaism has been open to the best that humanity has to offer, building this into its own structure.

In affirming God as the absolute One, Creator of the world and humanity, Judaism holds out the ideal of wholeness to a world torn by discord and to individuals split by inner conflict. Judaism proclaims the coming of the Messiah, a future in which humanity will be united in love and in peace. This messianic ideal offers an eternal challenge to every human being, calling all to do their utmost in promoting human welfare under God and to toil unceasingly for the improvement of society through social justice. *Shalom* is the goal Judaism envisions for all the children of God: *shalom* means peace, a peace that is more than the absence of war, for *shalom* also means perfection—in Jewish tradition, it is a name of God.

This book is not a Jewish history but the history of the Jewish experience. Whatever happened to the Jews at a given moment in history helped shape their outlook, their prayers and practices, their philosophy and hopes. The creative works of any Jew at any time became part of the living heritage. History, faith, and people are integrally unified, for Judaism sees God as Sovereign of history.

The arrangement of this edition differs from previous editions. The first part of the book deals with Jewish history from biblical times to the present. The second part discusses the spiritual life of the people; it deals with the centrality of Torah in the Jewish way of life—in prayer, in the cycle of the year, and in the rites of passage through the years of life. Jewish spirituality also finds expression in Jewish mysticism, philosophy, and theology; Jewish mysticism has its own visionary interpretation of Torah, while Jewish philosophy and theology confront the life and thoughts of the world with the eternity of Torah and the people of Torah. I invite the reader of the second part to refer to the first part for the period in history when the particular forms of Jewish life emerged and unfolded. I have tried to show that no part of Jewish experience can be fully understood out of the context of the whole. Many of the chapters can be read independently, but I hope that readers will approach the work as a whole.

A general, simply written presentation has to be selective in the choice and exposition of subject matter and ideas and necessarily omits details that may be relevant to the scholar. I have given special emphasis to the conditions and concerns of American Jewry. Belonging to the dwindling number of survivors who were molded by German-Jewish culture, I have also drawn on that tradition. I have generally not taken a stand in defense or advocacy of specific schools of thought or philosophies. In telling of halakhic decisions, I have merely described positions that have been taken by various schools of thought within religious Jewry. I have tried to relate the past to current issues and to include in general terms various answers to questions most frequently asked. My presentation should in no way be regarded as authoritative. In actual situations, the individual Jew will need the counsel of his or her rabbi.

Judaism has no central authority that could certify a work as an official presentation of its ideas. I have drawn from many sources, learned from many teachers, and am indebted to all of them. The greatest of my teachers have been my parents, who surrounded me with love and a home filled with Jewish devotion. My father led me into Bible and Talmud and opened my mind to Shakespeare and Mozart. My mother sealed her devotion to

Judaism with her life, dying a martyr's death in a Nazi camp. I have had inspiring teachers during my rabbinic training, men whose lives testified to their convictions. On December 15, 1999, the 6th of Tevet 5760, God took my beloved wife Miriam. For almost sixty-two years she shared with me the trials of life, in a courage born of faith, and in love that has given me strength. The caring love of our daughter Susan and her family is sustaining. Unanimously the family joined my wish that this book, up to now dedicated to them, perpetuate the memory of Miriam, her memory be a blessing.

I am grateful to all who have given me friendship and encouragement, especially my students, colleagues, and assistants at the University of Mainz where for years I have taught one semester annually. Professor Günter Mayer, Hebrew and talmudic scholar, teacher, and dear friend has given me numerous important insights. Other colleagues and the president of the university, Professor Joseph Reiter, have sustained me by friendship and support.

Most sincere appreciation is expressed to Behrman House, who anticipated my desire to rework the book by suggesting to me that I do so. The publisher has shown me great courtesy while giving me valuable assistance.

My editor, Jeannette Morgenroth, deserves my special thanks. A woman of learning and great stylistic ability, she has given me patience and understanding.

Most of the maps are adaptations of those used in Anderson, *Understanding the Old Testament* (Englewood Cliffs, N.J.: Prentice-Hall, 1957), based on maps in *The Westminster Historical Atlas to the Bible,* revised edition, © 1956 by W. D. Jenkins, the Westminster Press.

The *Tanakh* © 1985 by the Jewish Publication Society of America, is the translation generally used in this work. I have occasionally used an alternative translation when quoting biblical prayers (the Sh'ma, the opening of the Kaddish) that are best known in another translation. I have preferred to use the 1985 translation, rather than my own—unless necessary to avoid confusion—to show the Christian reader the similarities and differences between the Jewish translation and the authorized Christian ones. I hope to guide readers toward a renewed study of the Jewish version. Sincere appreciation is expressed to the Jewish Publication Society of America for the use of their translation. All other translations from the Hebrew, French, Latin, and German, except when indicated otherwise, are my own.

I would like to thank these other individuals and organizations that provided pictures used in the book (page numbers on which illustrations appear follow the name of the person or organization):

American Jewish Archives, 6, 230, 240
American Jewish Historical Society, Waltham, Massachusetts and New York, New York, 247
Anne Frank House, 274
Aron, Bill, 200, 366, 390, 401, 404, 421

Backer, Dennis, 364
Biblical Archeology Society, 72
Bibliothèque Nationale, 19, 57, 80, 208, 262, 307
Braun, Werner, 94
British Museum, 11, 237

Congregation Mikveh Israel, 221

Darmstaedter, Frank, 13, 52, 62, 86, 131, 136, 151, 207, 315, 362, 415, 418, 419, 441, 492, 508

Edinburgh University Library, 44

Gidale, T., 146
Giravdon, 64

Hatefutsoth, Beth, Photo Archive, Tel Aviv, 81, 317, 388
Hopf, John, 18, 216, 309

Israel Ministry of Tourism, 163, 291, 512
Israel Museum, 441
Israeli Office of Information, 472

Jewish Museum, 14, 165, 192, 248, 262, 379, 399, 456
Courtesy of the Library of The Jewish Theological Seminary of America, 460

Kulturinstitute, Worms, 126

I would like to thank these publishers, who provided poetry used in this book:

Beacon Press, 427
Bloch Publishing Company, Inc., 200

In joys and in sorrows God has sustained me. Blessed be the Holy One, who has permitted me to reach this moment—the completion of this work.

Erev Pesah 5760

INTRODUCTION

The Problem of Definition

Is there a single nation on earth like Your people Israel?
from Sabbath afternoon prayer

Judaism has molded men and women and children in its embrace. The Sabbath testifies to it. On this day, Jews feel divinely endowed with an additional soul that gives them peace amidst storms and the quietness of heart to meditate on God's greatness and love. Thus does a faith reach into the depths of its faithful, to mold them and to form them, to give them vision and courage and the unconquerable determination to be God's co-workers, and to contribute to the progress of humanity in the shaping of a better world.

It is an error to speak of a Jewish "race." Jews of every race live in every part of the globe. Although most Jews are Caucasian, there are also African Jews, Indian Jews, Chinese Jews, and Japanese Jews. From the very beginning of Jewish history there has been a mixture of many families united by their common bond.

Are Jews, then, a religious group? They are a religious communion, but they are more than that. The faith has shaped the people. But there are Jews who do not uphold any religious doctrines yet are proud of their Jewishness and the culture Judaism has produced.

Are they a nation in a political sense? Some Jews find themselves organized as a nation. Israel is a sovereign nation on its own free soil. In the former Soviet Union Jews had to carry identity cards that designated them as Jewish nationals. And throughout history, the internal structure of Jewish communities—with their guiding "officials," the rabbis, and well-developed legal, educational, and welfare systems—functioned in ways resembling a nation. But in the democracies of the West, where most Jews live, political government is not determined by religion. Ethnic identity and religious beliefs do not affect the rights and duties of citizenship. In the western world, the Jews, admitting ethnic values, consider themselves primarily a religion, and the synagogues are centers of Jewish life, with a variety of religious experiences finding expression in different religious branch movements: Orthodoxy, Conservatism, Reform, and Reconstructionism.

Yet there is one element that elevates Jewry in all lands beyond the character of a merely religious fellowship: the kinship and concern that Jews feel for each other. No political bond joins Jews in various lands, only the spirit of belongingness. The Bible expresses the nature of the Jews when it speaks of *Bet Yisrael,* the House of Israel.[1] Jews form a family linked by common experiences, a common history, and a common spiritual heritage. The family acquires its character by the spirit that unites it. The family unit includes those at home and abroad, those who have joined it by marriage, the children born to them. Whoever partakes of the spirit is part of the family. As the members share in common hopes and ideals, they develop the bond of love that holds them together. Like many families, world Jewry, composed of those who were born into it and those who have adopted it by choice, may be torn by disagreements, but love is its firm foundation.

---

1. In the first five books of the Bible, the Pentateuch, we often find the term *B'nai Yisrael,* the "Children of Israel," signifying an even closer family unity. The term *House of Israel* occurs most frequently among the prophets of the Babylonian Exile, Jeremiah, and Ezekiel.

The Covenant

The Jewish family spirit and will to survive has its roots in the conviction that the Jewish people are the people of the Covenant. Torah is the "Book of the Covenant," calling and guiding the people to function in a unique way for the sake of humanity as a whole.

At the conclusion of the biblical Book of Deuteronomy, Moses' farewell address, Moses summoned the people to enter into the Covenant as they had in connection with the revelation at Sinai (see Exod. 19:4–8 and Exod. 24:1–18). Now, in parting, he impressed upon the people that the Covenant, not linked merely to the generation that had witnessed Sinai, would endure throughout all generations:

> You stand this day, all of you, before the Lord your God—your tribal heads, your elders and your officials, all the men of Israel, your children, your wives, even the stranger within your camp, from woodchopper to waterdrawer—to enter into the covenant of the Lord your God, which the Lord your God is concluding with you this day, with its sanctions; to the end that He may establish you this day as His people and be your God, as he promised you and as He swore to your fathers, Abraham, Isaac, and Jacob. I make this covenant, with its sanctions, not with you alone, but both with those who are standing here with us this day before the Lord our God and with those who are not with us here this day. (Deut. 29:9–14)

Rabbinic interpretation offers us an insight into the meaning of Covenant. The Covenant will forever be an everlasting present, as alive as "this day." The Covenant is made not merely with the leaders, but with all, every man, woman, and child. It includes "those not with us this day," those yet unborn, and those who will affiliate themselves with the Jewish people in the future, the converts.

The Covenant created the bond between the Jews and God, thence between Jew and Jew. It has become so internalized that even those who may be unaware of its power have retained their allegiance to the Jewish people as its embodiment.

Covenant and Law

Out of the Covenant we come to understand the place and function of Jewish law. Law condenses the spirit of the Covenant into action. Law is both imposed and organic; it grew out of the encounter with God and out of the spirit of the Jewish people and its needs, hence it has evolved. Law has served as a unifying bond among Jews and contributed to their survival, deepening the spirit of unity and of purpose. Calling for an active response to the divine call, law has served as a life-giving force of self-identification and spiritual awareness. The law translated the Covenant into the deed, the Covenant's pledge into the reality of constant performance linking the Jew to God—hope becomes an action program that can lead to its fulfillment for the Jew and for humanity.

Contemporary Jewry in all its religious branches has affirmed the Covenant as the root element of its being. In 1992, America's leading liberal Jewish theologian, Eugene B. Borowitz, articulated Covenant theology in his work *Renewing the Covenant*. A living Covenant, it evolves out of the contribution of all the members of the Jewish people in all lands and at all times.

The Claim of Women

Jewish feminists have found in the *spirit* of the Covenant a strong foundation for the claim of recognition and equality. Every Jew, male or female, is equally embraced by it. The scriptural text, however, sees women as dependent on men, as wives following the children. At Sinai women were left out as equals. A distinction therefore has to be made between the spirit and the words. The text, which reduces the status of women, owes its formulation to the prevailing patriarchal character of Judaism and needs revisional interpretation. In the spirit of the Covenant, all hierarchical differentiation between the genders has to be abolished. In this spirit, women have claimed full recognition of their contribution in shaping Jewish destiny and have assumed full equality in the religious life. These claims need to be recognized; they may lead to a rewriting of Jewish history, and they have brought women equality in non-Orthodox Judaism.

JUDAISM AS AN EVOLVING CIVILIZATION

Women's claims and the response to them gives a living example of how dynamic Judaism is. Indeed, Mordecai M. Kaplan has defined Judaism as "an evolving religious civilization."[2] Judaism is religious: without finding God, it would never have come into being, nor would it have continued beyond a few generations. It is evolving, constantly changing and growing. It is a civilization, for it includes not only religious doctrines and practices but encompasses art and philosophy, language and music, folkways and cuisine, as well as a way of life. It expresses itself for some in a homeland in Israel, for others in ethnicity, secular culture, and social service, and for the majority—as in America—in religion. All Jews feel a deep emotional bond with Israel, and a two-way street has been built between the Land and the diaspora. Judaism cannot be understood without Jews, its living servants, the molders of its civilization.

JEWS IN THE WORLD

Numerically a tiny minority in the world, Jews have had a significant impact on the spiritual, intellectual, social, and economic life of every country they have inhabited. Of the approximately 14.5 million Jews, close to 6 million live in the United States of America, the largest Jewish community in history. They have become the leaders of world Jewry, giving it support and aid, offering spiritual guidance, and at the same time building a unique form of American Jewish religious life. (Canada has almost 300,000 Jews.)

Israel, with 4.5 million, is the second largest Jewish community. As a free and creative Jewish commonwealth, it is a focal point of the Jewish spirit and of Jewish hopes. It has been a spiritual magnet to Jews all over the world who have "made *aliyah*" (literally, have "ascended" to it) in the conviction that a full Jewish life was possible only in the Jewish Land, and it has

---

2. See Mordecai M. Kaplan, *Judaism as a Civilization* (New York: Schocken Books, 1967), pp. 173–85, 209. The idea is basic to all of Kaplan's writings and to the Reconstructionist movement, of which he is the founder.

offered a home to all Jews yearning to be free from persecution. American and Israeli Jews are closely linked.

In Western Europe, Jewish life is free, active, and flourishing but shows the tragic consequences of the Holocaust. The largest number live in France, 530,000; 320,000 live in England; 32,000 in Belgium; 32,000 in Italy; 26,000 in the Netherlands; 20,000 in Switzerland; 15,000 in Sweden; 10,000 in Austria; and 6,000 in Denmark. Approximately 80,000 Jews have settled in Germany, where the Jewish community may continue to grow due to the influx of Russian Jews.

In Eastern Europe, once the spiritual and numerical center of world Jewry, the number of Jews was tragically reduced as the result of the Holocaust. In the former Soviet Union live 1.75 million Jews; 60,000 live in Hungary; 19,000 are the remnant in Romania, only about 4,000 are left of the millions who once lived in Poland.

In Africa, we find flourishing congregations in the south totaling about 125,000, of whom the majority (115,000) live in the Republic of South Africa. The Jewish population along the Mediterranean coast is poor and decreasing.

On the Asian continent, outside of Israel, a Jewish community of about 20,000 exists in Turkey. Iran's once substantial Jewish community has dwindled to about 20,000, and in India live about 4,000 Jews. In Syria, the Jewish population of several thousand was held hostage by the country's dictators from the time of the establishment of the State of Israel; their release was begun in the fall of 1994, allowing them to settle in Israel.

South America has a substantial Jewish population, with a well-organized, active Jewish life: 220,000 Jews live in Argentina; 100,000 in Brazil; 35,000 in Mexico; 25,000 in Uruguay; and 15,000 in Chile.

Australia has 85,000 Jews, and New Zealand 4,500.[3]

Is there a single nation on earth . . . like Your people Israel?

---

3. These figures are based on *American Jewish Year Book*, copyright The American Jewish Committee and The Jewish Publication Society, New York and Philadelphia. They are adjusted annually.

BOOK ONE

Torah and History

 Chapter 1

TORAH

The Five Books of Moses

Judaism is a historical religion. Its history arches from its beginnings in antiquity to the day in an unknown future when the Messiah will be revealed. Jewish celebrations are tied to historical events. But past and present merge. A Jew can carry on a dialogue with a personality of the past, from the Bible and the Talmud on, confronting the other as a living presence. The Jewish family experience not only embraces the current generations but also extends into the distant past and the future as well.

Judaism has evolved and yet has remained constant. The past is both prologue and current reality. Judaism's achievements—the basic ideas of love and justice, of truth and righteousness, of civic duties and religious obligations, of faith and action, of dispersion and return, of purity of soul and individual responsibility, all proclaimed by the prophets and Sages—are part of the living heritage of Judaism and are guidelines for modern Jews.

The biblical and talmudic periods are not simply records of a majestic past but an account of our modern ideals and how they came into being. To the modern Jew, the Bible is a contemporary book whose ideals continue to be a personal challenge.

In daily prayer the Jew calls on "Our God ... God of Abraham." By being phrased in the plural the prayer emphasizes the link among all members of the present generation. At the same time, the praying Jew is conscious that his or her God, the One and Only, is Abraham's God, Sarah's God. Abraham stands at his side praying with him and for him; Sarah stands at her side, praying with her and for her. At the Seder, rehearsing the Exodus from Egypt, the word goes out to the Jew: "In *every* generation *every* Jew is to consider himself or herself as having been liberated personally and individually ... by God."

The Five Books of Moses—Genesis, Exodus, Leviticus, Numbers, and Deuteronomy—together are *Torah,* "the Instruction." The Torah is the core of Judaism, its guidance, counsel, and wisdom. But it is more. To some mystics it was the counselor and blueprint God consulted in creating the world, to others it was, in its entirety, a scrambled name of God. World, humanity and, above all, the Jew have their being in it. Every letter in it is therefore holy. Written on a parchment scroll with a goose quill—that the iron of war not touch its pages—the Torah scroll is the holiest possession of every congregation. It is read in public worship, but it is not merely a book. It is alive, and the Jew lives in it. When a scroll is so old that it cannot be repaired, it is buried like a human being.

BERESHIT, GENESIS: THE STAGE AND ITS HEROES

The first book of Torah is named for its opening word, *Bereshit,* "In the beginning." The book is also called Genesis. In its first eleven chapters the stage for the enacting of the historical drama of God's relationship with human beings and the world is erected and set, populated, dismantled, reconstructed and once again undermined. In the subsequent chapters, the patriarchs and matriarchs play leading roles in the founding of Judaism. Whether the events in Genesis are to be regarded as factual history, as Orthodox Jews believe, or as myths, stories that convey a philosophy of life, as many non-Orthodox Jews hold, the biblical drama offers moral guidelines for life to all.

CREATION. God is the Creator of the universe. The crown of the divine creation is the human being, man and woman, both created in God's image, both equal—"male and female God created them" (Gen. 1:27). The human being, created in God's image, is the divinely appointed steward of the world. All human life without distinction is sacred. In the words of the Sages, great Jewish interpreters of the Bible, "God created but one human being that no one may say to another, 'my ancestors were more distinguished than yours,' and in order to make it known that any human being harming or destroying another has destroyed a whole world" (Mishnah Sanhedrin 4:5). And already in Genesis the stage is set for the Land of Israel's history: "Should the nations accuse you of having displaced nations dwelling in the Land of Israel, you may tell them, 'the whole earth is the Lord's, because he created it; he may therefore give [any part of] it to whomever he chooses'" (Rashi to Gen. 1:1).

DESTRUCTION: THE FLOOD. The human stewards became corrupt. Murder, violence and tyranny became rampant. The mighty ravished the weak. World and humanity lost their right to exist and were destroyed in a cataclysmic flood. Only one person, Noah, proved himself true to the responsibility of human beings and was saved together with his family and specimens of all animal species.

At one time in antiquity a gigantic flood may well have destroyed large parts of the region. Such a flood is remembered in the great Babylonian poem, Gilgamesh Epic. In contrast to the biblical story, the Gilgamesh Epic shows the gods acting arbitrarily and at whim: they create the world because they are lonely and yearn for some entertainment, destroy it because they are bored and tired of it, and rescue one man because he is their friend and favorite. In the biblical account of the flood, however, the ethical message undergirds the story: God creates the world to impart blessing, destroys it because of its moral failures, and rescues Noah because he was upright.

RECONSTRUCTION: THE COVENANT. Upon its destruction the world was restored and firmed. God made a covenant with the entire world and all of Noah's descendants, the entire human race. The world will never be destroyed by a flood; the human race will survive if we abide by basic ethical principles, the

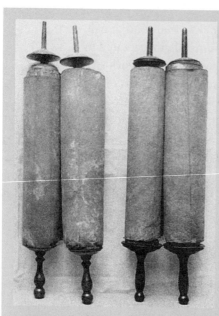

Torah scrolls.

In Israel, a Sefardic scribe patiently and in exacting detail inscribes the Torah on parchment.

What Is Torah?

The three main divisions of the Hebrew Scriptures are: Torah, or the Five Books of Moses, also called the Pentateuch; Nevi'im, the Prophets; and Ketuvim, the Collected Writings, also called Hagiographa. The Five Books hold the highest rank among these sacred writings. Using the first letters of the three sections, we speak of Tanakh. The Tanakh is the core text of Judaism. Each of these main sections is again divided into books, paragraphs, and verses. Originally, there were numbers for neither chapters nor verses. The numbers were added by Christian monks during the Middle Ages and have been universally adopted.

The Five Books of Moses are written on a parchment scroll by men who have devoted their entire lives to copying the words of holy writ. Each congregation needs to have at least one scroll but may have several. They are kept in the Holy Ark and form the congregation's holiest possession. Each scroll contains the full text. If a congregation has several scrolls, it can designate one for special holy day readings; if it has only one, it must be rolled to the place of special readings. It is wrapped in a precious mantle and may (in addition) have a breastplate, on which small, changeable silver plates tell of the place to which the scroll is rolled. There is a silver hand, *yad*, strung by a chain around its neck, to be used as a pointer. As Torah is the "crown of life," silver crowns are frequently placed on it.

The instructions of Torah are Israel's holy heritage and guide. Here is the primary source of mitzvot, the injunctions, that constitute the Jewish way. So basic is Torah that it is repeated in public reading year after year. The five books are divided into sections or portions, one of them to be read each Sabbath. The first words of each portion are used as its title, so every week of the Jewish year can be clearly marked. It is the week of such and such a portion, or Parashah (sometimes called Sidrah). "On the first day of the week of Shemot" then means, "on Sunday of the week leading up to the reading of the Sidrah Shemot" (the first of the Book of Exodus). The portion of Torah thus becomes motto for the week.

The Tanakh consists of the books that most Christians call "Old Testament." Jews consider this term condescending, for it indicates that the Hebrew Bible is but a forerunner of the "New Testament," in both its understanding of God and the ethical principles it proclaims. Jews feel strongly that no higher ethical principles have ever been expressed, no deeper love expounded, in any work that followed Jewish Holy Scriptures. Nor did God ever revoke the Covenant with Israel in favor of a new one. Many Christian scholars have therefore replaced the term Old Testament with Hebrew Bible, revealing a new approach to Judaism.

Every congregation treats its Torah scrolls with utmost respect, often clothing the living word in a beautiful mantle and adorning it with silver crowns.

"Noahide Commandments": recognition of God; respect and concern for human life, sexual morality, and property; the establishment of just courts handing down just verdicts; and concern for animals, which may not be made to suffer. Living by these commandments assures all human beings of ultimate salvation.[1]

DISARRAY: THE TOWER OF BABEL. Noah's guidance proved inadequate. Secure in the stability of the earth and blessed by being united in one common language, Noah's descendants built a tower to breach the heavens and dethrone God. Because human beings misused their unity in constructing the tower, God scattered the people and confounded their languages so that they could no longer understand one another (therefore the tower was called Babel, a play on the Hebrew word *balal,* to confound). The foundations of the stage and the historical drama to be enacted upon it had again been undermined. Stronger personalities than Noah were called for to give the drama stability and be the actors in history.

Patriarchs

The three generations of patriarchs and matriarchs in Genesis chapters 12 to 50—Abraham and Sarah, Isaac and Rebecca, Jacob with Leah and Rachel—forecast in their individual lives the destiny of their descendants, the people of Israel. They are role models and guides to all Jews, and their character traits are paradigms of the Jewish experience.

---

1. The "seven Noahide laws" establish the principle of recognizing ethical non-Jews. "The Rabbanan taught: Seven laws were imposed upon the descendants of Noah: (1) the establishment of justice, (2) the prohibition of blasphemy, (3) of idolatry, (4) of adultery and incest, (5) of murder, (6) of robbery, (7) of eating a limb torn from a living animal" (B.T. Sanhedrin 56a). This resulted in the rabbinic doctrine: "the righteous of the nations of the world [who abide by these laws] have a share in the world to come" (Tosefta Sanhedrin 13:2). Judaism acknowledges that "salvation" is granted to all who abide by the basic principles of human morality. Maimonides affirms this doctrine in regard to the faithful of the great world religions (Mishneh Torah, Hilkhot Melachim 8:11).

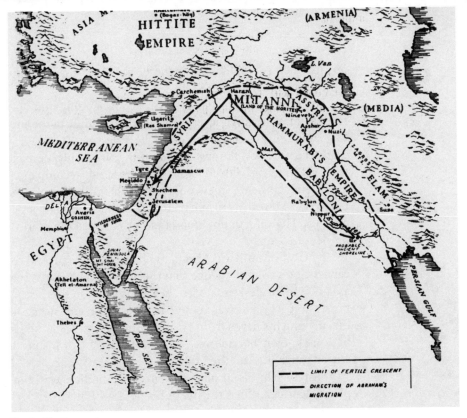

The Fertile Crescent.

Abraham: Model of Certainty and Trust

Living in a pagan world that worshiped idols, Abraham discovered the One and Only God who is invisible but all-powerful, all-loving, trustworthy, merciful and just. This revelation compelled Abraham to reject completely all the gods of his society, to commit himself exclusively to the One God and to construct his life by the divine norms he was to receive.

Abraham's homeland, Ur of the Chaldeans, as the Bible calls it, had a highly civilized society that possessed an advanced code of law, the Code of Hammurabi. But this law was supposed to have been handed down by the god Marduk and it placed property rights over human rights; it meted out different justice to the aristocrats than to the common folk, and none at all to the slaves. Abraham may have found some of the code's principles to be of value but in need of ethical transformation. We therefore find elements of the code in the legislation of the Torah, but with their principles altered.

Abraham heard the voice of God commanding him, "Go forth from your native land and your father's house to the land that I will show you ... and you shall be a blessing" (Gen. 12:1–2). He did not know the destination. He had to put his complete trust in God. His beloved, beautiful wife Sarah accompanied him. Being homeless, they found strength and stability in the family and won others to join their clan, their faith and their pilgrimage. Henceforth not blood but faith formed the unity of his people.

By God's command Abraham settled in Canaan, and received God's solemn pledge that this land had been divinely assigned to his descendants, a great nation, as an everlasting possession. As yet he was a sojourner, leading a semi-nomadic life, driving his herds from pasture land to pasture land. He became known as "Hebrew," "the dust raiser" (for his herds stirred much dust on their trek).[2]

Sustained by his absolute trust in God, Abraham was completely fearless. When the life of his nephew Lot was endangered, Abraham mustered an army and defeated the adversaries (he took no booty, for this would have perverted warfare from an act of rescue to an act of gain).

Abraham was absolutely obedient. Commanded to circumcise himself and the male members of his clan, he obeyed without question. He recognized in every human being, especially the stranger, an "angel," that is, a "messenger" of God (the literal meaning of the Latin word angelus, which translates the Hebrew malakh). When three tired, dusty and hungry men arrived at his tent, he immediately invited them to rest and refresh themselves. They were indeed angels.

---

2. The term Hebrew may have derived from a word for "over," meaning "across"; Abraham came from "across" the Euphrates and Tigris rivers. William F. Albright, however, derives the term from the word for "dust"; as donkey drivers or caravaneers, the Hebrews raised a lot of dust on the roads with their animals (The Biblical Period from Abraham to Ezra [New York: Harper Row, 1963], p. 5). On the relationship of the Hebrews to the Habiru, see B. W. Anderson, Understanding the Old Testament, 2d ed. (Englewood Cliffs, N.J.: Prentice Hall, 1966), p. 73; and H. H. Ben Sasson, A History of the Jewish People (Cambridge: Harvard University Press, 1976), pp. 18–20, 23, 41–42.

Abraham knew that God, the infinitely just and powerful, is equally merciful. When appraised that the city of Sodom was to be destroyed for its wickedness, he boldly approached God in argument. "Shall not the Judge of all the earth deal justly?" (Gen. 18:25). Because of Abraham's pleading, God agreed that if but ten innocent people be found in Sodom, the city would be spared, but this number could not be found.

Abraham never wavered in his obedience, even when commanded to offer his beloved son Isaac as a sacrifice to God. He bound his son on the altar. His knife was poised over his son's neck. Then, in a flash of revelation as a divine angel intervened, Abraham learned that God never demands any human victims, either as gift of appeasement or in token of absolute obedience. Abraham's trust in God found divine approval.

God demanded of Abraham, not the sacrifice of his son Isaac, but his life as a faithful partner of the Covenant.

ABRAHAM IN THE JEWISH EXPERIENCE. Abraham's character and life experiences have been realized in the collective life of the Jewish people. Absolute affirmation of the One God and absolute trust in God have been its foundations, unshaken by homelessness, expulsions, and even death. Jews' unquestioning willingness to sacrifice their own and their children's lives for the sanctification of God's name has stood the test throughout history. The family has been the source of strength, and charity one of the Jews' outstanding traits. Taught by God the sacredness of every human life, motivated by a deep love of all human beings and striving to be a blessing to all of humanity, they have fought against tyranny and oppression. The commitment to their Land as their God-given eternal possession has permeated their entire historical destiny, become enshrined in every prayer, and led to its restoration. Recognizing God as merciful and open to human appeals, they have assumed their right, borne of an unwavering faith, to "argue" with God in behalf of merciful justice. Circumcision is "the Covenant, sealed in our flesh." Even Abraham's openness to outside culture has prevailed, insofar as it conforms to Jewish tradition and values. "Because he put his trust in the Lord, He reckoned it to his merit" (Gen. 15:6): This assurance has guided and sustained the Jews, Abraham's descendants.

Isaac: Passive Transmitter of Tradition

Abraham's son Isaac was equally obedient to God. "Walking in unity" with his father, he accepted his destiny as his father's intended sacrifice willingly and without objection. His obedience expressed itself in his passive acquiescence; seared by his ordeal, he would always remain passive. He did not choose his wife Rebecca, she was found for him. She bore him twins, Esau and Jacob. Esau was self-centered and disinterested in the spiritual tradition of his family; Jacob was studious and this tradition was a driving force in his life. Perhaps seeing in the elder son Esau the compensation for the life that had escaped him, Isaac gave him his first love. He unquestioningly assumed that Esau would be entitled to the blessing which Isaac was to transmit, for this was tradition. He did not inquire into the merits of his sons. Isaac was physically and, perhaps, spiritually blind.

Rebecca, however, recognized that if Esau carried Isaac's blessing, the tradition and inherited values of Abraham's family would be dissipated and its spiritual future jeopardized, for Esau was unsuited to lead the family. The sacred heritage of the family could be perpetuated only through the studious and sensitive Jacob. And so Rebecca's insight preserved Judaism through her son Jacob.

Jacob: The Most Problematic and Tragic of the Patriarchs

Jacob himself described the years of his life as "few and hard" (Gen. 47:9). Few were the moments when he "lived," hard and tragic the rest. Described as a man of high character and studious, he has also been regarded as deceitful. He "purchased" the rights and obligations of the firstborn from Esau for a pot of soup—so much had Esau "despised the status as firstborn." And in obedience to his mother's instruction, Jacob secured his father's blessing by disguising himself as his brother.

Esau, deprived of the blessing and the right of the firstborn, vowed to kill Jacob, and so Jacob fled to his Uncle Laban at Paddan-aram. At Paddan-aram, Jacob fell immediately in love with his cousin Rachel and pledged her father seven years of service in place of the "fee" the groom had to give the father of the bride. On his wedding night he discovered that he had been cheated; the veiled bride was not Rachel but her sister Leah. For the pledge of another seven years' service he was given Rachel as well. While Leah bore him children, Rachel was barren for years until she bore him a son, Joseph, who became his favorite.

Ruthlessly exploited by Laban and his sons, Jacob took his flight with his family and his belongings to return home, where Isaac was still alive but Rebecca, his beloved mother, had died. Before reaching home Jacob had to make his peace with Esau.

Unlike Abraham, who knew that God was with him without knowing where he was going, Jacob knew where he was supposed to go but not whether God was with him or if he would ever reach his refuge. But in a dream, he had a vision of a ladder extending from earth to heaven, with angels going up and down; God assured him of divine protection and his eventual return home.

He sent him precious gifts of cattle and implored his brother to forgive him. Esau replied he would meet him with a large army.

The night before the meeting Jacob was attacked by a man emerging out of the dark. They wrestled until the break of dawn. The stranger could not prevail but he wrenched Jacob's hip out of its socket. When day was about to break, the stranger asked to be released from Jacob's grip and dismissed, but Jacob retorted, "I will not let you go unless you bless me." The stranger, who would not give his name, complied: "Your name shall no longer be 'Jacob', but *'Israel'*, for you have striven *(sarita)* with beings divine and human, and have prevailed" (Gen. 32:29). A heavenly being had wrestled with him, perhaps Esau's guardian angel, as some commentators assume. In another sense, Jacob's struggle with the angel was his struggle with himself, from which he emerged victorious, but lame. In the morning Esau arrived and the brothers were reconciled. Jacob could now safely go home. But on his way his beloved Rachel died while giving birth to her second son Benjamin.

JACOB'S SONS: FATHERS OF THE TRIBES OF ISRAEL. Jacob's twelve sons were the founders of Israel's twelve tribes. All were of different character. Reuben, the eldest, unable to curb his sexual impulses. Simon and Levi, impetuous hotheads. Judah, a man of contradictions, could be impetuous, rash, given to outbursts and sometimes cruel, but he was also a leader—intelligent, concerned, courageous and protective. To his tribe the leadership in Israel would fall.

And there was JOSEPH, Jacob's favorite, to whom the father gave a coat of many colors. Spoiled and pampered, Joseph dreamed of becoming the family's lord and master. His brothers came to hate him ever more bitterly. They sold him as a slave, and

Twelve tribes emerged from the sons of Jacob. The symbol of each encircles the tree of life in this nineteenth-century Palestinian silver relief.

he was taken to Egypt and sold to Potiphar, one of the king's courtiers. Potiphar's wife, enticed by Joseph's beauty, fell in love with him. Out of moral considerations he resisted her advances, and she, in spite, accused him of having tried to seduce her. He was thrown into prison. There he accurately interpreted the dreams of several courtiers who were being held for some offense against the pharaoh. When Pharaoh dreamed of seven fat cows and seven fat ears of corn, each followed and swallowed up by seven lean ones, a courtier had Joseph brought before Pharaoh. Joseph interpreted the dreams as predicting seven good years to be followed by seven years of famine. He proposed that the surplus of the good years be stored in royal storage houses to be administered by a royal administrator and, during the lean years, distributed to the people. Pharaoh, deeply impressed, appointed Joseph administrator and viceroy.

Blessing his grandsons, Jacob bequeathed a blessing to posterity: "By you shall Israel invoke blessings, saying: 'God make you like Ephraim and Manasseh'" (Gen. 48:20). These words are added to the blessing parents pronounce upon their sons every Sabbath. To the blessing of girls the words are added: "God make you like Sarah, Rebecca, Rachel, and Leah."

The predicted famine gripped the lands. Jacob's family was starving, and the father sent some of his sons to Egypt to purchase food. Joseph recognized them, but they did not recognize him. Testing them to find if the enmity between them had ceased, he found to his relief that, led by Judah, they stood up for one another. Tearfully Joseph revealed himself to his brothers and invited them and his father to move to Egypt. Most of the clan, seventy persons in all, settled there. Jacob enjoyed a few years of life in Egypt but requested to be buried in the land of Canaan. The rest of the clan remained in Egypt.

JACOB AND JOSEPH IN THE JEWISH EXPERIENCE. An athletic man who treasured learning, Jacob was worldly and pious, shrewd and naive, realist and dreamer, intellectual and emotional, impulsive and deliberate, sincere and deceitful. He was a good father, capable of bringing up his sons true to the tradition of the family, and a foolish father, splitting the family by an excessive preference for his son, Joseph. Both loving and profoundly self-centered, Jacob adored his beloved Rachel and loved Leah but least of all patriarchs saw women as equals.

Joseph closely resembled his father. He, too, was driven from comfort to abject misery. And he grew through adversity and was propelled by the dream of his youth. But no longer looking for power for its own sake, he became the provider of the starving and the unifier of his brothers.

SHEMOT, EXODUS: ISRAEL BECOMES A NATION

Retold in the second of the Five Books of Moses, the Exodus from Egypt, the birth of the nation of Israel and the beginning of its history, is the pivotal experience of the Jewish people, brought to mind in prayer and celebrated in the Passover Seder.

As was to happen so often in history, the "Jews," who had saved the Egyptians from starvation, were cast aside when no

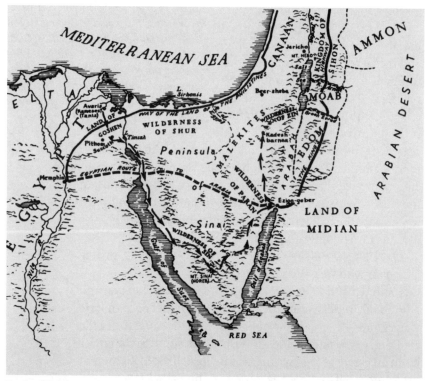

Route of Exodus

---

longer needed. Singled out as a subversive group with danger-ous ideas, they were enslaved and in forced labor had to build garrisons for the Pharaoh. But in slavery they became a people. During the reign of Rameses II (1290–1224), their harshest op-pressor, they gained their freedom and departed from Egypt to return home to Canaan.[3] Their leader was Moses.

HEROIC WOMEN. The survival of the Hebrew people rested to a large degree on the courage and compassion of women. Trying to extinguish the people, Pharaoh ordered the Jewish midwives Shiphrah and Puah to kill every male child at birth. They refused. He then ordered the male children to be drowned in the Nile. Moses' mother thereupon made a wicker basket, put him in it and placed it among the reeds on the bank of the river. His sister Miriam preserved his life by keeping a protective watch over him. Pharaoh's daughter, bathing in the Nile, discovered the baby. Knowing that he was a Hebrew child she set her motherly compassion over her father's orders, took the child, and gave him to Miriam to be cared for by his mother until he grew up and was taken to the royal court as the "son" of Pharaoh's daughter.

THE GOD OF MOSES: COMMAND AND RESPONSE. Moses' mother, Jochebed, instilled in her son a love for God and for his suffering kin. Egyptian religion, of which Moses may well have learned, had, at one time, stressed human responsibility and the immortality of the soul. After death, the soul was called to ac-count for all its deeds before the throne of the gods. Conduct was valued above sacrifices. For a fleeting moment, under Pharaoh Akhenaton, Egyptian religion even proclaimed the One God. But then the religion fell under the influence of Canaanite fer-tility cults, "abominations" to Scripture. Moses rejected all pagan rites. Deeply attached to his people, he went out to them to comfort them and renew their trust in the God of their fathers, who would liberate them. He had to flee after slaying an Egyp-tian taskmaster who was about to beat a Hebrew slave to death.

In the desert, Moses received in a vision the call to be his

3. If the biblical account is correct, that the pharaoh who had enslaved the Israelites died before their liberation (Exod. 2:23), then we shall have to place the Exodus during the reign of Pharaoh Mernepta (1224–1214 B.C.E.).

Like this 1828 Benjamin Howland painting in the Touro Synagogue in Rhode Island, a depiction of the Ten Commandments is often found near the ark in a synagogue.

The Ten Commandments

In categorical terms—you shall, you shall not—God commanded

1. *I am the Lord your God, who brought you out of the land of Egypt, the house of bondage.*
2. *You shall have no other gods before Me; you shall not make for yourself a sculptured image [to worship it].*
3. *You shall not swear falsely by the name of God.*
4. *Remember the Sabbath day and keep it holy.*
5. *Honor your father and your mother.*
6. *You shall not murder.*
7. *You shall not commit adultery.*
8. *You shall not steal.*
9. *You shall not bear false witness against your neighbor.*
10. *You shall not covet anything that is your neighbor's.*

See Exod. 20:1–7, also Deut. 5:6–18.

people's leader. He saw a bush ablaze in fierce flame, yet the bush was not consumed. In the midst of the fire he heard the voice of God revealing the divine Name—YHWH—"He Who Is What He Wishes To Be," or "He Who Causes What Is" (Exod. 3:14). The bush became the symbol of the people of Israel, surrounded by the flames of hatred, scorched by the heat of trials, yet never consumed as God speaks to them and through them. Theirs is the God of history, who calls events into being and shapes human destiny. History is divine revelation. It is dynamic, never static, hence God's voice can be heard but God's face never seen, for the vision is static while the call is everlasting motion.

Inspired by this insight, Moses returned to Egypt and gained the freedom of his people. When the Egyptians, regretting the release of their slaves, pursued them, Moses led the people through the Sea of Reeds (Red Sea), whose waves parted to let them pass but then drowned the Egyptians.

THE COVENANT OF SINAI. The Israelites arrived at Mount Sinai. Here God revealed to them their place and function in humanity:

If you … keep My covenant, you shall be My treasured possession among all the peoples. Indeed, all the earth is Mine, but you shall be to Me a kingdom of priests and a holy nation. (Exod. 19:5–6)

Surrounded by thunder, lightning and fiery clouds God gave them the Ten Commandments.

Something unprecedented and incisive happened at Sinai to the Hebrew people that transformed them. As they chose to enter into the Covenant with God, they came to accept the One God, not only as their personal God, as the patriarchs had done, leaving others to follow their own gods, but as the God of the whole universe and of all humanity as well, and this recognition gave them unity, the will and strength to prevail in history.

JUDAISM, A RELIGION OF MITZVOT. The Covenant of Sinai constituted the Jewish people as a kingdom of priestly spirituality through laws that make the nation and its people holy. Jewish religion binds spirituality to law. Torah contains 613 laws. But they are not simply abstract laws. They are *mitzvot*, "commandments," issued as a gift of love by the divine *Metzaveh*, "Commander," in personal relationship with the people. Judaism is primarily a tradition of mitzvot, holy deeds leading to holiness. As throughout this book we speak in detail of mitzvot as constituent elements of Judaism, we shall find them grounded in this Covenant of Torah, at Sinai.

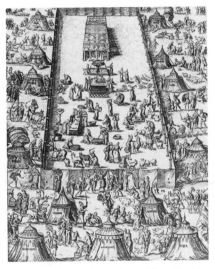

Following divine instructions, Moses built a Tent of Meeting to make God's dwelling with the people visible. The tablets rested in a sacred Ark within the tent. The people of Israel camped around the Tent of Meeting that held the Ark of the Covenant.

VAYIKRA, LEVITICUS: SACRIFICIAL LAW AND HUMAN LOVE

The third Book of Moses is named Leviticus because of its concern with the priesthood, which came from the tribe of Levi. The laws of the sacrifices and the sacrificial services are laid down, the dietary laws ordained and the festivals of the year appointed.

Of equal importance are the laws of human relations that

alone can make the people holy. Among them are these: do not deceive the unaware, bear no malice, seek no vengeance, be honest in business, be fair to the wage earner, honor the aged, sustain the poor, obey God's laws of sexual relations. They culminate in "Love your fellow as yourself" (Lev. 19:18) and "The stranger ... you shall love him as yourself" (Lev. 19:34).

The people are warned that disobedience to the mitzvot will bring disaster, exile and persecution, but they are given the comforting assurance. "Yet, even then, when they are in the land of their enemies, I will not reject them or spurn them so as to destroy them, annulling My covenant with them: for I the Lord am their God" (Lev. 26:44).[4]

BEMIDBAR, NUMBERS: WANDERINGS, UPRISINGS, PUNISHMENT, AND BLESSINGS

The Levites had been spread among the people to curb their impetuousness, inherited from their ancestor Levi, and they had been appointed servants of the sanctuary. Among them was Moses' brother Aaron and his sons, who were consecrated as priests. One of the sacred duties of the priest was to bless the people with the words:

> The Lord bless you and keep you. The Lord let His face to shine upon you and be gracious to you. The Lord lift up His face to you and give you peace. (See Num. 6:22–26)

A census of the people's numbers was taken, and chieftains were appointed for each tribe. From this the fourth Book of Moses received the name Numbers. The events related in this book concern many of the experiences of the Israelites in the desert. The account reveals the fluctuations in commitment among the people and its members. Highest commitment alternates with lack of faith, obedience with rebellion, trust with despair, unity with discord. The people were, after all, the "Children of Israel" and inheritors of his inner dissonances.

Scouts were sent into the land to explore it for the forthcoming conquest of the promised land. They so discouraged the people by their report of the enemies' invincible strength that

4. This divine pledge refutes the claim of the church fathers that God had canceled the Convenant with Israel when making a new one with Christianity.

the people despaired of ever defeating the enemy, even with the help of God. Only two scouts encouraged them, among them Joshua, their future leader. The people were condemned to remain forty years in the desert, until a new and more courageous generation would undertake the conquest. A rebellion, spearheaded by Korah, an aristocratic Levite, challenged the authority of Moses and Aaron, but their leadership was vindicated as the rebellion was crushed by divine intervention.

In contrast, the Israelites' unity is revealed in the blessings that Balaam, a famous heathen prophet is compelled to invoke upon the people. Frightened by the victories of the Israelites over some outlying nations, Balak, King of Moab, invited the prophet to curse Israel and thus assure its defeat. But Balaam could pronounce only the words God put in his mouth, and instead of cursing he had to bless. Beholding Israel harmoniously encamped and the spirit of God resting on it, he exclaimed:

How fair are your tents, O Jacob, your dwellings, O Israel. (Num. 24:5)

To this day these words are the greeting uttered to the synagogue by the entering worshiper.

DEVARIM, DEUTERONOMY: MOSES' FAREWELL

According to Torah, the fifth Book of Moses was composed as Moses' great farewell address to his people. He himself was not to be permitted to enter the promised land, for he had been found wanting. Moses reviews the history of the people since the Exodus, repeating commandments they have received and enlarging on them, including the Ten Commandments.

The key principle of justice is not law alone but justice and ethics: *Tsedek, tsedek tirdof,* which may be rendered "Ethics, ethics shall you pursue" (Deut. 16:20). Judges and magistrate were to be appointed. They were warned: You must not judge unfairly; you shall show no partiality; you shall not take bribes, for bribes blind the eyes of the discerning and upset the plea of the just. *Tsedek, tsedek tirdof.* This spirit must undergird all human relations at all times, including business, sexuality, marriage and divorce, and even the laws of war and peace.

The Sh'ma

"Hear, O Israel! The Lord is our God, the Lord is One" (See Deut. 6:4–5). This affirmation begins one of the most important prayers among Jews, the Sh'ma, which is recited daily, morning and evening.

Moses summoned the people to affirm and renew the Covenant. With a blessing to each tribe, according to its specific characteristics, he departed. Ascending Mount Nebo he was shown the whole land promised to Israel, then died alone. God buried him. "No one knows his grave to this day." His burial place was not to become a place of veneration. His living word was to be his monument. "Never again did there arise in Israel a prophet like Moses—whom the Lord singled out, face to face" (Deut. 34:10).

Chapter 2

NEVI'IM

The Prophets

Nevi'im, the Prophets, forms the second section of the Hebrew Bible, which consists of the Former Prophets and the Latter Prophets, also known as the Literary Prophets. The prophets had to speak out, for each was a *navi* (plural *nevi'im*)—a person with a divinely imposed "burden." They combined broad vision with such unequaled power of emotional, poetic, and ethical expression that their message belongs to the greatest treasures of world literature. The words of the prophets hold essential proclamations of social justice that continue to shape the Jewish experience and open the conscience of humanity. With the prophets, Judaism became a universalistic religion.

The prophets felt challenged by the events they witnessed to ask God about the purpose and meaning of life and history. They wanted to understand not as humans perceive but as God does. They asked about God's personal concern for humanity as well. They came to see the world from God's point of view and to feel as God feels:

> [T]he prophetic writings are filled with echoes of divine love and disappointment, mercy and indignation. The God of Israel is never impersonal.... [T]he fundamental experience of the prophet is a fellowship with the feelings of God, a *sympathy with the divine pathos*.... He lives not only his personal life, but also the life of God.

The prophet hears God's voice and feels His heart . . . speaking as he does out of the fullness of his sympathy [with God].[1]

The prophets had the burden of rebuking their people, not because their nation was worse than other nations, but because it was not better, did not set the world an example of a divinely inspired and guided nation. Every prophet found that the people were complacent and did not listen. So the prophets resisted their calling, for it made them lonely, despised, and led to their persecution. Nevertheless they could not escape their mission because in their hearts they felt the compelling force of the divine call. They suffered but carried on, hoping that people would cease to reject God, even if they abused God's prophet. The prophets' message would prevail: optimism in tears, hope in sorrow, faith in despair— part of the Jewish character and a Jewish message of encouragement to all who labor for a better world.

THE FORMER PROPHETS

Judges, 1 and 2 Samuel, 1 and 2 Kings

The Former Prophets tell the history of the Jewish people from the death of Moses until the fall of Jerusalem in 586 B.C.E. The Book of Judges, 1 and 2 Samuel, and 1 and 2 Kings chronicle the clash between ideal and reality in the Land of Israel. After Moses' death his disciple Joshua became the leader and general of the people. Israel, invading Canaan,

The Nevi'im in Worship
Selected chapters of the Prophets were chosen by the Rabbis to be recited after the reading from the Torah scroll on holy days. The selection is called Haftarah, *"conclusion," and is keyed to the special day on which it is read, or to the Torah portion which it follows. On the afternoon of the Day of Atonement, for instance, the Book of Jonah is read with its twofold message: no one can run away from the tasks God has set him or her, which includes helping "enemies"; and God's love extends to all creatures, even the animals—how much more so to human beings, even the wicked. On the Sabbath when the story of Jacob's death is read from the Torah scroll, the story of David's death is recited from the Prophets. The Haftarah is chanted, though the chant is slightly different from that used in reading the Torah.*

1. Abraham Joshua Heschel, *The Prophets* (Philadelphia: Jewish Publication Society, 1962), pp. 24, 26.

achieved some spectacular victories. The thinly populated hill regions were open for settlement, but in the heavily populated valleys the conquest was slow and rivalries for the best parcels began. The unity of the Israelites fell apart as tribal allegiances overrode national identity, and the Tent of Meeting, the national sanctuary, was but a weak rallying point. This weakness tempted their enemies—the Bedouins, who raided the farmlands, and the Philistines, a great warrior nation that had become masters of the coastal strip of Canaan.

In times of danger the Israelites chose charismatic leaders and pledged allegiance to God. Israel was ruled by these judges, who did their best to maintain unity and justice. Among them was a valiant woman, Deborah, who led the armies to victory and as "mother in Israel" held the people together as long as she lived. But as soon as the enemy had been repelled or a judge had died, the people's selfish interests and their desire to conform to the habits and religion of their neighbors arose again.

Eventually, the Israelites saw two paths to a permanent union in strength: A revitalized religious commitment would give them unity of purpose, as their judge, the prophet Samuel, counseled. Or they could choose to be governed by a king, and a hereditary monarchy would assure permanent leadership. They made the second choice. But God was to be Israel's sole King and Ruler. In choosing human rulers Israel committed a grievous error.[2] This is why the kings are depicted in the Bible as flawed, but those that followed God's word are characterized as good, while those who for political or personal ambitions followed their own designs are branded as evil.

Saul was proclaimed the first king. After several initial victories he lost both a decisive battle with the Philistines and his life, and once again the nation collapsed. David, a member of the tribe of Judah, succeeded him. A man of great ability, capable of making and holding friends, a statesman and excellent

2. Martin Buber, *The Kingship of God* (New York, Harper & Row, 1966).

The enormous altar from Solomon's palace at Megiddo, built during the tenth century B.C.E., attests to the magnitude and duration of the people's faith.

administrator, a warrior and a poet, David also had grave weaknesses, but he had the power to see them and the strength to repent. David took Jerusalem from the Jebusites and established the city as Israel's eternal capital, seat of royal power and the sanctuary. He entered history as Israel's ideal king.

David was succeeded by his son Solomon, who built the Temple in Jerusalem, which was also his royal chapel. When he died in 922 B.C.E., the people, groaning under the pressure of taxation and enforced service, appealed to his son Rehoboam for a redress of grievances. The king refused them, and the result was secession. Ten of the twelve tribes fell away to form the Kingdom of Israel. Only the tribes of Judah and Benjamin remained loyal to the House of David; they formed the Kingdom of Judah.

Judah and Israel, weakened by division, lay like a bridge between the great empires of antiquity, Egypt to the west and to the east the powers of the valley of the rivers Tigris and Euphrates. As long as these giants balanced each other, they left Israel and Judah alone rather than see them in the opponent's hand. As soon as either of the two great powers felt strong enough to subdue the other, the territory between them became a goal of their ambitions.

Divided Kingdom

THE LITERARY PROPHETS

Of the Latter Prophets, also known as the Literary Prophets, we speak of the *major prophets*—Isaiah, Jeremiah, and Ezekiel—of whose speeches major segments have been passed down to us. Twelve others are called *minor prophets*. Their message is also powerful, but only smaller works remain.

Amos: The Idea of Being Chosen

The prophets came from varying backgrounds. Isaiah may have been a royal prince, Jeremiah and Ezekiel were priests, Hosea was a member of the gentry. Amos was a lowly shepherd and dresser of sycamore trees. One of the twelve minor prophets, he flourished in the eighth century B.C.E. Duty compelled Amos to travel from his hometown, Tekoa, in the Kingdom of Judah, to the Kingdom of Israel, where he found a society living in splendor and luxury but lacking in compassion. He came to warn and to admonish but was not welcome and was ordered out.

The sins of the people were threefold and fourfold (Amos 2:6). Religious ideals had collapsed; "they have spurned the Teaching of the Lord" (Amos 2:4). As a result, society, narrowly guided by the letter of the law, had lost all sense of justice: the rich oppressed the poor; "they have sold for silver those whose cause was just, and the needy for a pair of sandals" (Amos 2:6). They had become morally corrupt (Amos 2:7). And organized religion, in all its solemnity, had become a mockery: "they recline by every altar on garments taken in pledge, and drink in the House of their God wine bought with fines they imposed" (Amos 2:8).

To his own kin, who had lulled themselves into false security, feeling that as God's chosen people they were assured of special privileges and protection, Amos brought a sobering message from God:

> To Me, O Israelites, you are just like the Ethiopians—declares the Lord. True, I brought Israel up from the Land of Egypt, but also the Philistines from Caphtor and the Arameans from Kir. (Amos 9:7)

Thus did Amos proclaim the God of Israel as the universal God, as he preached to the powerful nations of his day, and to all nations of all times. God's compassion and sympathy extend to all members of humanity regardless of national origin, race, or color of skin—the dark-skinned Ethiopians were equal to the Israelites in God's concern. Amos is the first to proclaim the principle of racial equality.

Under these conditions the concept of the "chosen people" acquires a new meaning. Israel is indeed chosen, but only to set higher standards, to assume greater responsibility, to lead the way: "You alone have I singled out of all the families of the earth—that is why I will call you to account for all your iniquities" (Amos 3:2). The "family of Israel" is called to prepare the way for all nations to become "families of the earth." If Israel fails it will be punished, said Amos; if it lives up to the challenge, it has but done its duty. Judaism has humbly accepted the heavy burden of its "chosenness" and hopes for the day when the rest of humanity, in all its distinctiveness, will accept it too.

Hosea: God's Love

Hosea, citizen of the Kingdom of Israel, who lived from around 784 B.C.E. to 725 B.C.E., was a tender soul but deeply afflicted. The wife whom he loved deserted him to be with other men and returned to him only when her charms had faded. Under the compulsion of the divine command he took her back. His emotions are symbolic of the love of God: "Go, befriend a woman who, while befriended by a companion, consorts with others, just as the Lord befriends the Israelites, but they turn to other gods" (Hos. 3:1). Hosea's love and compassion in his acceptance of his wife were unconditional and unsurpassed. They embody the Jewish concept of all-embracing love as an attribute of God and the duty of human beings.

Hosea rebuked the people in the Kingdom of Israel for their abandonment of God—which to him was "harlotry"— as well as for their dependence on political alliances, factionalism, and intrigues rather than on God. But love is the key to his rebukes, God's love will never be shaken. The prophet urged the people to find their way to God, and the road consists not of sacrifices but of a turning of the heart, for God would "desire goodness, not sacrifice; obedience to God, rather than burnt offerings" (Hos. 6:6). God responds to repentance in love: "I will heal their affliction, generously will I take them back in love; for My anger has turned away from them" (Hos. 14:5). "And I will espouse you forever," says God, "I will espouse you with righteousness and justice, and with goodness and mercy, and I will espouse you with faithfulness; then you shall be devoted to the Lord" (Hos. 2:21–22).

Isaiah: Rites and Righteousness—The Vision of the Future

While Amos and Hosea preached in the north, Isaiah raised his voice in the south, in the Kingdom of Judah. He did not speak all the prophecies that are contained in the Book of Isaiah, for it had at least two authors. One Isaiah, the man we shall presently discuss, is perhaps author of the first thirty-nine chapters, dating from around 740 B.C.E. to 701 B.C.E. At least one other man wrote chapters 40–66 at a later time; he is called the Second Isaiah, or Deutero-Isaiah. An editor unified both parts.

Isaiah's understanding of God's feelings and involvement with humanity is expressed in winged poetic language. His words reveal a man of power, a counselor of kings, and, perhaps, as some rabbinic commentators think, a prince. His position is reflected in the tone of his voice—his frankness, outspoken criticism, and undisguised cutting analysis. To him, faith in God and social justice are inextricably linked together. Israel is God's agent, but when it falls short, other powers may be divine tools to bring Israel back on the right road. In the end the whole earth will be filled with the spirit of God and walk in God's ways.

Isaiah recommended neutrality in the armed conflict between the great powers of Assyria and Egypt and counseled instead reliance on God's help. An exclusively political solution that did not take into consideration God's guiding power seemed to him an aberration. Having rejected the prophet's advice, the Kingdom of Israel was wiped out; Judah became a vassal state to Assyria but survived as Isaiah had predicted. Isaiah's admonitions transcended events and continue to have abiding meaning, for they rest on ultimate concerns. He was not so much interested in the immediate outcome of the struggle as in the survival of the people as a spiritual force. His view was directed toward "the end of days," toward the road leading to the future and the goal to be attained there.

For Isaiah, the strength of the people rests not in its Temple, prosperity, or victories but in its inner strength, its social justice. Worship without repentance and commitment to social justice is repugnant to God: "'What need have I of all your sacrifices?' says the Lord.... Learn to do good. Devote yourselves to justice;

aid the wronged. Uphold the rights of the orphan; defend the cause of the widow" (Isa. 1:11; 17).

At the end of days, all of humankind, led by Israel, will place itself under God's rule, and eternal peace will reign:

> For instruction [Torah] shall come forth from Zion, the word of the Lord from Jerusalem. Thus He will judge among the nations and arbitrate for the many peoples, and they shall beat their swords into plowshares and their spears into pruning hooks: Nation shall not take up sword against nation; they shall never again know war. (Isa. 2:3–4)

At that time Israel will be restored. This future of a renewed community of Israel is symbolized in the rule of a just king, a descendant of David, the son of Jesse:

> The spirit of the Lord shall alight upon him.... He shall sense the truth by his reverence for the Lord.... He shall judge the poor with equity and decide with justice for the lowly of the land.... Justice shall be the girdle of his loins, and faithfulness the girdle of his waist. The wolf shall dwell with the lamb ... nothing evil and vile shall be done; for the land shall be filled with devotion for the Lord as water covers the sea. In that day ... He will hold up a signal to the nations and assemble the banished of Israel, and gather the dispersed of Judah from the four corners of the earth. (Isa. 11:2–12)

Isaiah's utopia is not wishful thinking. Like a statesman, the prophet shows us the reasoned and attainable blueprint of a better world. The nations will retain their distinctions, each of them trying to promote the welfare of all of humanity by its own particular contribution. At the same time they will submit to the instruction going forth from Zion, namely, to restrict their sovereignty by placing it under an everlasting, universal divine law. They will not only make war no longer but abolish the teaching of war and all instruments of war, allowing every human being to live in peace and without fear. These are realistic aims that can be achieved by nations and governments that realize the futility of wars and the blessings of peace.

Isaiah's vision looks beyond time and space. It appears to address even the contemporary conflict in the Middle East:

In that day Israel shall be a third partner with Egypt and Assyria as a blessing on earth; for the Lord of Hosts will bless them, saying, "Blessed be my people Egypt, My Handiwork Assyria, and my very own Israel." (Isa. 19:24–25)

Isaiah's vision of the "end of days" has remained Israel's guiding light through the ages, shaping Jewish hopes, beliefs, and actions. It teaches that no nation can claim absolute sovereignty even in its "internal affairs." No state is a law unto itself; all nations stand under God's sovereignty and judgment. This principle was unknown to the world when it was first proclaimed by Isaiah; although it has remained largely unheeded by the human family throughout the ages, it remains a universal imperative. To the Jews it depicts the time of the Messiah.

Jeremiah: Tragic Prophet

Jeremiah's works date from around 626 B.C.E., during the reign of King Josiah of Judah, until after 582 B.C.E. The time of Jeremiah's life was tumultuous and ended in tragedy. Babylonia, having overthrown Assyria and taken its place as the most formidable eastern power, was locked in combat with Egypt. The kings of Judah, seeking full independence, switched their allegiance from one power to the other. When King Zedekiah of Judah (597 B.C.E.–587 B.C.E.) broke his solemn oath of fealty to Nebuchadnezzar, king of Babylonia, Nebuchadnezzar invaded Judah, occupied the country, and besieged Jerusalem. Briefly lifting the siege, he defeated Egypt, then resumed the siege. In 587 B.C.E. Jerusalem fell. The Temple, the royal palace, the great houses were burned to the ground, the walls razed, and the king and members of the aristocracy led into captivity. The land of Judah and

The Book of Lamentations, sometimes ascribed to Jeremiah, is recited on Tishah b'Av, the day Jews remember the fall of the Temple in 586 B.C.E. and 70 C.E.

the remnant of its population were then placed under a Jewish governor, Gedaliah.

God's call to Jeremiah, a lowly priest of Anatot in the territory of Benjamin, came to him when he was very young. He was told that he had been "chosen in the womb" and could not escape his burden. He was to speak to his countrymen in Judah, to rebuke and to comfort.

He boldly appeared in the Temple court to announce doom and disaster if they did not obey God, "abiding by the Teaching [Torah]" that God had "set before" the people (Jer. 26:4). He called for a return to God, to the observance of the Sabbath (Jer. 17:21–27), and to social justice (Jer. 21:12). He saw the political realities of the struggle between Egypt and Babylonia more clearly than the king and his court and knew that any hope of breaking the power of Babylonia was doomed. Only as Babylonia's vassals could the people of Judah avoid destruction and retain their spiritual independence.

To the king and the priests these words were treason. Jeremiah was ruthlessly pursued by the authorities, and, after many trials and fearing for his life, he went into hiding. Knowing that it was God's will that Judah should fall under Babylonia's overlordship, unless the king changed his policies, Jeremiah dictated the divine message that he had received to his disciple Baruch, who read the scroll to the people in the Temple. When the scroll was read to the king, the ruler burned it contemptuously. Jeremiah persevered, even though he knew his efforts to change the king's mind were in vain.

When disaster was inevitable and imminent, Jeremiah became the people's messenger of hope. On divine injunction, he bought a piece of land, now utterly worthless, and had the deed put into an earthenware jar to be preserved. He assured the people, about to go into captivity, that the land of Israel would be theirs again: "Houses, fields, and vineyards shall again be purchased in this land" (Jer. 32:15). Witnessing the tragedy of his people, he cried out in bitter pain at the fall of "fair Jerusalem."

After the fall of the Kingdom of Judah, Jeremiah remained and assisted Gedaliah, a dedicated Jew whom Nebuchadnezzar

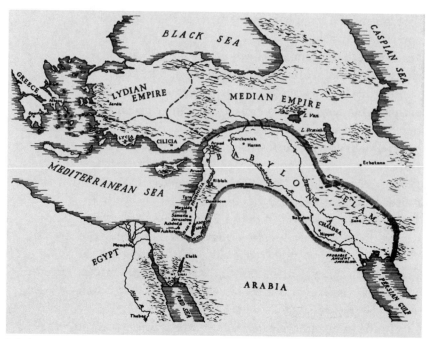

Babylonian Empire

had appointed governor of the territory, in the work of reconstruction. The remaining Jews were given assurances that they need not fear the Babylonians and could settle throughout the land. Jews who had fled to adjacent countries returned. When Gedaliah was assassinated by a member of the royal family of Judah, the people again ignored Jeremiah's advice and fled to Egypt. They dragged along the unwilling prophet, who abhorred the country and its cults. Against his urgent pleas, they turned to Egyptian deities. Jeremiah died in spiritual as well as physical exile, but not without hope in the future of his people.

Jeremiah was the most tragic of the prophets. The prophet's fate reflects God's pain. The people's deliberate blindness to and desertion from the truth of divine instruction caused great suffering to God. Jeremiah, as God's messenger, was caught in the middle. As God's spokesman to the people he had to convey God's just anger and rebuke them in the strongest words. As the people's advocate before God, he had to plead for mercy.

In his reactions to persecution and to the political events of his time, in his inner struggles and his spiritual victory, Jeremiah is the archetype of the Jewish people as a whole throughout history. This brings him close to us and makes his life and message relevant in our time. His life anticipates the life of the Jewish people through the centuries, including and above all during the Holocaust—in suffering, persecution, and extermination with courage, inner conflict, and doubt. For us as for him, life and message complement each other. Advocates of ethics and objective judges of reality, the Jews have suffered false accusations, unspeakable cruelties, and death. Like Jeremiah they could not give up, for God had enticed and overpowered them (Jer. 20:7). They have reaffirmed life by their will to survive even in a world of perverse heart, being certain in their hearts that they would ultimately return to the Land of Israel. Like Jeremiah, Jews trust God to bring them healing (Jer. 17:14).

The Amidah

"Heal me, O Lord, and let me be healed; save me and let me be saved; for You are my glory" (Jer. 17:14). In great wisdom, the Rabbis took this plea, translated into plural, as the text of the prayer for healing offered daily in the Amidah. In addition to clothing the prayer in biblical terms, they may also have wanted us to think of Jeremiah's life, for he rose from despair to spiritual victory, sought healing in God, and was a healer to others.

THE BABYLONIAN EXILE: THE HISTORICAL SIGNIFICANCE OF JEREMIAH'S LETTER. Jeremiah's own generation was not to see the prophet's hopes fulfilled. Family after family was led into captivity. At first they thought of it as a temporary exile, then, when the truth dawned on them, they lost themselves in unrelieved mourning and impotent hatred.

> By the rivers of Babylon, there we sat, sat and wept, as we thought of Zion. Upon the willows in the midst thereof we hanged our harps.... If I forget you, O Jerusalem, let my right hand wither; let my tongue stick to my palate.... O daughter of Babylon who are to be destroyed, happy shall he be that repay you as you have served us. Happy shall he be that takes and dashes your little ones against the rock. (Psalm 137)

Human but lacking the spirit of Jewish hope, these emotions dissipate in hopelessness; this is not constructive but,

At the destruction of the First Temple, Jews were forced into exile in Babylon, where the Gate of Ishtar stood near the Hanging Gardens, one of the seven wonders of the ancient world.

rather, is filled with hatred instead of love. While approving the people's love for Jerusalem Jeremiah had to check the elements of despair at their inception. He sent a letter to the exiled in Babylonia:

> Thus said the Lord of Hosts, the God of Israel, to the whole community which I exiled from Jerusalem to Babylon: Build houses and live in them, plant gardens and eat their fruit. Take wives and beget sons and daughters; and take wives for your sons, and give your daughters to husbands, that they may bear sons and daughters. Multiply there, do not decrease. And seek the welfare [shalom] of the city to which I have exiled you and pray to the Lord in its behalf; for in its prosperity you shall prosper. (Jer. 29:4–7)

This letter became basic to Jewish thinking. Dispersion was to be a condition of long duration. The Jews were therefore commanded to participate fully in the development of the countries where they were to live. They were to give the fullest measure of loyalty and devoted service, contribute constructively, and offer prayer for the countries of their home. This injunction, coming from the prophet Jeremiah, has been regarded by the Jews as a divine law. The promise of return also abides. That the "children shall return to their country" (Jer. 31:17) is Jeremiah's assurance.

Thus there was to be, from that day on, the diaspora, a worldwide Jewish community, even during the time of the Second Temple and commonwealth. The settlement in Babylonia continued to flourish and became a center of creativity, and the settlement in Egypt too would grow and develop. Babylonia and Egypt were the first two diaspora centers. Strong in numbers, faithful to their tradition, the Jews distinguished themselves as devoted citizens. Here lies the forecast of much of subsequent Jewish history.

Ezekiel: Individual Responsibility versus Inherited Sin

Ezekiel, a priest, was exiled to Babylonia in 597 B.C.E., before the destruction of the Temple. He had a terrifying mission: to extinguish all hope in his fellow captives that Judah and the Temple might still be saved.

A Jewish family from the town of Lachish is led into exile.

He was compelled to swallow a bitter scroll containing Israel's woes; it became sweet only as he obeyed God's will. Ezekiel came to be called the people's prophet and the individuals' shepherd. He was a mystic and told us about his mighty visions in great detail. He said of his first vision that it had come to him "in the land of the Chaldeans" (Ezek. 1:3), making it clear to his community that God was with them in their exile—the divine Presence was not bound to Jerusalem and the Temple but extended over all the earth. God can be envisioned in all glory wherever we seek the Presence.

Ezekiel emphasized individual responsibility. Every person is a "watchman" who must warn others and is responsible for sins committed by others insofar as the "watchman" has not tried to set the neighbor right through counsel and admonition. "But if you have warned the wicked man to turn back from his way, and he has not turned from his way, he shall die for his own sins, but you will have saved your life" (Ezek. 33:9).

The children of the first captives went to Ezekiel for counsel. Their minds were burdened. When Jerusalem was doomed, as Jeremiah and Ezekiel had predicted, their fathers and mothers saw its destruction as a punishment for their sinfulness; they had followed alien gods and committed other crimes and therefore had been sent

The Jews did not reject the culture of their Babylonian environment but took advantage of those elements that could strengthen Judaism. Thus the Hebrew months were now given Babylonian names, Nissan, Iyar. . . .

into exile. But then the children of the first exiles had tried to go in God's ways and yet were still far away from home. Were they, too, held guilty for the sins of their ancestors? Ezekiel, quoting Jeremiah, gave an answer that established the basic outlook of Judaism regarding inherited sin, including original sin. The answer is categorical: There is no inherited sin (Ezek. 18:1–29)—"The righteousness of the righteous shall be accounted to him alone, and the wickedness of the wicked shall be accounted to him alone" (Ezek. 18:20).

Judaism recognizes *Yetzer ha-Ra,* the inclination to yield to sinful temptation, but no inborn or inherited sinfulness, for everyone also has *Yetzer ha-Tov,* the impulse to do what is good. Victory over *Yetzer ha-Ra* is won through submission to Torah, the Rabbis maintain. No person can be held responsible for the sins committed by any ancestors. Judaism does not recognize any inherited sin, but it firmly upholds the principle of individual responsibility.

To those who came to Ezekiel, lamenting, "Our transgressions and our sins weigh heavily upon us: we are sick about them, how can we be restored to life?" he offered *teshuvah,* return to God:

A fresco at the synagogue of Dura-Europos (third century C.E.) tells the story of Ezekiel: first, the hand of God sets the prophet down in the valley of the dry bones, then God explains Ezekiel's duty, then Ezekiel prophesies to the bones, raising them to life.

As I live—declares the Lord God—it is not My desire that the wicked shall die, but that the wicked turn from his [evil] ways and live. Turn back, turn back from your evil ways, that you may not die, O House of Israel! (Ezek. 33:10–11)

This call to repentance has become one of the key admonitions in the liturgy of Yom Kippur.

To those who lamented that their future was lost, "Our bones are dried up, our hope is gone; we are doomed" (Ezek. 37:11), Ezekiel revealed his vision of the dry bones to whom God gave new life: "I will cause breath to enter you and you shall live again" (Ezek. 37:5). If Israel accepts God's warning and repents, then the dead bones will be filled with the spirit of the living God, will assume flesh and return to life. The future of the Jewish people is assured.

LIFE IN BABYLONIA. After their arrival in Babylonia, the Jews made a new life for themselves. They were occupied in agriculture or the building projects of Nebuchadnezzar, and other work. Strong leaders developed. Thirty-seven years after deportation from Jerusalem to Babylonia, King Jehoiachin was released from imprisonment (560 B.C.E.) and was appointed a member of the royal court, as an honored vassal king. He may have been the first of the "Exilarchs," scions of the House of David, who were for centuries the princely heads of the Jewish community in Babylonia (see Jer. 29:1, Ezek. 8:1 and 20:3).

The idolatry that had been endemic in the land of Judah during the time of the Temple disappeared. With the Temple in ruins and the sacrifices gone, the identity of the people had to be preserved by instruction and communality. The structure of family and society was strengthened.

Instruction and study in Torah, now the people's most precious possession, began to spread. Communality was achieved as groups began to gather, spending the greater part of every Sabbath listening to the reading of Torah and gaining a deeper understanding of it through the explanations of the leaders. Inspired by prophets, who were public preachers, they initiated the sermon. Torah reading and study were surrounded by prayers, hymns, and psalms expressing yearning, hope, and thanksgiving; giving expression to the spirit of repentance that permeated the community; and invoking divine protection for the "peace of the city" as Jeremiah and Ezekiel had enjoined them to do.

Those who joined together in the search for God eventually came to be known as a *synagogue*, a "gathering." It was not a building and could not be destroyed; it has remained immune to the ravages of time and the attacks of enemies, though many places where synagogues met have been reduced to ashes. The meeting house eventually acquired the name of those who met in it: the gathering, synagogue.

Another center of Jewish life gradually emerged, *Bet ha-Midrash*, the House of Study. A spiritual and intellectual movement was started that continued for centuries. The rabbi, teacher, distinguished by knowledge and conduct, took the place of the priest. Study became worship; the table with the Book became an altar; the family gathered around it in holy communion. Jewish love of knowledge emerged.[3]

THE END OF THE EXILE. Like Moses, who had been permitted to see the land but not enter it, Ezekiel was given a vision of the Temple of the future in all its splendor but would not live to serve in it as a priest. The events of the years following Ezekiel's prophesies are described in other books of the Bible—the Book of Daniel and the Book of Ezra. Dynastic power struggles and internal conflicts between rulers and priests brought an end to the Babylonian empire, whose last regent, Belshazzar (552–543 B.C.E.), is mentioned in the Book of Daniel.

Meanwhile Cyrus, a vassal of the king of Media, had defeated his overlord, taken the capital of Ecbatana (see Ezra 6:2), and founded the Persian Empire, which he set out to expand. Utilizing the dissension in Babylonia, he advanced against it, found an enthusiastic welcome, and was crowned King of Babylonia, King of the Lands. Having achieved his goal with the support of the Babylonian priests, his first step was the restoration and return to them of their temples, previously expropriated by the Babylonian kings, and the reinstatement of the ancient gods throughout his empire.

This included the restoration of the Temple at Jerusalem, around 516 B.C.E. In the first year of his reign, Cyrus issued a proclamation permitting the Jews to "go up to Jerusalem that is in Judah and build the House of the Lord God of Israel, the God that is in Jerusalem" (Ezra 1:3–4). The formal edict that was

3. The Talmud, B.T. Megillah 29a, finds a direct reference to the synagogue in the "small sanctuary" mentioned in Ezek. 11:16. Modern scholars also point to Ezek. 8:1, 14:1, and 20:1 ("the elders of Israel sitting before Me"). See Geoffrey Wigoder, ed., *The Encyclopedia of Judaism* (New York: Macmillan, 1989), "Synagogue."

stored in the royal chancellery gave the measurements of the Temple and provided that "the expenses shall be paid by the palace." The vessels that Nebuchadnezzar had carried away were to be returned (Ezra 6:3–5).

The Jews were permitted to go back to their land. This act of kindness provided the king with a grateful, friendly population in Judah, a border province of his empire facing toward Egypt.

The Second Isaiah: Israel's Future and the Meaning of Suffering

The returning Jews found prophets to guide them. One of them was the man whom we call the Second Isaiah or Deutero-Isaiah, whose messages form the second part of the Book of Isaiah, chapters 40 to 66. In inspired words he reviewed all of history—past, present, and future—as enacted by God, Israel, and humanity.

Isaiah reveals that God called on the whole universe to welcome the people home and bring them comfort: "Comfort, oh comfort My people, says your God. Speak tenderly to Jerusalem, and declare to her that her term of service is over, that her iniquity is expiated; for she has received at the hand of the Lord double for all her sins" (Isa. 40:1–2). God's love has never been withdrawn, nor will it ever be: "My loyalty shall never move from you, nor my covenant of friendship be shaken—said the Lord, who takes you back in love" (Isa. 54:10).

But God also loves all of humanity. Israel was therefore appointed leader and light to the nations and peoples, to bring all of them into the divine Presence, to Zion (Isa. 60:1–14). The splendor of Jerusalem, symbol of a restored Israel, spiritual capital of humanity, would be based on the fact that the city was the center of God's teachings. Israel was not simply to live in grandeur but to be the bearer of the Covenant, God's servant and model of social justice (Isa. 42:6–7).

To be true to its vocation Israel must not be elitist, accepting the gifts of others but holding itself apart from them. With open arms and hearts it must receive all non-Jews who wish to cast their lot in faith, fellowship, and destiny with it. They become Jews in the fullest sense to God and kin to the people they have freely chosen. They join the Covenant and become witnesses (Isa. 56:3–8).

Isaiah firmly rejected an idea that had just been advanced in the Persian Empire by Zoroaster (c. 660–583 B.C.E.), who had taught that two equal forces, God, who is light and goodness, and a dark, satanic Power, are constantly engaged in combat and determine the destiny of the world and humans. Addressing Cyrus, ruler of Persia, Isaiah declared unequivocally that Cyrus's deities had neither substance nor power, nor do any other gods that people may worship, for there is but one God, who is the sole creator of all and who sustains the entire world:

> I am the Lord and there is none else; beside Me, there is no god. I engird you, though you have not known Me, so that they may know, from east to west, that there is none but Me. I am the Lord and there is none else, I form light and create darkness, I make weal and create woe—I the Lord do all these things. (Isa. 45:5–7)

The concept of universal monotheism, enunciated here for the first time in the Bible, is the Second Isaiah's most radical contribution to Jewish theology. This affirmation of God's sole and universal power opens daily morning worship.

In a chapter about the Suffering Servant (Isa. 53), the Second Isaiah turns to the question, Why do the innocent suffer? The Suffering Servant is the metaphor for Israel, the Jewish people. The servant of God has, on behalf of the world's redemption, accepted disdain and untold suffering without demur. Isaiah hopes that humanity will eventually be transformed by the example of such heroic faith.

At the same time, the prophet made clear to his people and to all who suffer that suffering need not be regarded as the wages of sin; it may be a test of strength, a test of faith, a sign of being chosen. The Suffering Servant of God demonstrates to a calloused world that nothing can make him or her waver in dedication. Were she always blessed, she would not be a servant but a person of privilege; it would be easy for her to love God. Were he to know that reward and punishment are always linked to our actions as effect follows cause, he might serve God for selfish reasons, to escape suffering or find happiness. The true servant of God must be willing to be tested and maintain faith in adversity. He or she bears the wounds a sinful world has inflicted—for its sake, to make it eventually see the light, and that its children, too, remain steadfast amidst persecution. The reward is a humanity reborn in allegiance to God.

The Twelve Minor Prophets

The minor prophets enlarge our insight into the historical events we have traced and their spiritual meaning. Scholars have suggested that the number twelve under which these prophetical pronouncements were edited was based on the tradition of the twelve tribes of Israel; later on we find the twelve counselors of the community of Qumran and the twelve disciples of Jesus.

Hosea and Amos were contemporaries of the first Isaiah in the mid- to late eighth century B.C.E. Joel, Jonah, Obadiah, and Micah can also be said to belong to the eighth century, the time of the fall of the Kingdom of Israel. Jonah is mentioned in 2 Kings 14:25 as a contemporary of King Amaziah of Judah and King Jeroboam II of Israel (782–741 B.C.E.). Nahum, Habakkuk, and Zephaniah lived after the destruction of the Kingdom of Israel in 722 B.C.E. The activity of Haggai, Zechariah, and Malachi falls in the period after the Babylonian Exile and coincides with the return and the building of the Second Temple (539–516 B.C.E.). Malachi is regarded by the later Sages as a member of the Great Assembly (early Second Temple period).

AMOS and HOSEA have been previously discussed.

JOEL saw in a plague of locusts the prelude of future disasters and a cataclysmic battle from which Israel will emerge victorious, henceforth to dwell in security, while its enemies will be destroyed. Natural disasters, far from being accidents, are to be warnings calling for self-scrutiny.

OBADIAH—meaning "God's servant"—was, according to a late rabbic legend, a convert to Judaism. He equally predicts God's punishment upon the nations that have "dispossessed" the House of Jacob and will in turn be dispossessed. He reveals that the Jew by choice is indeed one with the House of Israel.

JONAH never preached to his own people. His primary mission was to the people of the "great city of Nineveh," capital of

Even after his journey in the belly of the fish, the reluctant prophet Jonah tried to evade God's command to call the people of Nineveh to repentance.

Assyria, to call them to repentance and thereby survival. Yet they were the greatest threat to Israel's survival. Jonah therefore faced the dilemma of either saving the people of Nineveh and thereby risk destroying Israel, or refusing to go to Nineveh and thereby possibly save his own people. He decided in favor of his own people and tried to escape by ship, but the Assyrians had to be given the opportunity to repent. And Jonah could not escape. In a storm he was tossed overboard and swallowed by a huge fish in whose belly he remained for three days and nights until he was spewed out at his God-ordained destination. In the fish, he called on God, but his prayer was not a plea but a hymn of thanksgiving for divine deliverance. He knew that his repentance would evoke divine pardon and acclaimed it as an already accomplished fact. Jonah succeeded in his mission, the king and the people of Nineveh repented, God forgave them, and they were spared destruction.

Jonah's trust while in the belly of the fish has guided the Jewish people, to whom Jonah's confinement has symbolized their life under the pressure of their enemies. And God's command to the prophet has guided Jewish obligations and tolerance toward non-Jews. Therefore the Book of Jonah has been chosen as the prophetic lesson on Yom Kippur afternoon to teach Jews love for enemies.

MICAH chastised the social injustice that had permeated all classes of society. The concluding verses of his book are recited on the first day of Rosh Hashanah, when the congregation goes to the banks of rivers and lakes, the members symbolically casting their sins into the water:

> Who is a God like You, forgiving iniquity and remitting transgression; Who has not maintained His wrath forever against the remnant of His own people, because He loves graciousness! He will take us back in love; He will cover up our iniquities, You will hurl all our sins into the depths of the sea. You will keep faith with Jacob, loyalty to Abraham, as You promised on oath to our fathers in days gone by. (Mic. 7:18–20)

NAHUM, ZEPHANIAH, and HABAKKUK paraphrase the prophecies of the major prophets, both against Judah and against Assyria and Babylonia.

Habakkuk's prayer was in the hearts and on the lips of the Jews during the Nazi years:

> O Lord! I have learned of Your renown; I am awed, O Lord, by Your deeds. Renew them in these years, Oh, make them known in these years! Though angry, may You remember compassion. (Hab. 3:2)

And the prophet's trust in divine redemption became the affirmation of the sufferers in the death camps: "Even if it tarries, wait for it still; for it will surely come, without delay" (Hab. 2:3).

HAGGAI and ZECHARIAH encouraged the building of the Temple after the return from the Babylonian Exile. Their writings are filled with the joy of restoration and the confidence that God will abide with Israel, and Jerusalem will become the center of all of humanity.

ZECHARIAH, a prophet who had many visions, issued a renewed call for social justice. Extolling the Temple, yet to be completed, he assured the people that God dwelled again in Jerusalem. A great battle would come, in which those who fought against Jerusalem will be routed and rot away. Then all nations will make pilgrimages to Jerusalem to celebrate Sukkot, the festival of divine sheltering.

The time will arrive when all the days of fasting and mourning, which the prophet enumerates, will become days for joy and gladness (Zech. 8:18–19). From this list, the fast days of the year have been derived.

Zechariah raised the issue of conversion and appears to have favored the admission of non-Jews:

> The many peoples and the multitude of nations shall come to seek the Lord of Hosts in Jerusalem and to entreat the favor of the Lord. Thus said the Lord of Hosts: In those days, ten men from nations of every tongue will take hold—they will take hold of every Jew by a corner of his cloak and say, "Let us go with you, for we have heard that God is with you." (Zech. 8:22–23)

In contrast to other prophets, Zechariah is addressed by an angel, not directly by God. In his book we also find mention of Satan, who is rebuked by God's angel for his enmity of Israel.

MALACHI—his name unknown, for the word simply means "My messenger"—rebukes the priests, but his message is universal: "Did not one God create us?" (Mal. 2:10). With Malachi's book, Nevi'im ends in a renewed charge to remain true to Moses' Torah (Mal. 3:22) and in a grand vision of history's consummation, when Elijah will come "before the coming of the awesome, fearful day of the Lord" (Mal. 3:23). Elijah, intrepid fighter against idolatry and compromise, bold antagonist of king and court, restorer of life and hope to the poor, had gone to heaven and never died (see 2 Kings 2). He is seen as God's ambassador, humanity's guide, Israel's protector, and the herald of redemption, the days of the Messiah. Referring to Elijah, Malachi offers assurance that there need be no cataclysmic battle at "the end of days" if the people, guided by Elijah's uncompromising commitment to God, return to the Torah of Moses.

Chapter 3

KETUVIM

The Collected Writings

Ketuvim, Collected Writings, the third section of the Hebrew Bible, contains, as its name indicates, a collection of writings, of varying character. It includes Psalms, Proverbs, Job, the Song of Songs, Ruth, Lamentations, Ecclesiastes, Esther, Daniel, Ezra, Nehemiah, and Chronicles 1 and 2—among these are some of the greatest achievements of the human spirit.

EZRA AND NEHEMIAH

The historical developments surrounding the return and reconstruction of the Jewish community after the Babylonian Exile and the building of the Second Temple are recounted in the Books of Ezra and Nehemiah. The reforms of these two men have had an abiding effect on Judaism. With the events told in these books biblical history comes to an end.

Jews began to return to Eretz Yisrael immediately upon the publication in 538 B.C.E. of the edict of the Persian king Cyrus that restored the Jews to Jerusalem. During Cyrus's and his successors' reigns approximately fifty thousand Jews arrived in several waves (Ezra 2:64). In 522 B.C.E. Cyrus's dynasty was overthrown, and Darius, member of a rival family, ascended the throne.

Persian Empire

Zerubbabel, a grandson of King Jehoiachin of Judah, was
appointed governor of the province of Judah (Ezra 4:3), and the
rebuilding of the Temple began. The returning Jews soon encountered the hostility of the Samaritans, named after the Kingdom of Israel's former capital city, who claimed the right to share
in the restoration of the Temple. But their faith and way of life
were regarded as dangers to the purity of Judaism, for they had
intermarried with foreigners and pagans and had fused Jewish
ideas with pagan customs and patterns of life (Ezra 4:2). Their
claim was categorically rejected by Zerubbabel. Despite the
Samaritans' attempt to block the Jews' erecting of the Temple,
Zerubbabel, inspired by the prophets Haggai and Zechariah,
continued construction. Eventually, Darius sanctioned the construction and ordered that it be funded by public taxes, ordaining that sacrifices for the king and the royal family be offered in
it (Ezra 6:1–12), an ordinance that was obeyed up to the rebellion of the Jews against Rome (68 C.E.). Haggai seems to have envisioned the restoration of the dynasty of David with Zerubbabel
as its first king, and Zechariah actually hoped to see Zerubbabel

crowned. But instead Zerubbabel suddenly disappeared from history.

With the departure of Zerubbabel and the completion of the Temple, dedicated with great joy in the sixth year of King Darius's reign (516 B.C.E.), exactly seventy years after the destruction of the first one, the power and authority of the high priest grew. The hostility between Jews and Samaritans abated for a time, and the Samaritans accepted the Temple and the high priest as the center and principal authority in their religious life.

During the reign of the Persian king Artaxerxes (464–424 B.C.E.) a revolt in Egypt had to be quashed. The king sought to strengthen the loyal Jewish population in adjacent Judah and so gave permission to Ezra, a priest and scribe in Babylonia, to lead a new group of settlers back to the land. "Expert in the Teaching of Moses which the Lord God of Israel had given" (Ezra 7:6), Ezra was given the authority to

> appoint magistrates and judges to judge all the people in the province ... who know the laws of your God, and to teach those who do not know them. Let anyone who does not obey the law of your God and the law of the king be punished with dispatch, whether by death, corporal punishment, confiscation of possessions, or imprisonment. (Ezra 7:25–26)

Endowed with absolute power,

Jerusalem and the Diaspora in the Second Temple Period

Close ties existed between Jerusalem and diaspora Jewry. Wherever they lived, Jews regarded Jerusalem and its Temple as their center and contributed regularly to its upkeep.

Babylonian Jewry, as Ezra and Nehemiah reveal, exerted a decisive influence on the community in the Land of Israel and became the leader of world Jewry during various periods of Jewish history.

Egyptian Jewry also flourished. A temple was built at Elephantine, the modern Aswan, where sacrifices were offered; but Egyptian Jews remained closely bound to Jerusalem, which was to them the authoritative source of religious instruction.

The Samaritans gave their allegiance to the Temple in Jerusalem but, under the strict rules imposed by Ezra and Nehemiah, were not considered trustworthy. When a brother of the high priest in Jerusalem took a Samaritan wife and was therefore no longer permitted to function as a priest in the Temple, his father-in-law, the governor of Samaria, built him a new temple on Mt. Gerizim and installed him as high priest. This marked the separation of the Samaritans from the fold of the Jewish faith. When Alexander the Great took the city of Samaria this temple was razed, but the small remnant of Samaritans still offers sacrifices on Mt. Gerizim.

Ezra arrived at Jerusalem around 458 B.C.E. In solemn assembly, he categorically ordered the people to separate themselves "from the peoples of the land and from the foreign women" (Ezra 10:11).

In about 445 B.C.E. Ezra found an associate in Nehemiah, an official at the Persian king's court. The king granted Nehemiah a twelve-year leave of absence to serve as governor of the province *Yehud* (Aramaic for Judah), where he would rebuild Jerusalem and help resettle the Jews returning from Babylonia. His first task was to restore the city walls of Jerusalem. Volunteers from all over the country, each group building a different section, completed the work in only fifty-two days, despite an increasing threat from the forces of Sanballat, governor of Samaria, who was determined to stop the construction (Neh. 3–4). Now that the walls were completed, Jerusalem had to be repopulated, and Nehemiah ordered that the magistrates and one out of every ten families throughout the country settle there (Neh. 11).

The greatest concern of Nehemiah and Ezra was the religious laxity they noted among the people who had not been exiled to Babylonia. Both leaders were dismayed by the association of the Jews with "the peoples of the land," that is, non-Jews, and their marriages to women not of Jewish descent. They also deplored the lack of observance of the Sabbath and the avoidance of financial obligations to the Temple and its priests. Therefore, on the 1st of Tishrei in the year 445 B.C.E., Nehemiah and Ezra assembled the people in a convocation that lasted several weeks. Standing on a tower built for the occasion, Ezra read the Torah to them, solemnly committing them to its injunctions (Neh. 8:1 ff.). The people then signed a compact "to observe carefully all the commandments of the Lord our Lord, His rules and laws" (Neh. 10:30), not to permit the marriages of their children to those of the "peoples of the land," to divorce their wives of non-Jewish descent (Neh. 9:2) so that "those of the stock of Israel separated themselves from all foreigners," not to transact any business with the "peoples of the land" on the Sabbath, to pay a self-imposed tax and fulfill all their obligations to the Temple and to make generous gifts to the Temple and those ministering there. According to the Sages of later centuries, Ezra established a permanent body with legislative and executive authority, the Great Assembly, which included a number of prophets in its ranks and existed for many generations; perhaps the great convocation of Ezra and Nehemiah was its precursor.

Under the influence of the teachings of the Second Isaiah and Zechariah (see especially Isa. 56:3–8 and Zech. 2:15, 8:20–23), a spirit of hospitality developed toward those who wished to affiliate with the Jewish people. The Jews of Babylonia, on the other hand, discouraged conversion, and their influence came to be felt as they returned to Judah. The position of Ezra and Nehemiah regarding converts was to create an inner tension in Judaism which has continued to the present day. In Babylonia, the Jewish community assured its coherence and survival through the family, its purity of lineage, and its undiluted obedience to the laws of Torah. The people in Judah, however, who had not had to endure the Exile, drew their sense of security from the land, which held the promise of survival. The young men and women married their neighbors' daughters or sons, whose lives and ambitions they shared, whether or not they were Jews. Ezra and Nehemiah saw in this intermarriage a danger to the Jewish people. Even if the spouses affiliated with Judaism, they had not been born as Jews; they would, Ezra and Nehemiah feared, inject elements of pagan culture into their families and weaken the law of Moses.

Without Judaism's absolute purity, the Jewish people could not long endure: this was the foundation of the ordinances of Ezra and Nehemiah. They therefore ruled that the foreign women would be dismissed without regard to the sincerity of their attachment to Judaism, and endeavors to bring converts into its fold were suppressed. Their ordinances, issued at a moment of crisis in the Jewish community, would have made Jews into a race; Judaism would have been deprived of the universalism proclaimed in Isaiah's revolutionary and unique concept that the stranger could become a Jew by pledging "to hold fast to the Covenant" for life.

THE BOOK OF RUTH

In Ezra's and Nehemiah's own time the Book of Ruth stood as a subtle protest against their exclusiveness and offered a testimony that converts, far from being a burden, can be an invaluable asset to Judaism and the Jewish people. The Book of Ruth tells a moving tale. A man of Judah and his sons went to Moab to escape a famine at home. The sons married two daughters of the land—non-Jews—but their joy was brief. Both husbands and the father died, leaving only the three women—Naomi, the old widowed mother, and her two widowed daughters-in-law, Orpah and Ruth. Naomi decided to return home, and said farewell to the younger women. But Ruth replied:

> Do not urge me to leave you, to turn back and not follow you. For wherever you go, I will go; wherever you lodge, I will lodge; your people shall be my people, and your God my God. Where you die, I will die, and there I will be buried. Thus and more may the Lord do to me if anything but death parts me from you. (Ruth 1:16–17)

As Ruth proclaims her faith to Naomi, she chooses to join Jews in their bond with God and the people.

Even in a foreign land the beauty of Judaism had wrought its miracle. By strength of conviction and nobility of love, Naomi had drawn Ruth to the inspiring fountainhead of Judaism. Ruth, in turn, like many later converts, brought great enrichment to Judaism. The story proudly relates that Ruth, the Moabite, became the great-grandmother of David, the ideal king of Israel. She became the paradigm of the convert to Judaism and of the blessings the convert can bring to the Jewish people (Ruth Rabba 2:22; B.T. Berakhot 7b).

THE BOOK OF ESTHER

Conversions continued in Judaism. The Book of Esther, written during a period of severe persecutions, relates with a kind of naive pride the story of many conversions. Esther, a Jewish girl, had been chosen by Ahasuerus, king of Persia, as his queen. She thwarted a plot to exterminate the Jews, and her uncle, Mordecai, was made prime minister. With this new regime in power, "many of the people of the land professed to be Jews" (see Esther 8:17). Although the historicity of this story, on which the minor festival of Purim rests, has never been proved, the spirit behind it—the happy acceptance of those who wished to join the faith—remains important.

CONVERSION IN THE JEWISH EXPERIENCE. Abraham and Sarah were converts. They migrated to Canaan with "the souls . . . gotten in Haran." Abraham, the Rabbis hold, instilled in those following him an unconditional attachment to God. They were Jews with full rights and privileges, which was confirmed by Isaiah (Isa. 56:3–6). From Abraham the Rabbis learned that a man who brings a single person under the wings of the divine Presence is regarded as if he had created him. Anyone seeking the security of Israel, even if it were only for the sake of marrying a Jewish woman, must be accepted and given all rights.[1]

---

1. Yalkut, *Shelah*, 745: "Abraham brought people into his home, dined with them, and befriended them, then converted them. . . . Hence you learn that a man who brings a single person under the wings of the divine Presence is regarded as if he had created him" (Gen. Rabba 39:14).

Later, we find Jacob proudly blessing his grandchildren, the sons of Joseph and Osnat, daughter of the priest of On, in Egypt; his blessing expressed the hope that all sons in Israel might be like Ephraim and Manasseh. Moses himself had married a Midianite woman and is praised for having first also converted her father Jethro, a pagan priest (Exod. Rabba 1:32). A multitude of mixed ancestry had joined the Israelites on their Exodus from Egypt; Canaanites and Philistines had become absorbed in the course of Israel's life. The Second Isaiah and Zechariah had even raised the ready acceptance of converts into a principle (Isa. 56:3–8; Zech. 2:15, 8:20–23). In the first century before our era, Queen Helena of Adiabene and her royal family accepted Judaism. So did the translator of the Torah into Aramaic (B.T. Avoda Zara 11a). During the period of the Roman Empire, Jews traveled as missionaries all over the known world; actually, the early Christian missionaries were able to build on the foundations laid by their Jewish predecessors.

With the fall of the Second Temple, when the Land and the Temple could no longer serve as unifying forces, the rules of admission to Judaism became more stringent and the arguments for and against conversion more pointed, but Jewish missionary work was brought to a halt only much later by the edicts of Christian emperors. Later still, the Church prohibited Jewish proselytizing, condemning to death the converting Jew and the convert alike.

A person became a Jew by studying the faith, by accepting it, by immersion, and—for men—by circumcision. A rabbinical court, assured of the candidate's sincerity, made the admission formal (B.T. Yevamot 47a–b). These rules have not changed. It was advised not to make the inquiry too detailed and not to impose too many commandments. That ruling is not followed in Israel and in some other countries, where conversion is very difficult.

The ideas of Ezra and Ruth are both operative in Jewish life today. Conversion is seen by some as a challenge and opportunity, and by others as a liability.

THE PSALMS

The Book of Psalms is an anthology of 150 poems and hymns which are divided into five books corresponding to the books of the Torah. In it we find plea and praise, jubilation and lamentation, triumph and defeat—the full range of human emotion. The book's name is *Tehillim*, "Praises," for both outcry and laud are praise; all prayer acknowledges God, to whom the Psalms are directed. The term "Psalter" derives from the psaltery, the harp that accompanied the recitation of the hymns.

Some of the Psalms give information about their history or use. The poems are by many writers, whose attributions are sometimes given, among them Moses (Ps. 90), Asaph (Ps. 50, 73–83), the sons of Korah (Ps. 42, 44–49, 84, 85, 87, 88), and Solomon (Ps. 72 and 127). By tradition, King David is regarded as the author of many, (Ps. 3–9, 11–32, 34–41). Some Psalms were composed for Temple worship and processions around the city and to the Temple mount (Ps. 24, 48). Others can be historically dated (Ps. 137: "By the waters of Babylon"). Some review Israel's history and envision the future and fulfillment of Israel's dreams (Ps. 126, 132). Every day of the week has its special Psalm; Psalm 92, for example, is designated for the Sabbath. Sometimes the instruments to be used for the performance of a Psalm are indicated, and the annotation "Selah" may be an instruction to the choir master to shift his voice into a higher key.

Alphabet Psalms and Parallelism
Some Psalms follow the Hebrew alphabet, each verse beginning with a successive letter. Parallelism, in which the second half of the verse paraphrases the first, is a widely used poetic form. Psalm 145 offers an example of an alphabet psalm and uses parallelism.

(Alef) *I will extol You, my God and King*
and I will bless
Your name for ever
and ever.

(Bet) *Every day will I bless You*
and praise Your name
forever and ever.

(Gimmel) *Great is the Lord and much acclaimed;*
His greatness cannot be fathomed.

(Dalet) *One generation shall laud Your works to another*
and declare Your mighty acts.

The Psalms are unique among the books of the Bible. God speaks to us in the rest of the Bible, but in the Psalms we respond. Our response runs the gamut of emotions: jubilation, "Bless the Lord, O my soul: O Lord, my God, You are very great" (Ps. 104:1); hope, "We set our hope on the Lord, He is our help and shield" (Ps. 33:20); longing, "Like a hind crying for water, my soul cries for You, O God; my soul thirsts for God, the living God" (Ps. 42:2–3); anguish, "Deliver me, O God, for the waters have reached my neck" (Ps. 69:2); repentance, "Have mercy upon me, O God . . . and purify me of my sin; for I recognize my transgressions, and am ever conscious of my sin" (Ps. 51:3–5); and, at the end, a climactic unison of a united humankind, "Let all that breathes praise the Lord. Hallelujah" (Ps. 150:6). No emotion is omitted; no situation in life is left out. Nature, humankind, individual, nation, Israel, past, present, and future— all are drawn into the circle of contemplation. So deep is the faith of the Psalms that even the Day of Judgment becomes a day of joy (Ps. 96).

This faith provides the context for all the states of the soul shown by the Psalms. The Psalms take up the question of why the wicked flourish and the innocent suffer. Again and again the human creature suffers and cries out, in agony, in despair. But in faith the person afflicted affirms God and sees a road to God even in suffering. Similarly, in this faith the sinner turns to God, who will surely forgive. The certainty of God's guiding presence gives the penitent confidence even in the face of death (Ps. 23).

Though he speaks in the first person, the Psalmist thinks not only of himself. The "I" of the Psalms may be the "I" of the person reciting the Psalms, or the "I" of the household of Israel, or the "I" of humanity as a whole, for the Psalmist's outlook is a universal one. The Psalms accept Isaiah's and Micah's vision of a world where the Torah will go forth from Zion and all humankind as one will receive God's blessing.

Israel is a household, and the family of Aaron is the priestly household within Israel, but the divine blessing extends to all who fear God. "He will bless those who fear the Lord, small and great alike" (Ps. 115:13). God is good to all creatures, as we pray in Psalm 145, which is recited three times daily in traditional Jewish worship. Significantly, the word "Israel" is not mentioned in Psalm 145; God is the God of "all creatures."

The Psalms affirm what the prophets teach. At the solemn consecration of the Temple, Israel's national sanctuary, Solomon proclaimed God's universality and called for ethics and a concern with every human being; we find the same ideas in Psalm 24, most probably composed for the procession to the Temple. Malachi complains of the loss of fellowship (Mal. 2:10); the Psalmist affirms its value (Ps. 133:1).

All the teachings of the Torah and the Prophets are found in the Psalms, once more repeated by the human being who has embraced them. The Psalms have thus become a second Pentateuch, a second "Torah" to the Jew, in their instruction, in their testimony to God's love and abiding goodness.

THE PSALMS IN THE JEWISH EXPERIENCE. The significance of the Psalms in the life of the Jew throughout history can hardly be overestimated. The Jew has found in the Psalms an outlet for the deepest feelings, an answer to all questions, a comfort in distress. In addition, public worship begins and ends with Psalms. The Sabbath is welcomed by reciting particular Psalms. Holy days are distinguished by the recital of "the Praise," the Hallel, consisting of Psalms 113–118. Psalms are quoted in the poetry of prayers. The very structure of the morning and evening prayers follows Psalm 19, as praise to God, the creator of nature, leads to thanksgiving for God's Torah.

PROVERBS

In Proverbs, *Hokhmah*, "Wisdom," speaks, personified by a woman. She conveys her insights in wise sayings. In her aphorisms we may seem to hear Plato's ideas as accepted by a Jew, but to the Jewish author the Platonic ideal of study and

Knowledge of King Solomon's wisdom was so widespread that he was credited with having written Proverbs, the Song of Songs, and Ecclesiastes. When he built the Temple at Jerusalem, he gave Israel a cultural and religious center.

example are rooted in reverence for God, Torah, and religious discipline. The wise find understanding through God's Torah; the true *sophia*, wisdom, builds all of life on divine instruction, trusting in God even in trials. Constituting the foundation of the world and of its order, Wisdom is equated with Torah.

THE BOOK OF JOB

The Book of Job is profoundly indebted to the Second Isaiah, who in speaking of the Suffering Servant of God (Isa. 53) determined that the suffering of the righteous may be a divine test of strength and faith; the sufferer may be a role model for others to guide them in their trust in God. The Book of Job illustrates the prophet's message.

As the story goes, Job was a good and pious man, yet he was deeply afflicted. He lost his fortune, his children, his home, and his health. Covered with boils, he sat in the dust. Why should he suffer? He was visited by three friends who wished to help him understand his suffering. With great audacity and harsh words, Job remonstrated with God. Cursing the day of his birth, he bitterly cried out, "Why does He give light to the sufferer and life to the bitter in spirit; to those who wait for death but it does not come" (Job 3:20–21). The friends were shocked, for they had the usual conviction that anyone who suffers simply reaps the fruit of sins. Eliphaz said: "Those who plow evil and sow mischief reap them" (Job 4:8). Bildad added, "Surely God does not despise the blameless, He gives no support to evildoers" (Job 8:20). Sin brings retribution, they thought, so if Job was punished, he must have sinned.

Job could have resolved the problem in two obvious ways: He could admit that there might be some hidden guilt in him; or he could simply have concluded that there is no God. He accepted neither solution. The deepest convictions of his heart affirmed to him the certainty that he was not a sinner. And he was equally convinced of God's existence, saying "I know that my Redeemer lives" (see Job 19:25).

The third friend, Elihu, presented an acceptable answer:

"God speaks time and again—though man does not perceive it—... Then He opens men's understanding, and by disciplining them leaves His signature" (Job 33:14–16). We must accept suffering as a test of faith and in accepting we will find insight and strength.

Here, the story might have come to an end, but instead, God personally spoke to Job:

> Where were you when I laid the earth's foundations? ... Do you know who fixed its dimensions ... Who set its cornerstone when the morning stars sang together and all the divine beings shouted for joy? ... Have you ever commanded the day to break, assigned the dawn its place? ... Have you penetrated to the sources of the sea, or walked in the recesses of the deep? Have the gates of death been disclosed to you? Have you seen the gates of deep darkness?... Can you tie cords to Pleiades or undo the reins of Orion? ... Who put wisdom in the hidden parts? Who gave understanding to the mind? (Job 38:4–36)
>
> Would you impugn My justice? Would you condemn Me that you may be right? (Job 40:8)

God reminded Job of the limitations of human knowledge and power; of our inability to understand the divinely ordained processes of the universe. No human being can understand God's actions. The human being must therefore acknowledge God's justice under all circumstances, accepting it willingly, as does the rest of creation.

Why did God speak directly, after Elihu had already made the point clear? God spoke to dispel three possible doubts. First, God appears as final arbiter among Job's three friends, to endorse Elihu's view against the others. Second, God's direct interference allays Job's and the reader's doubt that we can really be certain that God exists when we see so many good people suffer. Third, God reassures Job about his goodness; to hear the voice of God is the reward of the pious.

The Book of Job opens in heaven with a prologue in the form of a dialogue between God and Satan. Satan challenges God, who has delighted in Job's uprightness. Of course Job is good, Satan argues, since God has abundantly blessed him. "But lay Your hand upon all that he has and he will surely blaspheme You to Your face" (Job 1:11). Convinced of Job's unshakable faith, God permits Satan to test him.

The controversy between God and Satan as God's determined antagonist, indicates that Zoroastrian ideas had reached Judaism after spreading from Persia through the Hellenistic world. Zoroaster postulated the principle of dualism. God is the source of light and truth (Ahura Mazhda), and the angels are carriers of the divine will; Satan (Ahriman) is the source of darkness and evil, with devils as executors of destruction. The two forces fight for supremacy on earth, until, at "the end of days" light will win after a cataclysmic battle. In the Book of Job Satan obviously wishes to defeat God by weaning Job away from his faith, but the antagonists are not equal. Satan too is a servant of God. Not very powerful, Satan becomes the force that wishes to promote evil but is compelled by God to promote good. Satan has come to symbolize the human inclination toward evil, and Judaism feels that this inclination serves a good purpose as a necessary condition of freedom. God desires that all human beings have the freedom to choose between good and evil. If they could not make such a choice, and did not have the opportunity to overcome temptation, they could not consider themselves truly free. Freedom requires the choice between good and evil. God hopes that human beings will choose goodness. Human glory consists in the choice of good.

Did Job really exist, or is the book simply pious educational fiction written in the form of a Platonic dialogue? The prophet Ezekiel saw Job as a real person and listed him, together with Noah and Daniel, as one of the three truly righteous men (Ezek. 14:14). In contrast, some of the ancient Rabbis maintained that Job never existed (J.T. Sota 5:6) and that the Book of Job is fiction. Neither of these views affects the importance of the Book of Job, for it offers not only a justification of God but also a guideline for human conduct. Unlike Isaiah's Suffering Servant, Job violently remonstrates against God but is forgiven and his family and fortunes are restored to him "when he prayed on behalf of his friends" (Job 42:10). The Rabbis explain, he was restored only because he overcame his hostility against his friends, even though they had so grievously wronged him, and prayed on their behalf (Pesikta Rabbati 165a). The friends were severely castigated by God and enjoined to make atonement. The Rabbis see the friends' guilt and rule: "If sufferings and sickness befall a person, or his children die, we are forbidden to say, as Job's friends said to Job: 'Who ever perished being innocent?'" (B.T. Baba Metzia 58b).

THE FIVE SCROLLS

Five books—The Song of Songs, Ruth, Lamentations, Ecclesiastes, and Esther—are known as the "Five Scrolls." Written on individual scrolls, they are recited on special occasions of the year as part of public worship. They deal with various facets of love, both human and divine.

The SONG OF SONGS, one of the greatest love songs ever written, sings of the ecstasies of love. The bridegroom and bride are in love and share delights which even Solomon, in all his glory, can never experience. In unashamed rapture the bridegroom dwells on the beauties of his bride's body, her hair, her eyes, her lips, teeth, and breasts. He knocks at her door in the dark of the night, and she responds: "I had taken off my robe—Was I to don it again? . . . I rose up to let in my beloved" (Song 5:3–5). The power of love overwhelms them; it is elementary, it is life itself, it is eternity. It is one of the two forces which no human can escape, "for love is fierce as death" (Song 8:6), and they who love are dead to the world. But death is the end and love the beginning. Death is defeat and love is victory. And human passion, created by God, is good. To the Rabbis and according to tradition, the Song reflects the passionate love of God for the divinely created world and for the people of Israel.

The BOOK OF RUTH, mentioned earlier, speaks of the love for an ideal, the compelling force of Torah that calls forth a love that conquers all blandishments of life and all differences of nationality.

The BOOK OF LAMENTATIONS, sometimes attributed to the

prophet Jeremiah, reveals the agonies of unrequited love. Jerusalem has been destroyed, has become a widow. Her children, the people, have been carried into exile. Has God withdrawn love? Through bitter tears, Jeremiah, the supposed author, gives us a ray of hope. The people will renew their love for God, and God surely will respond.

ECCLESIASTES deals with love perverted into gloom and cynicism. There is nothing left when strength of passion has deserted the body; life has become a vanity. But the Rabbis would not let us yield to hopelessness. They added a last verse: "The sum of the matter, when all is said and done: Revere God and observe His commandments! For this applies to all mankind" (Eccles. 12:13). Resignation is the wisdom of advanced age; it can also bring happiness. Loving dedication to duty has its rewards, and spiritual love never dies but lives on to guide others.

The BOOK OF ESTHER, discussed earlier, glorifies sacrificial love. Esther risks her own life to rescue her people. Sacrificial love leads to heroism.

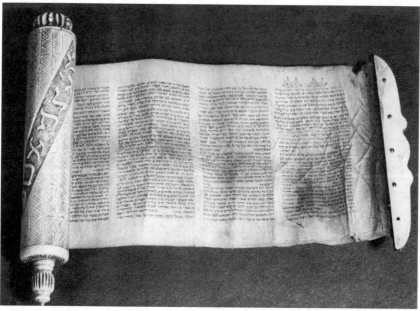

Esther's heroism is recounted every year as Jews read from a handwritten scroll, a *Megillah*, of the Book of Esther on the festival of Purim.

The Five Scrolls in Worship

Both nature and history demonstrate the workings of love, and so the Five Scrolls—the Song of Songs, Ruth, Lamentations, Ecclesiastes, and Esther—are read at appropriate times. The Song of Songs is recited at the spring festival of Pesah; this is the time of the year when Israel was liberated from Egyptian bondage and when nature bursts into bloom, when passion predicts new life, when divine and human love renew themselves. Shavuot, the summer festival celebrating the giving of the Ten Commandments, is a moment of loving rededication to the ideals of Judaism at a time when the harvest is on the way, promising fulfillment; the Book of Ruth shows us the importance of our strength of character. On Tishah b'Av, the fast day commemorating the fall of the Temple, we read the Book of Lamentations so that we remember that the agonies of the past will not lead us to despair but will rekindle in us that love which will call forth God's redeeming love in return. On Sukkot, the fall festival, the harvest is in, the leaves begin to fall, winter is at the gate, another year is gone, another round completed; not cynicism but loving dedication to the future must be the answer to melancholy and sadness, just as we read in Ecclesiastes. Purim brings us the Book of Esther, the only one of the Five Scrolls still read from a handwritten scroll, a *Megillah*; we give thanks for the rescue of our people and remember that it resulted from a heroic faith in God and a dedicated love.

THE BOOK OF DANIEL

The events in the Book of Daniel take place in Babylonia during the sixth century B.C.E., under the rule of the last Babylonian and the first Persian kings. Most Bible scholars, however, date the writing of the first half of the book to around 300 B.C.E. and the second half of the book to after c. 165 B.C.E. Daniel's "prophecies" then are in reality a review of past events.

The work, written partly in Hebrew and partly in Aramaic, tells us of Daniel's and his friends' steadfastness as faithful Jews in the face of persecution and the threat of death, and their

This seventh-century carving portrays Daniel safe among the lions.

deliverance by divine intervention, both from the fiery furnace (Dan. 3) and from the lions' den (Dan. 6). Attached to the royal court, they rejected the king's food and wine in order not to violate the dietary laws. Defying a royal order that forbade, under penalty of death, any prayer directed to any deity except the divine king, Daniel went to his house, "in whose upper chamber he had had windows made facing Jerusalem, and three times a day he knelt down, prayed, and made confession to his God" (Dan. 6:11). Daniel confirmed the duty of three daily prayers and established that the worshiper pray facing toward Jerusalem. Both practices are still appointed for Jews of all religious branches.

The book also contains apocalyptic elements, mentions guardian angels, and predicts cataclysmic battles at the "end of days," offering cryptic hints of the date of redemption. For the first time the Hebrew Bible speaks of a purgatory, an eventual resurrection of the dead, and a last judgment in which the righteous will be rewarded with eternal life of radiance and the sinners condemned to "everlasting abhorrence" (Dan. 12:2). These ideas are atypical of biblical thought. This may have been one reason for excluding the Book of Daniel from Nevi'im, the Prophets, the second section of the Hebrew Bible. On the other hand, Daniel's steadfastness in faith made him a role model deserving of emulation. As a compromise, the Book of Daniel was included in Ketuvim, the Collected Writings, the third section of the Hebrew Bible.

CHRONICLES I AND II

Chronicles summarizes the Books of 2 Samuel and Kings and draws on various genealogies, traditions, prophetic utterances, and the Books of Ezra and Nehemiah. Chronicles 1 and 2 offer details not mentioned in these other books. The main concern is the dynasty of David, especially David and Solomon, who are idealized and whose negative traits are omitted. It depicts the period of these kings as a time, when centered about the Temple, the priesthood, and the Levites, Israel was united and lived an exemplary life in observance of Torah and mitzvot.

Chapter 4

THE SECOND TEMPLE

The Rise and Fall of the Hasmonean Dynasty and the Jewish State

The Jewish commonwealth was restored in 516 B.C.E., which marked the end of the Babylonian Exile. Eretz Yisrael—the Land of Israel—was once again the spiritual center of world Jewry. It remained so until it was crushed by Christian rulers and most of the Jewish settlement was wiped out during the Crusades in the eleventh century C.E.

Following Nehemiah's return to the Persian court, the Land and the people enjoyed a period of benign neglect before being caught again in the cultural and political currents of history. Hellenism emerged as Greek ideas, art, architecture, philosophy, and political theory became dominant and fused with other cultures. Greek became the universal language. Alexander the Great, a disciple of Aristotle, was the driving political force. He saw himself both as conqueror and as champion of Greek thought. On his way to becoming the master of the ancient world, he took Jerusalem in 332 B.C.E. Receiving a strategic welcome, he spared the city and showed great kindness.

The conquering of Judaea began

Alexander's Welcome in Jerusalem
According to legend, Alexander the Great spared Jerusalem to express his gratitude to the high priest Simeon. Simeon had a vision, come to him in a dream, that promised Alexander great victories. Because of his kindness to the Jews, Alexander earned their eternal gratitude; they even named their sons after him.

Alexander's Empire

an influx of non-Jews into the Land of Israel. Soldiers, upon completion of their service at the garrisons, were given land amidst the local population. Greek landlords with new methods of cultivation were given large tracts of land. This infusion of Greeks led to the founding of Greek cities and the spread of Hellenistic ways of life.

Upon Alexander's death in 323 B.C.E. his empire was divided among contending generals. The provinces of their realms were internally autonomous and stood under the authority of a royal governor, who was also the high priest of the royal cult. *Yahud* (Greek *Ioudaia,* Judaea) was first attached to the kingdom of Egypt and ruled by the Ptolemies. Then it fell to the Seleucids, the kings of Syria (a large empire not identical with modern Syria).

Judaea was spiritually and politically governed by the Jewish high priest and an assembly of elders, the *Gerousia,* who represented the people. According to established tradition, the high priest served for life and the office was hereditary in the family of Zadok. He surrounded himself with the members of his family, who were therefore called Zadokites, or *Sadducees.* They were greatly attracted to Hellenism, and their influence was powerful.

The reign of the Seleucid King Antiochus IV (175–164 B.C.E.) brought conflicts that resulted in Jewish rebellion. The king called himself *Epiphanes,* "God made Manifest," and the Jews' rejection of his claim angered him. He also took special interest in the Jewish province because of its border with his archenemy, Egypt. Antiochus attempted to conquer Egypt but failed due to the intervention of Rome (168 B.C.E.). Encouraged by the king's defeat, the Jews of Jerusalem rose in insurrection. In response, Antiochus massacred the population of the city and replaced it with extreme hellenists among the Jews and with Greeks, who brought their gods with them. Realizing that the Jewish faith was the source of resistance and insurrections, Antiochus issued a decree in 167 B.C.E. forbidding, on penalty of death, the teaching and practice of the Jewish religion. Circumcision and the observance of the Sabbath were banned. Jews were forced to participate in pagan rites and eat pork in public. The Temple was rededicated to Zeus and thereby desecrated.

Antiochus had, however, greatly overestimated the influence that the extreme hellenists would have in swaying the rest of the Jewish population. The large majority of Jews, including moderate hellenists, remained loyal to Torah. The faithful felt required to rise up in rebellion to safeguard the Torah, their most precious possession.

THE MACCABEES

The revolt started in Modiin, a small rural community, when a Jew was forced to approach the pagan altar. Mattathias, an aged priest and head of the House of Hasmon, saved the man from blasphemy by striking him down in front of the altar. Having offended the authorities, Mattathias and his sons fled to the hills, and soon they were joined by a large number of followers. In revolt, they began to engage the enemy. The Syrians attacked on the Sabbath, whereupon Mattathias ruled that

Jews were permitted to take up arms in their own defense on the Sabbath, although they could not attack. This ruling, universally accepted, is of fundamental significance and has been followed as late as the Yom Kippur War in 1973.

When Mattathias died, his son Judah became leader of the rebels. Judah's banner displayed the initials of the scriptural quotation *Mee kamokha ba-elim YHVH,* "Who is like You among the mighty, O Lord?" (Exod. 15:11)—MKBY, which spells the word *Makaby,* giving Judah his title, Maccabee. (The word has also been interpreted as "Hammerer" of the enemy.) Not only an effective soldier and strategist, Judah was also a skilled diplomat. He gained allies, including Rome, whose Senate made a formal treaty with the Jews. Judah took advantage of the fact that Antiochus, engaged in other campaigns and internal dynastic struggles, could never deploy his entire military force against the Jewish army. Further, the king's armies could not cope with the rebels' guerrilla warfare tactics. Soon Judah severed Jerusalem from the rest of the land, isolated the garrison within the city, and defeated four Syrian generals who were trying to relieve the garrison.

Rejecting all compromise, even a promise of pardon for the fighters and freedom of religion, Judah, in the month of Kislev in the year 164 B.C.E., stormed Jerusalem, took it—except for Acra, the citadel—purified the desecrated Temple, and rededicated it in an eight-day festival, celebrated ever since as Hanukkah.

In the year 152 B.C.E. Jonathan of the House of Hasmon assumed the office of high priest. By this act the Hasmoneans deposed the dynasty of the Zadokites, which had held the office of high priest since the time of King David (1 Kings 1:33–35). The prophet Ezekiel had explicitly confirmed the Zadokites' priestly leadership in the name of God (Ezek. 44:15), but lately they had led the people astray, and the people approved the change. The aristocratic Zadokites, known as Sadducees, retained a significant influence.

Around this time, the Pharisees, a small, organized group of pious Jews, appeared on the scene. Their name derives from the designation they gave themselves: *Perushim* (*Pharisaioi,* in Greek), those "set apart" by strictest obedience to the laws of

Torah. According to the Rabbis, the group went back to the Men of the Great Assembly. Hoping to stop religious decay within the ruling house, they initially aligned themselves with pious Sadducees, but because of differences in *halakhah*, the practical interpretation of the laws of Torah, they parted ways. The Pharisees became the spiritual leaders of the people. The Sadducees followed different directions: One extreme group became worldly seekers of the good life. Another group split from the Temple and exiled itself to living an ascetic life near the Dead Sea (see below).

GROWING POWER AND SPIRITUAL DECAY

Within sixty years, the sons of Mattathias—Judah, Jonathan, and Simon—succeeded each other as rulers. They transformed the province of Yahud into Judaea, a strong, independent state. They renewed the treaty with Rome, under which Rome recognized the Judaean state as an equal and sovereign confederate.

Maccabean Palestine

They expanded their territory by conquest. From 140 B.C.E. on, they were affirmed as ruler, high priest, and commander in chief. In the process, the original goal of attaining religious freedom was forgotten.

Over time, the Hasmonean dynasty became increasingly absolutist and hellenistic. The *Gerousia*, hitherto an independent assembly representing the people's interests, was reduced to a monarch's council. As in the rest of the hellenistic world, this council was called *Synedrion,* or Sanhedrin. Attachments to foreign rulers increased, non-Jewish soldiers were hired, and the cities were strongly fortified, not only against enemies from without but also against internal restlessness.

John Hyrcanus (135–104 B.C.E.), one of Simon's sons and his successor, annexed so many territories that, at the time of his death, the boundaries of Judaea equaled those of King Solomon's kingdom. Among John's conquests was Idumaea in the south, whose entire population was converted to Judaism, an act of far-reaching consequences: because the Idumaeans became Jewish, Herod, an Idumaean, was born a Jew and could therefore become king.

John Hyrcanus, wishing to divide the power of king and high priest, willed that after his death his wife be regent and his son Aristobulus be high priest. Aristobulus, however, was determined to have unrestrained power. He imprisoned his mother and his brothers and proclaimed himself king. He died childless within a year, and his widow Shelomziyyon (Salome Alexandra) was compelled under Jewish law to marry the elder of the brothers, Alexander Jannai, who assumed the throne (104–76 B.C.E.). He further expanded the land.

Under Alexander Jannai the conflict between the Pharisees and the king came to a head. The Pharisees had grown in popu-

The Hasmonean Wall sheltered the city of Jerusalem even after the dynasty fell.

lar influence by virtue of their character and piety. In contrast to priests, a caste attached to the royal house, the Pharisees were democratic and their society was open to all, priest, commoner, recent convert, rich, poor; many of them were simple men, very poor, earning their livelihood by the work of their hands. The people found in them true role models and defenders of sacred tradition. The Pharisees insisted, for instance, that the high priest conduct the Temple service in accordance with their rulings rather than the rulings of the Sadducees.

When Alexander Jannai, officiating in the Temple, violated a halakhah of the Pharisees, riots broke out, and Alexander had a large number of Pharisees massacred. From then on he depended exclusively on the counsel and guidance of the Sadducees. On his deathbed, however, Alexander Jannai advised his wife Salome to make peace with the Pharisees. When she became reigning queen, she enhanced their influence and, with their help, gave the country several years of peace.

The conflict that arose after Salome's death was the beginning of the end of the Hasmonean dynasty. Hyrcanus II was given the office of king–high priest and was aided by the Idumaean Antipater, who hoped to become the power behind the throne. A struggle ensued between Hyrcanus and his ambitious brother Aristobulus for the position of king–high priest. The two brothers sent their competing claims to be adjudicated by the Roman general Pompey, who had arrived at Damascus in 63 B.C.E.

The Romans had annexed Syria and were now determined to incorporate the Jewish state as well. Pompey chose Hyrcanus, considering him the more pliable of the brothers to Roman requests. Antipater was assigned as royal adviser. When Pompey marched on Jerusalem, Hyrcanus opened the city's gates, but Aristobulus and his supporters gave strong resistance on the Temple Mount for three months. When Pompey finally gained control of the city, he murdered thousands of the defenders and even massacred the priests in the midst of their service.

Then Pompey entered the Temple and penetrated the holy of holies, the inner sanctum. To the Jews this was a sacrilege, for only the high priest was permitted to enter the holy of holies, and then only once a year, on Yom Kippur. Pompey found it empty. The Ark was not in the Temple, and probably had not been there since before the fall of the First Temple. The invisible God needed no visible reflection of the divine presence. Pompey, however, concluded the Jews prayed to nothing, were atheists, and from then on held them in contempt.

The Hasmonean king was now a Roman puppet. Judaea became a Roman dependent attached to the province of Syria and was stripped of most of the territories the Hasmonean kings had acquired. Soon Rome was torn by its own internal power struggles. Julius Caesar made himself dictator. He received valuable military assistance from Hyrcanus and Antipater, together with the Jews of Egypt. The grateful Caesar granted the Jews numerous privileges and enacted laws favorable to them that applied throughout the entire Roman Empire, which included much of the Jewish diaspora. He also confirmed Hyrcanus as king–high priest and appointed Antipater's son Herod as governor of Galilee.

HEROD

Herod acquired his office by craft and cruelty and with the help of the Roman legions. The Roman Senate bestowed upon him the title King of the Jews. In making Herod king, Rome followed its custom of appointing rulers who were wholly dependent on it, having no following among the people they governed. During his long reign (39 B.C.E.– 4 C.E.), Herod remained Rome's obedient servant. With the help of Roman legions, he succeeded in subduing all of Judaea (37 B.C.E.), and he was permitted to expand his land, whose borders once again reached those of Alexander Jannai.

Herod was haunted by a growing madness and suspicion of a reemergence of the Hasmoneans. On his orders Antigonus, the son of Aristobulus, was executed. Herod also executed as conspirators Alexander and Aristobulus, sons by his wife Mariamne, Aristobulus's granddaughter, whom Herod had married to give his rule legitimacy in the eyes of the people. Gripped by uncontrollable suspicion, he had Mariamne put to death as well. Of the House of Hasmon, only Herod's and Mariamne's grandson Agrippa remained. The Hasmonean dynasty had ended.

To eradicate all traces of Hasmonean influence, Herod executed forty-five members of the gentry who were linked to the Hasmoneans. To replace them, he brought in prominent Jewish families from Babylonia, including the high priest, who had no connections with the Hasmoneans. The old Sanhedrin was further stripped of its power, while Herod depended on a different Sanhedrin as a private council.

He reconstructed the Temple in such splendor that it came to be regarded as one of the wonders of the ancient world. This was no act of piety, however, for over the portals of the Temple Herod placed the Roman eagle, an abhorrent graven image and symbol of Roman dominance.

Herod favored the prevailing Greco-Roman culture, as could be seen in his building projects at Caesarea and Sebastos. Jerusalem became a magnificent capital, with the gymnasia and theaters typical of Roman cities. Herod also endowed temples to Greek gods. Combining his love for building with his lust for luxury and his constant suspicion of uprisings, he built several palaces far from the cities as retreats and fortresses—among them Masada and Herodion.

As Herod lived so did he die. From his deathbed he ordered the execution of two zealous Jews who had removed the eagle from the Temple gate. He jailed the leaders of the people with orders to kill them as soon as the news of his own death became known, so that no one would rejoice at his death; this was too much even for his henchmen, and his wish was not carried out. Herod's reign destroyed the last remnant of Judaean independence.

JUDAEA A ROMAN PROVINCE

Upon Herod's death, Emperor Augustus divided the kingdom into three parts: Judaea, Galilee, and the northeastern districts, all of them under Roman rule. Herod's eldest son

Archaelaus became ethnarch of Judaea, the people's ruler, but not king. His rule (4 B.C.E.– 6 C.E.) was so vicious that, after ten years, the emperor deposed him and transformed the territory into a province under Roman governors (6 C.E.). When Judaea became a Roman province, the administration of the territory was moved to Caesarea, the city and seaport built by Herod in honor of Caesar Augustus. Jerusalem remained the cultural and religious center; the higher ranks of the priesthood and the Jewish aristocracy had their residences there, the Pharisees their academies, and the Sanhedrin its seat, while the Temple was the focal point of world Jewry.

Herod's second son, Herod Antipas (4 B.C.E.–37 C.E.) held on to his power as tetrarch of Galilee by flattering Rome and engaging in vast building projects, the most important being Tiberias, which he named after his benefactor the emperor Tiberius. During the reign of Herod Antipas, Galilee became the center of religious ferment that was to transform world history. Many among the people saw their sufferings as the herald of messianic redemption and believed that "the end of days" was near and the coming of the Messiah imminent. They responded to John the Baptist, a wandering preacher, who called for repentance "for the kingdom of heaven is at hand" (Matthew 3:2). To symbolize renewal the penitents immersed themselves in flowing water and were baptized. At his hand the young Galilean carpenter, Jesus of Nazareth, received the baptism that marked the beginning of a ministry largely carried out in Galilee. John the Baptist rebuked Herod Antipas for his unlawful marriage to Herodias. Seeing the messianic movement as a danger and incensed at John's rebuke, Herod Antipas had him imprisoned and executed (29 C.E.).

Even though the Roman prefect had the power to appoint the high priest, religious life was as yet not disturbed. It was directed and supervised by the Sanhedrin, which consisted of seventy-two members, both priests and commoners, presided over by the high priest. The Pharisees assumed ever greater influence, and their opinions usually prevailed. The Sanhedrin issued religious ordinances, supervised the Temple service, and

Built by Herod Antipas in 26 C.E. and named in honor of the Roman emperor, the city of Tiberias is nestled on the western shore of the Sea of Galilee.

acted as city council of Jerusalem. It proclaimed the day of the New Moon and the leap years, by which the dates of the festivals were determined. World Jewry depended on its decisions. The Romans permitted the Sanhedrin to adjudicate civil litigations, which eased the burden of their own courts, but criminal jurisdiction, especially in capital cases, was taken from it.

When Pontius Pilate was appointed Roman administrator—procurator—over Judaea (26 C.E.–36 C.E.), he interfered in the people's religious life and treated the Jews' most sacred religious beliefs with contempt. Like Herod before him, he set up the royal eagles in Jerusalem. When the people appeared before him to ask for their removal, he surrounded them with his troops and gave them the choice to yield or die. The people bared their necks, ready to die for their faith, and Pilate relented. On another occasion, as they brought offerings to the Temple, pilgrims from Galilee were massacred, "whose blood mingled with their sacrifices" (Luke 13:1). Under his tyranny, the country seethed with unrest. Pontius Pilate responded by exciting the people to fever pitch and then slaughtering them. Without a moment's hesitation he could order the execution of Jesus of

Nazareth, whose beliefs and ideas he distrusted, seeing in him a man aspiring to be "king of the Jews." Pilate eventually carried his cruelties so far that Rome discharged him and called him home. Joseph Caiaphas, the high priest he had appointed, was also discharged.

Under the rule of Emperor Gaius Caligula (37–41 C.E.), people who despised Jews had an opportunity to vent their hatred. Caligula, convinced that he was a god, demanded that he be worshiped by all his subjects. The Greek population of Alexandria in Egypt, which had long envied the prosperity and privileged position of their Jewish neighbors, insisted that the Jews put up statues of the emperor in their synagogues. The Roman prefect Flaccus ordered the installation, turned the mob against the resisting Jews, suppressed a Jewish petition to Rome, and had thirty-eight Jewish community leaders publicly scourged. This is an early example of animosity against Jews based on their prosperity and cohesion.

Then, for a few years—41 C.E. to 44 C.E.—Jews enjoyed peace and tranquillity under the reign of Agrippa I, the grandson of Herod and Mariamne. Educated in Rome he became a member of high society and moved with ease among the aristocracy. As a friend of Caligula, he was given rule over the northern part of the land of the Jews and the title king. When Caligula died, Agrippa helped persuade the Senate to confirm Claudius as emperor, and the grateful Claudius conferred upon him the territory of Judaea. Agrippa now ruled as king over the entire kingdom of Herod.

Unlike his grandfather, Agrippa had the interests of his people at heart. He established contacts with diaspora Jewry and, above all, conducted himself as a deeply religious Jew. On the Sukkot festival in 41 C.E. he read the Book of Deuteronomy before the people in the Temple, as was the king's duty. When he came to the passage: "You may not put a foreigner as king over yourselves, who is not your brother," he wept, being himself of Idumaean descent. But the people called out to him: "You are our brother."

After Agrippa's death, Judaea once again became a Roman

province. Relations with Rome became worse and worse under the last Roman procurators. Their harshness can be traced to a number of factors: the resistance of the Jews, who chafed under Roman domination; the governors' corruption; their favoritism toward the Greek population; their contempt for the Jewish religion; their venality and greed to enrich themselves by confiscating the property of Jews; and their failure to demonstrate the power of Rome by successfully subduing insurrections. Harsh measures could not hide their inefficiency.

The last of the procurators, Cassius Florus (64 C.E.), schemed to incite the people to rebellion by taunting and humiliating them until their patience broke. Then, in the name of putting down the rebellion, he plundered whole cities, looted the Temple treasury, and "punished" the irate citizens, many of whom were crucified. But the people's rebellion was stronger than he expected. The daily Temple sacrifice for the emperor was eliminated, signifying secession from Rome. The Roman garrison at Jerusalem was wiped out. Riots between the Greeks and Jews broke out throughout the land. The countryside came completely under the power of the Zealots, Jewish patriots organized in rebellion against Rome.

The Rebellion and the Fall of the Temple

The emperor Nero, realizing that Roman rule in Judaea was threatened, ordered Cestius Gallus, Nero's governor of Syria, to break the insurgency. Unable to take Jerusalem, the Roman legions withdrew and on their retreat were routed by the Jews. The victory fused all classes of Jews in resistance, and a provisional government of Judaea was set up.

Nero decided to send Vespasian, his best commander, and Vespasian marched with sixty thousand men from Syria into Galilee (67 C.E.). To ward against the Roman advance, the fortress of Jotapa in western Galilee, the gateway to Jerusalem, had been strongly manned and put under the command of Joseph ben Mattathias. Upon Vespasian's arrival, Joseph surrendered, leaving the road to Jerusalem open. But then Nero died, and

Regarded as a traitor by his fellow Jews for opening the road to the Romans at Jotapa, Joseph ben Mattathias was given a stipend by the conquerors and was granted residence in Rome. Assuming the name of his benefactors, the imperial house of the Flavians, he called himself Josephus Flavius. Perhaps torn by remorse at his betrayal of the Jews and hoping to explain to the Romans that Judaism and Jews were worthy of respect, he became a historian. His works, *Jewish Antiquities* and *The Jewish War*, are important sources of information about Jewish life and the events of his time. In the medieval manuscript illumination here, curious crowds follow Josephus as the historian carries a volume of the *The Jewish War* to the emperor Vespasian and his son Titus, to whom Josephus dedicated his work.

Vespasian returned to Rome to become emperor and placed his son Titus in command of the armies. After devastating the countryside, Titus laid siege to Jerusalem, put up a wall around it, cut off its food supply, and made his assault.

While the enemy advanced, civil war raged within the city. Factions among the Jews could not agree about the conduct of the war. The Zealots eventually seized power. In the struggle, storehouses were burned and hunger became an ally of the enemy, who eventually broke through. Jerusalem fell. On the 9th day of Av in 70 C.E. the Temple was burned down by order of Titus, who wished to break the Jews' morale and destroy the center of their resistance. Jews remained ensconced at a few fortresses, among them Masada; the Zealots held out there for several years (73 or 74 C.E.) until they committed suicide, preferring death in liberty to capture by the Roman armies.

JUDAISM REBORN

After the defeat of the rebels, the Romans razed cities, devastated the land, carried tens of thousands of Jews into slavery, dispossessed Jewish farmers who had remained, settled non-Jewish colonists on their farms, and imposed crushing taxes on the Jewish population.

Having been stripped of its place as a nation, of the Temple, and of most of its political independence, Judaism no longer threatened the Romans. The Romans could therefore feel secure in granting the Jews a limited autonomy and in recognizing a *Nasi*, patriarch, as head of the Jewish community. We may discern

The Romans considered the conquest of Jerusalem in 70 C.E. so momentous that the pillaging of the Temple was depicted on the arch erected in Titus's honor after his triumphant return to Rome. The arch displays the holy candelabrum of the Temple, the menorah, being carried in triumph, followed by Jewish prisoners in chains.

two reasons for this change of mind on the part of Rome and for the miraculous revival of Judaism: the spread of the Jews and their power throughout the ancient world, and the leadership of the Pharisees and their successors, the Sages.

THE JEWISH POPULATION. During the period of the Second Temple the number of Jews is estimated at five million—one quarter of the entire population of the region. They were found throughout the entire Mediterranean basin. Babylonia had a very large, prosperous, self-governing Jewish community since the days of Jeremiah and was a center of Jewish scholarship. The Jewish philosopher Philo (c. 20 B.C.E.–50 C.E.), who lived in Egypt, claimed that the Jewish population there extended into the entire country and numbered one million (the exaggerated figure indicates that the population was large); Alexandria was an important center of Jewish learning. Syria, located on Judaea's border, had drawn large numbers of Jewish settlers. Jews were found throughout Asia Minor up to the Black Sea, on the islands of the Mediterranean, and in the larger Greek cities. In Rome a

Jewish patriots took their last stand against the Romans at Masada, one of the fortresses that had been built by King Herod.

Jewish community had existed for over a century and had grown into a powerful element of society. From there the Jews spread into all of Italy and into the Roman provinces as far as Gaul and North Africa. Throughout this part of the world, they engaged in extensive missionary activity.

Jewish communities throughout the world recognized the Land of Israel as the hub and ultimate authority of religious life, they transmitted their annual half-shekel to Jerusalem for the upkeep of the Temple, they made pilgrimages to Jerusalem, and scholars, traveling back and forth, exchanged ideas.

To commemorate the fall of Jerusalem in 70 c.e., Rome struck a coin bearing the inscription *Judaea Capta*. It shows the "widow" of Judah weeping under a tree whose fruits she will no longer enjoy. A conquering Roman soldier watches proudly.

The destruction of the Temple was traumatic for all of them but did not dislodge them or diminish their influence.

Judah will not again be captured. In 1958, the Israeli government struck a medal in celebration of the new state's tenth anniversary. One side shows a replica of the Roman coin. The reverse side, under the caption *Israel Liberata,* shows a mother proudly holding her child to the rays of the sun of freedom. She stands under the fruit tree, which has grown tall and sturdy. At her side is her husband, kneeling, planting a new seedling to grow to health and strength with the child and the Land.

THE SECTS

Caught amidst the political and intellectual currents during the time of the Second Temple, the Jews had several choices. They could yield to the prevalent intellectual and ideological trends of Hellenism, or they could seal themselves up against all external influences and resist them, or they could chart a course between the currents, remaining independent, yet open to them.

Each of these approaches was tried by one or another influential segment of Jewish society. These segments became the sects, each of them responding to the spiritual and practical problems of the period.

THE SADDUCEES. The Sadducees were a political and religious group of wellborn, wealthy, and conservative Jews of old lineage. Under the Hasmonean dynasty, they continued to exercise a dominant influence on the political life of the nation as counselors of the kings. Their influence on the people's religious life was gradually superseded by the Pharisees. The Sadducees were religious Jews who applied Jewish law rigidly and wanted to preserve Torah by strict obedience to the *written* word. For this reason they rejected the Oral Law as it had evolved through the Pharisees. They therefore came to halakhic decisions in pronounced contradiction to those of the Pharisees. The Sadducees denied the key pharisaic doctrines of a divine judgment and life after death, as well as the resurrection of the dead, for these were not found in the written Torah. The Sadducees held that the individual was in no way subjected to divinely ordained fate but was completely free in choosing good or evil. They saw in the Temple and its ritual the fundamental guarantee of Jewish survival. For the sake of the Temple their leadership was willing to ingratiate itself with the ruling power, Rome, and cooperate with its efforts to suppress popular opposition by force. Because of the Sadducees' close bonds with the priestly leadership of the Temple and their deference to Rome they were profoundly disliked by the people.

The Sadducees split into several groups. Holding that there was no divine reward or punishment after death, one group held that the Jew had to serve God with all his heart, soul, and might out of pure love, without expecting a reward. Another group held the exact opposite, feeling that they might follow their inclinations, since there was no reckoning after death anyway. A third group was so deeply shocked by the Pharisees' halakhic interpretations that they severed their bond with the Temple and established their own community at the shores of the Dead Sea, where they followed their own halakhah with extreme strictness; this would bring them life and liberation at the end of days in the final battle between "the Sons of Light and the Sons of Darkness."

If the perspective of the Sadducees had been held by all, Judaism would have fallen with the destruction of the Temple. Instead, with the fall of the Temple the Sadducees disappeared.

THE ZEALOTS. The Zealots, patriots organized against Rome, were committed to restore freedom by force of arms. In the spirit of the Maccabees, they were convinced that in times of need, God demanded aggressive armed resistance. And so they took action, sometimes violently, against the Roman authorities. They have been called Zealots because they were zealous for the Lord.

THE ESSENES AND THE QUMRAN COMMUNITY. The Essenes were another group of pious men who founded communities located in the Judaean desert and on the shore of the Dead Sea, far from any population. They originated between 140 B.C.E. and

130 B.C.E., or perhaps prior to the Maccabean uprising in 167 B.C.E. In the first century C.E. their membership numbered about four thousand. They saw in withdrawal from the world the way of preserving the Jewish people and its heritage. The turmoil of the time was to them a prelude to the fast-approaching day of judgment.

Communities were organized in the form of monasteries and followed a rigid discipline. The members were committed to absolute obedience to the superior's orders, to celibacy, to the denial of all pleasures, to total openness toward their brothers, to physical cleanliness and ritual purity. They immersed themselves daily to be purified by this act, which held spiritual symbolism. Daily common meals—strictly vegetarian— followed a prescribed ritual that made them sacred celebrations. The Essenes read the Torah with care and stressed ethics. The Sabbath was observed with great strictness. Only men were admitted, and then only after a probationary period of at least three years. All property was held in common and administered by elected officials for the good of the whole. The communities sustained themselves through the manual labor of their members, but never in commerce or the manufacture of weapons. In sickness and old age the members were cared for by the community. Some Essenes became hermits, clothing themselves in garments like those once worn by Elijah, or wandering preachers, like John the Baptist, calling the people to repentance before it was too late. Major violations of the rules were punished with expulsion. Generally, the Essenes acknowledged the Temple and sent gifts but did not offer sacrifices. The Essenes regarded the Pharisees and their interpretation of Torah as too worldly. The Essenes absolutely denied human freedom of will. Their doctrines and way of life, had it prevailed, would have sapped the strength of Judaism to evolve and change.

Beginning in 1947, scrolls preserved in clay jars were found by chance in caves surrounding the Dead Sea. They turned out to be one of the most important archaeological discoveries of the twentieth century. Subsequent searches in the Judaean desert and at Masada have brought thousands of scroll remnants to light. Scholars have held that these Dead Sea Scrolls originated within a community of Essenes and were written during the last century before the fall of the Temple. These documents provide significant insight into the period between the Hebrew Bible and the New Testament. They may yield valuable knowledge on the relationship of early Christianity to Judaism.

Excavations discovered a community center at Qumran at the shore of the Dead Sea. The scrolls revealed that its community followed the pattern of life of the Essenes, and scholars have held that the community was formed by Essenes. Another hypothesis maintains that this community consisted not of Essenes but of Sadducee priests who moved into the desert to live by the word of Torah as they interpreted it. Failing to persuade their priestly brothers in Jerusalem to return to the "true" interpretation and practice of Torah, they separated themselves from society, cut all contacts with the Temple and its ritual, and set up their community center as a sanctuary. After at least twenty years, they found a leader, a priest, whom they were sure God had given them, and he became their *Moreh Tzedek,* "Teacher of Righteousness"; he may have been the high priest whom the Hasmonean Jonathan deposed. This indicates the first half of the second century B.C.E. as the approximate period of the emergence of the sect. In seclusion from the world they devoted themselves entirely to the study of Torah and the performance of

The containers in which the Dead Sea Scrolls had been stored were unearthed in 1947, a few miles from Jericho. Most of the Dead Sea Scrolls are now in Jerusalem. Their full text became accessible only in 1994.

mitzvot. The community was wiped out by the Roman legions advancing on Jerusalem.

THE NAZARENES. The Nazarenes faithfully adhered to all Jewish laws, but they believed that the messianic time had come and Jesus was the *Christos,* the anointed Messiah (hence the name Christians). Some rites of the Essenes—governance by a priest and a council of twelve, immersion, the ceremonial meal presided over by the priest at which wine and bread were passed around, the monastic orders, and even the concept of predestination—may have had an impact on later Christianity. The Nazarenes left Jerusalem during its siege.

THE PHARISEES. The Pharisees gave Judaism its character and strength. As teachers and role models of high ethical standards they were among the great leaders of humanity. They forged a creative synthesis between assimilation and separation. Judaism has followed this road and proudly considers itself heir to pharisaic teaching. As we have seen, they gained political power under Queen Salome Alexandra, but their origin can be traced back to the days of Ezra and the men of the Great Assembly, when the interpretation of Torah became a major function of Jewish leadership. Fulfilling this role called for men of great intellectual ability combined with uncompromising faith and an exemplary life. Their name *Perushim,* or Pharisees, "separated ones," designated them as a group within the group, a congregation within the congregation. The term should be understood in the sense in which the Puritans or later the Mormons were to use it, a band of men utterly dedicated to the preservation of their heritage.

With the emergence of Pharisaism, the religious future of the people no longer lay in the hands of the priests, a caste composed of the descendants of Aaron, but in the hands of all those, irrespective of background, who wished to give their lives over to the task. Evaluating all ideas, including Hellenism, they were able to absorb the best that other cultures had to offer, insofar as it strengthened Judaism. In order that their intellectual openness not be misinterpreted as compromise they strictly observed the law. Being firmly anchored in tradition they had the flexibility to adjust Judaism as conditions changed. Able to accept the loss of national independence, they counseled political compromise, provided that the spiritual and religious independence of the Jews remained inviolate. In their spirit, the Sages undertook the rebuilding of Judaism after the fall of the Temple.

Chapter 5

THE JEWS ON THE LAND

From the Fall of the Second Temple until the Crusades

During the last days of the struggle for Jerusalem in 70 c.e., Rabbi Johanan ben Zakkai, a leader of the Pharisees, had himself smuggled out of the city in a coffin, since the Zealots would permit no one to leave the beleaguered city. Knowing that Jerusalem was doomed, he secretly met with Vespasian and asked his permission to lead the small school for Jewish studies in the little town of Yavneh. Vespasian agreed to the request. Rabbi Johanan's academy became the new center of religious authority. The academy established itself as the Sanhedrin, with the power to proclaim the New Moon and the leap years, and issued ordinances governing religious observance. As the academy became the focal point of worldwide Jewish observance, Rabbi Johanan achieved Judaism's transition to life without the Temple.

THE BAR KOKHBA WAR. When Hadrian became emperor (117–138),[1] he initiated a policy of appeasing the peoples in his realm, including the Jews, for whom he promised to rebuild Jerusalem and the Temple. Changing his mind, however, he decided to make Jerusalem into a modern Roman city. Considering circumcision barbaric, he prohibited it throughout the empire.

In 132 the Jews rebelled, the most concerted uprising among

1. All further dates are of the common era, c.e., unless otherwise mentioned.

a series of revolts following the fall of the Temple. Their leader was Simon ben Kosiba, who called himself "Prince of Israel." The greatest of the contemporary rabbis, Rabbi AKIBA BEN JOSEPH (c.50–135), hailed him as the Messiah. Simon gained control over the entire land. Jewish authority was reestablished; coins with the inscription "Year of the Freedom of Jerusalem" were minted; land expropriated by the Romans was taken back. Ultimately, however, the rebellion was crushed by Rome in the year 135. On the 9th of Av, the last bastion of the resistance, the fortress Betar, fell and Simon was killed. He was later called *Bar Kokhba*, "Son of the Star."

After the war the teaching and practice of Judaism were proscribed under penalty of death, and many Jews, including the most prominent rabbis, among them Rabbi Akiba, were martyred; their story is recalled in the liturgy on Yom Kippur. Thousands of Jews were sold as slaves. Jerusalem became the Roman city Aelia Capitolina, which Jews were forbidden to enter except on Tishah b'Av, when they were permitted to mourn the fall of the Temple. The Romans tried to wipe out any memory of the land as Jewish. Judaea was therefore renamed *Palestine*, after the Philistines, who had once lived there but had already disappeared by the time of King David.

RESTORATION. The emperor Antoninus Pius revoked the harshest laws, such as the prohibition of circumcision, and under Septimius Severus and his dynasty (138–235), Jewish internal autonomy under a Nasi, patriarch, was fully restored. The Rabbis, having been forced to abandon their school in Yavneh, established their center in Galilee, first at Usha and then, after several moves, at Tiberias. The Nasi, Rabban Simeon ben Gamaliel, who had stayed in hiding during the persecutions, restored the central importance of the Land of Israel in the hearts of communities of the diaspora.

RABBI JUDAH HA-NASI AND THE MISHNAH. Born while his father, the Nasi Rabban Simeon, was still in hiding, Rabbi Judah (c. 138–c. 217) raised the position of the Nasi to such heights that he came to be known as Judah ha-Nasi. He left so lasting a heritage of Torah study that he came to be remembered simply

During the time of Rabbi Judah ha-Nasi, Bet-Shearim thrived as a center of learning and the seat of the Sanhedrin, whose tombs from the second century C.E. are pictured here.

as Rabbi, or *Rabbenu ha-kadosh,* "our holy Rabbi." The Rabbi possessed great knowledge and wisdom, and he exercised real spiritual and temporal power. He held princely court, first at Bet-Shearim and then at Sepphoris. Roman emperors, among them Marcus Aurelius, Septimus Severus, and Caracalla, are said to have treasured his friendship, and he used his influence to improve the conditions of his people. His people loved and revered him. The Land returned to general prosperity, and the Jewish community in Palestine flourished.

Rabbi Judah systematically organized and edited the oral tradition of halakhah, evolved over many generations of

About Rabbi Judah ha-Nasi the Talmud says:

From Moses' days to the days of "Rabbi," Torah and worldly greatness have never been combined in one person (B. Gittin 59a). Beauty and power, wisdom and wealth, ripe old age and worthy children—these rewards are fitting for the righteous and good for society.... All these characterized "Rabbi" and his sons. (Tos. Sanhedrin XI:8)

Rabbi Judah's great wealth gave him the means to support worthy scholars. Some of the meditations that Rabbi Judah composed are part of daily worship.

predecessors, in order to create, around 200, a compendium of Jewish law. This work is the Mishnah (the "Review") on which the further development of Jewish doctrine was to rest (see ch. 23). Thereafter the Mishnah became a source of intense study and discussion. With the Mishnah as guide, the Sages of the academy insisted on sharing the Nasi's power to decide matters of law, while the Nasi continued as the political head of the community and as "first among equals" in deciding legal questions. Two of Rabbi Judah's disciples, Rabbi Arikha (Rav) and Samuel, went to Babylonia to establish great *yeshivot,* academies, thus creating a second great center of Jewish learning. The two centers remained in close contact.

FROM PAGAN ROME TO CHRISTIAN EMPIRE

The religious life of the Jews in Palestine was not disturbed for many years. The condition of the Jews changed, however, when the emperor Constantine (311–337), recognizing the spread and power of Christianity, made it the official religion of the empire. Judaism had widespread appeal throughout the ancient world, and the Church, fearful of its principal competitor, set to work worldwide to malign and debase Judaism and to deprive Jews of their rights and dignity. The Jewish community in the Land of Israel suffered grievously under the harsh restrictions imposed on it.

In order to disrupt Jewish observance, the emperor Constantius (337–360) banned the rabbis from proclaiming the New Moon and the leap years, so that Jews would not know the dates of their festivals. The Nasi Hillel II (320–365) therefore established a permanent calendar (358) that has been followed ever since.

Jewish rebellion against repressive imperial edicts was put down with great severity. Tiberias, Sepphoris, and Lod were destroyed but soon rebuilt; Bet-Shearim never recovered.

A brief respite was granted the Jews during the reign of Julian (360–363). Faithful to the old Greco-Roman religion and desirous of reducing the power of Christianity, he was gracious to the Jews and intended to restore the Temple and its sacrificial service. Having aroused the fury of the Christians, however, he was murdered, becoming know by the epithet Christians attached to him—Julian the Apostate. Upon his death Christians burned down numerous Jewish settlements in Palestine.

THE TALMUD. The Sages of the yeshivot of both Palestine and Babylonia each recorded and eventually edited their discussions and conclusions. The resulting work is the Talmud, the great source book for the study of Jewish law, life, and wisdom. There are two versions: the one that evolved in Palestine is called *Talmud Yerushalmi*, the Jerusalem Talmud; the one from Babylonia, the *Talmud Bavlee*, the Babylonian Talmud. (We shall take up the Talmud in more detail in ch. 23.) The Jerusalem Talmud was compiled under duress. Conditions in Palestine at the end of the fourth century were deteriorating so rapidly under Christian rule that the Rabbis feared being prevented from completing their work, and so in the yeshivot of Caesarea, Sepphoris, and Tiberias, they labored with great haste to complete and edit their work. They did not finish. The Palestinian Talmud, edited in Tiberias around the year 400, is only one-third the length of the Babylonian Talmud and is less comprehensive.

The Church had long resented that there was still a "scepter in Judah." More and more Christians had settled in Palestine and could not abide any Jewish authority over them. They accused the Nasi, Rabbi Gamaliel VI, of rebuilding synagogues, judging Christians, and circumcising slaves. The emperor Theodosius II (408–450) abolished the office of Nasi. Upon Rabbi Gamaliel's death (429), the emperor ordered the Jews to hand over the patriarch's official treasury, and the Jewish

This citadel of the Crusaders is now an Israeli monument.

patriarch was replaced by the Christian patriarch of Jerusalem. Babylonian Jewry, living outside the Roman Empire, now became the center of world Jewry.

THE YEARS AHEAD

In 614, the Persians, with the aid of the Jews, took Jerusalem from the Romans and returned internal autonomy to the Jews. But soon the Romans took it back, and in 629 the emperor Heraclius entered the city. The Jews, offering rich gifts, received his solemn pledge of pardon. On the request of the Christian clergy, he broke his promise, and the Jews were expelled from Jerusalem, or put to death, or converted by force.

A few years later, the Muslims conquered Palestine. Although they did not restore Jewish autonomy, they eventually permitted Jews to live in Jerusalem. The Muslims' attitude toward the Jews was more lenient than the Christians', even though Jews and Judaism were treated harshly in the Quran.

In the eleventh and twelfth centuries, the Crusades returned the land for a while to Christian domination. The Muslim population was slaughtered and the Jewish community of Jerusalem was massacred. The centers of Jewish life and creativity moved elsewhere, but Eretz Yisrael was never without a Jewish settlement and has always remained a force in the hearts and souls and minds of Jews everywhere.

ANCIENT ROOTS OF ANTISEMITISM

Resentment against the Jews existed even before the rise of Christianity although Jews were generally treated as equals and even admired. The strength of their union through law, customs, and family spirit brought them respect—but also misunderstanding or even hatred. By worshiping a just but loving God who could not be bribed or flattered and who turned to them in mercy, the Jews offered a spiritual religion to a disillusioned world. Some in influential Roman circles were interested in Judaism and even converted. Some Romans accepted Jewish beliefs without formally adopting the faith by undergoing circumcision; they were called "God fearers." Jewish missionaries were active throughout the ancient world, and the Jewish population in the time of the Roman Empire grew rapidly in numbers and influence.

What the strong admired was foolishness to others, and to some, accepting the creed of a conquered nation bordered on treason. Juvenal, who lived from around 60 to around 127 expressed it in satire:

> Some, sons of a father who observes the day of the Sabbath,
> worship nothing but clouds and a spirit in heaven,
> and differentiate not between human flesh and that of the swine
> from which their father abstained. Soon they shorten their
>   foreskin.
> Trained to hold Roman law in contempt,
> they study with care Jewish law to obey and revere it,
> and all that Moses transmitted in a secret book.
> It forbids them to show the right way to any but those who
>   accept the same rites,
> and permits them to guide to the well (of their wisdom)
> the circumcised only and none of the others.
> At fault is the father, however, who every seventh day
> turned lazy, taking no part in the tasks and duties of life.
>
> (Juvenal, *Satires,* 14.98–106)

When religion held the realm together, religious differences could easily be equated with disloyalty. Juvenal puts his finger on another problem. Jews could invite their neighbors to their homes and into their faith, but they could not reciprocate. They could not eat the Romans' food or respect their gods.

In fact, the fabric of Roman society was unraveling. Rather than admit their shortcomings, however, most Roman writers instead defamed the Jews. Detractors dismissed the Jews' God as a phantom in the sky; Jews might even be atheists. Attacking the Jews' religious practices, Juvenal, Tacitus, and other writers called them lazy because they observed the Sabbath—thus could the Romans disguise their relentless exploitation of the poor, to whom they never gave a moment's rest. The Jews were said to have no aesthetic sense because they rejected Roman statues, and the true reason, their enemies declared, was that the Jews' God was really an ass's head worshiped in the Temple of Jerusalem. Their accusers had an answer for why the Jews lived their own lives, often separate from the mainstream of Roman society: the Jews were really descendants of lepers expelled from Egypt at the time of Moses; they did not mix because they were outcasts. The contradictions among the slanderous statements made it difficult for Jews to refute them. If one accusation could be put to rest, another one could be leveled. Philo, the philosopher, and Josephus, the historian, together with others, tried to combat slander with fact, but they did not succeed. Jealousy of the Jews' prosperity was often at the root of the slander, for instance in Alexandria.

Actually, the causes of anti-semitism went deeper. The success of Jewish missionary activity showed clearly that many people were looking for a new way of life. Judaism was an implied rebuke of the private and public immorality of the late Roman Empire. Jews demonstrated that the moral principle cannot be suspended but will be victorious over license and tyranny. The Jews themselves were certainly not free from weaknesses, but their survival was a symbol of a divine providence unknown in the Roman state religion. Emperors and dictators could declare themselves gods, could rage and destroy, but in the end providence prevails. Jews pointed to the limitations of the tyrants' omnipotence. This may also be why Hitler could not tolerate the Jews, why communist Russia found them "inassimilable." Dictatorship and pogroms almost always go hand in hand.

Chapter 6

JUDAISM AND CHRISTIANITY

Dissent, Disruption, Dialogue

In order to understand the subsequent currents of Jewish history we must dwell briefly here on the character of Christianity and Judaism's response to it. Fortunately, after centuries of misunderstandings and disruptions, Jews and Christians have begun to move toward a genuine dialogue.

The great problem in the dialogue is that ideas that are self-evident to one religion may be strange to the other. Many religious ideas are caught rather than taught: they are linked to childhood recollections, holy traditions, books sanctified by the faith of believers, creeds and customs hallowed by the blood of martyrs. These ideas are "simply true" to the faithful, who cannot understand why others do not share them. People may be shocked to learn that someone could doubt such clear truths. Thus we must remember to respect the religious convictions of others even though they may surprise us or run contradictory to our own.

Jews and Christians worship the same God. But Jewish theology disagrees with some of the most fundamental doctrines of Christianity. In Judaism God is *absolutely* One.[1] The Trinity

---

1. As we shall see, even the mystics take great care to stipulate the ultimate, absolute oneness of God, the En Sof (see ch. 32).

is therefore not acceptable to Judaism. Further, the Christian doctrine that God took the form of a human being in Christ is contrary to the Jew's belief. To the Jew, God has no human form and no human being has been or ever can be the incarnation of God. The boundary between God and the human being is never eliminated. No human being has been or ever can be perfect; no human being in Jewish Scriptures has ever been described as perfect. The transcendent God is so near that the Jew does not believe in a divine intermediary between the human being and God. Everyone comes to the divine Author directly and has immediate access to the Redeemer and to salvation.

Christianity teaches a doctrine of original sin. Adam and Eve sinned in the Garden of Eden and all their descendants were thereby contaminated, all humans becoming sinful by nature; through them, sin and death entered the world. Judaism rejects this doctrine. As we saw in our discussion of Jeremiah and Ezekiel, the sins of the fathers are *not* inherited by their children. The expression "visiting the iniquities of the fathers upon the children" (Exod. 34:7) was, according to the Rabbis, revoked by Ezekiel, "The soul that sins, [only] it shall die" (Ezek.18:4; B.T. Makkot 24a). Given pure to every human being, the soul is not tainted in any way. Judaism therefore does not require a Messiah to atone for human sin, but, rather, the Messiah will restore the Jewish people and redeem humankind from war and hate.

Many Christians teach that only *faith* in Christ leads to salvation. Linking salvation to belief in Christ, Christianity is a missionary religion. Judaism, on the other hand, rests on the Jew faithfully living out the mitzvot, the commandments, that God has granted. Although Judaism accepts converts, it need not proselytize because "all the righteous of the peoples of the world have a share in the world to come." Salvation requires adherence to basic laws of justice and humanity. Judaism recognizes Christianity as a good and holy road to God—for Christians—and holds the same view with regard to Islam, Buddhism, or any other ethical religion. Jews see no reason for an adherent of an ethical religion to change his or her faith.[2]

Christianity, to various degrees, believes in sacraments,

physical means by which God reaches out to humankind. Judaism has no sacraments. Mitzvot are not sacraments but human actions in obedience to God.[3]

Christianity has considered Judaism as a "forerunner" with an inferior concept of ethics and a rudimentary ideal of divine and human love. Jews see Christian ethics and the Christian concept of love as restatements of Judaism's beliefs. Jews do not accept the Christian claim that the new faith and covenant have replaced and abrogated the Jewish faith and covenant.

Christianity regards the New Testament as divine revelation. The Jews do not. The Jew approaches it analytically, investigating it with the same objectivity that might be applied by both Jew and Christian to the study of the Quran. The New Testament rests on a substantial core of Jewish ideas. It was written at least fifty years after Jesus had died. During these years the life and acts of Jesus were transmitted orally. In the process of oral transmission, stories of miracles commonly told of many saintly people came to be ascribed to Jesus, and Jesus' life came to be told from the perspective of his resurrection.[4] The personality of the historical Jesus became obscured. His actual words cannot be ascertained. The New Testament by its

---

2. Joshua ben Hananiah in Tofseta Sanhedrin 13:2. Also: "Among the righteous of the peoples of the world some are priests of God, as for instance [Emperor Marcus] Antonius" (Tanna debe Elijahu Zutta 20). "I call heaven and earth to witness that on everyone, be he Jew or non-Jew, man or woman, manservant or maidservant, the holy spirit can rest; it all depends on his conduct" (Tanna debe Elijahu Rabba 10). The Second Isaiah calls Cyrus "Messiah."

The prophet Micah says: "Let all the peoples of the world walk, each one in the name of its god—but we will walk in the name of the Lord our God forever" (Micah 4:5). The Bible has contempt for the idolatrous and often immoral cults of antiquity (see Deut. 7:25–26). For later Jewish views and the relationship between Judaism and Christianity, see below, discussions of Moses Mendelssohn (ch. 12); Samson Raphael Hirsch (ch. 13); and Herman Cohen, Franz Rosenzweig, and Martin Buber (ch. 34).

3. Catholics and Protestants differ regarding sacraments; they also disagree about the idea of the necessity of faith in Christ without works. A detailed analysis goes beyond the scope of this book.

4. Leo Baeck, *Das Evangelium als Urkunde der Jüdischen Glaubensgeschichte* (New York: Schocken Books, 1928), p. 15 ff.

---

very name reflects the new religion's disengagement from its old Jewish roots. Written in part by non-Jews with no emotional ties with Judaism, it was composed when the new faith wished to distance itself from the old. This accounts for the anti-Jewish statements found in it, of which the Gospel of John offers the clearest example.

To the Christian the name of Jesus evokes deep stirrings of love. The Jew has deep reverence for the faith of Christians, sharing with them the love of God and a complete system of ethics. Jesus, however, is for the Jews a human personality, teacher, and reformer, whose influence has been a mighty force in bringing the knowledge of God to humankind. At the same time, Jews throughout history have dreaded the mention of Jesus' name, not on account of his personality and teaching, but on account of the untold suffering that was brought upon them in his name.

EARLY CHRISTIANITY: A JEWISH VIEWPOINT

The history of early Christianity may be divided into three periods: the life of Jesus, the ministry of Paul, the period of dissociation.

The Life of Jesus

Jesus came from the Hills of Galilee. He was a Jew, brought up in the spirit of pharisaic tradition. With deep faith in God, who is Israel's Father in Heaven, he went out to his people to teach and guide them. He believed that the end of days was near and established high ideals of conduct. At times he repeated— and at other times went beyond—the teachings of his pharisaic contemporaries. He had the wonderful gift of being able to simplify and bring near the commandments of ethical life as found in Jewish teaching. He was strong; anger could take hold of him; love reached out to all he met. He had the power to attract and hold followers, and a small band of devoted disciples attached themselves to him. The thought occurred to them that he may be the Messiah, and he did not discourage it, for he wanted to restore the people (Jesus was not the only Jew to regard him-self—falsely—as the Messiah, either then or later). Living as a Jew and interpreting Torah, he made it clear to his followers that Torah must be strictly obeyed:

> Do not suppose that I have come to abolish the Law [Torah] or the prophets; I have not come to abolish but to fulfill. For truly I tell you, until heaven and earth pass away, not one letter, not one stroke of a letter, will pass from the Law until all is accomplished. (Matt. 5:17–18)

This is Jewish thinking. The fulfillment of mitzvot, which is the duty of the Jew, means carrying them out.

When Jesus went to Jerusalem, his messianic preachings were brought to the attention of the Roman procurator Pontius Pilate. Taking no chance of having a potential troublemaker from the always rebellious Galilee on his hand, Pontius Pilate had Jesus arrested, sentenced, and executed.[5] Like many Jewish martyrs before and after him, Jesus accepted his fate in quiet dignity.

What was Jesus' relationship to his community, especially to those who disagreed with his messianism? If they knew of him, they had no argument with him on that issue. Some of the rabbis disagreed with his halakhic decisions, but he had the ability to defend them. This may have caused ill feelings, but at that time halakhah was still fluid. Those who heard of Jesus' death surely grieved for him as yet another Jew who had been murdered by the Romans—which had become a tragic monotony. Jesus was simply a man who expounded the Torah, teaching very much like other rabbis while giving his own point

---

5. The trial of Jesus by a Jewish court (Sanhedrin) is difficult to explain, as we would have to assume that Jewish law, as expounded in the Mishnah, did not yet exist. Samuel Sandmel points out in *A Jewish Understanding of the New Testament* (New York: KTAV and Anti-Defamation League of B'nai B'rith, 1956) that some Jewish scholars have refuted the procedures of the trial in detailed analysis; he continues, "The entire trial business is legendary and tendentious"(p. 128). We may assume the account of the trial to have been colored by later Christian antagonism against Judaism.

of view. He differed by thinking of himself as the Messiah who would free Israel from bondage. We must assume that the majority of Jews, both in Judaea and certainly in the diaspora, did not hear of him during his lifetime.

The Ministry of Paul

After Jesus' death a new personality brought leadership to the grieving disciples: Paul of Tarsus. He would indelibly imprint Christianity with his genius. Paul, an observant Jew of the diaspora and an obedient Pharisee, was influenced by some of the non-Jewish concepts he encountered, including oriental mystery religions. He also understood Torah, not as "instruction"—its actual meaning—but as "law," because the Septuagint, the Greek version of the Bible with which he was familiar, translates *Torah* as *nomos,* "law."

Paul says of the Jews: "They are the Israelites, they were God's sons; theirs is the splendor of divine presence, theirs the covenants, the law, the temple worship and the promises. Theirs are the patriarchs, and from them, in natural descent sprang the Messiah" (Romans 9: 1–5).

On the road to Damascus to persecute Jewish Christians who advocated the elimination of the law, Jesus revealed to him in a personal vision that the covenant of the Law has been replaced by the new covenant. Paul was compelled to carry this news abroad to a world yearning for redemption. Paul the visionary did not see just the man Jesus, walking and teaching throughout Judaea, but the risen Christ, the Lord. For Paul salvation rests on faith in Christ. Jesus, God's son, wholly without sin, was sent to humanity by God's grace to expiate universal sinfulness and to defeat death. He took his passion and death freely upon himself, and by his death and resurrection he assured salvation to all those who have faith in him. In baptism they undergo death with him and are raised from death to a new life of union with Jesus. The new spirit having been restored, the Christian will do what is right out of inner motivation and no longer live under the compulsion of the law. God, through Jesus, abolished the Law, replacing it by grace, thereby saving all of humanity.

The Jews did not accept Paul's theology, and he had to explain his opposition to them. Their faith was highly respected by seekers of a spiritual religion, and so in order to make progress converting the Gentiles, Paul had to distinguish between his faith and Judaism and demonstrate the Jews in error. Nevertheless, he was deeply attached to his own people and was torn between his pride in his ancestry and his mission to the Gentiles. He shifted between praise for the Jews and sharp critique.

Paul emphatically affirmed the Jews' zeal for God but condemned their way of life, for they followed their own way of righteousness—the law (Torah and mitzvot)—instead of serving God through faith in Christ who ended the law. Jews could abide by their observances but without faith in Christ these would be ineffective for salvation, meaningless, and harmful. Gentiles may not adopt Jewish law at all, and Paul rebukes any who do (Romans 9:6–33; Gal. 3).

Nevertheless God has not rejected his people. Christians are saved in order to stir Israel to "jealousy" by a Christian way of life so filled with love that it will rouse the Jews to emulation. Paul hoped that, in the end, the Jews would be saved. Paul says that the Gentiles therefore should never forget that they are grafted on the consecrated root of Judaism, by which they, as branches, were consecrated as well. The root sustains them, not they the root.

Paul's position regarding the Jews had a crucial influence on what was to befall Jews at the hands of Christians. It has allowed Christianity to emphasize the Jews' distinction in the eyes of God. But Christianity could also emphasize the derelictions of the Jews. Their misery was then ordained by God. It would clearly testify to the triumph of the Church. Throughout most of its history Christianity humiliated the Jews, on account of their supposed error. Only in our time has it come to recognize the distinction of the Jews and thereby has made a dialogue of equals possible.

Paul stepped beyond the bounds of Judaism. His doctrine that God became incarnate in Christ and his elimination of mitzvot were antithetical to Jews. Although he preached in the manner of rabbis, drawing conclusions out of scriptural verses, his principles were not Jewish. Internal tensions developed between him and the Jews to whom he spoke. Nevertheless, he had no animosity against his people, who, he hoped, would eventually accept Christ and be restored to glory. His counsel to the Christians, however, might have created an atmosphere of friendly, mutual adjustment, had Christianity accepted his guidance. Both religions might have lived peacefully together and given each other valuable inspiration. This relationship has opened up only very recently.

The Period of Dissociation

Until the defeat of the Jews in the Bar Kokhba rebellion, linkage to Judaism gave the new faith prestige and security. The Gentile world knew of Judaism and its missionary activities; the Christian messengers built on these foundations. After the defeat, however, Rome prohibited the Jewish religion for a while. Christian spokesmen now taught that the new faith had nothing to do with the old religion. Gentiles gradually assumed leading positions in the Church, and no affection or family spirit bound them to its Jewish past. Anti-Jewish statements found a place in Christian writings, including the New Testament. For example, the term "Pharisees" is used in a derogatory sense; by this time Pharisaism had become *the* central doctrine of Judaism and so all Jewry was implicated. "The Jews" are mentioned again and again as adversaries.

The Jews are said to have demanded the death of Jesus and to have taken on the responsibility for his death for all generations: "His blood be on us and on our children" (Matt. 27:25)— this created a new kind of inherited sin, which Judaism denies and no Jew could have said. The Jews were henceforth portrayed as a doomed people, cast out by God, who had abrogated the covenant with them and made a new covenant with the Christians. They were branded throughout the generations as killers of God. Jews have been unable to explain why they should be guilty, even according to Christian dogma, when it was ordained in the divine plan that Christ should die for the sins of the world. The Gospels themselves point out that he did not die on account of the Jews but in conformity with an eternal will.

Despite increasing dissociation and estrangement from Judaism, Christianity leaned heavily on Judaism, but without acknowledgment. The prayer Jesus taught his disciples—Our Father—is wholly Jewish and shows parallels to the Kaddish; it is inappropriate in Jewish worship only because of its key position in Christian liturgy. Quotations from the Hebrew Scriptures permeate the New Testament. The great commandment to love God and neighbor is quoted from Torah. And although the early Christians disdained the Temple and found the model for their religious life in the synagogue, they later copied the Temple service as they remembered it. This led to the Mass, a sacrificial service, with incense and vestments akin to those of the Temple priests. The liturgy reveals its Jewish background, and even includes Hebrew terms, such as *Amen* and *Hallelujah.* Up until the Second Vatican Council the cycle of appointed readings for the holy seasons were selected from the same chapters as the Torah and Haftarah readings for the corresponding Jewish festivals.

THE CHRISTIAN-JEWISH DIALOGUE RESUMED

World War II claimed six million Jewish martyrs. Theological antisemitism shored up the foundations on which racial antisemitism had been built. Christian conscience was aroused. Leading Christians felt theology must never become a source of Jewish persecution again. In 1958, Reinhold Niebuhr counseled Protestants against missionary work among Jews and upheld the dignity of the Jewish faith.[6] On the Jewish side, Martin Buber, among others, called for dialogue. But it was Pope John XXIII who changed the Catholic-Jewish relationship radically, and with it Christian-Jewish relations in general.

The Catholic Church

When Pope John called an ecumenical council for the purpose of "updating" the Catholic church, he specifically

6. See Reinhold Niebuhr, *Pious and Secular America* (New York: Charles Scribner's Sons, 1958), pp. 107 and 111.

ordered a statement on the Jews. It was promulgated by Pope Paul VI in 1965, bearing the title *Nostra Aetate,* the Declaration on the Relationship of the Church to Non-Christian Religions. It created new basic doctrines:

> The Church acknowledges the spiritual ties binding it to the Jews. ... God holds the Jews most dear for the sake of their fathers, for God does not repent His gifts.... What happened in Christ's passion cannot be charged against all Jews then alive without distinction, nor against the Jews of today.... The Jews should not be presented as rejected and accursed by God, as if this followed from the Holy Scriptures.... The Church decries hatred, persecution, and displays of antisemitism directed against Jews at any time and by anyone.

The decree had been prepared by the German Cardinal Bea, who sought the counsel of the distinguished Jewish thinker Abraham Heschel. Bishops in various countries, above all in America, pressed for clarification and additions and issued guidelines of their own. The French bishops, characterizing Judaism in Heschel's terms as "sanctifying time," held up to their faithful the Jews' "sanctification of God's name," their martyrdom throughout the ages and especially during the Holocaust. They emphasized the need for the recognition and study of the Talmud, Midrash, and Jewish exegetes, endorsed the restoration of the State of Israel, and emphasized that all the religious branches of Judaism must be regarded as legitimate. The German bishops called on Jews and Christians to come to grips both with the Holocaust—the possibility of believing in God after the Shoah—and with the significance of the State of Israel.

In 1974, the Vatican issued Guidelines and Suggestions for Implementing the Conciliar Declaration of *Nostra Aetate.* The guidelines further emphasize the links of the Church to Judaism through liturgy, the Bible, and shared worship of the same just and loving God. Duties emerge from the links, and the fight against antisemitism is emphasized as the duty of every Christian.

Education about Judaism "is important on all levels of

Christian instruction and education," and "research into the problems bearing on Judaism and Jewish-Christian relations will be encouraged." Prejudices acquired in childhood persist through life. Religious education for children can therefore be a powerful means of transforming Christians into fighters against antisemitism. Catholic colleges and universities are encouraged to develop programs in Jewish studies and to work alongside Jewish scholars: "in the spirit of the prophets Jews and Christians will work willingly together, seeking social justice and peace at every level."

Pope John Paul II has met with the Jewish communities in the countries he visited. In 1987, as a symbolic act, the Pope officially participated in a special service with the Jews in the synagogue of Rome, for the first time in history. It opened the way to joint worship throughout the world.

In 1992 a new catechism was promulgated, the first including concern with the Jews and translating the pronouncements of the Church into the teaching of the faithful on the grassroots level. In 1994 diplomatic relations between the Vatican and the State of Israel were established.

The Protestant Churches

The Protestant churches have followed the example of Catholicism. Their participation promises that Jewish dialogue with all of the Christian denominations will continue to grow and be a dialogue of equals. Significant works by Christian scholars have been written. For example, *A Theology of Christian-Jewish Reality,* by the Episcopalian theologian Paul van Buren, emphasizes the necessity of rethinking Christian theology in light of Jewish experience, teaching, and practice. The Protestant theologian Franklin Littell repeatedly confronted Christianity with its past, calling for acknowledgment of its guilt and renewal of spirit.[7]

In Germany, the Evangelical Synod of the State of Rhineland ordained the church to repent and actively renew itself, since

---

7. See, for example, Franklin H. Littell, *The Crucifixion of the Jews* (New York: Harper and Row, 1975).

German Christians stand "under the curse that Hitler's policies of *Judenreinheit* [total elimination of the Jews] had almost been fully realized." It called for the establishment of chairs on Judaism in the Protestant theological departments of universities. Other state synods have followed. State universities are increasingly establishing departments or at least chairs of Jewish studies. A remarkably large number of books on Judaism are being published. Regional and local conferences and lectures are widespread.

The dialogue with Islam is essential, due to its increasing influence worldwide and its close relationship to Israel, located in the heartland of Islam and counting a large number of Muslims among its inhabitants. Islamic fundamentalism may make this dialogue more difficult. The Quran, accepted as the unchanging word of God, denies full citizenship to "unbelievers" and is frequently harsh in its judgment of Jews and Judaism. But Mohammed also has words of praise for "the People of the Book," and Abraham is considered the ancestor of the Arabs, both physically and spiritually. These are among the starting points of a dialogue that needs to be extended without consideration of political factors.

Principles and Hopes

The task of implanting the new spirit of respect in a population conditioned by nearly two thousand years of anti-Jewish indoctrination will be long and arduous. Jews still offer convenient scapegoats for those suffering economic hardships. Within the churches, progress has often been slow. When the very existence of the State of Israel was in danger during the war of 1967, the churches stood silent. Liberal churches and theologians frequently show less understanding and forbearance with the State of Israel, its dangers, its needs, and the mistakes of its leaders, than do fundamentalist churches, which see the restoration of the Jewish state as an indication of the second coming of Christ. The increasing political power of the Radical Right in America, and its intent to "Christianize" America, has raised anxieties among Jews.

In 1996, the Southern Baptist Convention voted to extend missionary activity among Jews, and during the High Holy Day season in 1999 distributed a guide on how to pray for the conversion of the Jews. These efforts will create serious obstacles to a dialogue with evangelical churches.

Theologically based hatred of the Jews was the cause of antisemitism. A theologically based battle against antisemitism can be a powerful instrument toward its defeat. Dialogues can become very fruitful. They must be based on mutual respect and must reject any missionary intent—conducted between partners, committed to God. Participants must be rooted in a thorough knowledge of their own religious heritage and at the same time respectfully open to the convictions of the others.

In 1990, the Dalai Lama, expelled by the Chinese from his home in Tibet, invited a number of Jewish leaders to visit him and guide him and his people in how to survive away from a homeland. Subsequently he addressed Jewish gatherings in America, profoundly impressing them with his deep spirituality.

The faiths and practices of non-Christian religions also have valuable lessons to teach. Dialogues with non-Christian faiths, above all Islam but also Buddhism and others, acquire ever increasing urgency in our shrinking world. The Muslims can offer examples of unflinching devotion to God and religion. Buddhists and Hindus can teach the attitude of detachment from the illusions of the world and guide in the practice of meditation. Many religions, including Judaism, have begun to learn from them. Religious differences have been the source of wars. Spiritual reconciliation can lead to peace and universal human fellowship.

Chapter 7

THE GLORY OF SEFARDIC JEWRY

Two principal groups of Jews today are the Sefardim and the Ashkenasim, each with its particular rituals, traditions, and customs. The groups developed out of two great migrations.

Well before the end of the Roman Empire, Jews migrated from Palestine to Italy and throughout the Roman provinces, to Gaul and into the lands that were to be Germany and northwestern Europe, and, later, to Poland and Russia. This branch of Jewry is the Ashkenasim; the term *Ashkenas* in the Torah (Gen. 10:3; 1 Chr. 1:6) refers, according to folk etymology, to the German lands.

The State of Israel has two rabbinic bodies, Sefardic and Ashkenasic, each with a chief rabbi at its head. The groups pronounce Hebrew differently. Modern Hebrew, as spoken in Israel, follows the Sefardic pronunciation.

We shall take up the story of Ashkenasic Jewry in the next chapter.

As Islam advanced across the North African coast into Spain, many Babylonian Jews followed. This community is called the Sefardim because the prophet Obadiah speaks of the "Jerusalemite exile community of Sefarad" (Obadiah 1:20), a name applied to Spain.

In the eighth century, Spain came under Islamic rule. The Jews, as unbelievers, officially became *dhimmi*—tolerated without citizenship—but the Moorish kings recognized the benefits

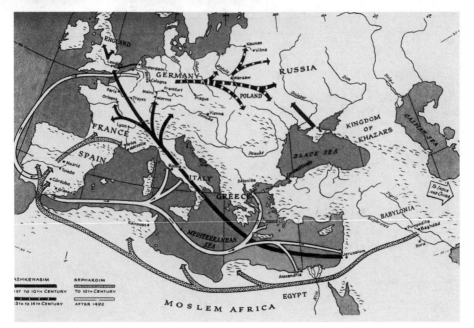

Jewish Dispersion

they could derive from the Jews and generally overlooked this law. On the whole, Jews were free to participate in the political, intellectual, cultural, and economic growth of society as a whole and were engaged in numerous trades and crafts. Jewish intellectual life flourished. Commentaries to the Bible and works in grammar, philosophy, and Talmud were published, a good many of them written in Arabic, later to be translated into Hebrew. Greek philosophy and Islamic thought were translated into Latin, and Greek thinking, especially the works of Aristotle, could thereby enter the western world. Without Jewish and Islamic thinkers, western scholasticism might not have developed.

SEFARDIC LEADERS AND THINKERS OF THE TENTH TO TWELFTH CENTURIES

Some Jews held high positions in service to the Muslim princes and were then called to political office as ministers. These Jewish leaders promoted the welfare and spiritual growth of Judaism and were leaders of the Jewish community, each calling himself by the title *Nagid,* "prince." For centuries to come, the Nagid cared for the poor, advocated for their people at court, and, being part of the general culture, contributed to its progress.

During the tenth century, Spanish Jewry had a great Nagid in HASDAI IBN SHAPRUT (c. 915–c. 975), who was described by ibn Daud as "the great *Nasi*, a prince and sage." Hasdai was a royal advisor, physician, and customs inspector, and in contact with Jewish communities everywhere. He surrounded himself with Hebrew poets and writers who brought about a revival of literature and poetry; the study of the Talmud flourished.

SAMUEL HA-NAGID (Samuel ben Joseph ibn Nagrela) (993–after 1056) was a trader and a scholar who knew Arabic literature well. He was also thoroughly familiar with Greek philosophy, an outstanding mathematician, a great astronomer, and a distinguished calligrapher. He spoke and wrote seven languages and composed inspired poetry. He came to the attention of the king of Granada, who appointed him vizier and general; in his service Samuel repeatedly led Muslim armies to victory. He was also a great talmudist, found time to direct a yeshivah, and wrote commentaries. Yet, the situation of the Jewish community was precarious; in 1066, the Jews of Granada were massacred by Muslims and Samuel's son Joseph murdered.

The historian, philosopher, and astronomer Rabbi Abraham ha-Levi ibn Daud (1110–1180) tells us in his work the Book of Tradition, *how Spain became a center of Jewish learning. Four Rabbis, each of them a great scholar, were sent out as envoys from Babylonia and were made captives when their ship was captured by pirates. Sold as slaves, each of the rabbis was redeemed by a different Jewish community, whose leader he became. One of them established the independent Torah center in Spain.*

A wondrous tale reached Hasdai's ears: On the steppes of southern Russia, a whole nation, the Khazars, had converted to Judaism after careful examination of the Christian, Islamic, and Jewish faiths. Bulan, the Khazars' king, decided around 740 that, "trusting in the mercies of God and the power of the Almighty, I choose the religion of Israel." The Khazars then followed the Torah and existed to the thirteenth century. This story is the frame for a great philosophical work, The Kuzari, *by Judah Halevi (c. 1075–c. 1141), in which the basic principles of Judaism are explained and contrasted with other faiths.*

SOLOMON BEN-JUDAH IBN GABIROL (c. 1021–c. 1057) was a contemporary of Samuel ha-Nagid. Indigent and frail, Gabirol was alive in mind and emotions. Because of him Hebrew poetry, from prayer to drinking song, acquired new beauty. His philosophical work, *Well of Life*, originally written in Arabic, was translated into Latin under the title *Fons Vitae*. For many centuries it was taken for the work of a Christian philosopher of the neo-Platonic school, until it was discovered that the Jew Gabirol and the non-Jewish philosopher Avicebron were one and the same.

JUDAH HALEVI (c. 1075 – c. 1141), was a physician. Born in Toledo, he traveled and studied for many years, finally setting down in Cordoba. He was an extraordinary poet, philosopher, and lover of Zion. (His philosophical work, *The Kusari*, is discussed in chapter 33.) Here he sings of spring, the beauties of love, the grandeur of nature, and the fury of the elements:

> But yesterday the earth drank like a child
>   With eager thirst the autumn rain.
> Or like a wistful bride who waits the hour
>   Of love's mysterious bliss and pain.
> And now the Spring is here with yearning eyes;
>   Midst shimmering golden flower beds,
> On meadows carpeted with varying hues,
>   In richest raiment clad she treads.
> She weaves a tapestry of bloom o'er all,
>   And myriad eyed young plants upspring,
> White, green, or red like lips that to the mouth
>   Of the beloved one sweetly cling. . . .
> Come! go we to the garden with our wine,
>   Which scatters sparks of hot desire,
> Within our hand 't is cold, but in our veins
>   It flashes clear, it glows like fire.[1]

Such poetry is remarkable, not only for its beauty, but also because a Jew wrote it. It reveals in Spanish Jewry an acculturation that did not deflect them from wholehearted allegiance to tradition.

There was for Judah another call more powerful than healing, another love more persuasive than spring's: Zion, the love of Jerusalem. He wished to go there, a humble pilgrim yearning for his God. Leaving his home, he reached Egypt after a stormy

---

1.Translation by Emma Lazarus, in *A Golden Treasury of Jewish Literature*, ed. Leo W. Schwarz (New York: Rinehart, 1937), p. 577.

voyage, then continued on toward the promised land. Whether he ever reached the holy city we do not know. According to legend he was killed by the galloping hoofs of a horse as he lay on the ground kissing the soil, his face turned in ecstasy toward Jerusalem.

Outstanding among the Spanish masters was Rabbi MOSES BEN-MAIMON, abbreviated Rambam, also called Maimonides (1135–1204), one of the leading philosophers of the Middle Ages. When he was born in Cordoba, a fanatic Islamic sect invaded Spain from North Africa to meet the Christian armies that were advancing from the North. The invaders were cruel to the Jews and forced them to migrate or accept Islam. Maimonides' family chose to leave. For ten years they moved from country to country, giving young Moses the opportunity to learn from all the masters he met. Talmud, philosophy, medicine, mathematics, and astronomy were among the subjects he studied. Following a sojourn in the Land of Israel he settled in Egypt, where he became court physician and head of the Jewish community of Fostat (Cairo). His grave is said to be found in Tiberias.

Finished in 1180, Maimonides' Mishneh Torah codified Jewish law. Many feared that its systematic summary of the Talmud and other legal writings would replace the Talmud.

Moses' first concern, the preservation of the Torah, is evident in all his works, including the two most extensive ones: the Mishneh Torah and the *Guide for the Perplexed*.

Mishneh Torah, "Repetition of Torah," or *Yad ha-Hazakah*, "The Strong Hand," is Maimonides' code of Jewish law; it embraces the entirety of talmudic legislation. He wrote the Mishneh Torah because he felt that the law of the Talmud needed clarification and codification. Having witnessed persecution and experienced homelessness, he realized the danger that threatens Jewish law in times of turmoil. He begins with the statement: "All the laws, given to Moses at Sinai, were given with their meaning." This is the first complete digest of the laws of Oral Torah. Culled from the vast expanse of innumerable opinions in the Talmud, the final decisions are systematically arranged by subject matter, enabling a rabbi to find an answer to any question quickly and authoritatively. Mishneh Torah has never lost its influence, although other codes were published later.

His great philosophical work, the *Guide for the Perplexed,* explained Judaism in the light of philosophy, especially to those who had become bewildered by the conflicting claims of Torah and Aristotle. He fused Jewish tradition and Aristotelian ethics. The *Guide for the Perplexed* established Maimonides as a leading philosopher. Praised and denounced by medieval Jewish thinkers and the Christian Church alike, this work influenced thinkers throughout the ages and entered the main current of western philosophy through the work of Thomas Aquinas. (The *Guide* will be discussed in more detail in chapter 32.)

Maimonides also condensed the basic beliefs of Judaism into a creed such as the Christians and Muslims had. Subsequently, his Thirteen Articles of Faith were given poetic form, and one version, *Yigdal,* is a hymn sung in the synagogue. To this day, his ideas express basic beliefs of traditional Judaism. Expressing them as a unified creed, however, has been attacked, for a creed would establish a dogma, resulting in eliminating from Judaism those who did not abide by all of the articles. Judaism has never insisted on such a body of belief. The principles constitute a foundation, however, and reinterpreted or maintained in their original meaning, they are guidelines for religious Jews of all denominations:

1. God created all and leads all creation.
2. God is One and there is no other Oneness.

3. God has no body, nor any bodily shape.
4. God is eternal.
5. To God alone and to no other is it meet to pray.
6. The words of the prophets are true.
7. Moses our master is chief of all prophets.
8. The Torah was given to Moses.
9. The Torah is not subject to change and there will never be another Torah.
10. The Creator is omniscient.
11. God rewards those who obey his commandments and punishes transgressors.
12. The Messiah will come.
13. God will raise the dead.

THE TRIALS AND END OF SPANISH JEWRY

Regarding the reconquest of Spain from the Moors as a sacred mission, the Christian kings of Castile moved slowly southward. In 1176 all Jews were declared to be "the serfs of the king and absolute property of the royal treasury" that could at any time expropriate them. The Christian rulers used Spanish Jews as counselors, tax collectors, and financiers. The tax gatherers were pressured by the kings to provide funds and therefore were hated by the populace as oppressors.

On an individual basis, relations between Jews and Christians were generally good, which disturbed the Christian clergy. Prompted by Pablo Christiani, a Jewish convert to Christianity who hated Jews, King James I of Aragon called the great halakhist and biblical commentator RABBI MOSES BEN NAHMAN (abbreviated Ramban, also called Nahmanides) to a disputation with the Dominicans at Barcelona in 1263. Nahmanides brilliantly used the Talmud and Midrash to prove the truth of Judaism and refute the claims of Christianity. He boldly asserted his right to speak freely, even if his arguments offended his adversaries. He won and received praise and an award from the king, but the Dominicans would not admit defeat. They asked the pope to intervene, accusing Nahmanides of blasphemy; he fled Spain for the Land of Israel.

Conversos - Marranos

Gradually, the Church succeeded in driving a wedge between Christians and Jews. In 1348 riots broke out in Aragon, and from then on Christian fanaticism led to ever increasing tensions. In 1391 mobs stormed the Jewish sections of many cities, and thousands of Jews were murdered. Tens of thousands of Jews allowed themselves to be baptized in order to save their lives and property; they were called *Conversos*. The populace still considered them wicked, however, and called them *Marranos,* swine. A new racist distinction emerged—"purity of blood," which the Marranos lacked because they were of a different "race."

Many Marranos practiced their Jewish faith in secret. To the Church this was unpardonable. Having once accepted Christianity, they had committed the mortal sin of apostasy. The Inquisition was organized and set up against them, and many were tortured and burned at the stake. Some families survived and retained their faith secretly throughout the ages, to profess it openly again only in the twentieth century.

A disputation at Tortosa, in 1413–1414, instigated by converted Jews, forced the Jews to defend both their belief that the Messiah had not yet come and the Talmud with its "errors, heresy, blasphemy, and abuse of the Christian religion." Realizing that they would not be permitted to win and were only harming their people by continuing, the Jews begged for an end of the disputation. Among the new restrictions was the yellow badge to be worn by Jews as a mark of "shame."

Torquemada and the Expulsion of the Jews

In 1483 the Dominican Thomas de Torquemada, a fanatical zealot, became Grand Inquisitor. Under his command, a Marrano could be brought before the Inquisition, tortured for a confession implicating himself, his family, and his friends, and sentenced to death. It sufficed that a neighbor claimed that there had been more smoke rising from the Marrano's chimney on Friday, indicating he had prepared a Sabbath meal; or that there was less smoke on Saturday, meaning he observed the Sabbath law against kindling fire and did not celebrate Sunday; or that he bought more vegetables before Pesah or purchased his meat regularly from a Marrano butcher. As the Church would not take a life, the accused was surrendered to the secular state, which burned him in a public auto-da-fe, act of faith.

Watching those whom the unbending will of Torquemada had sent into exile was Christopher Columbus, about to set sail for a new world. In his diaries he speaks movingly about the Jews and their plight. Was Columbus himself a Marrano?

When Ferdinand and Isabella married, the kingdoms of Castille and Aragon were united and the Moors pushed back until finally, in 1492, Granada, the last Moorish stronghold, fell. With that, Torquemada argued that the only non-Christians in Spain were the Jews, who subverted the Marranos. Because the Grand Inquisitor was the former father confessor of Queen Isabella and had great influence over her, she and Ferdinand issued the edict: the Jews must get out, leaving their property behind. The date set for the expulsion was the anniversary of the fall of Jerusalem.

This Sefardic synagogue was built in Venice in 1584, nearly a century after the Jews' expulsion from Spain and thirty years after the Jews of Italy were forced to dwell in ghettos.

Migration

The exiles, including large numbers of Marranos, found themselves in poverty and distress. Many fled to Portugal, but were forced to convert. During the following centuries, thousands of converted Jews secretly escaped from Portugal to confess their faith openly in freer countries.

Many rulers, however, welcomed the Jews as a cultural, social, and economic asset and gave shelter to the fugitives. Venice,

Bordeaux, Naples, Genoa, and Amsterdam were to profit from an influx of talented Jews, and a new settlement in Palestine was to emerge.

In the Ottoman Empire, the sultan Bayazid II, learning of the expulsion of the Jews, said, "How can you consider him [King Ferdinand of Spain] a wise ruler, when he impoverished his own land and enriched ours?" By religion Muslim, the Ottoman Empire was governed by a Turkish military aristocracy and encompassed numerous religious minorities. The minorities, especially the Jews, were entrusted with the economic growth of state and society—but as *dhimmis* and heavily taxed. The age-old local Jewish communities valiantly came to the aid of the newly arrived Spanish Jews, who settled throughout the empire—fifty thousand in Istanbul alone. Salonica, Adrianopel, and Smyrna (Izmir) became Jewish centers. In 1516–17 Palestine, Syria, and Egypt came under the Ottomans' power and were open to Jewish settlement.

SAFED. The Holy Land drew numerous Jews, especially to the city of Safed, which became a vibrant center of Jewish life and learning. Distinguished by its healthy climate and its location on the pilgrimage route to Jerusalem, the city was not claimed as a sacred spot by either Christians or Muslims. Safed became an agricultural center and developed a flourishing textile industry, a money market, and trade in grain and textiles.

In 1522 Safed had a Jewish population of three hundred families, equal to the Jewish population of Jerusalem. By the early seventeenth century it had grown to at least twenty thousand. The city is close to the grave of Rabbi SIMEON BEN YOHAI, regarded as the author of the *Zohar* (see chapter 32) and the graves of the Tannaim, the great authorities on the Oral Law (see chapter 23). The city attracted talmudists, halakhists, and kabbalists. Its rise to prominence brought tensions with the Jewish community in Jerusalem.

The talmudist and mystic JOSEPH KARO (1488–1575), author of the great code of Jewish law, the Shulhan Arukh, lived in Safed, as did the mystic ISAAC LURIA (1534–1572), whose teachings had an abiding impact on Jewish thought (see chapter 32).

THE FUTURE

Over the centuries, Sefardic Jewry remained deeply committed to Torah. Seeing themselves as exiles under God's will, the Sefardic Jews accepted their lot and their position as *dhimmi* within an unchanging Muslim world. By the end of the nineteenth century, the Sefardim constituted only one-tenth of the total Jewish population. Seeking to improve the well-being of the Sefardim, European Jews intervened, including establishing modern schools; but in doing so they created a wedge between the Sefardic Jews and the Muslim population, which was averse to change and hostile to foreign domination. This was the beginning of Muslim-Jewish tension.

Members of a Sefardic family, dressed in traditional costume, stroll at an Israeli festival.

RESTORATION IN SPAIN. After 500 years, the edict of expulsion was formally revoked. In 1992, the 500th anniversary of the expulsion, a commemorative service was held in the synagogue of Madrid, attended by the king and queen of Spain and the president of the State of Israel. A small Jewish community exists again in Spain.

Chapter 8

ASHKENASIC JEWRY IN THE MIDDLE AGES

Crisis and Learning

As soldiers and suppliers of Caesar's legions, Jews may have reached the Rhine River, and, following the routes of the Roman Empire, traveled as far as England. The Jews who then settled in Germany, France, England, and, later, Eastern Europe, are the Ashkenasim. The great accomplishments of the medieval Ashkenasim occurred in ever increasing isolation from the surrounding Christian communities and amidst threats of persecution.

Set apart from and yet interwoven with the society, the life of Ashkenasic Jewry in the Middle Ages demonstrates the history of the West itself, underscoring the clash between the universal claims of the popes and the ambitious expansionism of secular rulers. Although the Jews were sometimes welcomed as promoters of trade and commerce, they lost their status, which was dependent on the power of rulers and popes, as suspicion against them developed into prejudice, and prejudice and hatred were incited by the Church.

Hoping to convert the Jews, the Church claimed the right to determine their status. Pope Gregory I (590–604) hated the Jews. He knew, however, that they would find their way to the Church only if the Church exhibited a Christian spirit of love. Gregory therefore proposed economic inducements and at the

---

same time ordered the Jews subject to missionary pressure; he never restricted Jewish religious law but attendance at Christian sermons was often forced.

In the chaos that followed the collapse of the Roman Empire, Jews were exposed to the whims not only of popes but also of the rulers of the fragmenting empire. Under the Carolingian rulers Jews were welcomed. When Charlemagne (768–814) consolidated the realm, he showed kindness to the Jews. Charlemagne's son Louis the Pious (814–840) granted the Jews many rights, including protection of body and property, freedom of movement and of trade, and permission to build synagogues; he even ordered the transfer of market days from Saturday to Sunday. Jews were treated with favor at the royal court.

Several Jewish centers were established on the Rhine River at Mainz, Worms, and Speyer. When Otto II (973–983) saw the need to expand trade, he invited the Kalonymus family of Lucca, Italy, to settle in Mainz; a member of the family had saved Otto's life in a battle against the Saracens. When Jews were forced to flee

In the Middle Ages, for nearly one thousand years, the synagogue in Worms provided a place for learning, spirituality, and community.

Mainz in 1084, they were admitted to Speyer by Bishop Ruediger. In order to attract Jews to his city, he gave them land outside it, surrounded by a wall to ward off attacks. The bishop awarded them parcels of church land for a cemetery. He allowed them free trade in the city, permitted them to have Christian servants, and let them sell to Christians meat that was not kosher.

In his treatment of the Jews of Worms, Emperor Henry IV (1065–1106) also showed favor to the Jews. He fought bitterly with Pope Gregory VII (1073–1085) over the pope's claim to absolute supremacy over Christian rulers. The Jews were economically useful and politically supportive in the emperor's struggle against the papal demands. In 1074 Henry granted "the Jews and the other citizens of Worms" freedom from customs duties at the royal duty posts, placing the Jews on an equal footing with other citizens of the city.

In 1090, Henry granted the Jews of Worms and Speyer a special patent, in which he established his position as sole protector and supreme judicial authority over the Jews. No one was allowed to reduce their right to property, they could exchange money throughout the city, and they had complete mobility and freedom of commerce throughout the empire. They could be witnesses in the imperial courts and were to adjudicate litigations among themselves in their own court. They were permitted to have Christian servants and to sell wine, dyes, and medicaments to Christians. Forced conversion was strictly forbidden and put under penalty. A person who incited murder of the Jews or maliciously injured a Jew was punished severely.

These privileges were renewed by Emperor Frederick I, Barbarossa, in 1157, and in 1236 Emperor Frederick II extended them to all Jews of the empire. While these documents tell us that the relations between Jews and Christians must have been good in general, pressures on the Jewish community are equally revealed, including the threat of forced conversion, extortion, abuse, and murder. Jewish life remained insecure.

The emperor's exclusive authority over the Jews, while it offered protection, also opened the way for exploitation, as the emperors came to regard the Jews as personal property. A ruler might present a Jew's life and belongings to a friend or vassal. Further, a patent granted by one ruler—whether bishop or emperor—had to be renewed by his successor; there was no assurance of this, and it could always be revoked. Initially granted to a whole congregation, letters of protection, *Schutzbriefe,* were eventually awarded only to a few "useful" families, among them wealthy aristocrats who became advocates, *shtadlanim,* for the Jews at court and consequently exercised great power within the Jewish community.

As the power of the popes and barons increased, imperial power weakened—and with it imperial protection. Dukes, barons, and municipalities often acted on their own, dividing Germany among themselves. This saved the Jews many times. As one duke expelled them, another admitted them, and so the Jews never left Germany.

THE CRUSADES

To unify Christianity under his leadership, Pope Urban II, in 1095, called upon all Christians in the western world to go to battle against the infidels who had conquered the holy places in Palestine. This began the Crusades. Among the masses who answered the call were high minded knights and reckless profiteers. Some did not share the pope's need to go to Palestine to avenge the blood of Christ. There were infidels to be plundered and exterminated without risk right in their midst. And so Jewish communities along the Rhine were attacked. Many Jews, for the "Sanctification of the Name" of God, chose death over baptism. The centers of Jewish life in Western Europe—Mainz, Worms, Speyer, Trier, Cologne—were ravaged. In vain, and sometimes halfheartedly, the bishops tried to stem the mob's fury. The Jews themselves took up arms but were overwhelmed.

Surviving Jews reacted in two ways, either by insisting on having their own walled quarters, or by withdrawing from the culture of their surroundings, immersing themselves ever more deeply in the study of Torah and Jewish mysticism. These com-

In the wall of the ancient cemetery of Worms a simple plaque bore the words, "Ten Wardens of [4]856," the year of the Hebrew calendar corresponding to 1096. It recalls the sacrificial death of thousands who, following their leaders, went to their death for the "Sanctification of the Name." (The plaque was destroyed in World War II.)

munities recovered, and Henry IV, furious at the excesses against them, restored their rights. Relative peace returned, for a time.[1]

GERMAN LITURGICAL POETS AND THEIR PIYYUTIM. German Jewish poets composed liturgical poems, Piyyutim, for festivals and holy days. Their S'lihot, penitential prayers for the Yamim Noraim, and Kinnot dirges, for Tishah b'Av, are gripping poems that are frequently eyewitness reports of Jewish tragedies.

In this Piyyut, Kalonymus ben Judah laments the massacres of the Jews in the Rhineland during the Crusades:

> O that my head were filled with water, my eyes a well that I could
> weep all my days and nights for the slain of my children, from
> sucklings to aged of my congregations.... My eyelids overflow

1. On May 27, 1966, the nine hundredth anniversary of the massacre of the Jews at Mainz, the first restored synagogue at Mainz was rededicated by the author. Christians provided the funds and insisted on this date. The Catholic bishop and the president of the Protestant church publicly expressed deep shame and contrition at the deaths and cruelties inflicted by Christians on the Jews then and throughout the centuries.

with tears, and I raise bitter lament over the slain of Speyer. In the second month, on the eighth day, the day of rest, it happened, instead of rest they found a fiery death.... Jammed together, they fulfilled their lives in commitment to God to proclaim the unity of the One Name....With bitter pain I lift my voice in cry as I remember today the destruction of holy congregations. The congregation of Worms, tested and chosen, Master of the whole world and of flawless purity. Twice they sanctified the One Name in awe.... As they sang the Hallel, to render praise to God, they fulfilled their life linked to Him in love.... And over the towering giants of the famous congregation of Mainz, swifter than eagles and stronger than lions, fulfilling their lives in the proclamation of the awe-filled Name, over them I cry out in bitterness of soul.... On the day when Torah was given, I hoped to magnify it, but, as once it was given in fire, it returned, and ascended ... to the [heavenly] place of fire.... Heavy is my sigh from morning to night for the House of Israel and the people of God that have fallen by the sword.[2]

Pope Innocent III (1198–1216) saw it as his task to subdue the monarchs and humiliate the Jews. By restricting the financial business of the Jews he attained both goals—the monarchs lost a source of income and with it their interest in protecting the Jews. In addition, in 1215 the Fourth Lateran Council, convoked by Innocent, ruled that the Jews had to wear a yellow badge and a grotesque hat in order to be recognized immediately and given scorn and abuse. The council also proclaimed the dogma of the transubstantiation, which holds that at Mass bread and wine are transformed into the body and blood of Christ. This created new opportunities for slander against the Jews as they were accused of mutilating the sacred host, martyring Christ anew. The pope further declared, upon hearing a rumor of the death of a Christian student, that Jews ritually killed Christians. The libel of ritual murder spread all over Europe and led to massacres in Norwich, England (1144); Blois, France (1171); Lincoln, England (1255); Munich, Germany (1286); and many other places. It is mirrored in Geoffrey Chaucer's Canterbury Tales of 1340 (the "Prioress Tale"). Later

2. Kinnah for the 9th of Av

In the Middle Ages, Jews were tortured to produce "confessions" of ritual murder.

popes and emperors denounced the blood libels but to no avail. The two calumnies—ritual murder and desecration of the sacred host—were used to bring untold sufferings upon the Jews.

The Dominicans and the Franciscans, established as preaching orders, incited the populace by their sermons, with devastating effects. In 1240 an apostate Jew Nicholas Donin denounced the Talmud and forced the Jews to "defend themselves" at Paris in disputations with the Dominicans. The pope ordered that all copies of Talmud be confiscated and surrendered to the Dominicans on a Sabbath. Thousands of precious manuscripts were subsequently burned. Rabbi Meir of Rothenburg voiced his agony at the burning of the Talmud at Paris, addressing the Torah as a person:

> Torah, consumed by fire, will you not ask for the peace of those that mourn for you, who yearn to dwell in the courts of your house?... Woe, she, once revealed in consuming heavenly fire, was eaten up by human fire.... Tears I will shed until they become a stream and come to the graves of the two princes of your radiance, Moses and Aaron. (Kinnah for the 9th of Av)

As Christian art became propaganda, depictions of Jewish cruelty in Christ's passion were constantly before the illiterate population in images on stained windows and sculptures on church walls. The synagogue was portrayed as blind, her staff broken; the Church, as triumphant. Portrayals of Jews as swine and conspirators with horrible faces created stereotypes.

In the thirteenth and early fourteenth centuries in England and France, where royal power had broken the might of the barons and unified each kingdom, centralized royal power focused popular hatred and royal greed, which, together with the incendiary sermons of the friars, led to persecution. In 1255 a ritual murder trial took place at Lincoln, in England; and in 1290 the Jews were expelled from England—they could not return until the seventeenth century. The same occurred in France: in 1242 and 1248, Talmud manuscripts were burned at Paris; in 1288 Jews were subjected to a ritual murder trial at Troyes; in 1290 Jews were tried at Paris on the charge of desecration of the host; in 1306 they were expelled from France. The kings claimed all the debts owed the Jews for the royal treasury. In Germany, following a desecration charge in 1298, a nobleman named Rindfleish led mobs on a rampage through Bavaria and Austria; among the communities completely wiped out was Würzburg.

Jewish suffering reached a pinnacle during the Black Death, the bubonic plague. In the years after 1348, one-third of Europe's population perished. The Jews were made scapegoats, and for two years Jewish congregations were systematically exterminated. Fortunately, Poland had already opened her gates to German Jews, welcoming them as needed and useful. Thousands migrated to form great new centers of Jewish life, where piety and learning were to reach new heights.

But degradation continued in the Germanic lands. Squeezed out of trade, rejected by the craftsmen's guilds, and prohibited from owning and cultivating land, the Jews were permitted only one occupation—the lending of money. They were a ready source of exploitation by their rulers. For example, in Regensburg the Jews were held responsible for the economic decline of the city (actually a result of crime and corruption) and were maligned for engaging in various crafts and agriculture. In 1519 they were expelled after one thousand years of residence.

After an expulsion was over, the ruler often realized that he had lost a source of income and so resettled the Jews. The Jews had to live, however, in special sections of town that could be reached only through guarded gates. Locked up at night and on Christian holidays and insulted when they stepped out in their marked garments, they had lost access even to fresh air and the beauties of nature. As their numbers grew, many levels were added to the narrow houses, for the ghetto was never enlarged.

Segregation and Contact: Daily Inner Life

Under the constant threat of losing the consolations of their holy books, which the Inquisition could confiscate at any time and burn in public, and forced to listen to slanderous accusations that the Talmud contained blasphemies against God and Christ, the Jews withdrew into the realm of the Talmud. The small child, upon learning to speak, was taught an affirmation: "Moses charged us with the Teaching [Torah] as the heritage of the congregation of Jacob" (Deut. 33:4). Reciting these words, the child was told, "Close your eyes, little child, to everything around you, earthly goods and joys, but also the trials and the humiliation, all this is truly not yours. Your only assured heritage is Torah; no one can take it from you if you incorporate it in your mind and soul."

Yiddish is a German dialect into which have filtered terms from Hebrew, Polish, Russian, and other languages. Its development after the thirteenth century did not follow that of German, so it has retained an archaic character.

The Jews in their daily lives used the language of their countries. Rashi, the commentator on the Bible, gives French words for terms hard to explain in Hebrew—his people understood French. In Germany, they spoke German and dressed as much like the rest of the population as permitted (the caftan, the long black garb of the Polish Jew, was the dress of the medieval German). When driven out of Germany and fleeing to Poland, Jews took the German language with them and it became Jewish or Yiddish. They retained it through the centuries, a moving tribute to the culture which had helped form them and which they had helped develop.

German music entered the Jews' lives as well. Christian musicians played at Jewish weddings and festivities. They even produced a troubadour, a Minnesinger of their own, SÜSSKIND OF TRIMBERG (c. 1200–c. 1250), who visited the castles of the knights and struck his harp to sweet lyrical songs.

Except for the clergy, Jews were the only people who could read and write at a time when writing one's name was a mark of great literacy. Being able to read and write, they could help others. They gave philosophy and medicine to their Christian neighbors. Always famous as physicians, they served the rich and the poor alike. Jews' travel made them a link between cultures, transmitters of ideas and philosophies, even though they at times traveled against their will.

Fugitives were a common sight in a town's *shul*, as wave after wave of homeless poured in. Jews met the needs of their people, giving well beyond the tithe required in biblical law. Since talmudic times, collectors of charity have gone from house to house, week after week, to take up the collection for the needy. This giving is not "charity." It is *tzedakah*, "righteousness." To help a brother and sister in need is simply an act of righteous, decent living—nothing more. The spirit of *tzedakah* is one of the foremost distinctions of Jews.

The Jewish community of the Middle Ages met the challenge of its destiny by devotion to Torah and Talmud, by a deepening of both their inner life and their family love.

Chapter 9

ASHKENASIC JEWRY RISES TO EMINENCE

Upon settling in Northern Europe, the Jews developed centers of Torah. The traditional authority established at the yeshivot of Babylonia was far away. In addition, halakhic decisions had to take account of the new environment. Centers of learning were thus established in the Rhineland, where many Jews lived. The ordinances issued by the rabbis of the yeshivot of Mainz, Speyer, and Worms were binding throughout Ashkenasic Jewry, and questions about religious life had to be addressed there. These yeshivot attracted hundreds of disciples from all parts of the world, remaining centers of Jewish learning even after the massacres of the Crusades. From these schools, liturgical poets, philologists, experts in Jewish law, and mystics emerged.

These northern European yeshivot differed from those in Babylonia and Spain. In Spain, Jewish scholars frequently had close contacts with surrounding non-Jewish culture, as can be seen in their philosophical works. On the other hand, German Jews were influenced by their surroundings, but their rabbis excluded the culture of the non-Jewish world from their deliberations. In Torah and Talmud they discovered inner freedom.

The Masters

In the ancient Jewish cemetery, "Judensand," of Mainz the engraving on a simple stone reads, "Erected in memory of GERSHOM BEN JUDAH." Behind this name a history of great achievement unfolds. Rabbi Gershom (c. 960–1040) was likely born in Mainz and made his hometown a center of Jewish learning. Jews saw in him Rabbenu Gershom, "our" Rabbi Gershom; they called him *Meor ha-Golah*, "Light of the Diaspora." His influence rested on his personality, wisdom, and piety rather than on wealth or official standing in the community. He collected talmudic commentaries from various sources and began to combine, edit, organize, and sum up the work of generations, making new contributions as well. He also wrote liturgical poems still used in worship.

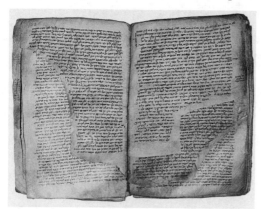

In the Middle Ages, Rashi's straightforward approach to commentary and interpretation opened up the text of the Bible and the Talmud, contributing to the democratization of learning that has characterized the Jewish tradition.

He became famous for the decrees ascribed to him. For example, he ruled that no letter may be read by anyone except its recipient, even if it is open; that no one may entice the customer of a competitor to oneself; that divorce requires the mutual consent of both parties; and that polygamy, not forbidden by Scripture but long out of use among Ashkenasim, was prohibited for the future. He also ruled that those Jews who returned to their faith after having left it were to be received in love and not reminded of their past.

The schools of Mainz and of Worms attracted to their ranks a man who was to become the greatest of all commentators, indispensable for the study of the Bible and the Talmud. His name was Rabbi SHELOMOH BEN YITSHAK—*Rashi*. Born in 1040 in the city of Troyes, France, he was drawn to the academies along the

Rhine to study under Rabbenu Gershom's successor, Rabbi Yaakov ben Yakar. Rashi returned home to Troyes at the age of twenty-five to open a school. Soon hundreds flocked to him, for he was a man of great kindness and humility. Not wishing to make his teaching a profession or to take money for it, he earned a comfortable living for himself and his family by cultivating vineyards and selling wine, an occupation and trade common among Jews.

In his love for his people and for tradition, he realized that they needed a guide through the Bible and the Talmud, and he set to work to compose it. He wished to bring comfort to his people out of the sources of tradition. He applied critical analysis to the text, revealing its inherent logic and grammar. Word by word, sentence by sentence, he went over the entire text of the Bible, explaining simply, elucidating deeply, combining his own words with those of the Talmud. The world of the Talmud was at his fingertips.

Behind the childlike simplicity of Rashi's style is a scholar of tremendous knowledge, a superb exegete, philosopher, theologian, and grammarian. For example, this is how he explained the first of the Ten Commandments.

Text: I am the Lord your God who brought you out of the land of Egypt, the house of bondage.

Rashi: Who brought you out of the land of Egypt: The purpose of your deliverance was that you be My servants. Or another explanation: At the Red Sea He appeared unto them as Lord of Battle, now—at Sinai—He appeared to them like a patriarch full of mercy. He wanted to make it clear to them: If I appear unto you in various ways do not say, these are different powers; I am He who brought you out of Egypt, I am the same.

Rashi asks why Egypt is mentioned in the first commandment, for it does not seem to belong. In giving his explanation, he presents the basic Jewish belief: God is the God of history. Israel is the servant of God, who alone is their ruler. Should God seem to act strangely toward the people of Israel, inflicting pain on them, they can remember that God is infinite, and infinite are the facets of the One God—knowing that their God is the One God, they will remain steadfast and true. This God of history will shape it mercifully and redeem them, as God did in Egypt. This is the meaning of the first commandment.

Rashi's thought is penetrating. To this day the talmudic scholar and the reader of the Bible depend on Rashi's commentary for a full comprehension of the sacred texts. To the simple or the hurried reader, he gives a satisfying answer; to the scholar, he opens new paths of research and study. Through his interpretation, Bible and Talmud become the common heritage of all. He is the commentator for all, and a man of true humility, who, at times said simply, "This verse I do not understand." When he died in 1105, he had given Jews a priceless gift.

This early printed edition of the Talmud from 1483 shows the text of the Mishnah (top), the Gemara (center), Rashi's commentary (right), and the *Tosafot* (left). The passage, from Tractate Berakhot, deals with when the Sh'ma should be recited in the evening.

THE TOSAFISTS. Rashi's commentary was so comprehensive and so influential that his immediate successors, rather than attempting new commentaries, wrote *Tosafot*, "additions," to Rashi. Outstanding among the Tosafists were Rashi's grandsons, Rabbi JACOB BEN MEIR (Rabbenu Tam, 1110–1171) and his brother Rabbi SAMUEL BEN MEIR (Rashbam). They were concerned with the development of halakhah, ethics in action, which guides all aspects of Jewish life and leads to theology and principles of ethical conduct.

Rabbi MEIR BEN BARUKH of Rothenburg, Maharam (c. 1215–1293), was the last of the Tosafists. Outstanding as a talmudist and liturgical poet, he shaped Jewish life by the large number of religious rulings he issued. Among them, he issued ordinances to improve democracy within the community; communal decisions were to be arrived at by congregational meetings, preferably by consensus, even though the ultimate halakhic decision lay with the rabbi. He strengthened the position of the Jewish woman by declaring Rosh Hodesh, the Day of the New Moon, as being special to women. This has been taken up by Jewish women again in our time. His deeply moving elegy on the burning of the Talmud in Paris is still recited on Tishah b'Av, the day commemorating the fall of the Temple.

Rabbi Meir tried to reach Eretz Yisrael but was recognized during his voyage and forced to return by the order of Emperor Rudolf of Hapsburg. In 1286 Meir was imprisoned for the rest of his life. He could have been ransomed, but he forbade his people to do so, for fear that it might set a pattern of Christian rulers capturing rabbis in order to extort ransom. Yet ransom had to be paid anyway, after the rabbi's death, for the privilege of burying his body. In 1306 Alexander Wimpfen of Frankfurt paid the enormous ransom demanded for the body. Rabbi Meir and Alexander Wimpfen are buried side by side in the cemetery of Worms.

HASIDEI ASHKENAS: THE PIOUS MEN OF GERMANY

The terrible tragedies that had befallen the Jews during the Crusades convinced some men to turn their backs entirely to the afflictions and joys of the world and to immerse themselves totally in an unconditional love of God. These men, the Hasidei Ashkenas, "Pious Men of Germany," lived in the latter part of the twelfth and the early part of the thirteenth centuries; their leaders were members of the aristocratic Kalonymus family. They were mystics, thus the term *hasid*, "pious," bears the additional denotation of "mystic." Jewish mysticism originated in the third century C.E. in Palestine and spread through the Roman Empire. In the eighth century, mysticism was brought to Lucca, Italy, where the Kalonymus family resided, and then members of the family brought it to Germany when they settled along the Rhine. The masters of the Hasidei Ashkenas were SAMUEL HE-HASID, the Mystic, who lived in the middle of the twelfth century; JUDAH HE-

*Judah he-Hasid was so deeply re-
vered that legends were woven
around him. Legend has it that the
mother of Judah he-Hasid, then
pregnant, found herself in the path of
the galloping horses and coach of an
approaching nobleman. Unable to
escape and certain to be run over, she
squeezed herself against the wall of
the synagogue, which receded forming a niche for her and the child in
her womb.*

HASID, who moved from Worms to
Regensburg, where he died in 1217;
and his disciple ELEAZAR BEN JUDAH,
who was born around 1176 at Speyer
and died in 1238 at Worms.

The collective work of these
three men, mainly ascribed to Judah
he-Hasid, the Book of the Pious—
Sefer Hasidim—is a guidebook showing Jews how to strive toward
becoming Hasidim. To the master, all
aspects of life—every emotion and action—must be ethical,
spiritual, and joyfully dedicated to God. In placing primary
emphasis on ethics and character development, *Sefer Hasidim*
deals with every aspect of worship, prayer, and study, and encompasses all human relations—family, education, and social interaction, including attitudes toward non-Jews. As well as striving
toward personal perfection, we are to instruct and guide others,
doing so with love, compassion, and gentleness; compassion
must also extend to animals.

The commandments and duties of ethical conduct are all
tests. Every mitzvah entails suffering; the more difficult a
mitzvah or an ethical action is, the more suffering it will involve
and the more valuable it will be. The highest mitzvah, being
absolute suffering—"Sanctification of the Name of God"—is
of supreme value for Jews and for God. A mitzvah attains its full
value when the person who performs it is filled by its spiritual
meaning and carries it out with joy and enthusiasm in
attunement to God.

The Hasidim emphasized the importance of *kavvanah*,
attunement to God in prayer. For themselves this meant a con-
centrated attention to every word and its secret meaning. For the
average Jew, devotion of the heart was sufficient. If a man or a
woman could not understand the Hebrew prayers, better that
they pray in the vernacular, but with deep feeling; God would
surely receive their prayer, which is properly not a plea that God
grant our desires but to ask what God desires.

Through example, the Hasidim gave the people strength

and endurance. Although the Hasidim belonged to the Jewish aristocracy, they eschewed the pleasures of the world, practiced severe asceticism,[1] and found highest satisfaction in serving God; the people believed their words, which were undergirded by their deeds. They emphasized that the love of God must entail love for every human being. They wished to open the hearts of all who would know God, seeking the welfare not only of their own families and fellow Jews but also of non-Jews. They reached out to the common people, who in turn loved them and

> *The* Sefer Hasidim *says that the pious person seeks no recognition. Having found an answer to a difficult point in a talmudic discussion he or she will never say, "I have found an answer," but "there can be this answer."*

tried to fashion their own lives by the Hasidim's example. To the question, why God made some people rich and others poor, they replied, to allow the rich the privilege of sustaining the poor, of promoting the study of Torah, of building synagogues and yeshivot, and of doing all this in secret. Never asking anything for themselves, they felt empowered to appeal to God on behalf of others. At times finding response, they came to be regarded as men of miracles.

THE STRUGGLE FOR SURVIVAL: THE CODES

Conditions had become less and less favorable for Torah study, beginning with the Crusades. Congregations were expelled, yeshivot closed, and the Talmud was in danger of being confiscated and burned. Once again, laws and customs had to be collected and concisely preserved. Individual communities frequently added their own customs and practices, adding minute details that wrapped the Jew in observances and practices. The more exquisite the details, the greater the spiritual protection against the outside.

Rabbi MORDECAI BEN HILLEL, a great disciple of Rabbi Meir the Tosafist, began to compile all these details, including decisions

1. The asceticism of the Hasidei Ashkenas is alien to Judaism and may have been influenced by the ascetic practices of Christian religious orders of the time.

from German and French academies. He and his family died martyrs' deaths at Nuremberg in 1298 at the hands of the Rindfleisch marauders. His colleague ASHER BEN JEHIEL managed to escape to Spain and was soon appointed Rabbi of Toledo. Asher undertook to compose the code begun by his martyred colleague and synthesized the teachings of the German and the Spanish masters. The work was completed in 1340 by Asher's son Jacob. It was compiled in four volumes and called Arba Turim, The Four Rows, after the four rows of precious stones that decorated the breastplate of the high priest of old. This work is usually referred to as the *Tur*.

The Shulhan Arukh

A little over two hundred years later a code was again established to unify all Jews. It was written by Rabbi JOSEPH KARO (1488–1575), who had been ordained rabbi at Safed. A solid scholar with a very systematic mind and a profound memory, he wrote in a simple and rather dry style, so that everyone could understand. He based his work on the Four Rows of Jacob ben Asher and the work was called the Bet Yosef. Karo later abridged his commentary to the Tur and the new code was called Shulhan Arukh—The Well Prepared Table. Published in 1556 and widely disseminated through the new art of printing, it covers every field of Jewish life, concisely stating the halakhah.

In rendering decisions in problematic halakhic cases, the rabbi will lean primarily on the Shulhan Arukh, yet may use all the source material at his disposal—Torah, Talmud, Rashi, Maimonides, Jacob ben Asher's Four Rows, Rema, and many others. Weighing the merits of a case, the rabbi hands down a ruling, often with a detailed opinion. This ruling, in turn, sets a precedent for the future. Thus the responsa of leading rabbis, from the earliest days to the present, have aided the evolving development of law and practice.

A Sefardi, Karo had followed the decisions of the Sefardic masters, which in many instances differed from those of Ashkenasic Jewry. Rabbi MOSHEH ISSERLES (1520–1572, known as Rema) of the Polish city of Cracow added annotations expressing the views of the Ashkenasic authorities and called his work the Mappah, the Table Cloth (for the Prepared Table). The code could serve both Sefardic and Ashkenasic Jewry and has remained the principle authoritative code for traditional Jews and their practices, thus fulfilling its authors' expectations and becoming a means of unifying world Jewry.

The four sections of the Shulhan Arukh are:

1. *Orah Hayim,* Way of Life, contains all the laws of religious observance from awakening in the morning to retiring at night, prayers, benedictions, Sabbath and festivals, and their rules.
2. *Yore Deah,* Teacher of Knowledge, deals with dietary laws and similar regulations.
3. *Even ha-Ezer,* The Stone of Help, contains the rules of family relationships, marriage, divorce, etc.
4. *Hoshen Mishpat,* Breastplate of Judgment, deals with civil law and similar items.

Chapter 10

FORCES AND COUNTERFORCES

The Renaissance and Protestant Reformation confronted the Jews with new issues and problems. The movements split society in two ways: secular life became disengaged from religion, and Christianity divided into several branches, each soon fighting the other.

Secularization of daily life and a spirit of individualism encouraged merchants' guilds to cast off restrictions on trade and business, including lending money on interest, which hitherto had been controlled by Church and state. Merchants proceeded to acquire the Jews' skills in trade and commerce and set out to eliminate Jewish competition and push the Jews into the lowest and most demeaning occupations. The majority of the Jewish population became desperately poor.

In Italy a Renaissance—"Rebirth"—took place as interest in Greek and Roman culture grew. This led to a rediscovery of the humanistic outlook of antiquity, an appreciation of ancient art and architecture distinguished by symmetry and harmonious proportions, and a reclamation of the works of classical writers, whose languages were admired. Among the classical languages to be preserved was Hebrew—one need not like the Jews to conserve their literary works. Pope Leo X ordered the printing of the Talmud.

Jews travel to meet the pope at the Council of Constance in 1417.

In Germany, which had been at the margins of the great classical cultures of Greece and Rome, "humanists" nevertheless dedicated themselves to the study of Latin, Greek, and Hebrew works, including the Bible. Generally, these humanists disliked the Jews but, doubting the accuracy of the Catholic version of Holy Scriptures, they consulted Jewish commentators such as Rashi and the works of the kabbalists. The humanists' discoveries added to dissent within the Catholic Church and contributed to the Reformation.

The Reformation changed the conditions of the Jews, bringing them some relief, now that they were no longer the only religious nonconformists, but also creating new hardships. The ecclesiastical and secular authorities became apprehensive that the Jews would use the split in the Church to make converts to Judaism. Expulsions from Lutheran principalities were the consequence.

Reformers and the Jews

Jews gratefully remember one exceptional humanist, the lawyer and Hebrew scholar JOHANNES REUCHLIN (1455–1522). One of his accomplishments was to refute Johannes Pfefferkorn, a converted Jew. Aided by the newly invented printing press and its potential for the broad dissemination of ideas, Pfefferkorn, who was sponsored by the Dominicans of Cologne, made vicious accusations that the Talmud was blasphemous and anti-Christian; he agitated for its burning. In response, Emperor Maximilian ordered the confiscation of copies of the Talmud but forbade their destruction until the opinions of the theological faculties of various universities and other experts, including

Reuchlin, had been obtained. Reuchlin came to a heroic defense of the Hebrew works and of the Jews. He argued powerfully that Hebrew was "a miraculous thing," that the Bible and Hebrew literature would yield their full meaning only when studied in their original language, and that the Kabbalah contained Christian mysteries, an opinion that was shared by the great Italian humanist Pico della Mirandola. In short, the preservation of Hebrew works was in the interest of Christianity. Reuchlin went even further, arguing that the Jews had held citizenship in the Roman Empire and therefore retained the same status in its successor, "the Holy Roman Empire of the German Nation." The Talmud was not burned and its copies were returned to their owners. The humanists, fired by their victory, took the offensive against their opponents, mocking the Dominicans as "obscurantist men."

The reformer MARTIN LUTHER (1483–1546) was a Renaissance man. An individualist, he proclaimed defiantly that neither pope nor church council could deflect him from his ideas. He turned to antiquity—the Bible—to find and apply its true meaning, as he saw it rather than as Church tradition taught. He was a nationalist, whose movement was welcomed by princes who wished to shake off the yoke of the pope and his influence in internal affairs and reduce the power of the emperor.

The young Luther wrote favorably of the Jews. He was convinced they would join his movement since he had cleansed Christianity from its accumulated dross; he himself would rather be a Jew than a Catholic, he said. When the Jews turned him down and some, according to his imagination, even tried to convert him to Judaism, he turned against them with unmitigated venom. In his pamphlet "Of the Jews and Their Lies" (1546) he advised:

> Set their synagogues on fire and what is left of them bury in dirt so that no one may ever be able to see a stone or cinder of it, destroy their prayer books and forbid by pain of death their rabbis to teach and preach. Smash and destroy their homes and put their inhabitants under one roof in a stable like the gypsies to teach them that they are not masters in our land. Ban them

from the roads and markets, seize their properties and then force these poisonous worms to work with hoe and spade to earn their bread by the sweat of their noses. Treat them with all unmercifulness. Ultimately, they best be expelled for all time as some countries such as Spain ... have already done.[1]

Luther's anti-Jewish sentiments smoldered in the minds of his faithful throughout the centuries until they erupted in twentieth-century Germany, when his blueprint for the eradication of the Jews was followed point by point by the Nazis. After the Holocaust the Lutheran Church, in repentance, rejected these teachings of its founder.

COURT JEWS AND THE UNRAVELING OF THE JEWISH COMMUNAL STRUCTURE

The empire regarded the Jews as a "nation," subject to their own jurisdiction. Authority lay entirely with the rabbis, assisted by a council, and extended to all facets of religious, personal, social, and economic life. Synods issued regional rabbinical ordinances, but neither they nor the local Jewish councils could overrule the local rabbi. His ultimate tool of enforcement was the imposition of the ban, *herem,* that would cast out any violator from contact with any member of the community. The ban, if need be, would be enforced by the secular authorities.

Despite widespread prejudice, some wealthy Jews with extensive trade connections enjoyed the benevolence of their sovereigns and were indispensable as providers of cash for the exorbitant needs of the rulers' courts and constant wars. These *Hofjuden,* "Court Jews," were permitted to dress like the Christian nobility and acquired the manners and language of the court. Their position was, however, precarious; they could be cast out or expropriated at any time, and they often served as scapegoats. Court Jews regarded it as their sacred duty to serve

1. Martin Luther, V*on den Jüden und ihren Lügen,* 1543. See trans. in Jacob R. Marcus, *The Jew in the Medieval World: A Source Book, 315–1791* (Cincinnati: Union of American Hebrew Congregations, 1938), pp. 167–69.

as their people's protectors and advocates, *shtadlanim*. They came to play a dominant role within the Jewish community, transforming the communities' inner life.

As the representatives and advocates of the Jews, the Court Jews could place themselves outside the power of the rabbis, which caused the corporate structure of the Jewish community and its internal autonomy to unravel. Christian rulers both welcomed and disliked the change. They had always mistrusted a community not subject to state jurisdiction in secular matters. The Jewish community's corporate character, however, could be exploited in order to hold Jews collectively responsible for the taxes of individuals; some rabbis who had been appointed by their sovereigns could be compelled to enforce the collection.

Unique among the *shtadlanim* was JOSEPH BEN GERSHOM (c. 1478–1554), called Joselmann of Rosheim, after his place of residence, a small, picturesque Alsatian city. Although not a rabbi, he had acquired a thorough Jewish education and was deeply pious. He remained utterly simple and at the same time became a very wealthy merchant and moneylender. From 1509, when his rabbi and congregation called him to be their advocate, he devoted his life and wealth to his people. He traveled from city to city—sometimes at great risk—to defend Jews against false accusations, to gain protection for them, and to settle internal conflicts within Jewish communities.

He also visited Lutheran principalities in order to explain to rulers and the people that the Jews were guided by the Bible even as Lutherans were. At times Joselmann succeeded in having expulsion decrees reversed; at times he failed. He had to combat Luther himself, however, only in printed pamphlets, for the reformer refused to receive him.

Joselmann's greatest benefactor was Emperor Charles V (1519–1556), who was both king of Spain and ruler of the Holy Roman Empire. In Spain Charles ruthlessly wiped out any traces of Judaism and persecuted the Marranos, but as emperor he protected "his" Jews in Germany and Flanders, thereby following the law of the empire and gaining access to their money. Joselmann provided the emperor with cash and in return was granted imperial audiences at which he was able to advocate for

Jews. He was permitted to attend—and even address in behalf of the Jews—several sessions of the Imperial Diet, the legislative body that all princes of the empire attended. The emperor granted Joselmann the title and powers of Commander of Our Jewry in the Holy Empire, gave him a letter of protection for all German Jews, and issued an order forbidding imperial troops to mistreat Jews on penalty of death. The Diet of Speyer, over which Charles presided, granted extensive rights and protections to Jews.

RELIGIOUS AND NATIONALISTIC WARS. In the wake of the Reformation, rulers, each claiming to be the defender of the true faith, sought to advance their own interests. For religious reasons they started wars, which soon became contests of power and instruments of political conquest. Initially a religious conflict, the Thirty Years War (1618–1648) eventually became a war for national expansion involving all the superpowers of the time. Alliances, made and unmade, crossed religious lines. The war brought utter devastation to Germany. Christians saw it as the apocalypse indicating the Second Coming of Christ. The Jews, needed by all sides as purveyors of cash, were given some protection, but general terror combined with abiding insecurity and oppression, and they came to regard these times as "birth pangs of the Messiah," whose coming was seen as imminent.

JEWISH LIFE IN VARIOUS LANDS

VENICE. The city-state of Venice opened its gates to Jews because they were valuable in expanding the city's international trade, and they had to pay exorbitant taxes. The Venetian Jews, eager to become an integral part of the Renaissance world, lived in all parts of the city, taught Christian Hebraists, and held philosophical debates with Christian scholars. They translated Italian works into Hebrew and engaged widely in the newly invented

Venice admitted Marranos, provided they return to Judaism and pay the taxes levied on Jews, thereby filling the city coffers. If they lost their wealth they were expelled. In The Merchant of Venice, Shakespeare, without knowing it, drew a perfect picture of an immigrant Marrano in the character of Shylock.

The invention of printing made the dissemination of the Hebrew Bible possible. In 1482, Hebrew scholars in Italy prepared this first edition of the Five Books of Moses.

art of printing. Christian printers of the city were also engaged with Jewish texts and were the first to issue the Hebrew texts of the Bible and Talmud. Jewish composers like Salomone Rossi wrote music for Jewish worship and made lasting contributions to baroque music. Eventually, however, the government, in reaction to the spread of the Reformation and fearful of Jews' taking advantage of the religious conflict, disrupted the close associations between Christians and Jews that had flourished there. The Venetian Jews were forced to move into a ghetto and their rights were restricted, but even so they continued their association with Christians. The Jews called upon the leading architect of Venice, Longhena, builder of the famous church of Santa Maria del la Salute, to build a synagogue for them—in the ghetto, on the second floor of a house; by city law, it had to be undetectable from without. Aristocratic Christians frequently attended services in the synagogue to hear the sermons of Leone de Modena, a renowned preacher.

UNDER THE POPES. Until the Catholic Counter-Reformation began, Italian Jewry, some fifty thousand strong and hospitable to the Marranos, had enjoyed the protection of the popes and lived freely in all parts of the cities within the papal state. The Council of Trent (1545–1563), however, convoked to reaffirm and strengthen Catholic dogma against the Protestant Reformation, ordained the utter degradation of the Jews, which the popes pursued as a matter of policy.

Pope Paul IV (1555–1566), a former Grand Inquisitor, and his successors segregated Jews into ghettoes. In Ancona, former Marranos were publicly burned. Jewish books were surrendered to the flames. Jews had to wear the yellow badge and were forbidden to hold real estate. In Rome they were allowed to have only one synagogue and were taxed in order to maintain shelters and schools for converts to Christianity. Christian preachers repeatedly invaded Jewish services and, under the sign of the cross, preached to the Jews from the pulpit before the Ark. Expulsions were frequent. Princes were pressured to take the same measures. Only in Leghorn could Jews live unmolested. The degradation and humiliation of the Jews remained in force up to the unification of Italy in 1870. Since the Second Vatican Council, opened in 1965, the Catholic Church has completely reversed its stand.

THE NETHERLANDS. After bitter struggles, the people of the Netherlands, whose religion was reformed following the teachings of Calvin, finally gained independence from Catholic Spain in 1590. Holland became a haven for refugees and a bulwark of independent thought. The study of natural science found a refuge, far from the doctrinal pressures of the Church that had just condemned Galileo. The Dutch created the atmosphere in which Benedict Spinoza (1632–1677) developed a philosophy that contradicted both Jewish and Christian teachings. The rabbis excommunicated him, but in Holland he lived undisturbed.

The Netherlands welcomed an influx of Marranos, who arrived by the thousands, to be followed by German Jews. Given full religious freedom and permitted to build splendid synagogues, the Jews helped to establish the stock exchange in Amsterdam, developed banks and insurance companies, and engaged in international trade. They were among the founders and stockholders of the Dutch East India and West India Companies, which gave them significant influence in the settlement of Jews in North America. ENGLAND. In England a militant sect of Calvinist purists assumed power—the Puritans, led by Oliver Cromwell (1599–1658). Cromwell accepted Manasseh ben Israel's arguments in favor of the Jews' resettlement in England; the British leader could see great economic benefits from having a Jewish class of merchants and traders. Jews were informally permitted to return, subject to the same laws as any other non-members of the established church of the land. Soon the Jewish community of London surpassed that of Amsterdam. A generation later, the English philosopher John Locke (1632–1704) laid the basic philosophical foundations for the civic equality of the Jews.

Manasseh ben Israel (1604–1667) paved the way for the readmission of Jews to England. A descendant of Marranos, a rabbi and theologian, and the founder of the first Hebrew printing press in Holland (1626), he had acquaintances among Jewish and Christian men of letters. Rembrandt, who used Jews as models in numerous paintings, was his friend and painted his portrait. In touch with leading Puritans in England, Manasseh ben Israel was able to convince the country's ruler, Cromwell, that Christ's Second Coming depended on the dispersion of the Jews throughout the world—including England, which had expelled them. Their readmission was required for humanity's salvation. A century later, the great Jewish thinker Moses Mendelssohn translated Manasseh's outline of Judaism in the hope that the work might move Germans to better understanding.

Eastern Europe

Russia admitted no Jews, but the kingdoms and dukedoms of Poland, Lithuania, and the Ukraine invited German Jews, gave them protective charters, and offered them new economic opportunities. A few settlements had been established in Poland during the Middle Ages, especially after periods of severe persecutions elsewhere, as during the Crusades and the Black Death, but the Jewish community remained small until about 1500, when it numbered about ten thousand. It increased rapidly to over one hundred fifty thousand by the end of the Thirty Years War (when the total Jewish population in the world came to about one million).

The Jews administered the vast estates of the nobility, increased their productivity, and exported their products. They became tax collectors and merchants and engaged in various crafts. They developed industries, among them the harvesting and export of timber and the production of flour and alcoholic beverages. A number of Jews became very wealthy. The barons even established new private cities, where Jews settled in large numbers. These became the *shtetl*.

The Jews' security depended on the strength of the rulers and their ability to hold an ever-hostile Church in check. Moreover, the merchants of big cities such as Cracow hated Jewish competition, spread false accusations, and incited riots. But the Jews had the protection of the nobility and could be neither expelled nor dislodged from their homes.

The nobles needed a middle class, promoting trade and commerce, and the Jews provided it. Subsequent social history in Eastern Europe moved in the opposite direction from the West. In the West ever more power devolved to the middle classes and eventually to laborers while in Eastern Europe the landowner became more powerful and the peasants sank deeper into the despondency of serfdom. Between the extremes of the lord of the manor and the serf, Jews were increasingly isolated and exposed.

COMMUNAL ORGANIZATION AND JEWISH LIFE IN EASTERN EUROPE. When moving into Eastern European lands, the Jews transplanted their traditions from Germany. They spoke German, which became Yiddish. They wore the German burgher's gown, which became the *caftan*. They also maintained the corporate communal organization, the *kahal* governed by the rabbis. They remained a distinct community and were eventually given autonomous self-government, supervised by the king. They developed regional synodal councils, and, above them, as central authority, the Council of the Four Lands, whose delegates, leading rabbis and lay persons, met twice yearly, allocated taxes, and issued ordinances binding on all communities.

Thus the Jews lived separated from the outside world, with which they had neither language nor culture in common. The culture of the Jews was Torah, and their life force, mitzvot. By living in their own *shtetl* they gave each other strength but also supervised one another. Great yeshivot emerged, where outstanding students, supported by the community, studied Torah under renowned talmudic masters. Life in Torah began in early childhood, when a boy was sent to the *heder*, the school room. If gifted, he would advance to higher yeshivot; if brilliant, the wealthy vied for him as husband for one of their daughters. The center of Torah had moved east.

Eastern European yeshivot explored the Talmud, analyzing in minute detail every phrase and word. Torah—written and oral—was the Truth and all legitimate interpretation was contained in it. The Sages of the Talmud could therefore never be wrong. Disagreement among them meant that each had expressed a different aspect of the same truth. The student of the Talmud had to reconcile contradictory views by means of *pilpel* (literally, "pepper"), making fine distinctions through dialectic reasoning and debate. In life, the commandments were taken literally. For example, the injunction, "You shall not round the corners of your head; neither shall you mar the corners of your beard" (Lev. 19:27), possibly designed originally to prevent effeminacy or practices of pagan worship, became a commanded practice: the "corners of the head," the sidelocks at the temples, could not be touched and the beard could not be cut at the side. Thus a Jew of self-imposed uniqueness emerged, who isolated himself beyond the isolation imposed from without.

THE CHMIELNICKI MASSACRES. In 1648 the peasants of the Ukraine revolted against their overlords. The Cossacks, regarding themselves as nobility in their own right, gave the uprising military strength. Religious hatreds added to the conflict, for the peasants belonged to the Russian Orthodox Church and the nobility was Roman Catholic. The Jews, religious outcasts from both sides and attached to the nobility as stewards of estates, were caught in the middle. The Cossack armies, led by their chief, Bogdan Chmielnicki, routed the forces of the nobility and then flung themselves upon the Jews, committing unspeakably inhuman atrocities.

The Chmielnicki massacres belong to the greatest of Jewish tragedies. One-fourth of the Jewish population of the

Ukraine was wiped out. Some Jews fled, only to be captured and enslaved by the Crimean Tartars; some moved back to the West. But the majority remained in the East, subject to increasing degradation and repeated raids. Seeing in their trial the birth pangs of the Messiah, for whom they yearned, Jews gave their hearts to the "Messiah" who now appeared (but turned out to be an impostor): Shabbetai Zevi.

MESSIANIC FERMENT

Immersion in Talmud, Kabbalah (mysticism), and, especially, the teachings of the mystical master Isaac Luria filled the Jews of the seventeenth century with messianic fervor. The Talmud had taught (B.T. Sanhedrin 97b ff.) that the coming of the Messiah would be preceded by periods of war, terror, and terrible sufferings. The Jews had experienced these "birth pangs of the Messiah" in the expulsion from Spain, the wars in Europe, and the Chmielnicki massacres. In addition, Luria taught that the Jews had been chosen by God for the special task of restoring the world to wholeness, bringing it *tikkun*, "restoration" (see chapter 32). Jews must transcend tensions within the Jewish community and find unity in *teshuvah* (repentance) and a universal outpouring of *kavvanah* (mystical prayer in harmony with God). The Jews felt that they must expect the immediate arrival of the Messiah. The time was ripe for the self-styled "Messiah," Shabbetai Zevi.

SHABBETAI ZEVI (1626–1676) was born of wealthy parents in the city of Smyrna (Izmir), in Turkey, on a Sabbath (hence his name Shabbetai) that fell on Tishah b'Av—according to tradition the birthday of the Messiah. Studying under renowned masters, he became an excellent talmudist and was ordained at the age of eighteen. He continued his studies, including Kabbalah, engaged in asceticism, and had mystical revelations. Young, handsome, charming, and charismatic, with a pleasant singing voice and a love for song, he quickly attracted disciples and became convinced that he was chosen to complete *tikkun*. He proclaimed his initiation by pronouncing the ineffable name of God [YHVH] in public.

Banished from Smyrna on account of this blasphemy, he traveled widely, gaining adherents and causing controversy. At Salonika he performed a wedding ceremony between himself and the Torah, a Torah scroll, under a huppah. Banished again, he now proclaimed that, as the Torah's husband, he stood above the laws of Torah. He publicly violated the laws of Torah, even pronounced his own berakhah on performing a forbidden act, "Blessed ... who permits the forbidden." Visiting Greece, Turkey, Palestine, and Egypt he gained more and more followers—but also enemies. In 1664, after having divorced two previous wives as not being predestined for him by God, he married Sarah as "the Messiah's consort," who was rumored to have been a harlot—just as the prophet Hosea had taken a harlot on God's command (Hos.1:2).

In the spring of 1665, Shabbetai met NATHAN BEN ELISHA HAYYIM (1643 or 44–1680), known as Nathan of Gaza. A young man of exceptional brilliance, Nathan was a mystic whose fame had spread. In a mystical vision he saw himself elevated to the rank of a prophet and Shabbetai standing as Messiah at the side of the divine throne. Shabbetai would take the crown from the sultan, bring back the ten lost tribes, and initiate an age of peace and bliss.

Nathan resolved any of Shabbetai's remaining doubts that he was indeed the Messiah. Claiming to have been anointed by the patriarchs, he made his messianic election public. At Jerusalem he applied the name God to himself. Fulfilling Zechariah's prophecy (Zech. 8:19), he abolished the days of fasting. During the Hanukkah festival, he entered the synagogue of Smyrna in royal robes. Some rabbis became his followers. Others were outraged but did not issue a letter of warning to world Jewry.

Nathan as Shabbetai's "apostle" helped the movement spread; letters were sent to the Jewish communities throughout the world. Prayers for the Messiah were introduced, and harsh *teshuvah* ordained. Doubters were threatened with divine punishment. Soon, news and rumors spread: The Ten Tribes had mustered a great army and were about to advance from their land (Midrash Gen. Rabba 73:6) to conquer Constantinople and dethrone the sultan. The Messiah would redistribute kingdoms. Jews sold their houses and belongings and bought carts for their return to Jerusalem. Excitement gripped all of Jewry, revealing the deep despondency that led them to follow a man who violated the norms of Torah.

In 1666, Shabbetai, utterly convinced of his power and his mission, set out for Constantinople to confront the sultan. He was arrested and confined to the fortress of Gallipoli. Soon his prison became his court as pilgrims arrived from all over the world. The sultan became alarmed, and in September of 1666 Shabbetai was given the choice between conversion to Islam and execution. He chose conversion.

Shabbetai's fall, his cowardice in refusing to accept a martyr's death, shook Jewry to its roots. Exultation led to agony. Life in exile had to be resumed. The disappointment was tragic beyond measure.

The movement collapsed, but was not extinguished. Nathan explained Shabbetai's apostasy as a divine necessity. The Messiah had to take shame and his people's contempt upon himself and descend into the deepest abyss in order to bring *tikkun*. By casting off the old form of Torah, valid in the *galut,* exile, Shabbetai had opened up the vista of the true Torah of liberation, laying the foundations of a new Judaism. Some groups of Jews holding this theology nevertheless strictly abided by the Torah and its commandments. Others formed sects for the purpose of completing Shabbetai's mission of *tikkun,* as they saw it, and fell away from Judaism.

CATALYST OF REFORM IN JUDAISM? The Sabbatean movement had consequences of great historical impact. In the 1750s Rabbi JONATHAN EYBESCHÜTZ (1690–1764), a renowned talmudist, kabbalist, and possibly connected in his youth with the Sabbatean movement, became chief rabbi of the communities of Altona, Hamburg, and Wandsbek in Germany. He wrote amulets for women to protect them from demons at the time of childbirth. In response, Rabbi JACOB EMDEN (1697–1776), an equally great talmudic scholar in the same city and a fierce enemy of the Sabbateans, accused Eybeschütz of having included Shabbetai Zevi's name in ciphers. Eybeschütz denied it. A bitter controversy ensued which eventually reached as far as

Poland. Leaders in the Jewish community were split and the government had to intervene. The conflict revealed grave superstitions and deep fissures in Orthodox Jewry and undermined its status among Jews committed to the Enlightenment. This loss of prestige aided Jews calling for reforms in Judaism. Shabbetai's movement had proved to them that Torah was open to reform and reinforced their view that Jewish faith called "for a deeper spiritual understanding of Judaism" rather than obedience to halakhah. GERSHOM SCHOLEM (1879–1982), the founder of the scientific study of Jewish mysticism, considers the movement a catalyst of reform:

> Sabbatianism represents the first serious revolt in Judaism since the Middle Ages; it was the first case of mystical ideas leading directly to the disintegration of the orthodox Judaism of "the believers."... [I]t encouraged a mood of religious anarchism on a mystical basis which, where it coincided with favorable external circumstances, played a highly important part in creating a moral and intellectual atmosphere favorable to the reform movement of the nineteenth century.[2]

2. Gershom G. Scholem, *Major Trends in Jewish Mysticism* (New York: Schocken Books, 1946), p. 299.

Chapter 11

HASIDISM

Tikkun *in* Galut

The Chmielnicki massacres and the failure of Shabbetai Zevi plunged Polish Jews into deep despondency. In response, a new form of Jewish mysticism arose in the eighteenth century, with the same name as the mysticism in Germany after the Crusades, namely, Hasidism. Its impact on Jewish life throughout the world continues.

THE GROWTH OF HASIDISM

Hasidism's founder was ISRAEL BEN ELIEZER, also called Baal Shem Tov (or Besht, from the initials BST), "Master of the Good (God's) Name" (c. 1700–1760). He was born in Podolia. In his youth he served as a synagogue sexton and assistant teacher in a *heder*. In his mid-twenties, after years spent in solitude, meditation, study of Kabbalah, and physical labor, he had *hitgalut*, a spiritual unveiling. His soul ascended to Heaven, where the Messiah pledged to arrive on earth as soon as Eliezer's teachings had been revealed and found worldwide acceptance. As a result of this vision, he became Baal Shem, "Master of the (mystical) Name (of God)," empowered to perform miracles and bring healing. He was a brilliant teacher but not a scholar, and he left no writings. After his death, his disciples published a work in

The Baal Shem Tov (Besht), founder of Hasidism, called Jews to recognize and rejoice in the beauty of every moment. This portrait is said to be of him.

1814, *Shivhei ha-Besht (The Praises of the Baal Shem Tov),* which contains his ideas and an idealized hagiography. His followers gave him and his successors the title Rebbe, in contrast to the title Rabbi given the Talmud scholar.

From the beginning the Besht aimed at creating a widespread, popular, revivalist movement, and he was highly successful. By stressing joy, in contrast to a life of penance, and the sanctification of daily toil, in contrast to the study of Torah, he attracted many followers. Adapting thoughts of kabbalism, the Baal Shem taught that *tikkun* and messianic redemption could not be brought about by waiting in fasting and asceticism but would come about only through the active cooperation of every Jew here and now, and in joy. Joy—not simple enjoyment but the delight that comes from doing everything for God—released the sparks of God's presence and should therefore permeate every act, be it eating or drinking, or manual labor, or pipe smoking, which the Baal Shem liked. God's presence is found in all places and all things and all acts. Joyful service advances *tikkun,* redemption, the gathering of the divine sparks scattered throughout the world.

The unity of the world, the Besht explained, had broken twice, first with Adam's sin and then again when Israel had to go into exile. This twofold exile must be removed and can be removed only through human actions. While everyone contributes to the fate of the world and even the fate of God, the Jews have been uniquely appointed as God's co-workers. Every Jew must be filled every moment with *devekut,* cleaving to God, and act filled with *kavvanah,* the intent to unite God with the divine Shekhinah (the indwelling presence of God in the world) and bring *tikkun.* This could be fulfilled by simple Jews and did not require talmudic learning. The mitzvot had to be performed but were meaningless unless filled with *devekut,* while a worldly act performed in the spirit of *devekut* and *kavvanah* could acquire greater value before God than an ordained mitzvah. The soul of every Jew is filled with joy and finds expression in a life of joy because he or she is conscious of being uniquely needed and at all times called by God.

Responding to God's call finds full expression in prayer with complete abandonment to God in *devekut.* In prayer the individual person spreads his or her total life in all details before God. The annihilation of personal existence and the ascent of the soul to God, prayer links the

Hasidic joy is celebrated with both dress and dance.

"world below" to the "world above" and is more important than the study of Torah. To reach God, prayer must be filled with *kavvanah,* bursting forth from the soul's innermost depth in ecstasy in the fullest sense of the word—to be beyond oneself. The Hasidim pray with their entire bodies, ecstatically reaching out for God; they dance before God with the same abandon.

A key element in the Baal Shem's teaching was his emphasis on the personality of the Zaddik. The Zaddik was the charismatic person who embodied the Torah, was the Torah; his power was unlimited, and he had messianic qualities. He stood between God and the people; his deep *devekut* bound him to God and enabled him to become the people's mediator. Without ever losing his state of *devekut,* he mingled with the people in order to release the divine sparks. This teaching had a long development. It was guided by the teachings of Isaac Luria and inspired by the charisma of Shabbetai Zevi.

Martin Buber (see chapter 34), has imaginatively related many stories out of the life of the hasidic masters, and his work, I and Thou *has roots in the spirit of the Hasidim.*

Proverbs 10:25 speaks of the *Zaddik*, the "righteous," as "an everlasting foundation" of the world. The Talmud narrows down the term: "For the sake of but one Zaddik the world endures." Therefore God assigns Zaddikim to each generation, for the Zaddik is the "pillar" of the world (B. Yoma 38b). Hasidism sees even God as Zaddik and Hasid, for the Psalmist says "*righteous* [*Zaddik*] is God in all his ways and *gracious* [*Hasid*] in all his works" (see Ps. 145:17). The Zaddik is therefore God's and the divine Shekhinah's partner.

By tradition and general acceptance outside of Hasidism, the spiritual leader of the community was the Rabbi, the Rav, who immersed himself in Torah and Talmud, pursued it in study, excelled in it, and out of its wellsprings taught the people the right way of life; he needed no charisma, nor did he mingle with the common folk. The Hasidim, in contrast, depended on the personality of the Rebbe, the Zaddik who had experienced a divine vision and been filled with the divine spirit. He bore responsibility for his people. He need not be learned, and he had to mingle with the people and speak with them, for he could change the world order only if he raised the people up.

Each Rebbe, it was held, transmitted his charisma to his descendants, and so Hasidic dynasties arose. The mantle of the Baal Shem fell on the Rebbe DOV BAER (1710–1772), the Great Maggid (preacher), who settled in Mezhirech in Volhynia, and sent his missionaries throughout Poland and Lithuania. He had outstanding successors, including the Rebbe LEVI ISAAC OF BERDICHEV (died 1810).

When a Rebbe established his court, the Hasidim in the area came to him as often as they could, especially for the holy days, to spend a few precious days in his presence, where they felt exalted and sanctified. The common meal, especially the Third Meal during the twilight hours of the departing Sabbath, became a hallowed institution. In these hours they tasted the moment of redemption amidst their daily toil and tribulations.

MITNAGDIM, THE OPPOSITION

By the time of the Great Maggid's death, the Hasidic movement had become powerful. Traditionalists had become alarmed at the doctrines and practices of Hasidism and decided to combat it.

The campaign began in Vilna, "the Jerusalem of Lithuania," and was spearheaded by Rabbi ELIJAH BEN SOLOMON ZALMAN (1720–1797), the Gaon of Vilna. Gaon, once the title held by the heads of the Babylonian academies, was bestowed on Rabbi Elijah in recognition of his greatness, for he was one of the greatest talmudists of all times. He combined knowledge of secular subjects with unparalleled mastery of Jewish sources; he regarded knowledge in the natural sciences as essential but rejected philosophy, including that of Maimonides. He realized that Judaism must use reason based on the tradition of Torah, and that talmudic study must be in line with sound principles of thought. His own commentaries followed this approach; they are lucid, simple, and clear. Worship in his synagogue was simplified, too, for he did away with a great many of the Piyyutim that had accumulated over the centuries and obscured the

Elijah ben Solomon Zalman, the Gaon of Vilna, was an influential opponent of the Besht and Hasidism.

clear pattern and meaning of the core prayers; he sought to improve fervor by greater use of unison prayer.

To the Gaon, the Hasidim were a dangerous sect. He saw a threat in their use of their own rites and in their use of the Sefardic prayer book used by Isaac Luria; their special form of ritual slaughter; their idea that God could be worshiped through worldly activity, thus erasing the boundaries between sacred and secular; their emphasis on *devekut* as inner, personal, devotion; and their belittling of the study of Torah for its own sake. Their rejection of the traditional rabbi in favor of the charismatic

Zaddik was to him heresy and raised bitter memories of the personality cult of Shabbetai Zevi. Fearing that Hasidism would undermine Torah as the foundation of Jewish life and break the unity of the Jewish people, he had the Hasidim at Vilna excommunicated and urged other congregations to follow suit. His followers were called Mitnagdim, "opponents."

Eventually, the Mitnagdim recognized that they had to find another way of meeting Hasidism's challenge. To this end, they established regional yeshivot, not to train rabbis but to create fellowships of students who would become leaders in their communities and be able to oppose the Hasidim. Recognizing and responding to the emotional appeal of Hasidism, Rabbi ISRAEL SALANTER (1810–1883) introduced *Musar*, "ethics," into the curriculum of the yeshivot. A movement addressing the general Jewish population emerged that emphasized the study of Jewish ethical works and the examination of the moral principles governing conduct and everyday life.

One of the great masters of the Musar movement was Rabbi Israel Meir Ha-Kohen (1838–1933), called the Hafetz Hayim, after the title of his widely read work on the sins of gossip, slander, and tale bearing. The title is taken from the Psalm verses, "Who is the man who is eager for life [hafetz hayim], who desires years of good fortune? Guard your tongue from evil, your lips from deceitful speech." (Ps. 34:13–14)

Traditional Jews and the Hasidim were brought closer together by the Mitnagdim's Musar movement and the Hasidim's growing emphasis on Torah study. The alienation between the two groups began to disappear. Having to face a new antagonist—the Maskilim, the "Enlightened," who wanted to reform Judaism to match the culture of the non-Jewish world—Hasidim and Mitnagdim became allies. In 1912 the rabbis of both groups, together with Orthodox rabbis from Western Europe, formed an Orthodox organization, *Agudas Israel*, the "Union of Israel."

THE IMPACT OF HASIDISM: HABAD AND THE CONTEMPORARY WORLD

The Hasidic school with the greatest impact on Jewish contemporary life was founded by Rebbe SHNEOUR ZALMAN BEN

BARUCH of Liadi (1747–1812), a great Lithuanian talmudic scholar who had joined the Hasidim as a young man but retained Judaism's intellectual approach to the study of Torah and Talmud. In his teachings, he toned down the importance of the Zaddik as intermediary between the human community and God. He founded the Habad movement—the letters are the initials of *hokhma, binah, deah* (wisdom, understanding, knowledge). Having turned from traditional Lithuanian Jewry, Rebbe Shneour Zalman became a primary target of the Hasidic movement's enemies. They accused him of having plotted the downfall of the tsar, and he was imprisoned at St. Petersburg, tried, and acquitted (1798). The day of his release, the 19th of Kislev, is still celebrated by the Habad Hasidim. Shneour Zalman was followed by his son DOV BAER (1773–1827), who moved to Lubavich in Byelorussia. He and his successors therefore became known as the Lubavicher Rebbe. Dov Baer's successor was Rebbe MENACHEM MENDEL SCHNEERSOHN (1789–1866), whose namesake was to play a significant role in modern Judaism.

Hasidic Jews meet in the streets of pre–World War II Poland. The Hasidim adopted their own garb, long black suits, a belt for prayer to separate the upper parts of the body from the lower ones. Some wore a wide fur hat, the *straymel* on the Sabbath, whose thirteen sable tails were to remind them to God's thirteen attributes of mercy.

Habad shows the continuing impact of Hasidism on Jewish religious life. When its headquarters moved from Lubavich to Brooklyn, N.Y., in 1940, the Habad transplanted Eastern European Hasidism to American soil—the garments, the swaying and the ecstasy, the spirit of joy, and reverence for the Rebbe, MENACHEM M. SCHNEERSOHN, 1902–1994, who led the movement from 1950 until his death.

The Rebbe made New York the hub of an unparalleled worldwide Jewish revival, as he saw that his function was to give Jews new pride and an awareness of the universality of Judaism and to reconvert lapsed Jews to Torah and tradition, making each a *Baal Teshuva,* "person of return." Unlike other Orthodox groups Habad has shown great love to non-traditional Jews, seeing in Habad a way to bring them back into the fold.

Non-Jews have to become worthy as well, and Habad reaches out to them. The Rebbe strove to make both Jews and non-Jews aware that the Jewish people is vital to the world, calling all to ethics and good deeds. Jews, as divine agents, must therefore return to true halakhic living and the world accept their message—then *tikkun* is at hand. To help the world move to that end, the Rebbe designated April 2, 1993, as the first Mitzvah Day for all humanity, when every human being was to do at least one special good deed. A humanity united in doing good would bring peace and love into the world and abolish war forever. In other words, the messianic age would arrive.

 Chapter 12

REASON, ENLIGHTENMENT, AND THE JEWS

The seventeenth and eighteenth centuries have been called the Age of Reason and the Enlightenment. Reason became the ultimate arbiter of thought and made freedom of thought, speech, and religion mandatory human rights—at least in theory. For the British philosopher John Locke (1632–1714), government served to protect life, liberty, and property; religion was a matter of mere personal conviction and lay outside the state's governance, for no religion could be proved by reason. Locke concluded, "neither pagan, nor Mohametan, nor Jew ought to be excluded from the civil rights in the commonwealth because of his religion."[1] In the Declaration of Independence, Thomas Jefferson (1743–1826), translated Locke's principles into political action, and the U.S. Constitution declared, "Congress shall make no law respecting an establishment of religion, or prohibiting the free exercise thereof" (Bill of Rights, Article 1).

BENEDICT (BARUCH) SPINOZA

Benedict (Baruch) Spinoza (1632–1677), born in Amsterdam as the son of a Marrano family returned to Judaism,

1. John Locke, *Letter Concerning Toleration*, (1689), ed. Mario Montuori (The Hague: Martinus Nijhoff, 1963), p.33.

was a trailblazer of the Age of Reason, developing radical concepts of God and religion. In his youth he studied Torah and Talmud and deeply immersed himself in both general and Jewish philosophy, including the rationalistic thought of Maimonides. Under these influences he developed a philosophy of his own.

To Spinoza, as to the great French philosopher René Descartes, mathematics is the key to the world, its absolute law. The universe is compelled to unfold as a matter of necessity, by inner mathematical logic. Perhaps as a result of his Jewish background, Spinoza affirmed the One God, but he rejected the personal, freely creating and sustaining, transcendental God of Judaism. Rather, he saw God as neither more nor less than all of nature and its immutable law, *deus sive natura*, "God who equals nature." God can be found only through reason and "loved" through the intellect, *amor dei intellectualis.*

Spinoza's thought was heresy to the rabbis of Amsterdam and resulted in his excommunication. It equally contradicted Christianity. He saw no need for religion, for the truth of philosophy alone leads to virtue and only the unenlightened need the consolations of faith and Holy Scripture, of obedience and piety. Whereas, beginning with Philo, philosophy had been the handmaiden of religion, with Spinoza, the two broke company, as in ancient Greece. Thus Spinoza reestablished the independence of philosophy from religion.

During his lifetime, Spinoza published only one work—and that anonymously—*Tractatus Theologico-Politicus, Theological Political Treatise* (1670). In it he approached the Bible simply as a literary document of antiquity. He thereby initiated a form of biblical criticism that created serious problems for all religions based on divine revelation.

In the *Tractatus,* Spinoza attacked Judaism. The Torah, he declared, was not given by God but, rather, was written by a number of men, and not necessarily those who are considered the authors of its various books. Its only spiritual value is the natural law it contains, which is implanted in human reason anyway and inherent in all human beings. The commandments do not promote "blessedness"[2] but are merely a practical human invention designed to preserve the ancient Jewish kingdom; they lost their binding character with the destruction of the Temple. The Pharisees preserved them to oppose Christianity; the later rabbis, as a means to maintain power over the people. Spinoza also argued, however, that their laws would be meaningful again if the Jews were to return to their land and kingdom.

In addition, Spinoza contended that the Jews hate the rest of humanity and in turn they are hated by the rest of humanity and even by God. He saw no rational meaning in the survival of the Jewish people. Their will to survive was the result of their persecution, which increased their hatred for non-Jews. Were they to be treated with kindness, their hatred would diminish.

A lonely spirit in his time, Spinoza came to have a profound effect on future generations, influencing both Christian and Jewish thought. Albert Einstein professed his belief in Spinoza's God, who "does not play dice with the universe"; like Spinoza, he saw a universe governed by the law of nature. But where Spinoza's philosophy denied the existence of the Jewish people as a spiritual body and tended to destroy the personal God, to whom every Jew can appeal, Einstein was a deeply committed Jew who loved his people.

The "Enlightened" Society and the Jews

By reason, Jews were entitled to civic equality, but laws that restricted their lives and livelihoods were maintained and "justified" by their enemies. According to Enlightenment ideals, universal humanity comprised all those who were imbued with "virtue," irrespective of religion, nationality, or class. Many prejudiced thinkers and statesmen maintained, however, that the Jews could not be regarded as virtuous because they were

2. Benedict Spinoza, *The Political Works*, ed. and trans. A. G. Wernham (New York: Oxford University Press, 1958), ch. 5, p. 95: "Sacred rites make no contribution to blessedness, and those described in the Old Testament, and indeed the whole law of Moses were concerned only with the Jewish state, and thus with temporal benefits alone."

guided by the Old Testament, a book filled with violence and vengeance. Spinoza confirmed this idea, having called the Jews haters of humanity—Jews were simply not human and therefore not entitled to equal rights. The Jews had their defenders, among them Locke in England, Montesquieu in France, and Lessing in Germany, but they were also viciously attacked by leading representatives of the Enlightenment, such as Voltaire and the Encyclopedists.

Trusting the spirit of the Enlightenment, the Jews hoped that their virtue would be recognized, once their true character became known. The wealthy elite began to reform itself: they cast off the alien trappings, the beard, and the garb; spoke pure German; established social contacts with non-Jews. These Jews opened themselves in general to the culture of the West and clamored for western aesthetics in the worship of the synagogue. Soon they found themselves squeezed between the culture that they were becoming a part of and the legal disabilities that set them apart. Jewish community organization became weak, as lay leaders lost interest. To find full integration, some Jews converted to Christianity. The Enlightenment was affecting Jewry and needed to be integrated with it. In Moses Mendelssohn, *Haskalah,* Enlightenment in Judaism, found its leader.

MOSES MENDELSSOHN

In 1672 the Jews founded a congregation at Dessau, in the tiny German state of Anhalt. Its most influential member was the duke's Court Jew, Moses Benjamin Wulff. A pious and enterprising leader, he founded a printing press where Maimonides' *Guide for the Perplexed* was reprinted for the first time in centuries. Next in importance to the Court Jew was the rabbi, David Fränckel. Close to the bottom of the hierarchy was Menahem Mendel, a Hebrew teacher and Torah scribe. But Mendel's son (Mendels-Sohn) Moses (1729–1786) was to lead Western Jewry in new directions and forge the synthesis of Judaism and Western culture.

Mendelssohn, a sickly child, hunchbacked from undernourishment, was brilliant as well as deeply religious, and Rabbi

Fränckel, impressed by the boy's ability and intellectual curiosity, accepted him for private instruction. Young Moses studied the work of Maimonides, just off the press, which influenced all his future thought. When the rabbi was called to be chief rabbi of Berlin, Mendelssohn, fourteen years old, followed him. At the city gate he paid the toll charged for cattle and Jews; he was so poor that he rationed his bread.

Moses loved Berlin, finding it a city alive with ideas, a metropolis of the spirit. From Talmud he moved to general studies—Locke, Leibnitz, Spinoza, and others. He met and formed a lasting friendship with Gotthold Ephraim Lessing, poet, critic, and playwright. In the play *Nathan the Wise*, Lessing used Mendelssohn as the model for the hero, through whom Lessing appealed to the conscience of humanity on behalf of religious equality. He helped Mendelssohn polish his German and persuaded him to publish his first book, *Philosophical Discourses*. The work created a sensation, and further distinction came in 1763 when Mendelssohn was awarded first prize for an essay that he submitted to a competition at the Prussian Academy; Immanuel Kant, also a competitor, was only given honorable mention.

Mendelssohn's fame grew, he married, and his home became a center for the literary world, but he had no permanent residence permit. For a long time Mendelssohn refused to "beg for that permission to exist which is the natural right of every human being who lives as a peaceful citizen."[3] Eventually, however, he applied to the King of Prussia, Frederick the Great. Grudgingly, the king granted the appeal to this man, now so famous that he was called the German Socrates. But when the members of the Prussian Academy petitioned the king for Mendelssohn's admission to their distinguished ranks, Frederick flatly denied them.

Mendelssohn was a new type of German Jew, devoutly pious and faithfully observant but also a liberal thinker, a philosopher of the Enlightenment who took his place proudly

3. Moses Mendelssohn to Marquis d'Argent, quoted in Joseph S. Baron, *A Treasury of Jewish Quotations* (New York: Crown Publishers, 1956), p. 420.

Lavater (right), through his challenge of Mendelssohn (left), provoked Mendelssohn's learned and insightful response. Lessing (standing) was so moved by Mendelssohn that he modeled the hero of his play *Nathan the Wise* on this important founder of the *Haskalah*, Enlightenment in Judaism.

among the guiding minds of his time. This combination of Jewish piety with philosophical free thinking puzzled many of his contemporaries, among them Johann Kaspar Lavater, a young Swiss pastor, who visited Mendelssohn and challenged him publicly: a work had just been published "proving" the truth of Christianity by arguments of reason; as a philosopher of reason, Mendelssohn must either disprove the argument or—if unable to do so—he must in honesty become a Christian. Mendelssohn would never give up his faith, yet he could foresee great harm for the barely tolerated Jews if he argued against Christian dogmas. And, as a man of peace he disliked controversy on principle, pointing out to Lavater, "It has been my hope to disprove the contemptuous views commonly held about a Jew by virtue rather than by controversial writings."[4] But Mendelssohn felt compelled to answer the challenge, and his reply is a ringing affirmation of Judaism:

> May I point out that I did not start yesterday examining my religion. . . . Years of examination have resulted in a decision wholly in favor of my religion; else I would have felt compelled to act publicly upon any negative conclusions. What indeed could tie me to a religion which is so extremely strict and, at the same time, so generally held in contempt, except the conviction of my heart that it is true. My examination . . . has strengthened me in the faith of my fathers. . . . I hereby witness before the God of truth . . . that I shall abide by these my convictions as long as my soul will not change its nature.[5]

4. Moses Mendelssohn, Letter to Lavater, in *Gesammelte Schriften*, ed. G. B. Mendelssohn (Leipzig: F. A. Brockhaus, 1843), vol. 3, p. 42.
5. Mendelssohn, Letter to Lavater, pp. 40–41.

The Torah, he explained, was binding only for the Jew, for "Moses charged *us* with the Teaching" (Deut. 33:4). The rest of humanity is dear to God if, guided by natural religion or other religious tradition, it leads a good life in accordance with reason and morality. Judaism therefore can admire the ethical teachers of all nations, whether Confucius or Solon; it rejoices in the knowledge that these, like all good persons, will find eternal salvation without change of faith.[6] Although Lavater had demanded an "either/or" decision, Mendelssohn replied in the spirit of tolerant understanding. To him, child of the Enlightenment, all ethical masters deserve admiration. Recognizing every ethical religion and its faithful, he demanded equal recognition of his faith by all humanity.

Lavater apologized for his hasty challenge, but Mendelssohn was deeply shaken. From then on his major efforts were devoted to the vindication of Judaism before a prejudiced world and to the improvement of his own coreligionists. In his translation of Manasseh ben Israel's outline of Judaism, Mendelssohn lashed out at bigoted statesmen who failed to see how all population groups are of value to the state:

> "People expendable to the State; useless to the State," these are statements unworthy of a statesman. . . . No country can dispense with even the humblest and seemingly most useless of its inhabitants without seriously harming itself. To a wise government not even a pauper is one too many; not even a cripple altogether useless.[7]

Mendelssohn's Political and Religious Philosophy

In 1783, Mendelssohn published *Jerusalem; Or, On Religious Power and Judaism*. Its first part expounds Mendelssohn's political theory; the second applies it to Judaism.

Mendelssohn clarified the relationship between state and religion. He held that society entered into a social contract for the purpose of promoting the common welfare, including spiritual welfare. In order to fulfill all their duties, the members of

6. Mendelssohn, Letter to Lavater, p. 44.
7. Mendelssohn, trans. of Manasseh ben Israel, in *Gesammelte Schriften*, vol. 3, p. 188. See also above, p. 153.

The German philosopher Johann Gottlieb Fichte (1762–1814), a founder of the University of Berlin and an agitator in the German uprising against Napoleon, implanted two ideas in the minds of Germans: he gave antisemitism respectability in the German universities, and he led people to believe that Judaism was racial.

society must perform the right actions but also must be filled with the right inner convictions. Through laws and institutions the state enacts and enforces right action. The state shapes good character and convictions through education. Education should, however, also include the citizen's relation to God. Religious bodies can be valuable allies to the state because, although ethics are instilled in humans by natural law, implanted by God in every person, religion can promote ethical conduct through *persuasion*. This is religion's function. Religious bodies are not included in the social contract but, rather stand outside, autonomous and without power. Because religion lies outside the social contract, which is the state's only sphere, the state has no right to distinguish among religions, or to grant rights and privileges to one, or to deny rights to others, or to inquire into any person's religion.[8] And a religious body has neither the power of coercion nor the right to enlist the state in its behalf.

> Divine religion ... Does not prod with an iron rod ... draws no avenging sword, dispenses no worldly goods, arrogates to itself no rights to worldly possessions, and usurps no external power over any person's mind. Its sole weapons are reason and persuasion; its strength is the divine power of truth.[9]

Consequently, church and state must be separate. Only the state has the power of coercion, while religion's appeal must rest exclusively on persuasion. The coercive power of religious leaders such as rabbis or priests must be abolished.

Mendelssohn's View of Natural Law and Revealed Law in Judaism

Mendelssohn maintains that ethical ideals, which the churches are to instill by persuasion, are found by reason, are

8. Mendelssohn, Jerusalem 1, in *Gesammelte Schriften*, vol. 3, p. 261.
9. Mendelssohn, Jerusalem 1, p. 296.

universal, and do not rest on revelation. God has given all human beings
the same power of mind to discover
them in nature. As part of the world
whose principles of religion are found
through reason, the Jew joins the rest
of humanity in establishing and pro-

Mendelssohn found support in his concept of the God of Reason in the book he had studied since childhood, Maimonides' Guide for the Perplexed. *He found that other Jewish philosophers also demonstrated that Judaism is the religion of reason.*

moting the ethical ideals of the religion of reason. But if ethics
as natural law are implanted in all human beings, then the revelation at Sinai was not necessary. On the other hand, if ethics
were *not* implanted in human reason, God would have been
unfair in singling out one people, Israel, revealing to it alone the
end results of reason. Mendelssohn therefore holds that

> The Israelites have a divine law, commandments, and ordinances
> ... but no dogmas, no saving truths, no general self-evident
> propositions. Those the Lord reveals to us as to the rest of man-
> kind by nature and by events, but never in words or written
> documents.[10]

Mendelssohn maintains that the Jews have the natural law, like
all of humanity, to which was added the revealed law. Christianity has the natural law, to which dogma was added. This constitutes the essential difference between Judaism and
Christianity. Judaism absolutely binds the Jew to the law when
it comes to practice but liberates his mind from the domination
of dogmas, thus making it possible to discuss and consider all
ideas and opinions with complete freedom of thought.

> There is not one single command in Mosaic Law telling us "Thou
> shalt believe" or "not believe."... Faith is not commanded. In
> questions of eternal truth nothing is said of believing, the terms
> are understanding and knowing. [11]

Mendelssohn can be a freethinking philosopher and yet a faithful Jew.

10. Mendelssohn, Jerusalem 2, p. 311.
11. Mendelssohn, Jerusalem 2, p. 321.

But Torah contains more than law. Torah also guides the Jews to put the natural law of ethics into practice. By placing the daily life of the Jews under the constraint of the law and its commandments, God made them teachers of morality to all of humanity. Jews obey the law solely in fulfillment of God's will that they be teachers of humanity. Obedience to Jewish law is a matter of free choice to the Jew, who need no longer fear any punishment for disobedience; no power exists to enforce the law. The Jew is morally bound, however, to remain faithful to it. By symbolizing in his life the spirit of obedience to God, the Jew becomes teacher of humanity. In word and life the Jews prepare the day when all humanity will serve God.

All humanity is equally beloved of God. Having the faith of reason, non-Jews need no commandments; should they go astray and worship symbols, the example of Israel will pull them back. The various families of humanity find numerous ways of approaching God. The divine plan for the world will be fulfilled only if society grants full freedom of conscience to everyone and permits all religions to unfold their ideals freely.

Mendelssohn and the Enlightenment

Mendelssohn followed the ideas of the Enlightenment in thinking that we can find God through reason. The greatest philosophical document of the Age of Enlightenment, the American Declaration of Independence, speaks of "the laws of nature and of nature's God." Nature reveals God; its laws testify to the divine presence and goodness. As a man of reason, Mendelssohn was skeptical about the revelations and miracles described in the Bible—except for the revelation at Sinai, which requires no speculation and is a publicly certified fact (an idea straight out of Maimonides). We can put faith in miracles only insofar as the content fully agrees with reason. Mendelssohn found that Judaism does indeed agree with reason, but the fundamental dogmas of Christianity—especially the Trinity, original sin, and the atoning death of Christ—are to him outside the realm of proof by reason and are therefore unacceptable. Unlike other representatives of the Enlightenment, who believed that humanity would progress in a straight line toward ethical perfection, Mendelssohn thought that reverses would always have to be expected—until messianic times when natural religion would be universally accepted.

Living in Two Worlds

Mendelssohn invited the Jew to live in two worlds—the world of Torah and the world of secular culture. But the Jews were not fully prepared to assume these obligations, in part because after years of ghetto life many had lost touch with German culture and language. Mendelssohn realized that communication creates the firmest link between people, and so in his view, the best way of fusing tradition and modern culture lay in a Bible translation. He gave his people a Pentateuch in modern German, together with a Hebrew commentary. Through Mendelssohn, German Jews stepped into German civilization holding in their hands the Bible, their proudest possession. They were protected from losing their heritage while adding a new culture to it.

Mendelssohn accomplished this synthesis: he was a Jew in the fullest sense of the word and also "a philosopher of the German nation and language."[12] Under the guidance of his thought, German Jewry set up an ideal that would give all of modern Jewry its character: to be devoted citizens and remain steadfast in tradition.

Some very rich Jews who provided Frederick the Great with the exorbitant amounts of money he needed for his wars were given permanent residence permits and allowed to live in palatial luxury. Their daughters received the education of the aristocracy with all its refinements. They made their salons into the center of the cultural life of Berlin. Here, from 1780 to 1806, members of the nobility, poets, philosophers, and artists gathered regularly. The disparity of being society leaders but legally only tolerated was glaring. To attain full equality, some of these women had themselves baptized and married Christian noblemen or poets. Mendelssohn's daughter Brendel, for example, changed her name to Dorothea, married the poet Friedrich Schlegel, and cut all her Jewish moorings. Had these women been given a share in the shaping of the communal Jewish religious life might the outcome have been different?

12. The German philosopher J. G. Herder, commenting on Mendelssohn's death, in Bruno Straus, *Moses Mendelssohn* (Berlin: Eschkol, 1929), p. 38.

Mendelssohn's Influence

As a philosopher of the Enlightenment, Mendelssohn entered general philosophy. This sets him apart from earlier Jewish philosophers, like Judah Halevi and Maimonides, who also wrote in the language of the land but built bridges from philosophy to Judaism rather than from Judaism to philosophy. As a person of high renown in German society, Mendelssohn became the advocate of the Jews; as an observant Jew, he reinforced obedience to halakhah. He therefore did not find too much opposition among the rabbis, even though he rejected the autonomy of the Jewish community and the power of the rabbinate, its jurisdiction, and its right to excommunicate members of the congregation. His radical definition of Judaism as revealed law and his denial of dogmas in Judaism came to be challenged, but his theories were the starting point for the development of modern Judaism.

Taking its cue from Mendelssohn, Western Orthodoxy was to give a considerable degree of freedom of thought to its followers, allowing them to enter many areas of western culture while adhering strictly to halakhah. Reform Judaism declared that laws and practices, being only symbols of eternal truths, can be subject to evolution and so can be changed or eliminated, especially if, as Spinoza had held, they had lost their validity for diaspora Jewry; the primary function of Judaism was to represent the great ideals of ethics and exemplify them among a struggling humanity. The freethinker, in turn, could equate the modern century with the period of universal reason; this Jew could cast off religion altogether, and Jews emerged whose only bond to Judaism was their emotional attachment, their family spirit. Some Jews seeing in Christianity a realization of natural religion and a ticket into society—a road to advancement—abandoned Judaism altogether. Mendelssohn's children followed this road.

In 1780, Mendelssohn received a desperate call for help from the Jews in the French province of Alsace. With Mendelssohn's help, Christian Wilhelm Dohm, a non-Jew, wrote the treatise On the Civil Improvement of the Jews. Mendelssohn was not happy with the title, but the treatise was a momentous document, a guide for fair-thinking leaders, and a lever for the emancipation and civil rights of Jews.

Chapter 13

CONFLICTS AND CONFERENCES

The Emergence of Denominations

"Reform" in Judaism is as old as Judaism itself. Tradition has never stood still. Hillel, Rabbi Johanan ben Zakkai, Rabbenu Gershom, the Hasidim, and others responded to the creative tension between tradition and life. What was new to the nineteenth-century reformers was a critical and questioning approach to Scripture itself, its divine origin, and the authorship of its parts. Jews of the past had always explained Torah in terms of "being," eternal and unchanging. Now Torah was explained in terms of "becoming," and Judaism seen as an evolutionary process. In addition, a new form of Orthodoxy was born that remained closely aligned with traditional Judaism while participating in the non-Jewish civic and cultural world. Other syntheses of Judaism and the surrounding culture were tried as well, several of which we know today as different "denominations."

With the abolition of Jewish internal autonomy, Jewish congregations became like churches, namely, exclusively religious institutions under state supervision. The state had jurisdiction over their organization, structure, and administration; the appointment of the rabbis and lay leaders; the enforcement of ordinances; and the collection of church taxes. King Frederick William III of Prussia (1770–1849) kept Jewish worship archaic, in order to alienate acculturated Jews from the services and entice them to Christianity. Other rulers favored reforms as a way of bringing Jews into the mainstream of society.

EARLY REFORM

Moses Mendelssohn, opposing the internal authority of the rabbis and their right of excommunication, cleared the way for reform, and many Jews who had embraced the modern age clamored for change. Their desire was to affirm Germany as their homeland in worship as in life and to gain the respect of their Christian neighbors by making Jewish worship comparable to theirs. Reformers pointed to the prevalent laxity in religious practice among acculturated Jews, citing the danger of large-scale defections from Judaism unless it was updated.

The first Reform temple, built by ISRAEL JACOBSON (1768–1828), a wealthy and charitable businessman at Seesen in Westphalia, was dedicated in 1810. The elegant structure deviated from traditional synagogues: the temple had a steeple with a bell; inside, the central bimah was eliminated and combined with the pulpit in front of the Ark; an organ was installed. The abbreviated liturgy, in Hebrew and German, centered on the sermon and included choral music and German hymns accompanied by the organ. Prayers for the government replaced those for the Land of Israel and the coming of the Messiah. Bar Mitzvah was retained, but the boy was not permitted to read from the Torah. Confirmation for boys and girls was introduced. Detailed rules were issued to give worship decorum and solemnity. Temple and worship now resembled the services of Protestant churches.

The designation temple was chosen for the Reform synagogue to indicate that for Reform Jews the local synagogue had fully replaced the ancient Temple in Jerusalem.

Jacobson moved to Berlin and opened a temple in his home, which soon became too small for the four hundred worshipers attending Sabbath worship. Services were transferred to the home of Jacob Herz Beer, the father of the composer Meyerbeer. Traditionalists became alarmed and prevailed on the king of Prussia to issue an injunction against "even the slightest innovation," which spelled the end of the new services.

In 1818 a group of Jews opened a temple at Hamburg that followed the practices in Seesen and Berlin and in 1819 issued a new prayer book with a shortened service in Hebrew and

German. The prayers for the coming of the Messiah and the ingathering of the Jews to their Land were eliminated as unpatriotic. Traditionalist rabbis throughout the Jewish world, considering this heresy, placed a ban on both the temple in Hamburg and the prayer book.

The Orthodox congregation at Hamburg realized, however, that only by modernizing its worship could it compete with the temple. The congregation called ISAAC BERNAYS (1792–1849) of Mainz to be its rabbi. He had studied at a university and was a scholar and an excellent preacher. In order to attract the sizeable Sefardic community in Hamburg he took the title *Hakham* by which the Sefardim call their rabbi. Being a militant foe of Reform, Bernays signified by his choice of title that the title Rabbi had become disgraced by the reformers. The battle between Neo-Orthodoxy and Reform had begun.

The Science of Judaism

Judaism had never been explored as a field of systematized knowledge, using modern research methods. The evolution of its worship, practices, and customs was largely unknown. If Judaism was to be modernized and gain general recognition, it had to be scientifically investigated. The father of this Science of Judaism, *Wissenschaft des Judentums*, was LEOPOLD ZUNZ (1794–1886). Zunz saw clearly that innovations in Judaism were appropriate and should be undertaken—but within the spirit of tradition. Trained in Jewish and secular subjects, he dedicated himself to the scholarly exploration of Judaism, hoping that knowledge of Judaism would give even marginal Jews new pride in their heritage. Zunz's research refuted deeply ingrained misconceptions and offered new insights into the literary sources and historical evolution of Judaism. In his work *The Religious Discourses of the Jews*, for example, he proved that the sermon was actually introduced into worship by the Jews. Zunz directed a Bible translation that became a standard work. His significance as trailblazer and master of the Science of Judaism endures and is reflected in this book.

Reform Finds Leaders and Becomes a Movement

The furious reaction of the traditionalists to the Hamburg temple rested in part on the fact that the young men of its leadership were uneducated in Judaism and yet dared to change Jewish law and custom. Soon, however, young and ambitious rabbis, well grounded in talmudic studies, undertook the task of reform. They followed reason, saw the problems of their time, and some, similar to Spinoza, held that with the fall of the Temple the mitzvot had lost their validity.

SAMUEL HOLDHEIM (1806–1860) was the radical of the group. Born in eastern Prussia, he spent his childhood and youth in the study of Talmud, pursuing it according to the medieval methods of the *pilpul;* only as a grown man did he come in contact with secular knowledge. When this new world burst upon him, he embraced it with all his heart.

Only the law of the state is binding, Holdheim proclaimed. The state had the right to deal with all laws governing religious observance and all issues arising in human relations. Originally, the Law had been given the Jews for the purpose of setting them apart, but under modern conditions the Law was outmoded, even harmful, and therefore had to be abolished. This applied to all Jewish laws but especially those that separated Jews from their fellow citizens and the surrounding culture. Sabbath worship was to be conducted on Sunday. Circumcision had to be eliminated. Dietary laws, all Sabbath prohibitions, and all dogmas without foundation in scientific fact—such as a personal Messiah, the resurrection of the dead, or the return to Zion—were to be abrogated. Disagreeing with Mendelssohn, Holdheim thought that science did not bear out revelation, but he agreed that Judaism had the mission to be humanity's leader in ethics. A small congregation in Berlin embraced Holdheim's ideas and called him as its rabbi. He conducted Sabbath services on Sundays and entirely in German, and he solemnized marriages of Christians to Jews.

To arrive at authoritative decisions, the Reform rabbis called conferences and synods. Guided by the spirit of the Science of Judaism the conferences sought to bring Judaism into conformity with contemporary needs and, above all, to enable Jews to live as both patriotic citizens and religious persons.

In ABRAHAM GEIGER (1810–1874) the Reform movement found its true leader. Born into an Orthodox family in Frankfurt, he began his studies of Talmud at an early age, while also receiving some secular education. He then pursued university studies, first at Heidelberg, then at Bonn, where Samson Raphael Hirsch, his future antagonist, became one of his close friends. Geiger received rabbinical ordination, accepted the call as rabbi of Wiesbaden, and obtained his Ph.D. He founded a scientific Jewish periodical in which he boldly called for a thorough reform of Jewish religion, and he convoked a small conference of liberal Jews. In 1838 he was called to Breslau. Although strenuously opposed by the Orthodox, he nevertheless became the leader of Reform at Breslau. Soon he was the recognized spokesman of Reform throughout Germany and published scholarly works advocating Reform. *The Original and the Translations of the Bible* [1] was, for example, dedicated to explaining Jewish religion as a developing and changing faith.

He was eventually called to Berlin, where he saw one of his great hopes fulfilled: the organization of a modern seminary for liberal rabbis, called the Lehranstalt (later, Hochschule) für die Wissenschaft des Judentums, the Institute (later, University) for the Scientific Study of Judaism. He was appointed one of its teachers. The school became one of the most distinguished centers of Jewish learning, until the Nazis destroyed it.

Geiger may be regarded as the spiritual father of Reform. He advocated drastic and systematic changes but did so in order to rejuvenate Judaism, to give it meaning under changing conditions, and to make it the true servant of humanity. The fundamental principles in Judaism had to be discovered and distinguished from nonessential elements that once had a purpose but later lost their validity. Geiger could not accept Torah as literally divine in every word; rather, it was to be the subject of critical study. Many biblical and postbiblical laws, resting on the needs of their time, were no longer justified; the Talmud had therefore lost its binding power, and the body of halakhah was to be dismissed. But Geiger also felt a deep attachment to his

1. Abraham Geiger, *Urschrift und Übersetzungen der Bibel*, 2d ed. (Frankfurt: Madda, 1928).

people Israel, and he never claimed to have broken with the past; he considered his reforms simply a historical development. Reform "preserves carefully the bond which connects the present with the past."[2] Where Holdheim had done away with Hebrew, Geiger, in his prayer book, retained it, for "the significance of the prayers consists not only in their content, but also in their traditional forms . . . in the Hebrew language."[3]

Geiger's ideas led to the formation of Reform Judaism, the first of the new "denominations." In it, education, sermon, and worship were the means to give Jews the strength to carry out their task of leading humanity to ethical living. Science was the guide in exploring Judaism, and individual conscience alone guided the performance of mitzvot. Contemporary Reform Judaism rests on Geiger's foundations but has moved closer to traditionalism and conservatism.

CONSERVATIVE JUDAISM

ZACHARIAS FRANKEL (1801–1875), the founder of Conservative Judaism, was born at Prague and received a thorough talmudic education; he acquired his earlier secular education by private study at home. When he was admitted to the University of Budapest, he had never been to school before. He obtained his Ph.D., was ordained, and eventually was appointed by the state of Saxony as the chief rabbi of Dresden, the state's capital. There he became a defender of Jewish rights, was revered, respected, and beloved. His writings were modern; his approach, scientific and critical.

Open to reforms made in the spirit of the Talmud, Frankel attended the Reform rabbinical conference at Frankfurt in 1845. But when the majority of the rabbis approved the elimination of Hebrew from worship, Frankel found the resolution too

2. Abraham Geiger, *Unser Gottesdienst,* 1868, quoted in Joseph L. Baron, *A Treasury of Jewish Quotations* (South Brunswick, N.J.: Thomas Yoseloff, 1956), p. 403; *Jüdische Zeitschrift für Wissenschaft und Leben,* quoted in D. Phillipson, *Centenary Papers* (Cincinnati, 1919), p. 102.
3. Abraham Geiger, *Israelitisches Gebetbuch,* 1854, quoted in Baron, *Treasury,* p. 370.

radical, for it denied the deep religious value of the language. He left the conference and became an opponent of the Reform movement.

As a man of science, Frankel was aware that the ideas and institutions of Judaism had evolved in the course of history, but reform had to be rooted in the spirit of the Jewish people, who had always brought change about, slowly, imperceptibly perhaps, but progressively. According to Frankel, a permanent inner creative tension exists between law and life—between halakhah and the spirit of the people—and this is constantly being resolved by the people themselves; Judaism evolves as the tension is worked out. By unspoken consent, the people differentiate between living precepts and those no longer having any meaning; they discard old concepts, introduce new ones, reinterpret others. Respecting this tradition, scholarly research must study Israel's evolving historical past while remaining in touch with the spirit of the people in the present. By being attuned to this spirit, by study and historical research, the leaders and members develop a traditional yet changing Judaism, bound by the laws that are living among the people and linked through Hebrew to the entire Jewish community of the world. Change, adjustment, and reform would take place while the unity of the Jewish people with the past, present, and future was preserved. Frankel called this principle "positive historical Judaism."

For example, use of the organ, when generally accepted, became permissible, as there was no objection to it in talmudic law. For centuries, the organ had been banned because the people had been opposed to it emotionally as the instrument of Christian worship. As long as such blocks existed they had to be respected; when they vanished, the road was open for the change.

Hebrew was another matter. While the Talmud permitted prayer to be offered in any language, the Jewish people were so deeply linked to Hebrew that it had to remain in the service. For Frankel, the Jews were a "nation"—not politically but religiously, as a spiritual union, a kinship—and Hebrew forged the link to its past, constituted a bond among the Jewries of many lands, and bound the Jew to his future, the restoration of Zion. The hope of redemption, the restoration of Zion, gave meaning to

Jewish existence. This hope enshrined all prayers for human improvement and perfection, for brotherhood and peace.

Frankel's ideas led to the second denomination in modern Judaism: Conservatism. In 1853 Frankel was called to be the rector of the newly founded Conservative Jüdisch Theologisches Seminar at Breslau, where he spent the rest of his life in education, calling to his faculty some of the outstanding scholars of his time, including the historian Heinrich Graetz. The generations of rabbis ordained by the seminary gave German Jewry its predominantly Conservative character. Conservatism extended into neighboring countries as well; in Hungary a Conservative rabbinical seminary was founded that still trains rabbis. American Conservatism is centered in the seminary that bears the name of its Breslau predecessor, the Jewish Theological Seminary of America.

NEO-ORTHODOXY

Neo-Orthodoxy attempted to bring about reforms in Judaism, especially Jewish worship, without encroaching on halakhah. Its forerunner was Isaak Bernays, its founder Nathan Adler, and its theologian Samson Raphael Hirsch. Adler and Hirsch were state rabbis (Landesrabbiner) in Oldenburg, making it the laboratory of a new Orthodoxy. I served as its last rabbi.

The school system under Adler's supervision was reformed to include secular subjects. Adler also required that women be given a Jewish and secular education, and even young girls attended services regularly.

Given unrestricted religious authority but no judicial power, NATHAN MARKUS ADLER (1803–1890) was elected by the Jews and appointed in 1829 by the grand duke with the specific charge to modernize Judaism. Adler instituted a number of changes in the services that increased orderliness, propriety, and decorum and decreased spontaneous, exclusive participation. Further, congregational officers could no longer hold their offices by virtue of their status; they had to be elected, and for limited periods. These and similar ordinances spelled reform to Adler's traditionalist contemporaries, pointing in the direction that Neo-Orthodoxy was to go. Adler left Oldenburg after fewer than two years and eventually became chief rabbi of the British Empire, where he organized British Jewry along the pattern he had begun in Oldenburg.

Before leaving Oldenburg in 1830, Adler succeeded in having his protege SAMSON RAPHAEL HIRSCH (1808–1888) elected and appointed as his successor. Born at Hamburg into a family belonging to the militant opponents of the Hamburg Temple, Hirsch realized that no traditional rabbi could meet the liberal movement on equal terms. He therefore pursued an education at the University of Bonn, where he met Abraham Geiger. The two men studied Talmud and languages together and became friends, although later they were to be bitter enemies.

Hirsch's Nineteen Letters on Judaism *is a stirring and powerful book. A fictitious young Jew, confused by the onslaught of modernity, asks for guidance and in response is given an interpretation of Judaism in nineteen letters. The true recipient of the letters, Heinrich Graetz (1817–1891), spent three years working and studying with Hirsch. Graetz was to become the author of the authoritative study,* A History of the Jews.

Hirsch was a prolific writer. He published his own translation and commentary to the entire Pentateuch—in German. Among his other works are *Nineteen Letters on Judaism* and *The Chorev: An Essay on Jewish Duties,* both written in Oldenburg. His theology, propounded in these works, still serves modern Orthodoxy as a basic guideline.

In 1851 Hirsch was called to Frankfurt to lead a newly established Orthodox congregation of great wealth—Orthodoxy in Hirsch's surroundings became fashionable. Hirsch founded a school system that combined absolute faithfulness to Torah with high scholastic and educational standards; students were expected to carry with them both a deep and abiding love for Judaism and an appreciation for German culture, music, art, poetry, and philosophy.

Under state law, however, the members of Hirsch's congregation had to belong to the larger city congregation that included all Orthodox and liberal synagogues. In 1876 Hirsch succeeded in having a law passed that permitted him to separate his congregation from the city community. From then on, Hirsch tried to persuade all Orthodox congregations that halakhah required their separation from the unified congregations. The greatest talmudist among the German rabbis, SELIGMANN BÄR BAMBERGER, disagreed with Hirsch, maintaining that if certain provisions were met, Orthodox Jews did not have to break with the city congregation. The majority of Orthodox congregations followed Bamberger's ruling, and *Einheitsgemeinde*, "United Congregations," emerged, thereby avoiding a split in Jewry.

Hirsch believed that the Jew's task was to elevate every human being to the fullest ethical perfection—exactly what Mendelssohn had said and the Reformers emphasized. But unlike the Reformers and in accord with Mendelssohn, Hirsch insisted that the task could be performed only by obedience to the laws of Torah. Neither a set of ethical values nor an emotional "religion," Judaism was practical performance of Torah. God created the Jews to give to all people an example of ideal humanity and to be their teachers. Through fulfilling the commandments, the Jew becomes the ideal human being and servant of God.

Jews throughout the diaspora are commanded by Torah to sustain their non-Jewish "brethren" in every way.

> Be a Jew, be it in all sincerity, strive to attain the ideal of a true Jew by fulfillment of Torah by justice and love ... practice justice and love as your Torah teaches you: be just in deed, true in word, bear love in your heart toward your non-Jewish brother as your Torah teaches you—feed his hungry, clothe his naked, refresh his afflicted, comfort his mourners, advise his seekers for advice, give aid by counsel and support in distress and danger, unfold the whole fullness of your "Israeldom."[4]

The Jew therefore affirms "peculiarity" through obedience to halakhah but equally is immersed in general society, which he or she serves as example. Hirsch therefore established the principle of *Torah im derekh eretz*, "Torah combined with worldly culture." He achieves this by boldly reinterpreting a statement

4. Samson Raphael Hirsch, *Neunzehn Briefe über Judentum* (Altona: Hammerich'sche Verlagsbuchhandlung, 1836), p. 76. See Karin Paritzky, trans., *The Nineteen Letters* (Jerusalem: Feldheim, 1995), p.205.

of the Mishnah: *yafe Talmud Torah im derekh eretz,* "the study of Torah is praiseworthy if combined with worldly occupation, for toil in both drives out sin"(M. Avot 2:2). Hirsch reads it, "the study of Torah is praiseworthy if combined with worldly culture," completely changing the meaning of the statement. The Jew must be open to all the achievements of humanity, for, at their best, they lead to a united humanity under God. But the truth and worth of Judaism must be judged by the eternal truths of Torah.

Samson Raphael Hirsch, leader of nineteenth-century Neo-Orthodoxy, all but denied the peoplehood of Israel, calling it a spiritual concept. Bound together by Torah alone, Jews are spiritually linked together but are otherwise fully immersed in the states of their citizenship.

Hirsch was actually more "reformed" than Frankel when it came to ideology. Understanding "nationhood" in purely spiritual terms, Hirsch rejected a physical peoplehood and Zionism as contrary to the word of God. The attachment to the secular state seems greater in Hirsch's Orthodoxy than in Frankel's Conservatism. Hirsch's ideal Jew is urged to maintain active contacts with "non-Jewish brethren" and commanded to aid them in every way, but in observance of halakhah even the smallest act is surrounded by divinity and attains almost cosmic meaning. We can understand why he could not permit contact with the other groups in Judaism; according to him, non-halakhic Jews were not only in error but also disobedient to all the laws of Torah. Hirsch's Orthodoxy, the third denomination in Judaism, could work only among a well-established, intellectually interested, and thoroughly emancipated upper middle class, to whom secular culture meant a great deal. It was so German in its forms that its image changed profoundly when it was introduced in America.

Adler transplanted Neo-Orthodoxy to England, and Hirsch's works have been translated into English. Neo-Orthodoxy continues to be challenged by pre-Mendelssohnian Orthodoxy, especially the Hasidic movement.

Frankfurt synagogue, built in 1711. German synagogue services were shaped by the aesthetics of German culture. Rabbis and cantors wore clerical robes. The Torah was carried from the Ark in slow measured steps following the beat of the choir leader's baton. The sermon quoted the Sages of old in conjunction with Goethe and Schiller. A mute congregation worshiped in silent prayer.

Hirsch's blueprint of a thoroughly acculturated Orthodoxy preserved Orthodox Judaism in Germany. To provide it with rabbis, Rabbi EZRIEL HILDESHEIMER founded an Orthodox seminary in Berlin, the Rabbinerseminar, which gave each denomination an educational institution—private education was no longer the only road to ordination. The seminary provided a thorough education in Talmud and codes, so its rabbis could render halakhic decisions. Rabbinical candidates were expected to acquire a university education, preferably culminating in the Ph.D. The seminary itself was dedicated to a scientific curriculum, differing from the Conservative school in Breslau in fundamental philosophy—the divinity of Torah and not the will of the people were the guiding principles of the Rabbinerseminar. Biblical criticism was rejected.

German Orthodoxy accepted all of Hirsch's ideas except separatism from other forms of Judaism. In retrospect, the differences separating Orthodox and liberal worship may not have been as great as their early proponents perceived them to be. The liberals used a modernized version of the prayer book, included

German prayers, had a shorter service, and above all, used the organ. (In the American sense, the liberal synagogue in Germany was generally Conservative.) The Neo-Orthodox synagogue, with its modern forms, was also far removed from old Orthodox forms. In both, women sat in a gallery separated from men (the mehitzah was later eliminated in Conservative synagogues). To the Eastern European Jew, both types of German synagogues and their worship might well have appeared very similar.

DENOMINATIONS AND IDEOLOGIES

These are the forms of Judaism that existed in Europe and America at the beginning of the twentieth century:

OLD ORTHODOXY. The Torah is divine and must be obeyed. Questions need not be asked. Judaism lives by itself without contact with the outside world, which is basically regarded as hostile. This Orthodoxy, which rejects all change, was practiced in Eastern Europe. Old Orthodoxy is the Judaism of official rabbinate in the State of Israel. Obedience to halakhah in all its details gives the people strength as they live with hardships and persecution; the expectation of a personal Messiah gives them hope.

NEO-ORTHODOXY. The Torah is divine, and obedience to it is service to humankind. Israel is the teacher of humanity. Secular culture is to be acquired; adjustment to modern conditions is essential but may not encroach on the observance of Torah, on halakhah. Good citizenship is a divinely ordained obligation. Aesthetic values are to be fostered in worship and in life.

CONSERVATISM. The divinity of Torah is anchored in the consent of the people, which will intuitively evolve it. Positive values are to be affirmed; historical study opens the gates to evaluation of Judaism. Halakhah has authority, but adjustment of halakhah is necessary and desirable within the framework of the people's acceptance. Israel constitutes a people. Spiritual and "national" bonds form a link; hope for restoration of Zion is a strong force. Aesthetic values are significant. Social action is emphasized.

REFORM. Torah is open to scientific study. The validity of the

Talmud is reduced. The conscience of the individual provides the yardstick in the performance of mitzvot. Ethical values are of supreme importance, for Israel is called to teach ethics to humanity. Social action is a basic duty. Aesthetic values are significant. Zionism, once attacked, has been implanted again.

RECONSTRUCTIONISM. Out of the experience of Jews in the U.S., a new, American denomination, emerged in the 1930s (see chapter 17).

SECULARISM. Orthodoxy in Eastern Europe categorically denied the right to secular studies. A new generation, especially those who had emigrated and been exposed to worldly culture, had no link to religion, but wished to remain Jews, so they took up the study of Judaism, its language and lore, without accepting religious obligations. They accepted the ethical teachings, especially in the field of social justice, and have come to be involved in social action. This has led to purely secular movements dedicated to Jewish culture.

ROMANTIC JUDAISM. In the nineteenth century, the God of Reason became the God of Emotion. Rationalism yielded to Romanticism. Since Mendelssohn's time, law and ethics had become separated, and many Jews, yielding to emotion, without practicing much, became "Jews in heart."

Chapter 14

THE AGONY OF RUSSIAN JEWRY

Rabbi Israel of Rizin used to say, "the Messiah will come first to the land of Russia," because nowhere else did the Jews suffer an exile equal in harshness. In contrast to Western Europe, no movement toward emancipation emerged in Russia. Under the influence of the Russian Orthodox Church, "Holy Mother Russia" had for centuries refused to admit a single Jew. Then, in 1722, 1793, and 1795, Russia, Prussia, and Austria divided Poland among themselves, and Russia found itself with the largest Jewish population of the world. The tsar's policy toward the Jews was summed up by one of his representatives: let one-third of the Jews be converted, another third die, the final third emigrate, and the problem is solved.

RIGHTS AND RESTRICTIONS. Empress Catherine II, the Great (1762–1796), classified her subjects, including the Jews, according to their usefulness to the state. Rich Jews were numbered among "merchants," and below them were the "burghers." Both groups had to reside in towns and were allowed to participate in municipal government, but this apparent rise in status meant that they were forcibly removed from the smaller villages where they had resided. Jewish merchants, free to trade throughout the land, expanded commerce deep into central Russia, where they encountered the hostility of the local Christian merchants, who resented the competition. Jews were therefore forbidden to leave the formerly Polish territory—the process of fencing in the Jews had begun.

THE PALE. To "protect" the Russian population from the "injustice" of Jewish competition, Tsar Alexander I (1801–1825) forcibly removed all Jews from the villages and defined an area that they were not permitted to leave: the territory of former Poland, the thinly settled parts of the Ukraine, and the shore of the Black Sea. After the defeat of Napoleon, this Pale of Settlement was reduced, and the Jews were expelled from a wide strip along the western border. The Pale remained a territorial prison for the Jews until 1917.

BRUTALITY AND FORCED CONVERSION. Tsar Nicholas I (1825–1855) determined to solve the Jewish problem by force. In 1827, he abolished the special tax paid by the Jews for release from military service and every Jewish community had to furnish soldiers. The poor, who were "useless," had to furnish three times as many recruits as the "useful" merchants, artisans, and farmers. Beginning at the age of 18, military service was for twenty-five years, to which six years of "preparation" were added. The young recruits were placed in special army units, and the military priests compelled baptism, with ever greater brutality against resisters. The only chance of relief was conversion or death. Some converted, at least outwardly; large numbers committed mass suicide "for the Sanctification of God's Name"; many others endured the years of torment remaining faithful to the teachings of Judaism. The tsar's plan to use masses of converted soldiers as a Christian nucleus among the Jewish population failed.

An imperial edict (1836) closed the Jewish printing presses, except those at Vilna and Kiev, and placed all Hebrew works under government censorship. A tax was imposed for wearing a skull cap or the caftan; wearing of sidelocks was forbidden. Local officials, bribed to overlook "offenses," found a lucrative source of income.

In various cities the government established rabbinical seminaries whose directors and teachers were Christians; Jews were allowed to teach only Hebrew subjects. The traditional schools, the *heder*, were harassed, and under the pretext of acculturating the Jews, the government established elementary schools. A young German rabbi, Max Lilienthal, was called to develop the school system. Discovering that the aim of the schools was to convert the Jewish children, Lilienthal fled in 1845; he went on to have a distinguished career as a liberal rabbi in America.

LIBERAL GESTURES, NATIONALISTIC OPPOSITION. Alexander II (1855–1881), called the Liberator, abolished forced conscription and permitted a small minority to leave the Pale and settle in cities throughout the land. These Jews included merchants paying high taxes, university graduates, artisans, and soldiers who had served under Nicholas; within the Pale they were allowed to settle in all towns and to purchase real estate. But the majority of Jews, crammed into the Pale, grew poorer and poorer. In 1866, after an attempt on his life, the tsar became more reactionary, and after his assassination in 1881, the liberal course was reversed.

In Russia as in the West, nationalism, superimposed on the anti-Jewish attitude of the Church, gained widespread popular appeal. Many books and pamphlets branded the Jews as corrupters of Slavonic and Ukrainian national purity. The government gave up policies designed to convert the Jews and, committed to "ethnic cleansing," pursued extermination. In 1871 a pogrom broke out in Odessa. In 1878 the blood libel was resurrected in some cities.

UNSUCCESSFUL INTERNATIONAL PRESSURE. In 1878 the great powers met at the Berlin Congress to settle conflicts and recognize new states in the Balkans. The recognition of these states was linked to the granting of civil rights to the Jews. Russia was also pressured to give the Jews civic equality. Bulgaria and Serbia accepted the resolution. Russia categorically turned it down and intensified discrimination and persecution.

Romania's parliament, pressured by mob uprisings, denied civil rights to Jews. Pogroms ensued, and the great synagogue at Bucharest was sacked. The government decided to force the Jews out of the country. A group of Jews was driven with bayonets across the river into Turkey, only to be met by bayonets and to be driven back. Romania's barbarism brought international protest, and two international Jewish leaders, Adolphe Crémieux and Moses Montefiore, went to Romania to negotiate an end to the persecutions. Romania promised to comply, but the promise was never kept.

POGROMS AS POLICY. Tsar Alexander III (1881–1894) instigated brutal measures against the Jews, and his minister of churches, Pobetonostsev, was so cruel that he was known as the modern Haman. Pogroms became the instrument for distracting the Christian populace from its misery and uniting it in a nationalistic spirit behind the tsar, reinforcing his absolute autocracy. The government secretly incited and guided pogroms, sponsoring the publication of incendiary anti-Jewish material that called the pogroms "a spontaneous uprising of the population against Jewish exploitation." In 1881 pogroms started in Odessa quickly spread to more than one hundred communities from Warsaw to Nizhni Novgorod.

In May 1882, the government issued the infamous Temporary Rules, known as the May Laws. Even in the Pale, Jews, forbidden to settle in the villages, were forced into the cities, where they became easy targets. Cities were then declared villages and the Jews expelled. Jewish schools were closed. Universities enacted severe quota restrictions. Heavy fines were imposed upon families whose sons failed to report for military service, although the authorities knew that the young men had already emigrated to the West. To purge the "sacred historical capital" of "foreign elements," twenty thousand Jews were expelled from Moscow and carried in chains beyond the city limits.

POGROMS. Nicholas II (1894–1918) used antisemitism as a potent political instrument. His government established secret antisemitic organizations, whose incitement led to a pogrom in Kishinev in 1903. The tsar also provided secret funds for incendiary pamphlets, among them the infamous *Protocols of the Wise Men of Zion*. In 1904, pogroms were used to deflect the attention of the people from a defeat that the Russians had suffered in their war with Japan. The tsar's authority was briefly threatened in 1905, when he was forced to establish an advisory parliament, the Duma, in which some Jews were to participate.

Hoping to reestablish his absolute rule by uniting the Christian masses behind him, the tsar sought to provoke the people to action against the Jews. Armed gangs, the Black Hundred, supported by the army and the Cossacks, spread riots and pogroms throughout the land. In Odessa three hundred Jews were murdered; in Bialystok, Russian workers aiding the Jewish defenders were put down by the police and army, who were decorated for patriotic service. By 1907 the tsar had fully restored his autocratic rule.

The blood libel was revived. In 1911 a Christian boy was murdered, and a Jew, Mendel Beilis, was accused of ritual murder. The world was shocked and protested, but the trial dragged on for two years before the jury finally acquitted Beilis.

In 1905 the pamphlet, The Protocols of the Wise Men of Zion, *was published by tsarist agents. Originating in France as a lampoon on the grasping French emperor Napoleon III, the work was altered and "Napoleon" was replaced with "Wise Men of Zion." It purported to reveal that a worldwide Jewish leadership existed that secretly conspired to dominate the world by setting the Christian nations against each other in order to acquire economic supremacy and to corrupt the social, moral, and political fabric of nations. The work became central in antisemitic circles and has been used to this day to spread hatred of the Jews throughout the world.*

In World War I the Jewish Pale became a battlefield. Jews were accused of being spies for the Germans, and some were court martialed and executed. The Cossacks carried out pogroms. All Hebrew publications were forbidden as "containing treasonous material." As Russia faced defeat, trains needed for the pursuit of the war were diverted to expel hundreds of thousands of Jews from the war zone. Attacks against "Jewish treachery" became a cornerstone of post-war policy.

The Russian Revolution of 1917 brought the downfall of Nicholas II and eventually his execution. The hopes of the Jews that the revolution would end their persecution were not to be fulfilled.

FORCES OF RESISTANCE

TORAH AND THE SHTETL. Over these one hundred fifty years most of the Jews of Russia created their own world of the

Despite all odds, Jews continued to meet for prayer and study at the synagogue in Minsk.

shtetl. Deeply impoverished and deprived of self-government, the Jews of the shtetl had only Torah to sustain them, and they clung to it with heroic tenacity. Rabbis were the highest guides, and mastery of the "sea of the Talmud" was the ideal for the truly gifted. This ideal of the Talmud scholar, disciple of the Sages, created a unique type of personality, a man dedicated since childhood exclusively to the study of the Talmud, "a prisoner, self-guarded, self-condemned, self-sacrificed to study the Law."[1] This man built the inner defenses that all the Jews needed as a way to retain their sanity and emotional balance.

HAYIM NAHMAN BIALIK (1873–1934), considered the greatest twentieth-century Hebrew poet, himself a product of this environment of Torah, Russian persecution, and poverty, wrote:

> And shouldst thou wish to find the Spring
> from which thy banished brethren drew,
> 'midst fear of death and fear of life,
> their comfort, courage, patience, trust,
> an iron will to bear the yoke,
> to live bespattered and despised,
> and suffer without end?...
> then enter thou the House of God,
> the House of Study old and gray...;
> perchance the eye may still behold...
> in some dark corner hid from view...
> the profile of some pallid face,
> upon an ancient folio bent,
> who seeks to drown unspoken woes
> in the Talmudic boundless waves.[2]

1. Hayim Nahman Bialik, "The Mathmid," trans. Maurice Samuel, in Leo W. Schwarz, ed., *A Golden Treasury of Jewish Literature* (New York: Rinehart, 1937), p. 613.
2. Hayim Nahman Bialik, "The Fountain," trans. P. M. Raskin, in *A Book of Jewish Thought* (New York: Bloch Publishing, 1943) p. 57.

EMIGRATION AND HASKALAH. In a different response to the terrible conditions faced in Russia, hundreds of thousands of Jews emigrated to the West, especially to the United States, where they built the largest and strongest Jewish community in the world. For other Russian Jews, the *Haskalah*, Enlightenment,— which since Moses Mendelssohn had taken hold in the West— became attractive and led in turn to socialism and Zionism.

SOCIALISM. A response to the exploitation of workers during the Industrial Revolution, socialism grew to a worldwide movement. It struck a responsive chord in many Jews, not only because they were oppressed but also because social justice had been instilled in them by the teachings of the prophets. The Jewish socialist movement became the strongest workers' association in Russia, and in May Day celebrations at Vilna (1892, 1895) the association called for the establishment of a social-democratic organization for all workers.

In 1897 representatives of Jewish socialist groups founded the General Union of Jewish Workers in Lithuania, Poland, and Russia, known by the Yiddish term *Der Bund* (the Union). Training its members for self-defense against the pogromists, the Bund saw itself as a segment of the general democratic movement in Russia. Increasingly, the group demanded that all nationalities in Russia be given autonomy, including the Jews, whose official language was to be Yiddish. The Bund hoped to become the sole representative of the Jewish proletariat, despite the fact that Jewish socialists, among them Trotsky, tolerated only one party representing the workers—the Bolsheviks. Regarding itself a nation with autonomy within Russia, the Bund condemned Zionism. Eventually, however, the ideas of the Bund merged with those of Zionism and this synthesis became the foundation of society in Israel.

 Chapter 15

THE EMERGENCE
OF ZIONISM

As long as Jews have been scattered throughout the world, they have yearned to return home. Their daily prayers give voice to this desire, and throughout history, Jews have sought to return to Palestine, alone or in groups. Early in the nineteenth century, the idea of a return to Zion (Palestine's poetic name) started to become a practical reality, and by the end of the century developed into a worldwide movement. This movement supporting the restoration of the historic Jewish homeland and the creation of a free, Jewish nation-state is known as Zionism. Jews suffering unbearable oppression found strength in Zionism's idea of Jewish nationhood, of freedom, of a land where one could enjoy life and self-respect. Rising above martyrdom, Jews time and again have retained the qualities that would help give birth to the new nation.

> In 1862, Moses Hess, a German socialist thinker, advocated the creation of a Jewish state that would be a model of social justice to the world.

Initially Zionism caused deep divisions. Western European Jews opposed it at first, out of fear that they would lose their civil rights if they were suspected of lacking loyalty to their countries. Orthodoxy, including its leader Samson Raphael Hirsch, regarded any constructive effort toward the restoration of the

Moses Leib Lilienblum, one of the founders of the Hibbat Zion (Love of Zion) movement, believed that Jews could find freedom only in their homeland.

Land of Israel to be prohibited by Torah. But over time, Zionism came to unite world Jewry. On the one hand, the Maskilim (adherents of *Haskalah*, Enlightenment), who opposed traditional Judaism, found the fulfillment of the call for social justice in Zion, a Jewish commonwealth rooted in the social ideals of the prophets. On the other hand, the traditional religious Jew prayed daily for the return to Zion and found this perennial hope enshrined in sacred literature, thereby coming to perceive Zionism's deep religious roots.

THE HIBBAT ZION MOVEMENT

The Hibbat Zion movement was the first international group advocating the migration of Jews to Palestine and the establishment of a Jewish state there. The pogroms in Eastern Europe had brought many Maskilim to a new understanding of their heritage, and many advocated for a resettlement of Jews in Palestine. To this end, the movement Hibbat Zion (Love of Zion) was formed, whose members called themselves Hovevei Zion (Lovers of Zion). One of them, MOSES LEIB LILIENBLUM (1843–1910), a former social radical and religious reformer, asserted that there was no hope for Jews in the diaspora; only in their ancient homeland could they expect to live in freedom. Most extensive in Eastern Europe and Russia, the movement also attracted followers in Germany, France, England, and the United States.

LEON PINSKER (1821–1891), a distinguished military physician who had advocated Jewish Enlightenment in Russia, pointed out in his pamphlet *Auto-Emancipation* (1882), that

Jews would never be free unless they emancipated themselves. Antisemitism was a psychosis, and

> as a disease carried down the ages for 2,000 years it cannot be cured. As long as we do not have our own homeland as the other nations, we may as well give up hope once and for all of becoming equal human beings.[1]

In 1883 he joined the Hovevei Zion and became one of the organizers of its first conference at Kattowitz in 1884. The Hovevei Zion was made a religious movement when Rabbi Samuel Mohilever joined, and eventually half of its board members were required to be rabbis. The group joined the World Zionist Organization when it was formed near the turn of the century (see below).

CULTURAL ZIONISM

AHAD HA-AM—"One of the People," the pen name of Asher Ginsberg (1856–1927)—found Pinsker's desire for a place for Jews to live in decency and freedom severely wanting. A homeland would simply normalize the Jewish people, making them like all other people. Could the Jews become truly free by means of a nationalistic movement that would lead to an "ingathering of exiles" in a national state? What would become of the spirit of Judaism and the Jews' future contribution to the spiritual and cultural growth of humankind? Physical survival, important as it was, did not

Ahad Ha-Am, pen name of Asher Ginsberg, leader of cultural Zionism. By his pen name, Ahad Ha-Am modestly wished to indicate that he claimed no distinction but merely wished to give form to the people's ideas. Born in 1856, he started life as a Hasid and was an excellent talmudic scholar who found himself drawn to general philosophy and culture. *Haskalah*, the philosophy of Enlightenment, attracted him.

1. Leon Pinsker, *Auto-Emancipation*, 1882; reprint (Berlin: Jüdischer Verlag, 1934), p. 8.

spell the ultimate goal of the Jewish people. The spirit—Jewish culture—must find a home. This was Ahad Ha-Am's theme, voiced again and again. Thus Ahad Ha-Am became the father of cultural Zionism, which, while never fully accepted by the official Zionist movement, had great influence upon it.

Ahad Ha-Am's thinking stimulated the development of Israel as a world center of Jewish culture. He believed that every nation possesses a national spirit. The national spirit of the Jews found expression in the prophetic ideals of justice and righteousness, and it developed when people and soil were united. To preserve the spirit in foreign lands of exile, a wall of religious laws had been erected to shelter the people from alien influences. The emancipation, the granting of civil rights to Jews in most European countries, tore down the wall and left the Jewish spirit unprotected; it could flourish again only with a national home in Palestine, which was to serve as a haven for the persecuted, as the wellspring of Judaism, and as an inspiration for diaspora Jewry. This home would be the spiritual core of Hebrew culture. Perhaps not all Jews would move to Palestine, but all would be revived and sustained by the spirit of Judaism that would emanate from Zion.

JEWISH IMMIGRATION. In 1881 young Jews from Russia began to make *aliyah,* "ascent," as the successive waves of immigration to the Land of Israel were called. One group, the BILU—*Bet Yaakov Lekhu Venelkha,* "O House of Jacob! Come, and let us go" (see Isa. 2:5)—immigrated as a whole. In 1882 and 1883 they established the colonies of Rishon le-Zion, Zikhron Yaacov, Rosh Pinah, and Petah Tikvah. The land was poor and malaria infested; the work, backbreaking. Baron Rothschild of France provided the sorely needed funding, but he ran the colonies in a paternalistic fashion. The Turkish government became increasingly disturbed by the large-scale immigration of Jews and eventually prohibited it. Many immigrants were smuggled in. A second *aliyah* between 1904 and 1914 brought an additional forty thousand Jews to Palestine, among them David Ben Gurion and the generation that would provide leaders at the birth of the State of Israel. In 1909, the city of Tel Aviv was founded. By then Zionism had gained its foundation through the leadership of Theodor Herzl.

POLITICAL ZIONISM

THEODOR HERZL (1860–1904) became a messianic personality for Jews. Born into a highly assimilated family in Budapest, he had nevertheless been exposed to antisemitism as a student. On completing law school he wanted to become a judge, but that was impossible for a Jew. Instead, he gained popularity as a writer, essayist, journalist, and playwright. Vienna's leading newspaper, the *Neue Freie Presse,* sent him to Paris to cover the Dreyfus trial. This was the turning point of Herzl's life, for the Dreyfus process deeply shocked him. If antisemitism could reemerge so quickly and with such terrifying impact, and of all places in France, then there was no cure for it and no hope for diaspora Jewry, except in the establishment of an independent Jewish state.

Theodor Herzl's *Der Judenstaat—The Jewish State*—became the bible of political Zionism.

In 1896, Herzl's brochure *Der Judenstaat, The Jewish State,* appeared. This small work became the bible of political Zionism. In it, Herzl considered

> the Jewish question neither a social nor a religious one, even though it sometimes takes these and other forms. It is a national question, and to solve it we must first of all establish it as an international political problem to be discussed and settled by the civilized nations of the world in council. We are a people—one people.[2]

2. Theodor Herzl, *Der Judenstaat* (1896), in Arthur Hertzberg, ed., *The Zionist Idea* (New York: Atheneum, 1970), p. 209.

The Dreyfus Affair
The treatment of Captain Dreyfus convinced Herzl that there was no cure for—or hope against—antisemitism. Dreyfus was a captain in the French army, a career officer, and the only Jew attached to the headquarters of the French general staff. In 1894, a secret document was stolen and transmitted to the Germans. Without further inquiry, the cry went up. "Le Juif, voilà l'énémi" ("The Jew, there is the enemy"). Dreyfus was arrested. Documents were forged and defense witnesses intimidated. Prosecution witnesses perjured themselves. Dreyfus was convicted and degraded in a public ceremony on January 12, 1895 (shown here). A special law was passed permitting his deportation and imprisonment at the isolated penal colony of Devil's Island. Appeals were rejected and champions of justice persecuted, among them the famous French writer Emile Zola. Dedicated men pursued the search for truth, and eventually it came to light; the real criminals were brought to justice. Dreyfus was reinstated and promoted, but the specter of antisemitism once again had risen.

He described the distress of the Jews in progressive and repressive countries alike. And for him, there was only one answer:

> Let sovereignty be granted us over a portion of the globe adequate to meet our rightful national requirements; we will attend to the rest.[3]

Herzl began to organize. In 1897 he called the first Zionist Congress to Basel, Switzerland. After lengthy debates, the congress established a permanent World Zionist Organization and

3. Herzl, *Der Judenstaat*, in Hertzberg, p. 220.

formulated its platform: "Zionism seeks to secure for the Jewish people the creation of a national homeland in Palestine, which shall be recognized and guaranteed publicly and legally by international law."[4] A trust fund was set up and a Jewish National Fund organized. All land acquired was to belong to the people as a whole, not to individuals. Nor was the Jewish state to become a theocracy, Herzl declared; it would simply be a political entity. This was political Zionism.

He traveled to meet with statesmen, the emperor, the pope, the sultan, even Russian ministers, and wherever he went governments rejected his proposal. He also faced opposition from within the Zionist community. His diplomacy was a one-man project on behalf of the Jewish people, without asking for their advice and consent. Herzl demanded that only Zionism be empowered to engage in political activities but the Jews of Eastern Europe wished to act for themselves.

In his novel *Altneuland, Old-New Land* (1902), he expressed his vision of the achievements of the new settlements in the social and technological fields, but without mentioning cultural accomplishments. He envisioned a *community of Jews*, whereas many of his followers wanted a *Jewish community*—and with Hebrew as its language, not German, as Herzl anticipated.

The Maskilim demanded a national state with a national culture and Hebrew as the national language, but without any religious character. The Orthodox, fearful of a secular Jewish state, founded the religious faction Mizrachi to advocate for a Torah-true culture within Zionism. The Poale Zion, the socialist Workers for Zion, desired the Yishuv, the Jewish settlement in Palestine, to be founded on socialism.

Herzl's primary concern was the establishment of a refuge for his distressed brothers and sisters, but he did not care where it was. Relying on vague promises from the British government, he surprised the Zionist Congress of 1903 with a proposal to accept Uganda as a homeland for the Jews. The Jews would have none of it. Palestine was the land promised by the Torah,

4. Theodor Herzl, in *Proceedings of the First Zionist Congress.*

enshrined in the hearts of the Jews. Herzl yielded. In 1904 he realized that his proposal had been a mistake. In the same year he died.

Herzl's autocratic attitude caused divisions within the Zionist movement, but a less determined personality could not have provided the dynamic leadership that was needed. Herzl, the practical visionary, became the father of the State of Israel, a liberating personality in Jewish history. His chief assistants assumed the leadership of the movement, among them Chaim Weizmann, who would be the first president of the State of Israel.

Reaction and Opposition to the Zionist Movement

Herzl regarded Jews who would not follow him as lost. He saw no future or value in diaspora Jewry. Eastern European Jewry, considered a nation among nations already, generally welcomed his plan. Ahad Ha-Am, however, could not accept a purely political Zionism. German and American Jewry were even more outspoken. German Jewry, which had developed a Judaism that emphasized religion and regarded civic duties and love of country as part of one's religious obligations, could not accept the polarity position of Herzl's program: either come with me or sever all ties with Judaism. The Neo-Orthodox and many Orthodox in Eastern Europe believed that the return to Zion was in God's hand and could be promoted only through prayer and mitzvot; the struggle of the Zionists, many of them non-religious, to achieve this end by secular means was seen as disobedient to God's will.

American Jewry, while rejecting Herzl's either/or stance, gradually came to feel the deep kinship that binds it to all of Jewry and above all to the Yishuv. Perhaps influenced by Ahad Ha-Am's ideas, American Jewry recognized a mutual cultural influence. From its ranks, especially from Reform Judaism, came those who fought for the international recognition of the State of Israel, and its financial support has been of vital importance. American Jewry has come to see itself as an ethnic-religious body of Americans closely bonded to Israel, but with its future in America.

Between World War I and World War II early settlers struggled to reclaim the Land. Hasidism contributed to the spirit of the non-religious but deeply Jewish *halutzim,* pioneers preparing for the foundation of modern Israel. These Jews worked to build and bring redemption to the Land. Giving their utmost, every person counted and therefore was equal. The pioneers exhibited unparalleled endurance and unflinching dedication to their goals and lived with joy and exuberance.

Life in the Yishuv

EARLY ACHIEVEMENTS. The period around World War I witnessed some remarkable achievements within the Yishuv, progress made possible in large part by the kibbutz. The technical institute (Technion) was established at Haifa, and in Jerusalem the Bezalel school of arts and crafts was founded, named after the architect of the Tent of Meeting in the desert (Exod. 35:30–35). Eliezer ben Judah modernized Hebrew, restoring it as a living language and making it the common language of Jews in Palestine. In 1925 the Hebrew University in Jerusalem was opened.

THE KIBBUTZ: EXPERIMENT WITH A NEW SOCIETY. The kibbutz, founded by the earliest immigrants, was a wholly new concept of societal living, a collective community based on democracy and the love of Zion. Its members joined the communal settlement by their own free will and could resign at any time. They submitted to the democratic decisions of the community, shared everything, held all property in common, and accepted whatever task the community assigned them. The children were brought up communally. In turn, once accepted, the members were sheltered and protected for the rest of their lives. The land, assigned to the kibbutz by the Jewish National Fund, was held in trust, and the kibbutz developed it using the latest technological means. The kibbutz members reclaimed the land—poor, barren, dried out, or swampy and malaria infested—and made it fertile, healthy, and beautiful. The kibbutz is a model for underdeveloped nations.

DEALING WITH NEIGHBORS AND WORLD POWERS. Its power waning, Turkey hoped to maintain its hold on Palestine by stirring nationalist sentiment in the Arab population and by kindling hostility against the Jewish settlements and further Jewish immigration. Jews were persecuted in many parts of the region; Arabs were permitted to arm themselves. Jewish settlers attempted dialogue with Arab leaders but were unsuccessful. Raids on kibbutzim increased.

THE BALFOUR DECLARATION. In 1917, the British Foreign Office, in part to counteract the overtures made by Germany and its allies to the Jews, issued the document signed by Arthur James Balfour, Secretary of Foreign Affairs, known as the Balfour Declaration:

> His Majesty's Government view with favour the establishment in Palestine of a national home for the Jewish people, and will use their best endeavors to facilitate the achievement of this object, it being clearly understood that nothing shall be done to prejudice the civil and religious rights of existing non-Jewish communities in Palestine, or the rights and political status enjoyed by Jews in any other country.

At the end of World War I, Palestine fell to the victorious allied powers, and they carved up the defeated Ottoman Empire. In December of 1917, on Hanukkah, General Allenby entered Jerusalem at the head of a British expeditionary force: the Arabs were to establish several independent states; the Jews were to receive Palestine as a homeland and to dwell as friends among their liberated Arab neighbors. After the war, all of the members of the newly formed League of Nations and the United States endorsed the Balfour Declaration. The League of Nations appointed Britain to administer Palestine and implement the Balfour Declaration under the League's mandate.

As supervising power under the mandate, the British were principally concerned with their own interests, which called for appeasement of the Arab states that held the wealth of the region. Britain began to restrict immigration, which nevertheless continued. A new chapter began in the struggle of the Jews for their land and the rescue of their brothers and sisters, soon to be caught in the flood of terror and extermination.

Chapter 16

ENTER AMERICA

On August 3, 1492, three days after the Jews had been expelled from Spain, Christopher Columbus set sail. For the native population of the Americas the arrival of the Europeans
meant exploitation, the destruction of flourishing cultures,
enslavement, and extermination. But for the persecuted masses
in Europe, the discovery of the New World would bring liberty.
As America opened, a new land was established that would offer
refuge to Marranos, to thousands of Jews from Germany, and
to millions of Jews from Eastern Europe. A Jewish community
emerged that could claim full rights of citizenship and that grew
to become the largest and freest in the world.

Jewish settlement in the New World had humble beginnings. Many Marranos sought refuge in the Spanish and Portuguese colonies, but the Inquisition was soon established there;
the first burning of a Jew in America took place at Mexico City
in 1574. When the tolerant Dutch took Recife (Pernambuco),
however, they welcomed Jews as pioneers in the colony. By 1645
Recife had a Jewish congregation of 1,450 and a famous rabbi,
Aboab de Francesca. But in 1654 Recife fell back into the hands
of the Portuguese, and the Jews had to leave.

Also in 1654, two prosperous Jews, with the permission of
the Dutch West India Company, settled in New Amsterdam,

capital of the Dutch colony in North America. Twenty-three Dutch Jews from Brazil arrived in September of the same year. So began the settlement of Jews in what would become the United States of America.

COLONIAL AMERICA

From the moment of their arrival the Jews fought for civic equality, aided by their own courage and the strong support of the Dutch West India Company, many of whose leading stockholders were Jews. Peter Stuyvesant, governor of the colony, appealed to the company in Holland on many occasions for permission to limit the rights of the Jewish settlers, and each time he was rebuked. They were allowed to remain in the colony, for they promised to take care of one another, a promise that American Jews have kept ever since. They were permitted to conduct their worship in their homes, and they had the right to bear arms and join their fellow colonists in the defense of the colony. From the very beginning they rejected "toleration" and strove instead for equality and full citizenship. In 1764, New Amsterdam fell to the British and was renamed New York.

This first immigration, a ripple rather than a wave, resulted in the settlement of no more than fifty Jews by the end of the century. Almost all of them were Sefardim, including many former Marranos. The first Torah scroll was brought to the colony in 1773, and shortly thereafter the Jews built their first synagogue—they laid the foundations on which their descendants could build.

In Massachusetts the Puritans built a community on the principles

One of the first synagogues in America, the Touro Synagogue, was built in Newport, Rhode Island, in 1763. It is constructed in Georgian style, based on the English adaptation of classical forms as promoted by Inigo Jones, the famous British architect. The architect, Peter Harrison, also designed King's Chapel in Boston. Today the Touro Synagogue is a national shrine.

of the Old Testament but had no room for the children of the Old Testament. Nevertheless, the Puritans did much to weave Jewish ethics and morality into the permanent fabric of America. Every year, as we celebrate Thanksgiving we are reminded that the holiday is based on the biblical festival of Sukkot, the Feast of Tabernacles, which celebrates the fall harvest and commemorates the wandering in the desert during the Exodus.

Few in number but deeply committed to freedom, the majority of colonial Jews rallied to the cause of the Revolution. Haym Solomon was the broker of the new United States government and had the job of selling its bonds. Aaron Lopez, a former Marrano, became a leading ship owner and armed his ships against the British. Solomon and Lopez sacrificed so much of their funds in support of the new country that they both died destitute.

Virginia and Maryland excluded Jews for religious reasons. Rhode Island, founded on the principle of toleration, admitted them early. The Quaker state of Pennsylvania opened its gates to them but without giving full equality. In giving them the right to build a synagogue, South Carolina followed the advice of the philosopher John Locke, who had drawn up the state's constitution: "If we permit the Jews to have private houses and dwellings among us, why should we not allow them to have synagogues?"[1] Georgia also admitted Jews.

By the time of the Revolutionary War there were fewer than three thousand Jews in the United States, with five synagogues in all. The synagogues were located in New York; Newport, R.I.; Charleston, S.C.; Savannah, Ga.; and Philadelphia, Pa. Newport had the most enduring of them. Philadelphia's synagogue was built with contributions from Christians as well as Jews, and Benjamin Franklin was the largest contributor to its building fund.

By 1812 New York had a Jewish population of about fifty families and thirty unmarried men, Philadelphia had thirty families, Charleston had about six hundred Jews, Richmond had thirty families, Savannah a small number.

1. John Locke, *Letter Concerning Toleration*, in *Works* (London, 1740), vol. 2, p. 273.

Democratic Ideals

The United States Constitution provided full liberty and equality to all citizens regardless of religion (Article 6, and Bill of Rights, Article 1), and Jefferson and Madison bent all their efforts to establish a "wall of separation between Church and State." They succeeded on the federal level. The states, however, were slow to adopt this policy, and as late as 1840, New Hampshire, Rhode Island, New Jersey, and North Carolina refused to grant full rights to Jews. The battle for equality was not over, but the Jews were not alone in their fight. In Maryland, for instance, a Scotch Presbyterian, Thomas Kennedy, took up their cause:

> There are no Jews in the country from which I come, nor have I the slightest acquaintance with any Jew in the world. . . . There are few Jews in the United States; in Maryland there are very few, but if there were only one, to that one we ought to do justice.[2]

And George Washington categorically supported the Jews. In a reply to a letter sent him by the Jewish congregation at Newport, he wrote:

> The citizens of the United States of America have a right to applaud themselves for having given to mankind examples of an enlarged and liberal policy—a policy worthy of imitation. All possess alike liberty of conscience and immunities of citizenship.
>
> It is no more that toleration is spoken of as if it were the indulgence of one class of people that another enjoyed the exercise of their inherent natural rights, for, happily, the Government of the United States, which gives to bigotry no sanction, to persecution no assistance, requires only that they who live under its protection should demean themselves as good citizens in giving it on all occasions their effectual support. . . .
>
> May the children of the stock of Abraham who dwell in this land continue to merit and enjoy the good will of the other inhabitants; while everyone shall sit in safety under his own vine and fig tree and there shall be none to make him afraid.[3]

2. Quoted in Lee J. Levinger, *A History of the Jews in the United States* (New York: Union of American Hebrew Congregations, 1949), p. 137.
3. The letter from the Hebrew Congregation of Newport to President Wash-

Some Personalities

GERSHOM MENDES SEIXAS (1745–1816) was minister of New York's synagogue, Shearit Israel. When the British took New York, he refused to remain in the city. Carrying with him the scroll of the Torah, he left for Philadelphia with the majority of his congregation, and he immediately built a new synagogue there. After he returned to New York in 1783, he became one of the founders of King's College (now Columbia University). He stood next to George Washington when he was inaugurated as the first president of the United States.

JUDAH TOURO (1775–1854), was born at Newport, Rhode Island, but moved to New Orleans, where he fought under Andrew Jackson in the Battle of New Orleans. A successful businessman, he became a philanthropist, founding the synagogue at New Orleans and donating to churches. He is especially remembered as the man who sparked the building of the Bunker Hill Monument at Boston by donating one-fifth of its costs.

MORDECAI MANUEL NOAH (1785–1851) was a playwright, social leader, sheriff of New York County, judge, and United States consul at Tunis. In response to a letter by the great Jewish scholar Leopold Zunz and friends, which explained the plight of European Jews and pleaded with him to bring a large number of them to America, Noah devised a plan to let the Jews come to America and establish a colony that would eventually become a state. He purchased land near Buffalo, New York, and founded the community of Ararat, named after the mountain on which Noah's ark finally found rest. Noah called the Jews to the refuge, saying

> Therefore I, Mordecai Manuel Noah, Citizen of the United States of America ... and by the grace of God governor and judge of Israel, have issued this my proclamation, announcing to the Jews

ington (1790) and Washington's reply appear in Jonathan D. Sarna and David G. Dalin, eds., *Religion and State in the American Jewish Experience* (Notre Dame, Ind.: University of Notre Dame Press, 1997), pp. 77–80 (quote above, pp. 79–80).

of all the world that an asylum is prepared and hereby offered to them.[4]

The cornerstone, still preserved, reads

Ararat—City of Refuge for the Jews
Founded by Mordecai Manuel Noah in
the Month of Tizri,
September 1825
and in the 50th Year of American
Independence[5]

One of the earliest advocates of establishing a Jewish state in Palestine was Mordecai Manuel Noah, who proposed it as early as 1818.

His project failed. Persuaded that Jews would rather go to Palestine, he asserted, "Palestine must revert to its legitimate proprietors ... the descendants of Abraham. ... Their eye has steadily rested on their beloved Jerusalem."[6] Noah became a Zionist long before the Zionist movement was organized. While the Jews in Europe were being told that "as a nation" they would be granted no rights at all, this religious American Jew could call himself "governor of the Jews," be a Zionist, and proudly proclaim himself "citizen of the United States."

At a time when in Europe conversion was the only ticket into society, an American Jew, URIAH P. LEVY (1792–1862), rose through the ranks to the highest commission in the navy of the time. Commodore Levy abolished flogging in the navy. In 1836, he purchased Monticello, Thomas Jefferson's home, and donated it to the United States in gratitude for Jefferson's determined fight for religious liberty. The Jewish chapel of the United States Naval Academy at Annapolis today bears Levy's name.

4. Museum at Buffalo, N.Y., quoted in Anita L. Lebeson, *Pilgrim People* (New York: Harper, 1950), p. 206.
5. Lebeson, *Pilgrim People*, p. 207.
6. Mordecai Noah, quoted in Lebeson, *Pilgrim People*, p. 209.

Problems of Acculturation

Under conditions of expanding freedom, the Jewish community grew. By 1840 their number had risen to approximately fifteen thousand and by 1850 to fifty thousand. English and German Jews arrived, and congregations were founded wherever Jews moved. Freedom created the challenge of fully entering into the American way of life without losing the sense of belonging to Judaism, its tradition and values.

American synagogues were free from state supervision and exerted considerable influence upon the Jews of the community. A spiritual haven, the synagogue gave emotional security to the immigrants and perpetuated the customs of the old country. It undertook the education of the young, provided kosher meat, and su-

The Gratz family from Silesia soon became successful merchants in Philadelphia. The American writer Washington Irving, a frequent visitor to the family, described Rebecca Gratz (1781–1869) to Sir Walter Scott in Scotland, who made her the heroine in his novel *Ivanhoe*. Rebecca spent her life aiding the poor. Deeply concerned with Jewish education, she founded the Jewish Sunday School movement. Her published letters bore her pen name, A Daughter of Israel.

pervised the religious life of the community and the individual. Until roughly the middle of the nineteenth century, there were no rabbis in the United States, and so laymen were the arbiters of religious observance and practice. When rabbis eventually appeared, they found themselves subject to the laity, even in spiritual matters. Worship, shaped by a congregation's customs or nostalgia, tended to permit different standards of religious conduct: a person was Orthodox in an old-fashioned way when attending the synagogue, but outside, went with the world. Eventually the gulf between life and worship grew so wide that worship became meaningless, even distasteful, to many.

Some Jews clearly saw the need for reform. One of them was ISAAC HARBY of Charleston, South Carolina. As an educator, he realized that only a synthesis of Judaism, Americanism, and the

Enlightenment could save American Judaism. This he expressed in a letter to Thomas Jefferson, dated January 14, 1826:

> With patience and industry we hope, in a few years, to be able to establish a mode of worship, simple and sensible; suited to the liberality of the age, improving to the Israelite and acceptable to the Deity. The example set by the University [of Virginia], which owes its noblest characteristic to your judgement and philanthropy, offers a bright pattern to any similar institution in our country. May you, honored sir, live to see your warmest wishes realized in the results.[7]

In his reply, Jefferson wished Harby well and discussed his own view of religion as an instrument of moral improvement.[8] The form of religion mattered little, as long as it served the moral education of the worshipers. Education for all, Jefferson's deepest concern, had inspired him to found the University of Virginia. He fought for the abolition of required courses in Christian doctrine at universities because they prevented Jews from enrolling in higher education.

German Jews in America

By 1875, the number of Jews in America had risen to about two hundred fifty thousand, the majority of them immigrants from Germany who wished to escape oppression. They began to arrive early in the century, and more sought refuge after the failure of the German revolution of 1848, when the German states enacted severely repressive laws against the idealists who had attempted to establish democracy. The German Jews, poor but enterprising, settled along the Eastern Seaboard or moved west to Cincinnati and St. Louis, where large settlements of Germans already existed, or to the South, where as whites they were more or less accepted. Following the gold rush to California, Jews founded congregations there even before the Golden

7. Lebeson, *Pilgrim People,* p. 208.
8. Lebeson, *Pilgrim People,* p. 211.

Judah P. Benjamin, after serving as a U.S. senator, became the Secretary of State of the Confederacy.

State had become part of the country.

Spiritual leaders and rabbis arrived. ISAAC LEESER came in 1824 and, although not a rabbi, assumed the spiritual leadership of the Jews of nearly the entire country. After fleeing tsarist Russia, MAX LILIENTHAL saw in America a new and creative future. The year 1846 saw the arrival of ISAAC MAYER WISE, the future organizer of the Jewish religious community and founder of the Reform movement. He was followed nine years later by DAVID EINHORN, an advocate of radical reform. The work of these men will be discussed in the next chapter.

THE CIVIL WAR. The Civil War found Jews on both sides. Six thousand served in the Union Army, twelve hundred in the Confederate Army. JUDAH P. BENJAMIN rose to a cabinet position in the Confederacy. DAVID EINHORN, rabbi of Baltimore, had to flee for his life after having preached in fiery wrath against the crime of slavery. There was also antisemitism, then, as there so often is, as a result of general tension. When Jews were accused of crossing the lines between North and South, General Ulysses S. Grant signed Order Number 11, which ex-pelled all Jews from his sector of operations. Abraham Lincoln intervened, and the order—the only anti-Jewish government regulation in

The Jewish War Veterans of the United States of America, founded by Jews who had served during the Civil War, is the oldest veterans' association in the U.S.

American history—was revoked immediately. When a Jewish delegation submitted its protest to him, the president listened carefully and said, "and so the children of Israel were driven from the happy land of Canaan." "Yes," was the reply, "and they have come to father Abraham's bosom to seek protection."[9]

Some Personalities

Among the Jewish immigrants from Germany were those who saw opportunities in the Industrial Revolution, were capable of building great fortunes, and were willing to put their wealth at the disposal of their brothers and sisters. The massive philanthropy of these "patricians" established a system of charitable institutions unparalleled in Jewish history. Millions of Jews were eventually rescued and transformed into proud and creative American citizens.

LEVI STRAUSS arrived at San Francisco with a load of canvas and a riveting machine to make tents for the gold diggers in California, but, finding the gold rush over, instead produced canvas pants held together by rivets—Levi's. MEYER GUGGENHEIM, a very pious man, started as a peddler and ended up as mine owner and multi-millionaire; the Guggenheim Museum and the Guggenheim Foundation testify to his civic spirit. Typically German in their thoroughness and organizational ability, Jewish immigrants became leaders also in the garment industry (Hart-Schaffner & Marx), founded department stores (Bloomingdale's, Macy's, Filene's, Gimbel's, Sears Roebuck), and established newspapers, including the *New York Times*. Linked by a common background, common aspirations, and success, they saw themselves as the patricians of American Jewry and as advocates of world Jewry. They were the modern *shtadlanim*, dedicated but also autocratic, and not inclined to tolerate opposition.

The acknowledged leader of Jews in America was JACOB HENRY SCHIFF (1847–1920), spokesman and advocate of Jews throughout the world. He financed the American Telephone and Tele-

9. Quoted in Levinger, *History*, p. 199.

graph Company, Westinghouse, U.S. Rubber, Anaconda, and the Union Pacific, and he supported Japan in its war against antisemitic tsarist Russia. During the peace conference of Russia and Japan that was held at Portsmouth, N.H., in 1906, Schiff personally remonstrated with the tsar's ambassador on behalf of the beleaguered Russian Jews. He decided that official pressure by the United States government was required and so approached President Theodore Roosevelt and his successor President William Howard Taft to ask them to abrogate the U. S. treaty with Russia until Russia granted civil rights to all its Jews. The treaty was canceled, but the tsarist government, preferring grave economic damage to justice for the Jews, did not yield.

In the wake of the Kishinev pogroms, Schiff and other distinguished Jewish leaders founded in 1906 a small defense organization, the American Jewish Committee, in order "to prevent infringement of the civil and religious rights of Jews and to alleviate the consequences of persecution" all over the world. The committee has continued to be active, especially in interfaith dialogue.

Schiff also founded and generously supported the Bureau of Jewish Education. Its function was to improve the education of the teachers in Jewish schools, assure them an adequate salary, and provide better curricula and means of instruction. The bureau established branches in every large city, and has continued to provide valuable leadership. Recognizing that many immigrants did not feel at home in Reform Judaism, Schiff became instrumental in building a firm foundation for the Conservative Jewish Theological Seminary.

Antisemitism and Jewish Defense

Throughout American history we find organizations, such as the Klu Klux Klan, that are directed against non-whites, foreigners, Catholics, and Jews. Racial theories found acceptance and were reflected in the official immigration policies of the United States. As early as 1843 Jews were blocked from membership in fraternal orders. Mass immigration from all parts of the world led to increased hostility from white Anglo-Saxon

Protestants, who saw their supremacy endangered, and from the trade unions, who were afraid of the ever-growing immigrant labor supply. During economic disturbances, the Jews were held as scapegoats, with Jewish merchants being branded as swindlers.

Deeply embedded theological antisemitism was preached from a number of Protestant and Catholic pulpits. The main impulse against Jews, however, came from Germany. Books and pamphlets were exported from there to the United States, and several rabid antisemites arrived in America to incite the masses and spread "Aryan" ideology.

Even Jewish patricians were affected. Newly rich Christians, hoping to gain admittance to the old upper class, distanced themselves from the Jews, excluding them from many neighborhoods and resorts and refusing them employment. Jews found themselves in a gilded ghetto. They learned that even in America they had to stand up for each other, defend and sustain each other. Their cohesion grew. "All Israel is responsible, one for the other" became the motto.

At the same time American Jews cast their roots ever more deeply in American soil. And they had the support of many of their fellow citizens. Like other forms of discrimination, antisemitism is contrary to the law as well as the spirit of America—a perversion of American ideals, and a subversion of the Constitution. This has given American Jewry the will and legal means to fight against it and against all forms of discrimination.

Emma Lazarus, who wrote the poem on the base of the Statue of Liberty, was also an ardent Zionist. She urged Jews to restore their strength and their homeland:

Let our first care today be the re-establishment of our physical strength, the reconstruction of our national organism, so that in future, where the respect due to us cannot be won by entreaty, it may be commanded, and where it cannot be commanded, it may be enforced.

Emma Lazarus, "An Epistle to the Hebrews" (1883), quoted in Ellen M. Umansky and Diane Ashton, eds., *Four Centuries of Jewish Women's Spirituality: A Sourcebook* (Boston: Beacon Press, 1992), p.103.

EASTERN EUROPEAN JEWS IN AMERICA

Between 1881 and 1920, a total of two million Jews came to the United States, most of them victims of persecution in Eastern Europe and desperately poor. Many were pious, others were inspired by the Jewish socialist movement, but all of them found in Judaism the strength to endure. Tightly knit, they found strength in mutual support. The Jewish poet EMMA LAZARUS (1849–1887) found the inspiration for her great poem, which is emblazoned on the base of the Statue of Liberty, from working among Jewish immigrants from Eastern Europe. The poem expresses her compassion for her brothers and sisters as the statue speaks:

> "Keep ancient lands your storied pomp," cries she
> with silent lips. "Give me your tired, your poor,
> your huddled masses yearning to breathe free,
> the wretched refuse of your teeming shore.
> Send these, the homeless, tempest-tossed to me;
> I lift my lamp beside the golden door."

Staying together as they had lived together in Eastern Europe, the new immigrants settled along the Atlantic Seaboard, the majority remaining in New York. Each group organized its own synagogue, where it followed the same customs and spoke the same language as in the shtetl whence it had come. Their rabbis, who had come with them and remained their leaders, were schooled in Talmud but were strangers to American secular culture. The masses had a strong sense of *Yiddishkeit*.

Problems of Transition

The number of immigrants was almost ten times larger than the entire Jewish population of America up to that time. The American German Jewish patricians wanted to Americanize the new immigrants as quickly as possible. Apprehensive that the newcomers might jeopardize their position in American society and not wishing to be identified with the newcomers, the German Jews helped but remained aloof. While

Many Jews became labor movement organizers and leaders. One such Jew was Samuel Gompers (1850–1924), cigar maker from London and founder and first president of the American Federation of Labor (AFL).

appreciating the generous help given them by the established Jews, the newcomers wanted to become Americans on their own terms and by their own efforts. They wished to retain their own distinctive Jewish characteristics. German and Eastern Jews drifted apart emotionally.

There was demand for labor only at the lowest levels of employment, such as in the sweatshops of the garment industry; some new immigrants peddled notions, old clothes, or vegetables. The Jews worked, learned, and organized. But their concern for improvement did not blot out the Jewish ideal of social justice. A type of Jew emerged in America: idealistic, imbued with a social conscience, but no longer religious; proud to be a Jew, but having little contact with the synagogue. For many younger Jews, Judaism became primarily an emotional attachment, expressing itself in deep devotion to their parents, or in the fight for Jewish rights, or perhaps in a love for Jewish food and a nostalgia for Yiddish tunes. As the new generation acquired means, Judaism came to the fore in their charity, however, and eventually found an outlet in Zionism.

Facing Prejudice

Prejudice had made itself felt in the United States even when the number of Jews had been small; it increased with the growth of the Jewish population. Jews themselves were often blamed for the prejudice, as if it were caused, not by bigotry, but by the presence of more Jews. As Jews' status improved and they moved to better sections of town, Christians moved out and then accused the Jews of clannishness. The Jews' emphasis on education was also turned against them. By 1925 the Jewish students at Harvard accounted for fully 13 percent of the student body; President Lowell introduced a quota system, "to curb the antisemitism which so large a number of Jewish students could generate among the rest of the students." Yale, whose Jewish students had distinguished themselves, changed its admission policy to focus on the "character" of the applicant, and that criterion was misused to exclude Jews. Jews were hardly ever appointed as professors. Jewish hospitals had to train Jewish physicians, for non-Jewish ones rarely accepted them as interns and residents.

The Communist revolution in Russia led to a witch hunt of so-called Communists among the immigrants to America at the end of World War I. Since Jews like Trotsky had attained great power in the USSR and since a number of Jews believed that socialism would spell the end of prejudice, Jews in general were accused of being Communists or holding socialist inclinations. "Of twenty Bolsheviks in the United States nineteen are Jews. The bulwark of Bolshevism in America is the Yiddish speaking element on the East Side of New York," a representative declared in Congress. Hate of Jews was fanned when Henry Ford published the infamous "Protocols of the Elders of Zion" in his daily paper, the *Dearborn Independent*, giving publicity in the U.S. to this vicious forgery. Louis Marshall, on behalf of the American Jewish Committee, issued a declaration that all Jews condemned Bolshevism, and he pressured Ford to apologize publicly. But antisemitism cannot be eradicated by declarations and apologies.

The soil was prepared for the anti-Jewish atmosphere that permeated the American public in the following decades. Antisemitism was financially supported by German funds streaming into the country after the Nazis had come to power, and it was further encouraged by hatemongers, including the growing Ku Klux Klan and the German American Bund, a uniformed Nazi organization. At a time when millions of Jews were desperately seeking escape from extermination, "the golden door" was slammed shut by new immigration laws.

IMMIGRATION LAWS. Immigration laws restricting free access to the United States had long been advocated by racists in order to favor the immigration of "desirable" northern Europeans and to block the immigration of "unhealthy elements," such as Jews, Slavs, and southern Europeans. Over the vetoes of several U.S. presidents, increasingly restrictive laws were passed. In the heated atmosphere after World War I, a quota system was introduced in 1921; only 3 percent of the various national groups that had lived in America in 1910 were to be admitted annually. In 1924, the census year used to calculate the quotas was changed to 1890, when smaller groups of "undesirables" had been in the country; only 2 percent of these groups would be admitted. The quotas allowed for a large influx of British and German immigrants but a very limited number of immigrants from Poland, Russia, and Romania—countries from which Jewish immigration came.

JEWISH AMERICAN LIFE

Immigrations from Germany and Eastern Europe have given American Jewry both the numbers and the resources for creative and constructive efforts in every field of endeavor, making it a leading Jewry in the world today.

Jewish Organizations

American Jewry found a dynamic leader in Rabbi STEPHEN S. WISE, a committed Zionist (he had attended the Second Zionist Congress at Basel in 1898) and a militant spokesman for the Jewish people and for Zionism. Wise's appeal to President Wilson prevailed in gaining U.S. endorsement of the Balfour Declaration. Imposing in stature and a dynamic speaker, Wise had been called to Temple Emanuel at New York, but when he was told that his sermons

Stephen S. Wise, Reform rabbi and Zionist, was an articulate spokesman for the Reform movement and founder of the Jewish Institute of Religion.

had to be submitted to the board for approval, he protested against this "corruption of Judaism"; as a result of his efforts, no American rabbi would henceforth be subjected to censorship by the congregation. Wise opened a Free Synagogue that imposed no membership dues, assigned no seats, and affirmed the freedom of the pulpit. His weekly services at Carnegie Hall were attended by thousands of all creeds.

His experiences taught him that American Jewry needed unity and democracy. To give it unity, Wise founded, in 1922, the Jewish Institute of Religion, a rabbinical seminary designed for all branches of Judaism (later it merged with the Hebrew Union College). To give democracy, he founded in the same year the American Jewish Congress so that the Jewish community would have broader popular representation than it possessed under the American Jewish Committee. Elected democratically, Wise became the president of the congress, gave it its Zionist character, and expanded it in 1936 into a World Jewish Congress. The purpose of the organization was to defend all minorities and fight antisemitism throughout the world, a task that the congress has carried out with energy as they have pressured their enemies to yield to justice.

In 1843 Jews founded B'nai B'rith, Sons of the Covenant. Started as a benevolent organization of German Jews, it cast off its exclusiveness, grew rapidly, and has spread all over the world. B'nai B'rith entered the field of defense through its Anti-Defamation League, which has helped many minorities and combated antisemitism. B'nai B'rith also established the Hillel Foundation at colleges and universities, which is designed to offer Jewish students a home away from home and access to Jewish religious, cultural, and educational programs. The Hillel Houses, corresponding to the Newman Clubs or Wesley Foundations sponsored by Catholics and Protestants, have brought Jewish inspiration to students in America and abroad.

The Jewish Welfare Board, a lay organization, began by organizing Young Men's Hebrew Association and Jewish Community Centers. It expanded its scope by becoming the official agency certifying chaplains for the armed services, drawing equally from all branches of Judaism. Ultimately, the Jewish

Welfare Federations, or Community Federations, emerged in communities nationwide and have been a unifying force among American Jews of all denominations. The organizations raise funds for Israel and local needs and sponsor educational activities.

Zionism

Stephen S. Wise and several outstanding Reform rabbis became prominent in the Zionist movement, holding that loyalty to America did not exclude loyalty to Zion any more than loyalty to family excluded loyalty to country. Professor Horace Kallen advanced the concept of cultural plurality: all ethnic groups are members of a "symphony of culture," each playing its instrument in contributing to a harmonious whole.

Louis Brandeis became one of the most distinguished justices of the Supreme Court of the United States. His confirmation by the Senate was bitterly opposed, for he was an advocate of labor and a Jew, but President Wilson, who had nominated him, prevailed.

LOUIS DEMBITZ BRANDEIS (1856–1941) gave American Zionism its character and philosophy. A brilliant lawyer and a defender of workers, he settled a strike between the mainly Jewish workers in shirt factories and their Jewish bosses. This, his first contact with the Eastern European Jews, gave him a deep inner compulsion to identify with his people. He joined the Zionist movement, and when its center moved from war-torn Berlin to neutral America, he assumed a leadership position. A deeply committed American, Brandeis firmly asserted that American Jews had their home in the United States but should support and defend the Yishuv with all their heart and strength.

Among the most prominent American Zionists was HENRIETTA SZOLD (1860–1945). Daughter of a

Baltimore rabbi, she became a co-founder and secretary of the Jewish Publication Society, editing Jewish works which would bring inner strength to American Jews out of the sources of Judaism. Imbued with a deep love for Palestine, she founded Hadassah, the organization of Zionist women. In 1920 she moved to Palestine to lay the foundations of the medical work which was to bring healing to Jew and Arab alike, culminating in the Hadassah Hospital completed in 1960. When the Nazis overran Germany, she organized Youth Aliyah, bringing thousands of youngsters to Israel and a new life.

Contemporary American Jews

The majority of American Jews today are native born, and a high percentage are the children of native-born Americans. Jews are free to move in society, to choose any university for which they are intellectually qualified, and to associate freely with adherents of other faiths. American Jews have a strong sense of community, of *Yiddishkeit*, and have come to understand themselves as a religious-ethnic community. Jewish self-esteem has found expression in proud affirmation of Jewishness, militant advocacy of Jewish rights, and an openness toward converts—"Jews by choice"—who come to Judaism in sincerity to accept the privilege of belonging. Jews have prospered and have surpassed all ethnic groups in charitable giving and in giving of themselves in the struggle for social justice. They have enlarged every frontier of human achievement. ALBERT EINSTEIN proudly both affirmed his newly won American citizenship and placed himself at the service of the Jewish people. JONAS SALK invented the polio vaccine. BETTY FRIEDAN, mother of the feminist movement, drew consciously on her Jewish inheritance of social justice.

The work of many renowned literary figures is rooted in the Jewish

Close to 80 percent of Jews attend universities, many of which have a large number of Jewish professors. Jewish refugee professors from Europe were instrumental in elevating American higher education to true university standards. Many universities have established chairs and programs in Jewish studies, attracting not only Jews but also non-Jews of all faiths. The Jewish sponsored Brandeis University, accepting students of all religions and races, has gained great distinction.

experience. SAUL BELLOW, 1976 Nobel Prize winner, speaks of Jews to reveal alienation and loneliness and the search for spirituality in a world out of shape (*Augie March, Herzog, Humboldt's Gift*). BERNARD MALAMUD analyzes the Jew in urban America, who will suffer, either for the law or for nothing (*The Assistant, The Fixer*). PHILIP ROTH reveals the anxieties of the Jew striving to assimilate (*Portnoy's Complaint, Good Bye Columbus*). ARTHUR MILLER, in *Death of a Salesman*, reveals the insecurity of a man who finds strength only from outside approval, while *The Crucible* demonstrates the power of slander, fear, and hysteria in dealing with non-conformists. ISAAC BASHEVIS SINGER, 1978 Nobel Prize winner, wrote in Yiddish; his world of Eastern European Jewry explores the struggles and conflicts of human beings everywhere.

American Jews have made lasting contributions in the field of music, where they have given America some of its leading composers, conductors, and virtuosos. The violin virtuoso ISAAC STERN, a deeply dedicated Jew, saved Carnegie Hall from the wrecker's ball. YITZHAK PERLMAN, born in Israel, has been counted among the greatest violin virtuosos of his generation, and JAMES LEVINE, the artistic director of the Metropolitan Opera at New York, is among the outstanding conductors. AARON COPELAND, composer of *Appalachian Spring* and *Fanfare for the Common Man* has been regarded as one of America's foremost composers. Jews—among them the composers and lyricists HAMMERSTEIN, HART, LERNER and LOEWE, HAMLISH, and SONDHEIM— transformed the European operetta from a vehicle of frothy escapist entertainment into the musical with a social message. GEORGE GERSHWIN brought the condition of African Americans to the attention of white America in his opera *Porgy and Bess,* and the great conductor and composer LEONARD BERNSTEIN, who steadfastly refused to change his name for the sake of a career, addressed the issue of racial conflict in *West Side Story.* Jewish composers also presented Jewish tradition and life to the world. Bernstein, in his *Chichester Psalms,* set the Hebrew text of Psalms into music and he gave us his *Kaddish Symphony.* In *Fiddler on the Roof,* HARNACK and BOCK presented the life and trials of the shtetl to the western world, as did BARBRA STREISAND in the film *Yentl*. STEVEN SPIELBERG, one of the innovative filmmakers of his time, stirred the world with *Schindler's List*, an overwhelming portrayal of the Holocaust that reveals both the suffering of the Jews and the heroism of a Christian who saved many concentration camp victims from extermination.

In 1996, many Jews held high elected and appointed offices in state and federal government. Two Jewish women, Diane Feinstein and Barbara Boxer, represented the State of California as its senators, and two Jews, Ruth Bader Ginsberg and Stephen Breyer, were justices on the Supreme Court.

We have mentioned but a few especially well-known names and works from the large list of distinguished Jewish contributions and omitted many others of equal stature. Jews have felt obligated to serve America and humanity in return for the gift of freedom and equality. Prejudice has not been eradicated, but life, law, and society are constantly creating a new environment with new challenges for all Americans, and American Jews have accepted them.

Chapter 17

THE RELIGIOUS DYNAMICS OF AMERICAN JEWRY

In America, Judaism grew in a new environment. The roots of this religious evolution lay in Europe, but ideas from other lands came to life when transplanted to American soil. Life in the United States has given American Jewry a unique and dynamic character that has influenced Jews throughout the world.

REFORM JUDAISM

Diversity and individual autonomy are fundamental to Reform Judaism. Every Jew must study Judaism carefully, for the Jew must choose wisely the obligations to which he or she is committed, find the reason for rejecting others, and always be mindful that the Jewishness of future generations depends on his or her own. This individual autonomy can lead to highly committed Jewish living, provided individual Jews and Jewish communities constantly and conscientiously evaluate the pattern of their lives as Jews. The process requires a thorough knowledge of Judaism and its traditions, personal sacrifice, and a view of the world through the sight of Judaism.

Building Reform

ISAAC MAYER WISE (1819–1900), born in Steingrub, Austria,

came to America as a man of twenty-seven, inspired by the vision of civil liberties and hoping to graft modern Jewish thought onto the tree of Judaism in the United States. In his journal, *The Israelite,* Wise stated his basic convictions: Oppression has demoralized the Jew.

> It has robbed him of his self respect, has killed all pride in him. . . . He must, within himself, develop the self reliance and self assurance for which America stands.[1]

Isaac Mayer Wise, a pioneer of Reform Judaism in America, founded the Union of American Hebrew Congregations (1873) and the Hebrew Union College (1875).

Dedicating his life to Americanization and Reform, Wise intended to give Judaism more power and to restore the faith of the Jews. These aims were to be served by his new prayer book *Minhag America, An American Ritual.* Even Isaac Leeser, the pioneer of Neo-Orthodoxy in America, approved, saying that Wise's prayer book would unify divergent customs and lead to a uniform practice among congregations; undue attachment to the old country would be eliminated and Judaism strengthened.

Wise attempted to organize an "Association of Israelitish Congregations in North America" in order to "defend and maintain our sacred faith."[2] In 1855 he convoked a conference to formulate the articles of this Union of American Israel so that they would be acceptable to all Jews. This article stated, for example, that

1. Jacob R. Marcus, *Memoirs of American Jews,* vol. 2 (Philadelphia: Jewish Publication Society, 1955), p. 133 f.
2. Isaac Leeser, quoted in Anita L. Lebeson, *Pilgrim People* (New York: Harper, 1950), p. 311.

the Bible is of immediate divine origin; the Talmud contains the Traditional, Legal and Logical Expositions of the Biblical Laws which must be expounded and practiced according to the Comments of the Talmud.[3]

Radical reformers like David Einhorn rejected the position as too conservative.

DAVID EINHORN (1809–1879) was forty-six years old when he came to Baltimore from Germany. Having a thorough talmudic education, he had also studied at various universities. His ideas belonged to the radical wing of Reform Judaism and are expressed in his prayer book, *Olat Tamid (Perpetual Sacrifice)*.

For Einhorn, monotheism was not a Jewish discovery but had existed in all of humanity since Adam. Sinai created a new people, the Jews, with the universal mission to teach and exemplify ethics in the love of God and humanity. Fulfilling this mission would lead to the messianic age of peace and universal human brotherhood—Israel collectively becomes the Messiah, the world's redeemer. Laws were given to the Jews so that a balance between unity and individuality would create harmony and purpose, but these laws had validity only as long as they held symbolic power. As revelation continued to open the human spirit to God, laws lost their relevance as symbols. They became outdated and had to be abolished. In this way, the Talmud, in its time an important phase in Israel's development, had become obsolete. The fundamental principles of Judaism, however, remained divine and had to be maintained and taught. For example, Sabbath rest with its many injunctions had lost relevance and therefore was invalid; Sabbath *sanctification,* an absolute principle, was indispensable.

Einhorn saw that Israel's mission could be realized within the context of American equality, and he called on his people to embrace their Jewishness but to abolish most forms of religious observance and to cast off the laws of the Talmud.

3. Isaac Mayer Wise, quoted in Ismar Elbogen, *A Century of Jewish Life* (Philadelphia: Jewish Publication Society, 1944), p. 124.

THE COMPROMISE. Wise was apprehensive that Orthodox congregations would not follow him even in moderate changes. He was also aware that he needed the liberal congregations in order to build an American Judaism, and so he moved toward Einhorn's radical reform. Believing that unity and cooperation could still be preserved through a union of congregations, as long as each congregation's religious individuality was explicitly confirmed, Wise was urged by followers to found in 1873 the Union of American Hebrew Congregations. Among its aims were the establishment of institutions of higher Jewish studies, relief for Jews from oppression and discrimination, and the promotion of religious instruction. The Orthodox congregations, however, refused to affiliate, and the Union became a Reform Institution.

Facilitating the education of Rabbis of all denominations, Isaac Mayer Wise established the Hebrew Union College in 1875. A 1947 merger of Hebrew Union College with Rabbi Stephen Wise's Jewish Institute of Religion at New York created Hebrew Union College–Jewish Institute of Religion. The institution has campuses in Cincinnati, New York, Los Angeles, and Jerusalem. It has produced rabbis, cantors, and educators who have ranged from radical Reform to traditional Conservative. It was the first school to ordain women as rabbis and invest them as cantors.

The Union grants its members great freedom and responsibility in matters of worship and practice. No central body or code—such as Torah, Talmud, or Shulhan Arukh—is relied upon as a decisive authority on law and custom. Rather, each individual congregation establishes the forms of religious practice and observance to be followed, and each individual is responsible for deciding the particular form of his or her Jewishness. This platform allows all congregations to join, regardless of their religious convictions.

In 1875 the Wise established the Hebrew Union College, a theological seminary where rabbis would be prepared and ordained. The school was to be free from any specific denominational doctrine, and its graduates equipped to serve all branches of American Jewry. The College, the oldest rabbinical school in

America, did not attract traditionally oriented students. In 1889 Wise added a third organization, the Central Conference of American Rabbis. The organization was established to perpetuate Jewish teaching, unify worship, and pursue the development of law.

Wise was a visionary and the master builder of American Jewry. Conservative, Orthodox, and Reconstructionist groups, seeing the need for union and regeneration, copied his pattern in every detail—each has a union of congregations, a theological school, and a rabbinical organization.

The Theological Development of Reform Judaism

After Wise, the Reform movement found its leader in KAUFMANN KOHLER (1843–1926). He was born in Fürth, Bavaria, into a strictly Orthodox family. Among his early teachers was Samson Raphael Hirsch, the central theologian of Neo-Orthodoxy. Later, his university studies changed his views so radically that he could no longer hope for a pulpit in Germany. He immigrated to America at the age of twenty-seven and became Einhorn's son-in-law and adherent. Succeeding Wise as president of the Hebrew Union College, he molded generations of Reform rabbis.

THE PITTSBURGH PLATFORM. In 1885 Kohler convoked an unofficial conclave of fifteen rabbis at Pittsburgh, Pennsylvania. Its resolutions, the Pittsburgh Platform, constitute the high water mark of Classical Reform. The conference acknowledged the Bible as "the most potent instrument of religious and moral instruction"[4] but rejected the binding force of Torah, Talmud, and halakhah and denied the peoplehood of Israel. While maintaining the sanctity of the traditional Sabbath, Sunday services were also allowed; worship was to be in English. The platform would "extend the hand of fellowship to all who cooperate . . . in the establishment of the reign of truth and righteousness";[5] at the same time, a vision of Judaism as fostering

4. Pittsburgh Platform, quoted in Michael A. Meyer, *Response to Modernity: A History of the Reform Movement in Judaism* (Oxford: Oxford University Press, 1988), p. 387.
5. Pittsburgh Platform, in Meyer, *Response*, p. 388.

a purely ethical culture without religious commitment was rejected. More radical than the resolutions of the German reformers except perhaps Holdheim, the platform guided Reform for the next five decades.

THE COLUMBUS PLATFORM. Over the next fifty-two years, the Conservative movement drew large numbers of Jews, Mordecai Kaplan's ideas made inroads (see below), and Zionism grew. Persecution of the Jews in Europe dispelled exuberant hopes in the progress of justice.

In 1937, in Columbus, Ohio, Reform Jews responded to these changes by formulating a new platform. It affirms Jewish peoplehood and Israel's universal message, which will lead to the perfection of humanity under the sovereignty of God who transcends time and space and is an indwelling Presence in the world. The genius of the Jewish people lies in its religious insight—the Torah. While revelation is indeed a continuous process, all of the ancient laws have not become outdated.

The Columbus Platform places new and significant emphasis on Jewish practice: in the home, "hallowed by the spirit of love and reverence, by moral discipline and religious observance and worship"; and in the synagogue, "the oldest and most democratic institution in Jewish life," which "links the Jews of each community and unites them with all Israel." Education is crucial for "the perpetuation of Judaism as a living force"; prayer at home and in the synagogue is necessary "to deepen the spiritual life of our people." The Sabbath, festivals, and Holy Days are to be observed, and "such customs, symbols and ceremonies as possess inspirational value" to be followed, including "the use of Hebrew, together with the vernacular, in our worship and instruction."[6]

The Columbus Platform affirms the responsibilities of American Jewry as an emerging center of world Jewry. Jewish at-homeness in the lands of the diaspora is affirmed, the non-religious "cultural" Jew recognized, and the convert welcomed. In addition, the bond with the Yishuv and obligations toward the upbuilding of the Land of Israel are prominently emphasized.

A CENTENARY PERSPECTIVE. Seared by the Holocaust and

6. Columbus Platform, in *Meyer, Response,* p. 390–91.

uplifted by the establishment of the State of Israel, the Reform rabbinate knew that American Jewry and Israel were the heirs to the annihilated centers of Jewish life in Europe. Jewish unity had to be affirmed. At the same time, in the spirit of Reform, Jewish diversity had to be asserted. And so in 1976, close to the one hundredth anniversaries of the founding of the Union (1873) and the College (1875), the Central Conference of American Rabbis marked the occasion by passing a new platform, called A Centenary Perspective.

The platform asserts that the Jewish people, faith, and peoplehood are one, joined with God, and "always in the process of becoming." The survival of the Jewish people, bound up with the evolving Torah, rests on specific Jewish obligations as well as ethics. The platform stresses the imperative of Judaism as a way of life for every Jew.

The platform also confirms the State of Israel and even endorses *aliyah*. At the same time it insists that Reform Judaism be given complete legal status in Israel, which had been denied it. The platform asserts that loyalty to both America and Israel sets an example to humanity, leading it from a narrow nationalism to an ethical nationalism that embraces other peoples. Loyalty to Israel therefore expresses the ideal of Judaism to be a light to the nations.

The dilemma of two loyalties resolved, the Reform Jew faces a different dilemma:

> A universal concern for humanity unaccompanied by a devotion to our particular people is self-destructive; a passion for our people without involvement in humankind contradicts what the prophets have meant to us. Judaism calls us simultaneously to universal and particular obligations.[7]

Having been taught to serve Judaism by serving humanity, the Reform Jew now finds that service to humanity and to the vital concerns of Jewish survival may at times be in conflict.

REFORM PRINCIPLES, PITTSBURGH, MAY 26, 1999.[8] In 1999, the annual convention of the Central Conference of American

7. A Centenary Perspective.
8. Quotations from Reform Principles, Pittsburgh, May 26, 1999, with permission, Central Conference of American Rabbis.

Rabbis issued a new platform: Statement of Principles for Reform Judaism. In contrast to the Pittsburgh Platform of 1885, this statement views Judaism, not from the standpoint of the surrounding world and culture to which it had to be adjusted, but from within, stressing the spiritual strength and the healing that Judaism can give to its faithful and to the world. Resting on the three pillars of Judaism—God, Torah, and Israel—the statement emphasizes *b'rit*, God's Covenant with the Jewish people; accentuates *k'lal Yisrael*, the invisible community of Israel; and underscores the need for the performance of mitzvot. The great contribution of Reform Judaism is its ability "to introduce innovation while preserving tradition, to embrace diversity while asserting communality, to affirm beliefs without rejecting those who doubt, and to bring faith to sacred texts without sacrificing critical scholarship."

To meet their special obligations, Jews have to "respond to God daily: through public and private prayer, through study, and through the performance of other mitzvot." Lifelong study of Torah is an obligation, because "through Torah we are called to mitzvot, the means by which we make our lives holy." The rabbis dwell on the importance of sanctifying "the times and places of our lives" by observance of Shabbat, the festivals, and days of remembrance, as well as by marking the personal milestones of a person's life. Jews also have obligations as God's partners in restoring the world to wholeness.

The Principles boldly affirm the singularity of Jewish people in the world:

> We are Israel, a people aspiring to holiness, singled out through
> our ancient covenant and our unique history among the nations
> to be witnesses to God's presence. We are linked by that covenant
> and that history to all Jews in every age and place.

This entails the mitzvah of love for the Jewish people, for according to Jewish teaching "all Jews are responsible for one another." Therefore Jews must reach out to all Jews across ideological and geographic boundaries. As an inclusive community, Reform Judaism will open the doors of Jewish life "to people of all ages, to varied kinds of families, to all regardless of their sexual orientation, to *gerim,* those who have converted to Judaism, and to all individuals and families, including the intermarried, who strive to create a Jewish home." It is committed to supporting individuals and families in creating Jewish homes, rich in Jewish learning and observance, and to making the synagogue central to Jewish life.

Commitment to the State of Israel includes encouragement of *aliyah,* immigration to Israel, where life offers unique qualities to Jews. It is envisioned and expected that the State of Israel will grant full human religious rights to all its inhabitants and strive for a lasting peace with its neighbors. Through progressive Judaism the spiritual life of the Jewish state and its people will be enriched.

Reform Judaism Today

The Central Conference of American Rabbis passed the platforms we have discussed. In addition, numerous *responsa,* responses founded in halakhah, to questions on Jewish law and customs, have been issued and collected. Halakhah is scrutinized for the guidance it can offer. The Reform rabbinate has given women equal rights, from initiation rites for girls at birth, to Bat Mitzvah, to the ordination of women as rabbis and their installation as cantors.

The Conference has also issued prayer books and periodically revises them. The *Union Prayer Book,* strongly influenced by Einhorn's *Olat Tamid,* has, in turn, been replaced by *Gates of Prayer* for the year and *Gates of Repentance* for the High Holy Days. Egalitarian versions of prayers are available, as are prayerbooks for children and for numerous occasions. Hebrew has been restored in many prayers, and many blessings are included; prayers for Jerusalem and services commemorating the Holocaust and Israel's Independence Day are found as well. Individual Reform synagogues, free to construct their forms of worship, have brought back many traditional customs and ceremonies, such as wearing the tallit and head covering. Bar Mitzvah and Bat Mitzvah have become universal.

The movement trains and certifies men and women as

mohelim, in order that circumcision be truly observed as a religious act. It has established synagogues, sent rabbis and prayer books to Jews in the former USSR, and guided Jewish immigrants from Russia. It reaches out to the non-affiliated, the intermarried, and to non-Jews in search of meaningful faith. In view of the large number of interfaith marriages, Reform is prepared to recognize the children of a Jewish father and a non-Jewish mother as Jews, on the condition that they have been brought up in a Jewish home environment and have received a Jewish education. This resolution has caused great controversy within the other branches of religious Jewry.

One of the great achievements of the Union of American Hebrew Congregations has been in the field of education. From primer to advanced texts, the movement's education series have blazed new paths. Summer camps for children and adolescents, retreats for adults, and institutes for the laity have been developed in all regions of the country; Jewish day schools have been initiated by a number of congregations. Following the ideal that Judaism be a light unto the nations, the Union has developed a program to explain Judaism and teach ethics to the community at large; its center in Washington, D.C., and the social action committees of individual congregations transmit the Jewish ethical point of view to lawmakers and the nation. The Union is a member of the World Zionist Organization and has established Reform kibbutzim. The World Union of Progressive Judaism encompasses liberal congregations throughout the world.

CONSERVATIVE JUDAISM

Conservative Judaism has fused religion with ethnicity, the wisdom of the world with the abiding principles and norms of Judaism, the past with the present. It considers ethics—the duties of human beings toward each other—to be as important as those mitzvot that bind the Jew to God. It joins a universalism to nationalism, and Zionism to American patriotism. It stresses the peoplehood of the Jews and retains bonds with all Jews, including Jewish denominations with which it disagrees and non-religious Jews.

The Jewish Theological Seminary

Conservative Judaism's growth can be linked to the immigration of two million Jews from Eastern Europe. Eager to blend into American life, they found the European style synagogue inadequate for their needs but desired its warmth and intimacy. Although they admired the decorum of the Reform synagogue, they could not accept its departure from tradition.

In response, Isaac Leeser's successor, SABATO MORAIS, founded a traditional rabbinical seminary, whose beginnings were slow and faltering. JACOB SCHIFF and his associates, themselves Reform Jews but vitally interested in the acculturation of the Eastern European immigrants, secured its fiscal stability. Under the leadership of SOLOMON SCHECHTER (1850–1915), called by Jacob Schiff and his associates to assume the presidency of the seminary, it acquired status and strength.

Isaac Leeser (1806–1868), a religious pioneer of American Jewry, was both deeply Orthodox and a follower of Moses Mendelssohn's teaching. Responding to an article in a Richmond paper that attacked Jewish customs, he exhibited such learning, clarity of thought, and dignity that the synagogue in Philadelphia appointed him its cantor. He translated the Bible and the prayer book into English, founded a periodical, *The Occident and American Jewish Advocate*, and traveled all over the country to guide and inspire his widely scattered coreligionists.

Schechter was deeply influenced by German Jewish scholarship and philosophy. He had studied at the rabbinical seminary developed by Abraham Geiger but ideologically was a disciple of Zacharias Frankel and the school of "positive historical Judaism" (see chapter 13). The seminary would bear the same name as Frankel's in Breslau, the Jewish Theological Seminary.

Like Frankel, Schechter was interested in the organic growth of Judaism and was convinced that each generation must participate in the unfolding destiny of the living body of the Jewish people. The theology of the "historical school" holds that "it is not mere revealed Bible that is of first importance to

Solomon Schechter was born in Romania and brought up as a talmudic scholar. He acquired his secular education in Vienna and Berlin and was eventually called to Cambridge University in England. By accident, a few scraps of medieval manuscripts were brought to his attention, and following their lead to an ancient synagogue at Cairo, Egypt, he discovered a *genizah*, a hidden storage place of discarded books, that the Jews, forbidden by religious law to destroy even scraps of sacred texts, had deposited there. The discovery was momentous. It included the works of Ben Sirah, never known in their Hebrew version, original manuscripts of Maimonides, and many other priceless manuscripts. Schechter took them to Cambridge and began to edit them. He gave up his position as one of the world's great scholars at one of the world's great universities when he was called to become the president of a small, struggling school in New York: the Jewish Theological Seminary.

the Jew, but the Bible as it repeats itself in history, in other words as it is interpreted by Tradition." The center of authority is removed from the Bible and placed in some living body. This living body "is not represented by any section of the nation, or any corporate priesthood, or Rabbihood, but by the collective conscience of Catholic Israel as embodied in the Universal Synagogue."[9] The Jewish people as a whole (catholic, that is, universal Israel) fashion a pattern of life and interpretation of Torah.

9. Solomon Schechter, quoted in Norman Bentwich, ed., *Selected Writings of Solomon Schechter* (Oxford: East and West Library, 1946), p. 35 f.

Conservative Judaism has grown to great strength, both in numbers and in spirit. Organizationally, Schechter followed Wise's pattern but centered the movement in the seminary, around which he built the congregational organization of the United Synagogue. The Rabbinical Assembly became the body of the conservative rabbinate. The Jewish Theological Seminary, in addition to its rabbinical school, also has schools for cantors, teachers, and general Jewish studies; an extensive program for the ongoing education of rabbis; training for selected rabbis to issue bills of divorce; and halakhic instruction and certification for mohelim. The seminary's Institute of Religious and Social Studies gathers scholars of all religions for research into social problems and the solutions offered by religion. It holds the greatest collection of Jewish manuscripts ever assembled in the world, and its Jewish Museum has become one of the showplaces of New York. The University of Judaism in Los Angeles, with a branch in Jerusalem is also linked to the seminary.

The Character of Conservative Judaism

Conservative Judaism in the U.S. rests on "positive historical Judaism" as defined by Frankel and Schechter but also reflects American pragmatism. Conservative Judaism constantly tries to combine the old and the new as it lives in the tension between tradition and change. Its growth is based on the organic evolution of the spirit of Judaism through the Jewish people. As new ideas and practices are accepted and incorporated, they become part of the structure of Judaism. Changes are formally sanctioned only after they have been adopted by the people. A Committee on Jewish Laws and Standards is entrusted with rendering authoritative decisions as it interprets halakhah in consideration of the needs of the people. If the opinion within the committee is split, congregations may follow either the majority or the minority opinion. The process of change has created a wide variety in the practices of Conservative congregations. Some may for all practical purposes be Orthodox; others may come very close to Reform.

Theological Development

The basic laws of Judaism may not be changed. Daily prayer, the observance of the dietary laws, of the Sabbath, and of the festivals and holy days are compulsory. Through them and through Hebrew, the unity of the Jewish people is symbolically expressed and physically maintained. Modifications in halakhah are, however, possible. This is achieved by investigating how a given halakhah came into being and how it developed. How would it be different had it been enacted in our time?

One of the most important Conservative halakhic decisions, arrived at in this manner, gave full equality to women. This was instituted after consultation with all member rabbis and congregations and by ratification by their majority in a process that lasted for years. The change was motivated by Conservative Judaism's commitment to ethics, whose source is Torah itself. Through the Conservative method of halakhic adaptation, answers were sought to halakhic problems that imposed real sufferings on women. As a result of this process of change, Conservative women are now counted in the minyan, educated at the Seminary, ordained as rabbis, and installed as cantors. Ceremonies, such as Rosh Hodesh, are promoted that are especially geared to women. Women are full participants in the liturgical life of their congregations, and in most congregations women and men sit together. The Bat Mitzvah is observed. A condition is included in the marriage contract that can force the man, under law, to grant a *get* to his wife, thus aiding women who could not remarry without their husbands' initiating divorce.

Conservative Judaism considers the experiences of the Jewish people as the basic source of revelation. It equally affirms contradictory positions on revelation such as the absoluteness of Sinai. The Bible need not be regarded as literally revealed; it must, however, be regarded as true, for it is the revelation of the Jewish people's communion with God. The truth of the Bible lies not in its historical accuracy but in its meaning for the life of the Jew and the life of humanity.

Conservative Judaism understands the appeal of both

Reform and Orthodoxy but finds that Reform rejects halakhah and relies on individual autonomy while Orthodoxy, in resting on the dogma of the unchangeable Torah, gives spiritual security but rejects the insights of modern scholarly research and lacks concern for critical contemporary issues. Conservative Judaism sees itself as bound to both tradition and modernity, halakhah and science.

TRUTH AND FAITH. In order to reaffirm its unique position, the Conservative movement published its first platform in 1988 under the title *Emet Ve-Emunah*, Truth and Faith, which contains the guiding principles of Conservative Judaism. As its name indicates, it wishes to find a living synthesis between *emet*, the truth revealed by critical judgment, and *emunah*, the inherited faith.[10]

Acknowledging and tolerating differences in order to provide a spiritual home for Jews of widely divergent opinions, Conservative Judaism has wholeness as its ideal, to be reached by full adherence to three basic principles. First, the Conservative Jew is willing to see all of life through Jewish eyes and construct life around absolutely binding mitzvot, among them daily prayer, kashrut, observance of Sabbath and holidays; this Jew is committed to ethics and especially the family. Second, the Jewish person is learning by integrating general knowledge into the basically essential Jewish knowledge; the gate to Jewish knowledge is Hebrew. Finally, the Jewish person is a striving Jew who attempts to grow at all times in knowledge, mitzvot, and ethical conduct.

Numerous publications carry information and religious instruction to almost every Conservative home. The prayer book—Siddur Sim Shalom—the Mahzor for the High Holy Days, and the Haggadah for Passover are distinguished by their outstanding English.

Conservative Judaism sees its strength, not in giving its members the security of established ways, but in challenging them to grow, ascending to "God's holy mountain." Tradition and change constantly confront each other in eternal, creative

10. *Emet Ve-Emunah: Statement of Principles of Conservative Judaism* (New York: Jewish Theological Seminary, the Rabbinical Assembly, the United Synagogue, 1988).

tension. Conservative Jews are called to develop the strength necessary to confront this challenge in their lives.

The Conservative movement has spread worldwide, its congregations united in the World Council of Synagogues. Conservative rabbis have also settled in Israel, where the movement, Masorti, has created an educational system, youth movement, summer camps, and a kibbutz. In 1984 a rabbinical seminary was established in Jerusalem that ordains Israelis as conservative Rabbis who serve some fifty synagogues in the land. In spite of its traditional character, Conservative Judaism has not gained recognition by the Orthodox State Rabbinate.

RECONSTRUCTIONISM

Reconstructionism, the only Jewish religious movement rooted in America, sprang from Conservative Judaism as a school of thought that grew into a denomination. It aims to make Judaism meaningful for modern, scientifically oriented Jews who are committed to the Jewish people but cannot in honesty accept the supernatural elements of the Jewish religion.

The Character of Reconstructionism

Reconstructionism's founder, MORDECAI M. KAPLAN (1881–1983), was motivated by his own intellectual honesty and his deep love of the Jewish people and of every individual person. He expounded his thoughts in a number of books, organized a congregation in New York, and founded the periodical *The Reconstructionist*. In 1955 he established a Federation of Reconstructionist Congregations and Fellowships (Havurot). In 1968 the Reconstructionist Rabbinical College was opened, located now at Wyncote, near Philadelphia. The movement has its own Rabbinical Association, press, and prayer books.

Kaplan was influenced by John Dewey (1859–1952), Ahad Ha-am, and the French Jewish sociologist Emile Durkheim (1858–1917). To Dewey, the value of an idea is to be measured by its effect on the lives of its adherents; for Kaplan, Judaism is to be measured by the help it gives the Jew to fulfill the promise of his or her life as a person, as a member of both the Jewish people and humanity. Also like Dewey, Kaplan was a naturalist, rejecting supernatural revelation and dispensation. To Ahad Ha-am, Israel is the hub of Jewish life; Kaplan, a Zionist, sees a mutual cultural interaction between Israel and diaspora. For Durkheim, a people, more than the sum of its members, develops a collective ideal by which its individual members are united and toward which every member is challenged to strive. The individual person thereby transcends small, self-centered concerns and becomes linked to ultimate concerns, receiving in return an orientation in life and the security and courage that result from a sense of belonging. Kaplan applied these insights to the Jewish people.

To Kaplan, the Jewish people is not a chosen people. Claiming chosenness would be both arrogant—other peoples have equally unique qualities—and scientifically unconfirmable. The Jewish people acts as all other peoples do, expressing themselves creatively in language, art, music, literature, and so forth; they create civilizations. The Jewish people form a civilization that has grown continuously, and its roots are in religion. Judaism therefore is not simply a religion but an evolving religious civilization that enhances the lives of its members and makes life more meaningful. Ethical nationhood is its supreme value. When we speak of a *value* we mean something that *ought* to come into being. The value gives orientation to the person, who now strives with every thought, motivation, and action to attain the goal. Within everyone is a power to transcend himself or herself to attain that goal. For the Jew, the highest value is the realization of ethics for individuals and in society. The ultimate *power*—by which humans transcend themselves to reach ethics, the ultimate value—is *God*. This leads Kaplan to what he called his Copernican revolution: We cannot say that God created Israel. Distinguished by the quality of striving for ethical nationhood, the Jewish people, out of its collective ultimate concern, created its God concept: the God of ethics. God is the power within every Jew that compels him or her to transcend himself or herself in striving for the realization of universal ethics.

In the official seal of the Reconstructionist movement, the binding elements of Judaism emanate from Zion to unite Jewish communities throughout the world.

The Jewish God must be a living force for ethical growth, a real presence and power in every Jew's consciousness, not merely a theological idea. Because the Jewish God concept emerged from the Jewish people collectively, the Jewish people must exist as an organic whole and must evolve organically in order for the spirit of the people to unfold within the body of a living community. Divisions within world Jewry must be overcome. Israel and diaspora must enrich each other. The collective spirit must govern every individual life.

To make God's presence real and in order to maintain its creative peoplehood, the Jewish people—out of its own genius—developed observances and rites. All mitzvot are expressions of the people. They remind every member of his or her belongingness and awaken—through God—the power, the spirit of self-transcendence found in striving for ethics. These sacred symbols Kaplan calls *sancta*. The Sabbath, for instance, one of the *sancta*, removes from the Jew the burden of work and makes the Jew feel free. It gives the Jew the will and strength to use his or her freedom on behalf of others, to build a world in which more and more people shall be free, until all are free and may rest. If Jews find that a practice or ritual no longer has meaning for them, cannot be reinterpreted and given new content, then it may be eliminated. As long as a Jew commits himself or herself to the survival of the Jewish people, be it through art or literature or another commitment, even if this Jew rejects all religious observances, he or she remains a member of the Jewish people. In this manner Judaism is "reconstructed," hence the term *Reconstructionism*.

Reconstructionism is absolutely egalitarian. Women are ordained as rabbis and the woman can give her husband a *get*.

The children of a Jewish father and non-Jewish mother are recognized as Jews if they have been brought up as Jews. Its richly annotated prayer book *Kol Haneshamah, Every Soul* (1989 and 1994), features "Meditations," with instructions on posture and breathing, as alternatives to the traditional text. It is absolutely gender neutral and seeks to eliminate the purely masculine character of references to God. God is addressed by the gender-neutral *Yah* plus the attribute of God suitable to the context and placed below in English, for example, Yah / The Incomparable, Yah/The Ultimate , Yah/The Caring One, Yah/The Dear One, etc.

For the Reconstructionist, God is not a personal God; neither can God be discovered through science, for science tells us how the world came into being and what it is. Awareness of God leads us to aspire to what the world ought to be, namely, ethical. God is transnatural. The authors of Scripture, the Sages of the Talmud, and their successors could not yet perceive this fact. A demythologization of Scripture will reveal it and, at the same time, make Scripture and tradition meaningful for the scientifically oriented Jew who cannot accept any supernaturalistic theology.

Kaplan's ideas have been strongly attacked, primarily by the Orthodox, especially for his denying a personal God and the chosenness of Israel. Nevertheless, Kaplan compelled all Jewish denominations to grapple with his ideas, his practical solutions, and his intellectual honesty. Reform and Conservative rabbis have acknowledged his impact.

THE HAVURAH MOVEMENT. The Havurah movement emerged within Reconstructionism in the 1950s and 1960s; subsequently, independent Havurot were founded. A *Havurah*, "fellowship of friends," is a small group of Jews who are closely bonded in life and come together for Torah study, prayer, and activities. The Havurot are democratic and egalitarian. To make Judaism relevant, they create new forms and expressions of Judaism in their worship and lifestyle. Eventually, Conservative and Reform synagogues also promoted the organization of Havurot. The warmth of these gatherings of intelligent and committed Jews has given new vitality to congregational life and new inspiration to rabbis. Thousands of Havurot exist in America; a National Havurah Coordinating Committee has been established.

ORTHODOXY

Most Jewish immigrants from Eastern Europe followed a pre-Mendelssohnian Orthodoxy—a faith that did not doubt. Life in America tended to erode this way of life, and many who felt close to tradition were attracted to Conservatism. Several elements contributed, however, to a resurgence of Orthodox Jewry: many later immigrants from Europe, fleeing Nazi terror, were Neo-Orthodox and considered Conservatism too liberal; numerous American-born Jews, disillusioned with the country's pleasure-driven materialism looked for a firmly disciplined, divinely sanctioned way of life; in addition, the principles, vitality, and warmth of the Hasidic Lubavitcher Rebbe and his school appealed to many Jews.

Orthodox Jewry on its arrival to the U.S. was deeply split, each group having its own synagogue, rabbi, and intensity of practice and observance. The effects are still felt, for the organization of American Orthodoxy is far from the unity found in Reform and Conservative Judaism. Differences exist between rabbis trained in Europe and those trained in America, between the college-educated and those who would consider this kind of training unjewish, between the "centrist" (Hirsch-oriented) and the pre-Mendelssohnian.

Two rabbinical organizations encompass the majority of Orthodox rabbis: the Union of Orthodox Rabbis in the United States and Canada, and the Rabbinical Council of America. The outstanding rabbinical training school for "centrist" Orthodox rabbis is Yeshivah University in New York. Starting as a small yeshivah, it has developed into a full-fledged university not restricted to Orthodox students, and the rabbinical seminary at the center is surrounded by other schools: a liberal arts college, a college for women, and graduate departments; its Albert Einstein Medical School is outstanding. The university and the numerous Orthodox day schools throughout the country reflect Samson Raphael Hirsch's belief that only a synthesis of Judaism and worldly education and culture could make the Jew whole. Of several congregational organizations, the Union of Jewish Orthodox Congregations is the largest and is also the primary agency certifying kosher food. Like Conservatism, Orthodoxy has—at some remove—followed the pattern established by Isaac Meyer Wise: rabbinical organization, seminary, and congregational organization.

The Character of Orthodoxy

Orthodoxy regards itself as the only true Judaism; any Jew who does not fully accept its principles is a sinful Jew. It maintains that God personally revealed Himself at Sinai, choosing Israel as a holy people. The function of the Jewish people in the world is whatever the Eternal had in mind—perhaps a mission, but not necessarily; it is simply God's will that they exist. God personally directs and guides the affairs of the world and of every single person, listening to prayer and answering it in accordance with the divine decision.

God gave the Jewish people the Torah, which contains 613 divine and eternal commandments for the Jews, 248 mitzvot demanding performance of religious acts and 365 prohibitions. Although Maimonides had enumerated each of them, no Jew can observe them all, but their divinity is beyond doubt. The words of the Written Torah are literally God's words, so major changes to the law are impossible. The Written Torah is accompanied by the equally divine Oral Torah, the discussions and halakhic decisions in the Talmud. Within the framework of written and oral Torah, rabbis are invested with a certain limited authority to interpret the law, and this makes some development possible. Ultimately the Shulhan Arukh remains the basic halakhic code to be followed. Changes will therefore be few and limited to individual situations.

Obedience to Torah not only regulates religious practices but also affects every moment of life—rising and washing, food and business, weekdays and holy days, sex, marriage, and divorce—and shapes the Orthodox Jew's outlook in philosophy, psychology, social sciences, and all the other disciplines of life. In reward, the Jew has the assurance of life eternal and resurrection in days to come. The Orthodox expect the coming of a personal Messiah, a God-appointed man who will gather Israel from the "four corners of the earth" to its homeland, restore the Temple and the sacrificial service, and bring peace and brotherhood to all humanity.

The majority of Orthodox Jews are Zionist; a small minority feels that Israel's redemption must not be attempted by human means but must await God's intervention. Those approving of the State of Israel have hailed it as a place where Torah can be lived fully. In a prayer, composed by Israel's Chief Rabbinate and recited in Orthodox congregations, the renewal of the state has been called "the beginning of our redemption." The Orthodox expect that Torah will become the constitution of the land.

The prestige of Orthodoxy as the state religion in Israel, and the power of its rabbinate to determine who, in Israel, is a Jew and who is not, and to decide worldwide who is to be recognized as a rabbi, have given Orthodoxy new strength and determination. Small Orthodox Jewish communities all over the world depend on the Israeli rabbinate for their acceptance as Orthodox. In America, the spirit of k'lal Yisrael, the community of all Jews, has, at times, been weakened by Orthodox Jewry's exclusion of other denominations.

SOME PRACTICAL IMPLICATIONS IN SYNAGOGUE AND WORSHIP

THE POSITION OF WOMEN IN WORSHIP.
Orthodoxy: Minyan of ten, men only. Women, seated in the gallery behind the mehitzah, do not participate in conducting worship.

Conservatism: Minyan, men or women or both. Families usually seated together. Women participate in worship, are ordained as rabbis and function as cantors.

Reform and Reconstructionism: Minyan desirable but not required. Women have equal status, are ordained as rabbis and installed as cantors.

PRAYER AND THE PRAYER BOOK. The basic structure of the traditional service is maintained in each. The three non-Orthodox groups have regarded revision of their prayer books and creation of egalitarian texts as an ongoing concern.

Orthodox: Hebrew, translations have been made, and readings in English are provided in some of the more recent books.[11] The English sermon has also been introduced in a great number of congregations. Traditional service is offered in its entirety.

Conservative and Reconstructionist: designed for shorter services, large selections of readings, including alternate prayers in English.

Reform: more abridged and has large alterations in the traditional text. Hebrew and English are used, large sections of English only.

HOMOSEXUALITY.

Orthodoxy: excludes homosexuals completely.

Conservatism: will not ordain open homosexuals, permits congregations to sever relationship with rabbis who "come out" after being ordained and appointed, helps these rabbis to find a congregation willing to accept them.

Reform and Reconstructionism: no restrictions, Reform has accepted specifically gay congregations into its congregational organization.

Some Problems of Religion in American Jewry

The Hitler period made overwhelming demands on the financial resources of American Jews that forced them to push religion to the background for the sake of fundraising that saved millions of lives and made the State of Israel possible; during this "moratorium on religion," study and observance held minor importance. Each branch of Judaism has found that not all of their members live up to their obligations. Even a synagogue operating along strictly Orthodox lines may have members who follow non-Orthodox ways outside of the synagogue. Many Jews, be they Orthodox, Conservative, or Reform, have moved away from the synagogue and from a consistent observance of religious duties. Knowledge of Judaism is small and membership

11. See David de Sola Pool, ed. and trans., *The Siddur*, publication of the Rabbinical Council of America, Inc. (New York: Behrman House, 1960).

in synagogues patchy, fluctuating with region, generation, marital status, family income, and country of origin.

Many Jews lack the basic knowledge required for deeply religious Jewish living and are unaware of the proud heritage which is theirs. Nevertheless, many parents have come to feel that their children should know at least something about Judaism, and the majority of Jewish children receive some Jewish education, in one-day schools on Sunday and increasingly through weekday Hebrew instruction and in day schools. Practically every child observes Bar Mitzvah or Bat Mitzvah. Congregations and national organizations have emphasized adult education, which is meeting with widening response. Since Hebrew has become the official language of Israel its study has been pursued. Havurot have given new vitality to Judaism and congregations. The influx of rabbis, scholars, and well-educated Jewish laypersons from Europe due to the Nazi persecutions has been helpful and enriching.

Jews have found reasons for survival in the Land of Israel, the Holocaust, and *Yiddishkeit*. But only Jewish religion can give full spirituality and the strength to bear witness in mitzvot. The synagogue, to regain the centrality it has had as the force of Jewish survival, must become active in reaching out to all Jews, vital as a center of learning, innovative in worship, affordable to all Jews, and fully democratic in governance. Competition among the Jewish denominations can strengthen the synagogue when they engage in dialogue on the crucial issues of Jewish life and survival.

Chapter 18

INSECURE CITIZENSHIP

While American Jewry, in spite of reversals, made progress, the experience of Western European Jewry was turbulent. Civil rights were granted reluctantly, consistently attacked, often reversed, and, in the end, wholly annulled. In the end both Western and Eastern European Jewry were wiped out in genocide. Jews desperately fleeing for their lives found both Palestine and America largely closed to them.

FRANCE

The Jews of France were granted civil rights by the French National Assembly in its last session, September 28, 1791. The French armies, fired by revolutionary fervor, swept over Europe and everywhere broke down the walls of the ghettos. But Napoleon Bonaparte, assuming dictatorial powers as First Consul (1799) and subsequently crowning himself emperor (1804) soon whittled down the rights of the Jews. To assure himself of a submissive Jewry, he called an Assembly of Jewish Notables to Paris in 1806 and submitted twelve questions for them to answer, in his favor. The rabbis' answers laid bare the quandary of Jews obligated to balance the demands of the state and religious obligations. In the following year Napoleon convoked a Grand

After proclaiming himself emperor, Napoleon hoped to establish himself as patron of a grateful and submissive Jewish population.

Sanhedrin, supposedly endowed with the same authority as the ancient one, to make the Jewish assembly's responses religiously binding. Judaism was subjected to the same limits as a "church." Further, the government-directed Grand Consistory, an imperial council founded to oversee religion, now supervised regional consistories that oversaw the life and activities of every congregation and all Jews. Napoleon placed all financial transactions of the Jews under government control, required them to obtain annually a letter of "honest conduct," and set additional limitations as well.

Napoleon suffered a devastating defeat when he attempted to conquer Russia, and his foes formed a grand alliance. In Prussia, young Jews streamed to the colors of the Armies of Liberation.

In 1807, Napoleon continued his campaign to control Jewish affairs by convoking a Grand Sanhedrin. He claimed authority over this religious assembly, which in ancient times had been a meeting of the highest Jewish court.

The German States

The Jews were grateful to Prussia. In 1812 it had granted limited citizenship rights to the "protected" Jews in its heartland, excluding, however, the masses living in territory acquired from Poland. At the Congress of Vienna, convened by the victors of the Napoleonic wars, the "Jewish question" came up. A resolution was passed that, for the time being, "the rights already given the Jews in the various states shall be preserved." A recorder, who possibly had been bribed, nullified the resolution by changing the words "in the states" to read "by the states." The rights had been granted *in* the states but *by* Napoleon, not *by* the states—the states themselves had not granted any rights, and so the Jews lost the rights they had.

The reactionary states, especially Bavaria, imposed such heavy restrictions that many Jews emigrated to the United States. Encouraged by the governments' anti-Jewish position and incited by a rabidly antisemitic press, mobs rioted, attacking Jews, plundering their homes and businesses, burning down synagogues, and expelling them from some cities.

The German Reich

Gradually, the German states united, in spite of the failure of revolutions in 1830 and 1848. In 1869, the parliament of the North German States passed an emancipation law that gave Jews full citizenship rights, and Chancellor Otto von Bismarck saw to its implementation. In 1871 all the German states formed the German Reich (empire) and were henceforth bound under one law; even Bavaria had to emancipate its Jews. But Germany was officially a Christian state.

Having been imposed from above and against the will of large segments of the population, the emancipation law remained under assault. Legally equal, the German Jews were still denied access to the civil service, the officers' corps, full professorships, etc. A relentless hate campaign was launched, fueled by an embrace of pan-Germanism and envy of the Jews' prosperity. For example, Houston Stewart Chamberlain (1855–1927), son-in-law of the rabidly antisemitic composer Richard Wagner, claimed in *The Foundations of the Nineteenth Century* to have established the "scientific rationale" for antipathy against the Jews. Based on pseudo-scientific social Darwinism, racial principles, and eugenics, the work "explained" that there were lower races, especially the Jews, and higher ones, culminating in the Germans. The destructive Jewish race had to be removed. Emperor Wilhelm II read nightly to his children from this book and recommended it for the education of officers and government officials. The historian Heinrich von Treitschke (1834–96) coined the slogan, "The Jews are our misfortune," which the Nazis later adopted.

In 1881 a petition called for "the emancipation of the German people from alien domination" and demanded that all Jewish immigration from Eastern Europe be prohibited. The appeal was signed by 250,000 persons and submitted to Bismarck, but he refused to take notice of it. During this period, the Jews of Western Europe had to care for masses of immigrants fleeing pogroms in Russia. But despite giving aid, the Western Jews remained distant from their Eastern European brothers and sisters, mainly from fear that the pronounced hostility of the Germans against the immigrants would lead to general anti-Jewish measures.

THE TREATY OF VERSAILLES AND ITS EFFECT

World War I began in 1914. Continuing discrimination even in war, the German government ordered a Jew census to "prove" that Jews shirked their military duty and were exploiting the people. The results proved the opposite and were withheld.

The Americans entered World War I in 1917, resulting in the defeat of Germany. On November 9, 1918, Emperor Wilhelm II abdicated, and two days later the German armies surrendered. Germany became a republic whose representatives had to sign the peace treaty of Versailles in 1919; henceforth the republic would be maligned for having accepted the harsh treaty.

Eastern Europe

The treaty restored a number of independent states—among them Poland, Latvia, Lithuania, Estonia, Hungary, and Czechoslovakia—that had previously been absorbed by their more powerful neighbors. The states' newly won independence led to an upsurge of nationalism. With the exception of Czechoslovakia, the new states sought in every way to circumvent the provisions of the treaty, which gave minority rights to the Jews and called for the improvement of their civil rights. The new states boycotted and discriminated against the Jews and forced them to emigrate. Repressive laws and heavy taxes deprived the Jews of their livelihood. They lost contact with the non-Jewish population, lived in ever-increasing fear, and were afraid to speak out against the injustice.

In Poland, pogroms broke out and thousands of Jews were murdered. In Romania, antisemites were sustained by the press and secretly supported by the government; in 1937 the king entrusted the government to the antisemitic party, which immediately introduced laws similar to those of the Nazis. The worst pogroms took place in the Ukraine, whose nationalist faction, the Whites, went on a rampage; between 1917 and 1920, at least 75,000 Jews were murdered and many others tortured and raped, in spite of formidable Jewish resistance.

Germany

The Treaty of Versailles condemned Germany as solely guilty of the war, severed large sections from it in both the east and the west, reduced its army, eliminated the navy, deprived it of its colonies, ordained the occupation of the Rhineland, and imposed a huge payment of reparations. This resulted in economic distress and popular resentment.

The collapse of the German army and the abdication of the emperor resulted in a power struggle between monarchists, the democratic leadership, and extreme left-wing socialists. In Bavaria, a left-wing government under a Jewish prime minister, KURT EISNER (1867–1919), assumed power. Eisner was assassinated, as was ROSA LUXEMBURG(1871–1919), the Jewish socialist leader in Berlin.

To fashion a new republic, its founders called a constitutional convention at Weimar, the city of Goethe and Schiller, hoping that their spirit would undergird the new constitution and assure its acceptance among the people. A Jewish lawyer, HUGO PREUSS (1860–1925), was the chief architect of Germany's first truly democratic constitution. But the Weimar Republic rested on shaky foundations, and the people, crushed by reparation payments, were in distress. To reduce its debt, the government devalued the German Mark between 1920 and 1923 to the point where the value of one dollar was equal to over four trillion Marks.

Jew haters blamed the Jews for the misery of the people. The Jews, they claimed, had shirked their duty during the war and had caused the defeat of the German army. In vain did the newly organized Jewish Veterans Organization point out that 100,000 Jews, about one-fifth of all German Jews, had served, 12,000 lost their lives, and 35,000 received decorations.

In 1922, WALTER RATHENAU (1867–1922), a Jew, was made foreign minister and began the difficult task of convincing the Allied Powers to ease their pressure on Germany. Less than six months later "the god-damned Jewish sow" was assassinated by nationalists.

Judges, teachers, professors, army and police officers, and many other officials were holdovers from the imperial period; they hated the republic and bent every effort to destroy it. Resentment was widespread and Germany became a fertile ground for agitators. In this atmosphere Hitler made his first, abortive putsch at Munich in 1923. He was given "honorary confinement" by a sympathetic court and was soon released, having used his confinement to write his book, *Mein Kampf,* his program for the extermination of the Jews.

During a few good years after a currency reform in 1924, agitation abated. Jews took hope, fully immersed themselves in German culture, and became prominent in art, architecture, literature, music, science, and journalism. The universities of Frankfurt and Hamburg owe their beginnings to Jewish initiative and money. The Jewish community also experienced a new flowering in its own spirit. The influence of MARTIN BUBER

(1878–1965) grew; FRANZ ROSENZWEIG (1886–1929) founded the Freies Jüdisches Lehrhaus (Free Jewish Institute). German Jews trusted the sacredness of the Weimar constitution and regarded the antisemitic disturbances as outbursts of rabble. The Jews relied on the "educated" citizens, failing to see that they too were infected by racism and reserved humanism for members of the Germanic "super race."

In 1929, the world economy collapsed as the Great Depression began. Germans were not told that this was a worldwide phenomenon and were persuaded that only Germany was suffering. "Scientific" anti-Jewish publications found increasing resonance. They proclaimed the German people's spirit of shared race, blood, and soil; Jewish participation in German culture was, they said, an attempt to corrupt Germanic purity. The Nazis escalated social tension with ever greater ferocity. The republic was in its death throes. In 1930, the Nazis increased their number of deputies in the German Reichstag, Parliament, from 12 to 107. By 1931, the Nazis had already started persecuting the Jews of Berlin.

THE NAZIS IN POWER

In 1932 the Nazi party won 230 seats. On January 30, 1933, the president of Germany, General Paul von Hindenburg (1847–1934) appointed Hitler chancellor of Germany. Within a few months the entire Weimar constitution was set aside. At the following election, the Nazis garnered 228 seats, which was only 44 percent of the representatives. A fire in the Reichstag building on February 27, 1933, gave the Nazis a pretext for arresting all "communists" and placing them in already established concentration camps. The Nazis dissolved all other parties and instituted one-party rule. By a vote of the streamlined Reichstag, Hitler was given full powers to enact any and all laws he saw fit. The Nazis now used three techniques to rid themselves of their enemies: administrative decrees implemented in secret, open violence, and arrest of all opponents.

The headline of *Der Stürmer*, Nürnberg, 1939, accuses the Jews of ritual murder. The footer quotes Heinrich von Treitschke, "The Jews are our misfortune."

A general boycott of Jewish businesses took place on April 1, 1933, as the paramilitary Brown Shirts stood guard in front of Jewish stores, jeering at those who wished to enter them. On May 10, books by Jews and some by non-Jewish "subversive" authors were publicly burned at bonfires in Berlin, with the help of university students. Decrees in April and May dismissed "non-Aryan" civil servants, public school teachers, and university professors; excluded "non-Aryan" physicians, lawyers, and artists from public institutions, workers from public employ, and journalists from the media; and introduced a quota system at universities. Smears against the Jews filled the press, the most rabid among the papers being, *Der Stürmer* by Julius Streicher. Cities and towns began to post notices at their entrances, "Jews are not wanted here." Under Nazi pressure Jews were forced to "sell" their businesses and properties to "Aryans" at ridiculous prices, and the pitiful proceeds were held by the Nazis. Jews were no longer permitted to occupy an apartment in a house if a single Aryan wished to live there.

The Jews turned to each other for aid. In 1933, they organized the Reichsvertretung der deutschen Juden, the Representative Agency of the German Jews. It was designed to unify all streams of Jewry and represent the entire Jewish community in its dealings with the Nazis. It was led by Rabbi LEO BAECK (1873–1956), renowned scholar and community leader, and OTTO HIRSCH (1885–1941), a distinguished lawyer. Both men refused to leave their people and to emigrate when opportunities were given them. Baeck survived the concentration camp, Hirsch was murdered.

As the Jewish community began to collapse, the tasks of the

organization assumed gigantic proportions. It had to feed and house thousands who, forced from their work and their homes, had become poverty-stricken and homeless. Jewish schools had to be established so that children no longer had to endure the taunts and violence to which they were subjected in public schools. Above all, the agency had to find ways and means for emigration.

To give moments of inspiration and surcease, a system of adult education, led by Martin Buber, and a Kulturbund— Society for Culture—were created. Strictly supervised by the Nazis, they were, for a few years, permitted to offer lectures and courses, plays, concerts, and operas, sending throughout the land first-class performers and teachers, many of whom had been dismissed from their positions. They were forbidden to discuss German culture or perform works by German play-wrights or composers.

With the passage of the Nuremberg laws in 1935, the sys-tematic destruction of the German Jews moved into high gear. Along with many repressive measures, the laws defined just who would be excluded from society: a Jew was defined as a person who had three Jewish grandparents; those with fewer Jewish grandparents were placed in different categories of "mongrels." New restrictions eliminated all rights of the Jews in every sphere of life. Finally, they were placed under the domain of the "secu-rity police" without any legal rights whatsoever.

In May of 1938, Hitler annexed Austria and was received jubilantly by the population, which immediately engaged in savage atrocities against the Jews. More and more Jews were confined to concentration camps. At the end of October, all Jews who were Polish citizens were rounded up in the middle of the night and deported to the Polish border, where they had to spend weeks in no-man's land, hungry and freezing; the Poles refused to take them until forced by international pres-sure to accept some of them. The rest were placed in concen-tration camps in Germany. On November 7, a young Jew, Herschel Grynszpan, incensed at his parents' deportation from Germany to Poland, assassinated a councilor at the German embassy in Paris. This was the pretext for the Nazis to carry out their long-planned pogrom against all Jews. Claiming to be part

The Fasanenstraße synagogue, Berlin, after *Kristallnacht*, November 9, 1938.

of a spontaneous popular uprising, Nazi Stormtroopers and mobs burned down hundreds of synagogues. The night came to be called *Kristallnacht*, night of glass. Jewish homes were attacked, 90 Jews murdered, 7,500 Jewish businesses vandalized, 26,000 Jews rounded up and placed in concentration camps. I was among them.

Following the *Kristallnacht*, Jews were fined one billion marks and ordered to repair the damage. They were expelled from all economic enterprises, their children thrown out of the schools. They were forbidden to attend cultural events or visit parks. Their organizations were dissolved, including Baeck and Hirsch's Reichsvertretung, which was replaced by the Reichsvereinigung der Juden in Deutschland, Association of the Jews in Germany, under the control of the Gestapo, the secret police. Pressure for emigration was increased.

Emigration

In the winter preceding World War II, over half of the German Jews still lived in Germany, one quarter of them on relief.

The world powers, including the U.S., refused to accept more than a trickle of emigrés into their countries. For a short while, Zionists obtained permission from the Nazis for emigrating Jews, who had obtained a visa to Palestine, to buy German goods and export them at the time of emigration. By selling the goods in Palestine, these Jews were able to obtain "capitalist certificates" permitting them to emigrate despite the rigid quota. With permission of the British government, a Youth *aliyah*, directed by Henrietta Szold, brought 3,400 young people from Germany to Palestine. Britain admitted 7,500 children to England. The separation of the children from their parents, which I witnessed, was heartbreaking but saved their lives.

Palestine under British Mandate

As the distress of the European Jews grew, Britain, intent on appeasing the Arabs, closed the doors to the Jewish homeland. From the beginning the British government had resisted the full implementation of the Balfour Declaration. The first High Commissioner Sir Herbert Samuel, a Jew, worked hard to appease the Arabs and made it clear that Arab interests were to determine policy. Jewish efforts to negotiate with the Palestinians brought no results, in part because British officials incited them to rise up. In 1920 Palestinians rioted in Jerusalem, in 1921 they attacked the immigrant center at Jaffa. Samuel suspended Jewish immigration but was overruled by Winston Churchill, then Colonial Secretary.

Between 1920 and 1929, Jewish immigration to Palestine grew by approximately 80,000. The Yishuv established self-rule institutions, some of them clandestine, including a defense force, the Haganah; the chief rabbinate was given authority over matrimonial matters. The Arab movement became more extreme and rejected all compromise under the influence of Amin el-Husseini, a fanatic Jew hater whom Samuel installed as Mufti of Jerusalem. In 1929 a dispute over Jewish access to the Western Wall provoked violent attacks in a number of areas. For the most part, the attacks were repelled by the Jewish defense forces, but in Hebron scholars and yeshiva students were massacred. Orthodox world Jewry appointed a day of fasting.

A British investigation, headed by Sir Walter Shaw, blamed the Arabs for the attacks but saw the cause of their hostility in Jewish immigration and expansion. Immigration and land purchases were to be restricted. Despite the rejection of the new policies by the League of Nations and the protest of the Yishuv, Britain halted all Jewish immigration. In 1930 Britain declared that as long as there was any unemployment among Arabs, Jewish immigration should not be permitted. Under the impact of numerous protests, however, the British government retreated; it would honor its obligation to facilitate Jewish immigration.

Between 1933 and 1939 the Yishuv had doubled its size. In 1937, the British proposed the dividing of the land: Israel was to receive the coastal strip, Jezreel, and enclaves in Jerusalem, Lydda, Bethlehem, Ramleh, and Jaffa; the rest of the territory was to be assigned to the Arabs, and Jews forbidden to acquire land there. Jewish immigration was to be reduced to 8,000 per year. Incensed by having to yield any land, the neighboring Arab states came to the aid of the Palestinians, and Jews, the British, and moderate Arabs were attacked. The Mufti took up residence in Germany, where Hitler received him as an honored guest. The British offered wider concessions, attempting to appease Hitler and fearful that the Arabs would link themselves to the Nazis.

In 1939, shortly before the outbreak of World War II, Jews and representatives from the Arab states were invited to London. This marked the recognition of the Arab states as parties to the Palestinian-Jewish dispute. Britain proposed that a Palestinian state was to be established and gain full independence in ten years. In the first five years a total of 75,000 Jews were to be admitted, after that, none without permission of the Arabs. The Arabs rejected the proposal, demanding an immediate end to immigration and a shorter transition period. The Yishuv violently protested. David Ben-Gurion proposed non-cooperation with Britain; Rabbi ABBA HILLEL SILVER, an American Zionist leader, counseled keeping up the protest but not deserting Britain, which was facing Hitler's attack. In September, World War II broke out, and the Yishuv expressed its readiness to join Britain in the struggle against Hitler. The Homeland, surrounded by Arab enemies and abandoned by Britain, appeared to be doomed.

Chapter 19

WAR AND HOLOCAUST

POLAND. On September 1, 1939, the Germans invaded Poland and rapidly conquered it. According to a non-aggression pact with the USSR, the two countries divided Poland and the Baltic states among themselves. Western Poland was declared part of Germany, and Jews throughout the territory were expelled to Lodz, which became a ghetto. Forced to travel on foot, hundreds froze to death on the road.

In 1940, another ghetto was established in Warsaw, and Jews were forced to live in either Lodz or Warsaw. All the restrictions in effect for German Jews were imposed on them, and they were placed in the custody of the special security police.

WESTERN EUROPE. In Germany the yellow star was introduced and, forced to wear it, Jews were more completely isolated. The possession of a telephone was illegal. Automobiles were confiscated, use of public trasportation was prohibited.

The destruction of the Warsaw ghetto after the uprising of 1943.

The Jews of the Warsaw ghetto acted to retain their human dignity. They purchased arms secretly from left-wing partisans, and on January 13, 1943, Jews destined for deportation fired on German soldiers and escaped. The Nazis, determined to wipe out the ghetto, surrounded it. When they entered it on April 19 with armored cars and artillery, they found determined resistance. It took five weeks to wipe out the Jews. The Warsaw ghetto uprising became a symbol of resistance and a witness to the heroic defenders' unshaken faith in the future of the Jewish people. The fighters gave strength to the rest of Jewry under siege, as did Jews who formed partisan groups in various parts of Poland and Russia; revolts broke out even in concentration camps.

Radios were banned and newspapers forbidden. A curfew was imposed. Evicted from their dwellings, Jews were crammed together in "Jew Houses," ready for deportation. They received no milk, meat, fish, or eggs; they were allowed only a small amount of food, for which they could shop only after all other customers had been served and the stores were already empty.

In a *Blitzkrieg*, "lightning war," Germany overran Holland, Belgium, Luxembourg, France, Denmark, and Norway. The Germans divided France into a northern occupied region and a semi-autonomous southern state, whose capital was Vichy. In the occupied region, special registration for Jews was initiated and 40,000 "alien" Jews, most of them fugitives from Germany, were placed in concentration camps. The Vichy government chose to adopt Nazi measures; French Jews were deprived of all public activities, alien Jews lost all civil rights, and Polish Jews who had become naturalized French citizens were arrested.

In Holland, Jewish property was confiscated, civil rights rescinded, and the Jewish quarter of Amster-

Among the Jews sheltered by the Dutch were Anne Frank and her parents. Her diaries, written in the midst of terror, reveal a moving faith in the goodness of human beings. Denounced by a Dutch collaborator, she died in a concentration camp. Photo credit: ©AFF/AFS, Amsterdam, The Netherlands.

Rescued in small boats, Danish Jews were among the few to survive.

dam invaded by Germans and Dutch collaborators. Jewish hostages were tortured and murdered. Most of the Dutch resisted, however. The workers of Amsterdam showed solidarity with the Jews by calling a general strike. Many Jews were secretly harbored by Dutch citizens, who risked their lives doing so.

The Danes exhibited full solidarity with the Jews. King Christian refused to permit any anti-Jewish laws. He died when he was thrown from his horse, which had probably been drugged. Appraised of a forthcoming roundup of the Jews, the Danes secretly transported them in trawlers and fishing boats across stormy seas to neutral Sweden. Their humanity has set an everlasting example.

Finland did not hand over its Jews. Bulgaria firmly resisted German pressure, and its Jews were saved. The Jews of Yugoslavia fled to Italy, where they were placed in concentration camps. A number of Jews found refuge in the Vatican.

EASTERN EUROPE. Having completed their conquest of western Europe, the Germans, breaking their treaty with the

USSR, attacked Soviet Russia on June 22, 1941. In preparation the Germans had trained within its SS (storm troopers) special *Einsatztruppen,* "Action Brigades," whose task it was to murder officials, Jews, and gypsies, with the full cooperation of the army.

In 1944, Admiral Horty, the ruler of Hungary, saw the defeat of the Nazis at hand and granted a stay to Jews who had visas to other countries. The Swedish representative at Budapest, Raoul Wallenberg, issued visas to thousands and saved their lives. On entering the city, the Russians arrested him, and he vanished. The United States made him an honorary citizen.

The Germans organized local gangs to assist in pogroms. Usually the Action Brigades would enter a city, send for the rabbi, and order him to assemble all the Jews for registration and resettlement. The Jews assembled and then were taken outside the cities to be murdered by the Germans and their Ukrainian, White Russian, Lithuanian, and Latvian collaborators. Between September and December of 1941, close to 150,000 Jews were murdered, 34,000 of them on Yom Kippur at Babi Yar, near Kiev in the Ukraine. No memorial marked the place of their martyrdom, but the Russian poet Yevtushenko courageously reminded his country of this deliberate silence, and President George Bush insisted on visiting the spot when he traveled to the Ukraine.

Concentration camp bunks at Buchenwald.

Extermination made room in the ghettos for more Jews from the West. The ghettos were governed by Nazi-imposed *Judenräte,* "Jews' Councils," composed of prominent Jews. Faced with the task of selecting the daily contingent for deportation and death, some warned their people, others sought to gain postponements, committed suicide, or went with their people to the crematoria. A few cooperated with the Nazis, hoping to gain privileges for themselves.

THE "FINAL SOLUTION." On January 20, 1942, a group of Nazi leaders meeting in a villa at the

Wannsee, a lake near Berlin, determined the speedy *Endlösung*, "final solution" of the Jewish question—the extermination of 11 million Jews, including those of England, which they were certain of conquering. Adolf Eichmann was in charge. Theresienstadt was the transit camp to the extermination camps. Gas chambers and crematoria were built at Auschwitz, Majdanek, Belzec, Chelmno, Sobibor, and Treblinka. German chemists found a cheap and effective poison gas.

Wedding rings confiscated at Auschwitz.

The Judenrat of Warsaw had to furnish a minimum of 6,000 Jews daily for "resettlement," the Lodz ghetto a similar number. By the end of 1942, 1,274,166 Jews had been "resettled." They were joined by the Jews of Germany, Holland, Belgium, and the German satellite states of Greece, Slovakia, and Croatia.

LIBERATION. The liberation of the pitiful remnant of European Jewry came with the invasion of Germany and Eastern Europe by the Allies. The first to enter the extermination camps were Japanese and Black soldiers of the American army, which at that time was racially segregated. They were aghast at the sight of living skeletons and heaps of dead. Knowing all too well the pain of the discriminated, these American soldiers opened their hearts and hands to the Jews, whom racial hatred had condemned to death, embraced them and brought them to freedom. To the Jewish inmates they were and have remained angels of mercy, messengers of God.

The extermination of the Jews of Europe, Hitler's most determined ambition, largely succeeded, for its execution was supported by the common people, the army, the civil service, scholars and scientists, legislators, and courts.

After the war, Nazi ringleaders were brought before an international court at Nuremberg, tried, convicted, and sentenced as criminals. This legal process was necessary, but it also gave the impression that only those convicted as "war criminals"—and not the people as a whole—were responsible. We hear too often, "I did not know!" People may not have known the extent of the atrocities, but all were aware of them. I was among the Jews publicly marched through the city streets of Oldenburg past the burned out synagogue, to jail and then to the train that took us to Sachsenhausen; the population flanked the sidewalks.

THE CHURCHES AND THE PEOPLE. The official German Lutheran Church became nazified; the Confessional Church, although organized in opposition to the Nazis, saw no Christian duty to take a stand against the persecution of the Jews. Among the Catholic bishops, some showed courage, others embraced Nazism. Among the religious orders and lower clergy, in Germany and especially in France and Italy, were staunch defenders and helpers of the Jews, men and women who gave their lives for them. The dean of the Catholic cathedral of Berlin, Bernhard Lichtenberger, publicly prayed daily for the Jews; he died being transported from one concentration camp to another. In 1996 he was beatified by Pope John Paul II. Among the public opponents of the Nazis was the Protestant pastor Dietrich Bonhoeffer, who was executed by them. A number of high army officers, led by Colonel Count von Stauffenberg, attempted to assassinate Hitler; they all were executed. And among the common people were a few with the courage to save Jews. In Munich, two students—Hans Scholl and his sister Sophie—their professor, Kurt Huber, and a group of followers organized the White Rose in opposition to the Nazis; they were all executed. Their idealism indicates that the striving for *tikkun olam*, the restoration of the world, was alive even in Nazi Germany. After the war, I met a Mrs. Gerschütz in Stadtlauringen, an old lady who had saved the lives of two Jewish women. "I am no hero," she told me, "I only did my Christian and human duty." But in addition to these few resisters was a larger number of people who opposed the Nazis but were too weak to voice opposition, being under relentless surveillance by the Secret Police, and a very large number that identified and cooperated with the Nazis to varying degrees.

APPROXIMATE NUMBER MURDERED

Total between 4.5 and 6 million

Country	Before the Holocaust	After the Holocaust	Victims
Germany	300,000	30,000	270,000
Holland	130,000	30,000	100,000
Belgium	80,000	45,000	35,000
France	300,000	200,000	100,000
Austria	90,000	10,000	80,000
Hungary	450,000	150,000	300,000
Czechoslovakia	275,000	35,000	240,000
Italy	60,000	30,000	30,000
Yugoslavia	75,000	15,000	60,000
Greece	75,000	10,000	65,000
Romania	800,000	425,000	375,000
Russia	3,000,000	2,000,000	1,000,000
Poland	3,300,000	70,000	3,230,000

CONCENTRATION CAMPS

Country	Camp
Germany	Bergen-Belsen, Buchenwald, Dachau, Dora, Grossrosen, Neuengamme, Niederhagen, Ravensbrück, Sachsenhausen, Stutthof, Westerbork
Austria	Mauthausen, Theresienstadt
France	Drancy, Gurs, Natzweiler, Pithivier, Rivesaltes, Vittel
Holland and Belgium	Malines, Vaught
Italy	Fossoli
Yugoslavia and Romania	Jasenovac, Kluj, Samjiste, Zemun
Latvia and Estonia	Klooga, Riga

Extermination Camps, all in Poland: Auschwitz, Belzec, Chelmno, Majdanek, Sobibor, Treblinka

THE WORLD'S RESPONSE

THE UNITED STATES. In the United States, the impact of German propaganda was profound. At no other time was antisemitism in America as widespread. Franklin D. Roosevelt, primarily concerned with retaining popularity and votes among all groups, hedged. The State Department instructed its consulates to reduce the number of visas issued to Jews; only after the *Kristallnacht* did Roosevelt order that the quotas be filled. A ship, the *St. Louis,* filled with Jewish refugees and destined for Cuba, was turned away as Cuba reneged on its pledge to admit them. The captain slowly sailed along the Florida coast, hoping that the United States would accept the refugees, but the beaches were manned with military guards to prevent any of the passengers from swimming ashore. The ship returned to Germany, delivering its Jewish passengers to their fate.

When the first news of the exterminations became known, the State Department warned the Jews of America not to publicize them. Neither the U.S. nor England nor any of the allies tried to destroy Auschwitz by bombing the death camp or the railroad tracks leading to it. When the atrocities increased, the State Department forbade its foreign representatives to inform Jewish leaders. The Jewish leadership, caught between fear of antisemitic reaction and concern for its Jewish brothers and sisters, vacillated between protests, appeals, and silence. An American Jewish Emergency Committee was established in 1943. Insistent Jewish protests and the intercession of Henry Morgenthau, Jr., the Jewish Secretary of the Treasury, led to the creation of a War Refugee Board in 1944. By then practically all Jews had been deported to death camps. Even so, the War Refugee Board rescued thousands. A more humane U.S. policy could have saved millions.

ENGLAND. While Winston Churchill advocated rescue for the Jews, his foreign secretary, Anthony Eden, successfully thwarted it. When the British learned that Germany would accept a ransom to free 70,000 Romanian Jews, Britain obstructed it. In 1941, the *Struma,* a rickety ship filled with Romanian Jewish refugees, was driven back by the British from landing in Palestine. It sank and only one of its 770 passengers survived.

RUSSIA. While being allied with Germany, Russia surrendered Jews to the Nazis. After the outbreak of the war, the invading Germans found their most active accomplices among the Ukrainians and Lithuanians. The Russian government gave the Jews no protection and never acknowledged their extermination. It provided no support to Jewish partisans and never acknowledged their contributions. When two Jewish leaders,

Erlich and Alter, proposed the establishment of a Jewish anti-fascist committee, they were executed.

THE YISHUV. The Yishuv faced two tasks, aiding the British militarily and rescuing Jews. When the advance of the Germans in North Africa threatened the British, the tension between the British and the Yishuv abated and the repression of the Jewish defense force, the Haganah, eased. Jewish forces attached to the British army contributed to Rommel's defeat at El Alamein in 1942. Later, Jewish parachutists were sent behind enemy lines in Europe. A Jewish brigade of 25,000 men participated in the Allied invasion of Italy. When the immediate danger had passed, however, the British renewed their harassment of the Yishuv and confiscated the arms of the Haganah. The Irgun Tzevai Leumi, a secret Jewish military force, and other clandestine Jewish defense organizations gained in strength.

In 1942, the Zionist Organization, meeting at the Biltmore Hotel in New York, passed the Biltmore Declaration. It demanded the immediate opening of Palestine for Jewish immigration under the exclusive jurisdiction of the Jewish Agency and, above all, called for the establishment of a Jewish commonwealth in Palestine immediately after the end of hostilities. In 1944 the U.S. Congress passed a resolution demanding the opening of Palestine and calling for the establishment of a democratic Jewish commonwealth. President Roosevelt, always vacillating, expressed his support but also assured King Ibn Saud of Arabia that nothing would be done that could be considered hostile by the Arabs. Some immigrants arriving in Palestine were banished by the British to Mauritius, an island in the Indian Ocean; others were admitted as an "act of grace." The conflict was to escalate.

THE RETROSPECTIVE VIEW OF A VICTIM

I was abruptly arrested in the *Kristallnacht* and subsequently taken to jail and hence to the Sachsenhausen concentration camp. The sudden transition to captivity was shattering. I beat the cell walls with my hands crying out, "What have I done?" We were supposed to be treated well and to be released as soon as we could prove that we had visas for immediate emigration. But I was beaten and saw others beaten, tortured, and kicked to death. As I grow old I cannot get out of my mind the torture that the old people suffered, standing at attention, like all of us, for twenty-four hours, in bitter cold, after being chased into the camp by storm troopers and vicious dogs. Could I do it today? Running, I severely hurt my ankle falling over a stone, and still suffer from the effects. I would have been kicked senseless or shot had my friends not lifted me up and supported me. The indignities of being publicly examined standing naked, of being shaven, beaten, put in flimsy prison garb, being crowded in icy barracks, the hunger, were crushing. The counting and recounting, especially in the drizzle before dawn, lasted for hours and exhausted body and mind. Purposeless slave labor ravaged body and soul. There was the grinding uncertainty regarding our fate, the consciousness of being wholly surrendered to the ruthlessness of our tormentors. The harangues of the commandant repeatedly impressed upon us that we were the scum of the earth. Our treatment, the total absence of rest, the knowledge conveyed to us by our tormentors that we had no right to live—all were designed to transform us into automata wholly devoid of human dignity. These were "good conditions." We were warned never to "slander" the camps, for Hitler's hand would reach us, even across the seas. We signed that we had been treated well.

One early morning, dark, drizzly, when the search lights played over the silent mass to be counted and the commander screamed that we deserved execution, I expected the machine guns to mow us down at any moment and said "Sh'ma." At that instant I experienced the Presence of God as I had never experienced it before or was to afterwards. God was there, in exile, with us, suffering. I was ready to die for God and my people.

These experiences have given me some idea of the immensely more brutal ordeal endured by those who knew there was no hope—and a regard for their faith. They did not become automata. Among them was my mother and many relatives. I know they went to their death in dignity, giving their lives as martyrs of God. I must believe that, must believe in God, for the thought that they all died in vain would be intolerable.

No report or description can fully convey the suffering, humiliation, heroism, and faith of the martyrs. We may acquire an inkling as we identify with our people.

Chapter 20

ISRAEL REBORN

Out of Shoah, the catastrophe of the Holocaust, the State of Israel emerged. Some Jews have seen in the rebirth of the State of Israel the renewed presence of God in history, after the divine absence during the Holocaust. The rebirth was accompanied by bitter struggles.

RISING TENSIONS AFTER WORLD WAR II

The post-war British Labor government pursued a harsh anti-Jewish policy. By 1946, Britain had placed 200,000 liberated European Jews in displaced persons' camps instead of admitting them to Palestine. Jews were banished from the British occupation zone in Germany. President Harry S. Truman requested that 100,000 immigrants be immediately admitted to Palestine. His request was rebuffed by the British Foreign Secretary Ernest Bevin on the grounds that Britain could not antagonize the Muslim world. Bevin cynically proposed that European

The Haganah, a volunteer army of the Jewish settlers before the establishment of Israel, patrol the salt hills at the southern end of the Dead Sea.

When in July of 1947, the ship Exodus, *with 4,500 immigrants from France, approached Palestine's shores, it was attacked by British destroyers, brought under escort to Haifa, and the passengers forcibly returned to Germany.*

Jews should return and give aid to their former countries—where they had been tortured and their families killed—"but without getting too much at the head of the queue."

With Britain unable to resolve conflict in Palestine, the United Nations sought a solution. Strongly supported by the United States and the USSR, the UN General Assembly, on November 29, 1947, ordered that Palestine be partitioned between Jews and Arabs. Britain was to evacuate by August 1, 1948, and to open one port to Jewish immigration. The Arabs immediately organized a "Liberation Army," to which the British granted entry into Palestine. While the Haganah realized it had to hold as much territory as possible and advanced in all areas of the land, Arab hostilities steadily increased, abetted by Britain's refusal to intervene. To open the road for an Arab invasion before the Yishuv could muster its forces, the British declared that they were evacuating the country prematurely, on May 15.

Centuries of expectation were fulfilled when Israel's first president, David Ben-Gurion, read the country's Declaration of Independence in 1948.

Israel Declares Independence

In the midst of this danger, Israel declared its independence when delegates assembled at Tel Aviv on May 14, 1948. DAVID BEN-GURION (1886–1973) read the Declaration of Independence, saying,

> By virtue of our national and intrinsic right and on the strength of the resolution of the United Nations General Assembly we hereby declare the establishment of a Jewish state in Palestine, which shall be known as the State of Israel.

They chose as a flag a blue Magen David on a white ground and two broad blue stripes, the colors white and blue being mentioned in Torah (Num. 15:38) for the tzitzit, the fringes along the edge of the prayer shawl. The seven-branched menorah was its coat of arms. CHAIM WEIZMAN (1874–1952) became Israel's first president, Ben-Gurion the prime minister. The U.S. and USSR were the first nations to recognize Israel.

Immediately, Egypt, Lebanon, Syria, Iraq, and Jordan attacked Israel from all sides. Under severe pressures, the Yishuv expanded its fighting force, and immigrants joined as soon as they arrived. A navy and air force were created with the help of supplies purchased abroad. In June, an armistice was mediated by the UN that imposed unacceptable conditions on Israel, including the eventual annexation of the Jewish state by Jordan. On July 9, fighting resumed.

Mediated by the American Ralph Bunche, truce agreements were concluded with Egypt, Lebanon, Jordan, and Syria. The truce was to be only the first step toward a future, negotiated peace agreement that would give

Chaim Weizman, first president of Israel, urged a synthesis of Hebrew culture, political Zionism, and democracy.

Israel secure borders. With the truce, the borders followed the accidental positions of the opposing armies when the truce was called. The land was serrated, Jerusalem divided, and no security was provided. Free access to Jewish holy sites, now located in Jordan, was one of the provisions of the armistice; the Arabs did not keep this pledge.

The State of Israel and World Jewry

The rebirth of the State of Israel was a watershed for world Jewry. With Jews all over the world, I felt personally "reborn" when independence was declared. The perennial prayer of the Jewish people had been answered. The restoration of Israel gave world Jewry new unity, strength, and pride in being Jews. Affirming Jewish peoplehood, Israel has found the courage to fight in defense of Jewish and human rights. Israel has become one rationale for survival.

The sovereign state envisioned by the Yishuv, more than a politically independent entity, was to become a spiritual and cultural center. A remarkable number of institutions were created while the Yishuv was still under siege, both before and after the establishment of the State of Israel. Hebrew, modernized by ELIEZER BEN-YEHUDAH (1858–1922), became the national language and the medium of expression for poets, playwrights, novelists, scholars, and scientists. The arts flourished: Habimah (the national theater), and a national Philharmonic, inaugurated by Arturo Toscanini, were established. The universal school system culminated in the Hebrew University at Jerusalem, the Technion (the Technical University at Haifa), and the Agricultural Research Institute at Rehovot (later bearing Weizman's name), to which later the Universities of Tel Aviv, Haifa, and the University of the Negev South (now Ben-Gurion University) were added. The Hadassah medical network and the medical school were initiated. Histadrut, the union of workers, guided by its first secretary, David Ben-Gurion, encompassed both management and labor and established a universal health insurance. In Rabbi ABRAHAM ISAAC KOOK (1864–1935), its first Ashkenasi Chief Rabbi, the Yishuv found a leader of great spirituality, a poet and mystic filled with the deepest love for his people and all of humanity. New yeshivot emerged. Democratic governmental institutions were put in place on every level.

The new state began to recognize that its internal consolidation had to be combined with welcoming all Jewish refugees from every part of the world. A primary task was the "Gathering of the Exiles"; recognizing that millions of Jews could have been saved during the Holocaust had there been an Israel, the state opened its doors wide, greeting the arrivals with enthusiasm. First came the homeless Jews, who were waiting in transit camps in Cyprus and Germany. Jews from Arab lands—Egypt, Yemen, Libya, Iraq, Morocco, and Tunisia— followed. Jews arrived from Bulgaria, Poland, Romania, and Czechoslovakia. The Jews from Ethiopia, having

Rav Abraham Isaac Kook, first Ashkenasi Chief Rabbi in Palestine, left behind him a legacy of spirituality and poetry that demonstrates his deep love for Zion and humanity.

suffered persecution over thousands of years, were finally brought home. A Law of Return was passed, granting Jews Israeli citizenship from the moment they set foot on its soil. The absorption of these large masses of immigrants, including entire liquidated diaspora communities with their aged, infirm, and even criminals, imposed heavy burdens on Israel. The immigrants had to be settled, taught Hebrew, and acculturated to the modern world and Israel's way of life.

THE SINAI CAMPAIGN

War against Israel united Arab leaders and rallied their people. Every offer by Israel to negotiate was rejected. Israel retaliated against roaming bands of terrorists, the Fedayeen, but was called the aggressor. In 1955 the USSR, together with its satellites, supplied vast quantities of arms to Egypt. This allowed Egypt to arm the entire Arab world for an attack against Israel and to assume leadership of a joint Arab command. The Gulf of Aqaba was blockaded, depriving Israel of access to the Red Sea and its southern port of Eilat.

In 1956, the U.S. refused to provide funds for the building of the Aswan Dam. In retaliation, Gamal Abdul Nasser, the ruler of Egypt, nationalized the Suez Canal, an international waterway built by the French and the British that links the Mediterranean Sea with the Indian Ocean. The canal was closed to Israeli shipping, and open to ships of other nations only by permission of the Egyptian authorities. France and Britain invaded Egypt, and with Israel's assistance lifted the blockade and liquidated the Fedayeen camps. To forestall an international war, with the USSR on the Arab side, President Eisenhower called for a withdrawal of all troops, and Israel had to retreat. Eisenhower was unable to keep his pledge to keep the Suez Canal open to Israel. A UN force was placed along the borders to assure calm. Nasser had won Israel's withdrawal, gained prestige in the Arab world, and armed his country and its allies.

THE SIX DAY WAR

In 1967, Syria increased its shelling of Israel from the Golan Heights and sent saboteurs into the land. Retaliating, the Israeli air force shot down Syrian aircraft stationed at Damascus.

On Egypt's demand, the protective UN border force was removed. Egypt, Jordan, Saudi Arabia, Kuwait, and Iraq united their forces and prepared for war. The Arab press predicted the extermination of Israel. On May 15, a huge Egyptian army took positions in the Sinai peninsula; by June 5, Egypt's air force and all the Arab armies were poised for attack.

Fearing for its life, Israel took the offensive, destroying the air forces of Egypt, Syria, Jordan, and Iraq, thereby obtaining domination of the skies. In a gigantic desert battle the mobile Israeli tanks encircled and destroyed the heavy enemy tanks and

For many Jews, the Six Day War of 1967 reaffirmed belief in the presence of God in history.

moved toward the Suez Canal, where they enclosed Nasser's forces and incapacitated them. Israeli forces took the Golan Heights and advanced to within a few miles of Damascus. They took the Sinai peninsula, the Gaza strip, the Old City of Jerusalem, and the West Bank of the Jordan River. In six days—June 5–10—the enemy had been routed.

Having won the war, Israel declared its readiness for direct peace negotiations with the Arabs. But the UN condemned Israel as the aggressor and demanded Israel's immediate withdrawal behind its prewar borders as the precondition for a cease-fire. The borders offered Israel no security. No peace agreement was reached.

Israel's Prime Minister GOLDA MEIR (1898–1978) and President Nixon worked out a cease-fire formula. Israel would withdraw to new but secure borders, to be agreed on in direct peace negotiations among all parties. The United States promised to provide Israel with weapons to defend itself. On these terms, President Nixon obtained a cease-fire from Egypt in 1970.

The Six Day War changed Israel's relationship with many nations. Because of its dependence on America, Israel was

At the end of the Six Day War, Jews rejoiced at the Western Wall of Jerusalem. For the first time since the establishment of the State of Israel, Judaism's holiest place, Jerusalem's Western Wall, was accessible to Jews.

branded an enemy of the developing world, and Third World countries, even those to whom Israel had given help, severed diplomatic relations. Israel's new, defensible borders, had not been secured through international agreements, and the world was to speak of "occupied territories."

The Six Day War also changed the relationship between Israelis and diaspora Jewry. Recognition of diaspora Jewry by the Israelis has unfolded gradually. The native youth of Israel, called *Sabras* after a cactus that is prickly on the outside and sweet on the inside, considered the period between the fall of the Temple in the year 70 C.E. and the rebuilding of the Land as non-history; they saw diaspora Jewry as uncreative, unjewish, and decadent. During the Six Day War, they came to recognize the identification of diaspora Jewry with Israel and the value of its commitment to Israel's survival and welfare.

THE YOM KIPPUR WAR

Anwar Sadat, Nasser's successor, remained under pressure to free Arab territories from "Israeli occupation." But the Israelis had an armistice with Egypt and saw no threat from the Arab armies, which were being supplied steadily by the USSR. The Arab countries also exerted a growing influence in the West, which was ever more dependent on Arab oil.

In 1973 Egypt and Syria launched a massive surprise attack on Yom Kippur, the holiest day of the Jewish year. Israel's initial losses were high, and the country was in grave danger. Eventually, the Israelis stemmed the attacks. An armistice was arranged by the United States, and a United Nations force was again placed between Egypt and Israel. Israel's victory was bought at grave costs in lives and matériel.

The danger to Israel sealed the bond between Israel and the diaspora, which in turn led to an unparalleled reawakening of the Jewish spirit. Jews knew that their souls and their destiny were bound to Israel. Israel stood alone, and with it all of Jewry. Widespread demonstrations took place, and donations poured into the Land. Students and people from all walks of life clamored to interrupt their studies and their work to go and serve in Israel. The great Jewish thinker ABRAHAM HESCHEL (1907–1973), whose entire life had been dedicated to Judaism, expressed this rich upwelling of commitment to Israel: "Up to this moment I had not known how Jewish I was."

TERRORISM. Arab terrorism continued and claimed many innocent victims in Israel and throughout the world. The Palestine Liberation Organization, PLO, provided terrorism with a centralized, coordinating force. Headed by Yasser Arafat, its constitution was committed to the annihilation of Israel. The PLO gained recognition as the only legitimate representative of the Palestinians. Eventually, it was accepted by western countries, who depended on Arab oil.

PEACE BETWEEN ISRAEL AND EGYPT

In 1977, President Anwar Sadat of Egypt, who had spearheaded the Yom Kippur War, sought the way of peace. Sadat

In 1979, Israel's Menachem Begin and Egypt's Anwar Sadat celebrate the first peace agreement to be reached between the two countries.

came to Jerusalem, was enthusiastically received, and addressed the Knesset, Israel's parliament, endorsing the peace dialogue. In 1978, he sent an open letter to American Jews, asking them to assume responsibility for creating peace between Israel and Egypt. President Carter invited Sadat and Israel's Prime Minister MENACHEM BEGIN (1913–1992) to Camp David, to hammer out a peace treaty. Israel was in principle prepared to return "occupied" Arab territory as a price of peace, but it had to retain some areas for security reasons and had to keep all of Jerusalem, its only holy city. The treaty was a compromise—Israel would return the Sinai Peninsula to Egypt—and the statement on the Palestinians was vague enough to be acceptable to both parties. On March 26, 1979, the treaty was signed. Sadat had broken the unanimous Arab hostility against Israel. He was assassinated in 1981; under his successor, Hosni Mubarak, relations cooled, but the peace has held.

Confrontations

The late 1970s witnessed profound changes in the Middle East. Islamic fundamentalism spread throughout the Muslim world as groups like the Hezbollah, "Party of God," campaigned for a return of all Islamic states to the rule of the Quran in its fundamentalist interpretation. Lebanon was plunged into a civil war, and terrorism spilled over into northern Israel as far as Tel Aviv. To protect itself against the threat of terrorists, Israel advanced repeatedly into Lebanon. Wholly devastated, Lebanon, the only other non-Muslim state in the region besides Israel, collapsed.

Following the war with Lebanon, a small Israeli peace movement, calling for *Shalom Ahshav*, "peace now," gained momentum and followers; its members were prepared to surrender land in exchange for a secure peace. In turn, Jewish fundamentalists founded in 1973 *Gush Emunim*, "Block of the Faithful"; to them, the conflicts of the time were the "birth pangs of the Messiah," whose arrival was conditional on Jewish sovereignty over all the territory defined by Torah. The group's members, seeing themselves as God's army, settled in the "occupied territories" and took violent actions against Palestinians. The Israeli government similarly opposed any territorial concessions. Frustrated, but certain of Arab support, Palestinian groups, in 1978, formed the Intifada, an insurrection using frequent street attacks to wear down the Israelis. After the dissolution of the USSR, Jews from Russia streamed into Israel, and additional settlements emerged in the "occupied territories." The Palestinians became more apprehensive and Intifada activities increased.

ROADS TO PEACE

In spite of conflict, peace began to become possible. Following the war with Lebanon, Yasser Arafat slowly began to seek compromise with Israel. In 1988, he endorsed UN Resolution 242, recognizing Israel within defensible borders, and Resolution 338, calling for the evacuation of all "occupied territories." This was the PLO's first acknowledgment of Israel's right to exist. Following the Gulf War in 1991, Arab states turned to the United States and became more amenable to negotiations with Israel.

Meanwhile, the conservative government of YITZHAK SHAMIR (b. 1915) had been replaced by the labor government of YITZHAK

RABIN (1922–1995), who was open to compromise. President Bush pushed for an Arab-Israeli peace conference, which was convened in October of 1991; no resolution was reached until 1993.

In 1993, an agreement, whose architect was Israel's Foreign Minister SHIMON PERES (b. 1923), was hammered out. Before a surprised world, peace between Israel and the PLO was announced. A peace treaty was signed by Israel's Prime Minister Yitzhak Rabin and Chairman of the PLO Yasser Arafat, in the Rose Garden of the White House. President Clinton presided and the former enemies shook hands. Arafat, Rabin, and Peres received the Nobel Peace Prize in 1994.

Toward the end of 1994, King Hussein of Jordan and Prime Minister Rabin of Israel signed a peace treaty. It was ratified by both countries' parliaments.

On September 28, 1995, the fourth day of the Jewish year 5756, a peace accord between Israel and the Palestinians was signed at the White House by Rabin and Arafat. It was presided over by President Clinton and witnessed by King Hussein of Jordan and President Mubarak of Egypt. The accord granted the Palestinians eventual self-government in territories of the West Bank, to be added to full authority over the Gaza strip and the city of Jericho.

Many problems remained. Syria and Lebanon refused to join the accord. Jerusalem, whose Old City holds Judaism's holiest places and is claimed by Israel as its indivisible capital, was equally claimed as capital by the Palestinians. It is a sacred place to them because the prophet Mohammed had ascended to heaven from there. The commitment of the PLO to exterminate Israel had not been eliminated from its charter, but its deletion was promised. Boundary adjustments giving Israel defensible frontiers had yet to be worked out. The Palestinians saw in autonomy the prelude for an independent state, which Israel has rejected.

Terror and Assassination

Fundamentalists on both sides challenged the agreement. An Islamic fundamentalist movement, the Hamas, engaged in widespread terrorist activities in order to abort the peace. Israel had similar problems. Baruch Goldstein invaded Moslem worship at Hebron and massacred the worshipers. And Jewish settlers of the West Bank, determined to resist resettlement, claimed a God-given right to live within the biblical borders of Israel. The majority of Israelis supported the peace efforts, but those vehemently opposed engaged in vicious propaganda attacks against Rabin. On November 4, 1995, after a peace rally in Tel Aviv, Yitzhak Rabin was assassinated by a young fundamentalist Orthodox Jew. The young man claimed to have acted on God's command to kill the "traitor" and end the surrender of Jewish land to the Arabs.

For Israel, the inconceivable had happened: a Jew had murdered a Jew. The entire world was gripped by shock. Leaders of great and small powers attended the funeral. Arab leaders took part. King Hussein of Jordan called Rabin his "brother," President Mubarak of Egypt expressed sympathy. In deeply moving words Rabin's granddaughter tearfully expressed the feeling of the family and of Israel. "You were our pillar of fire, and now we are in darkness" (alluding to Exod. 13:21).

Shimon Peres, Rabin's close colleague, became Prime Minister. He pledged to carry the peace policy forward. Israeli opinion, however, was sharply divided. Large segments were prepared to make wide concessions to gain "Peace for land." Israeli groups engaged in joint projects of goodwill, working with the Palestinians to break down prejudices and suspicions. On the other hand, some Israelis grew uneasy that the concessions might go too far. Secure borders were needed and giving up old Jerusalem was categorically opposed by all Jews. Because the Arabs had broken their pledges and had denied Jews access to their holy sites, the PLO's promise to preserve and keep open Jewish holy sites was met with distrust.

The split in Israeli society was expressed in the general election of 1996, when the conservative Likud party gained just enough strength to form a government in coalition with the "religious parties." BENJAMIN NETHANYAHU (b. 1949) became prime minister. The transfer of territory to the Palestinians was delayed. Eventually, armed struggle ensued, and the peace process came to the verge of collapse. President Clinton called Netanyahu, Arafat, Hussein, and Mubarak to Washington. Mubarak refused to go; the others agreed to ongoing talks until various issues could be settled. Netanyahu declared that Israel would abide by all agreements previously signed. In early October the talks began again.

On October 23, 1998, a peace accord between Netanyahu and Arafat was signed in Washington. Israel pledged, among other points, to evacuate more territory; to grant free transit of Arabs through Israel from the West Bank to Gaza; and to permit the building of an airport at Gaza. The Palestinians pledged to combat terrorism and to remove from their charter the destruction of Israel as a fundamental principle.

Arafat had the provision calling for the extermination of Israel removed from the charter of the PLO but was unable to curb terrorism against Israel. Netanyahu hedged on his pledges and had new housing developments started near Jerusalem in territory claimed by the Palestinians. Peace was again endangered. In the elections of May, 1999, the Israelis defeated Netanyahu and the Likud party and elected EHUD BARAK (b. 1942) prime minister, which gave leadership to the Labor Party in the parliamentary coalition that had to be created. The election of Barak, previously a high officer and a protégé of Yitzhak Rabin, was welcomed with relief by the population of Israel and the world. The peace process was back on track and additional territory was ceded to the Palestinians as Barak combined caution and concern for Israel's security with an earnest striving to reach a lasting peace with the Palestinians.

IN ISRAEL

Israelis face a great task within their own country. They must balance the competing demands of a modern democratic state and adherence to religious obligation.

Orthodoxy in Israel and Its Effect on World Jewry

In Israel, Orthodoxy is the only official expression of Judaism that is recognized and fully funded by the state. This has historical roots. Under Turkish and British mandate, each religious group was placed under the jurisdiction of its clergy and was funded by the government. The Jews were under the Orthodox rabbinate. The State of Israel did not wish to change this. While non-Jewish religions in Israel are therefore still given government subventions, non-Orthodox Jewish communities were for many years excluded. The Israeli rabbinate follows a pre-Mendelssohnian Judaism. Many Israelis, unable to follow Orthodox Judaism, have therefore abandoned religion altogether. American sponsored Conservative and Reform synagogues, designed to reach these Jews, have faced an uphill fight under strenuous opposition by the official rabbinate. The power of Orthodoxy rests on its small political parties in the Knesset, the parliament, that frequently hold the balance of power in coalition governments and demand concessions for their alliance.

Marriage, family, and inheritance laws are governed by religious law, and all legislation of the government is scrutinized by the rabbinate for its conformity with halakhah. Non-Orthodox rabbis are not permitted to officiate at functions such as weddings. The school system is divided into religiously oriented and secular schools. Conversions in Israel and abroad are recognized only if performed by Orthodox rabbis recognized by the Israeli rabbinate. There exists but one exception. Every Jew has the right to claim citizenship on arrival in Israel. This includes converts admitted by any rabbinical court abroad, even a non-Orthodox one. The Orthodox parties have made great efforts to have this law changed and to exclude converts under non-Orthodox auspices. This would affect American Jewry with its hundreds of thousands "Jews by choice."

Otherwise, the state and its Supreme Court follow Western law, which differs markedly from Torah. Orthodoxy would like to see this changed. The state claims that it is impossible to operate a modern society on principles and legislation enacted under totally different circumstances. The problem has not been solved, and is a source of continual conflict. Voices have been raised in the Zionist movement demanding recognition of Jewish religious pluralism in Israel.

The Modern State

Israel's existence has unfolded amid war and violence, and a major portion of its revenues has had to go to armaments. Men and women are subject to military draft and, after their years of duty, to annual military exercises. The absorption of large masses of immigrants has imposed additional heavy social, religious, and financial burdens. Tourism, a major source of income, fluctuates depending on the degree of security perceived by would-be visitors. Israeli citizens accept the austere conditions of their homeland.

Yitzhak Rabin gave his life advocating peace for the Land and people of Israel. The late prime minister pointed out in an address on September 28, 1985, that Israel has been guided by the spirit of the prophets and has earnestly striven to live up to the ethics that Judaism has given to the world.

Remarkably, the country has remained democratic. No leader has, in the face of abiding emergency, made himself or herself dictator. This uncompromising adherence to democracy and its processes makes Israel the only true democracy in the region and a trustworthy ally of the United States.

The consciousness of living in a democracy has shaped the people. It has helped alleviate the social tensions between immigrants and native born, between the different lifestyles of Western and Oriental Jews. It has guaranteed universal and free elections, a free press, and free expression of protest. It has given freedom to all religions and cared for their holy places. To be sure, conflicts among competing groups exist. For example, the rabbinate and the secular Supreme Court have issued conflicting rulings on the rights of non-Orthodox religious groups. The *Charedim,* "God fearers," exempt from military service while yeshivah students, have assaulted laws, institutions, activities, and persons not following what they consider halakhah. Substantial numbers of Israelis have even emigrated to the West. Nevertheless, amid constant insecurity, the population has remained remarkably calm, leading a "normal" life. Israel is their country, whose destiny they alone determine.

Israel has fused modern dynamics with its past, as discovered from ongoing archaeological discoveries and the unearthing of documents. In this manner, the country has built a modern society whose social justice and universal welfare system reflect the spirit of the prophets. Through an enduring peace with its neighbors, Israel can become the hub of the region, a generator of physical and spiritual prosperity.

BOOK TWO

Torah, Mitzvot, and Jewish Thought

INTRODUCTION TO BOOK 2

Jewish traditions sanctify place and time. Jews are bound to each other and to the history of the Jewish people through traditional forms of religious study, worship, and humanitarian service, all centered around the Torah—the text itself, its interpretation, and its concrete working out in day–to–day life. The synagogue and the home are the focal points of Jewish life, where the individual Jew finds meaning within the context of family and congregation. Through the study of Torah, prayer, the celebration of holidays, and the observance of life-cycle events, Jews join their lives to their community and to Jews of generations and ages past, whose lives unfolded in the same religious context, reading the same texts, saying the same prayers, keeping the same calendar, and marking the same milestones. All of this has and does occur within tremendous diversity of place, time, surrounding culture, and specific expression.

Ceremonial objects are outward symbols of Jews' faith and reverence for God and their unity as a people. Picart's 1724 engraving depicts the lulav, etrog, tzitzit, eternal light, shofar, yad, and matzah.

In addition to building unity among Jews of many different places and times, the sharing of traditional forms of study, worship, and service has also created a long tradition of reflection and writing about the meaning of Jewish life and its relation both to God and to humanity. Through mysticism, philosophy, and the scholarly study of Jewish sources, Jewish thinkers have explored how to live a full Jewish life and the impact that such a life can have on humanity.

Individual Jews may seek guidance in the perplexities of our times and may find answers in the philosophers studied here.

Chapter 21

SYNAGOGUE

The term *synagogue* originally stood for an "assembly" or "meeting" of Jews who gathered for prayer and the reading and study of Scripture. The word may have been used to refer to the groups of Jews who gathered in private houses for worship and study during the Babylonian Exile (586 B.C.E.–516 B.C.E.). The place of worship was originally called *proseuche.* Eventually *synagogue* applied to both the place and the people of the assembly.

Exactly when synagogue buildings were first built is not known, but Jewish literature and archaeological excavations testify to the existence of imposing synagogue buildings in antiquity. The first-century Jewish historian Josephus (c. 38–c. 100), for example, speaks of the reading of Torah within the synagogue. A synagogue existed in Masada during Temple times.

Few aspects of the appearance of the synagogue building were regulated. According to the Babylonian Talmud, the synagogue was to stand on the highest place in the city, commanding all the other buildings (M. Megillah 4:22 ff.). And it was to be beautiful: "This is my God and I will enshrine Him" in beauty (Exod. 15:2) was the Rabbis' guideline (B.T. Shabbat 133b).

Built between the second and the fifth centuries, the synagogue at Capernaum gives us a good idea of a synagogue building in antiquity and shares many features with synagogues through the ages. Architecturally, the Capernaum synagogue follows the style of the surrounding Greco-Roman culture, just as synagogues ever since have been built in the style of their own place and time. The synagogue at Capernaum was entered through a courtyard that led to the Bet Midrash—the House of Study—and to other meeting rooms; still today synagogues are houses of prayer, study, and meeting.

Like all synagogues, the synagogue at Capernaum shows the importance of the Torah reading during services, with reverence shown in the housing of the scrolls and a prominent place marked for their reading. Because, during the week it was used for assemblies, as a courtroom, and for similar secular purposes, the synagogue at Capernaum, like others of its time, had no permanent shrine for the Torah scrolls. Rather, as a wall sculpture at Capernaum shows, the scrolls were kept in a large ceremonial cabinet on wheels that was rolled into the room for the Torah reading; no one was to leave the synagogue before the Torah had been removed, as the Talmud says (B.T. Sota 39b). The cabinet was called *aron,* "cabinet," in allusion to the *aron* in which the tablets of the Ten Commandments had once been kept. The housing for the scrolls might also be called *tevah,* "Ark," alluding to the ark that protected Noah. It was veiled by a curtain (B.T. Megillah 26b). Ashkenasi Jews call the place where the scrolls are stored *Aron Hakodesh,* "Holy Shrine," while Sefardic Jews call it *tevah.*

Torah scrolls being taken from the Ark in the synagogue of K'ai Fung Foo, China.

In Capernaum, the worshipers turned their faces at prayer toward Jerusalem, as Daniel had done (Dan. 6:11); in Europe and the New World synagogues face east, still towards Jerusalem, with a permanent, elevated Aron Hakodesh built into the eastern wall, and an "Eternal Light" in front of the shrine. The light, like the eternal flame on the candelabrum in the Temple of old, is symbolic of God's eternal presence.

The synagogue in Mainz.

While the interior of a synagogue is shaped by the style of the surrounding culture and time of its design, several features are prominent: the Ark (Aron Hakodesh) where the congregation's Torah scrolls are kept, on the east wall; the Eternal Light (Ner tamid) that burns in front of the Ark; the platform or area from which Torah is read (the bimah); and seats for the congregation, in front of the Ark. This basic structure expresses architecturally the centrality of Torah in the life of the congregation.

The central feature of every synagogue are the Torah scrolls, protected in the Ark. The Eternal Light burns before them.

Next to the Eternal Light, facing the people, sat the congregational officials. The *shaliah tzibbur*—"messenger of the congregation," prayer leader—stood on the same level as the congregation and faced the Torah shrine. The Torah was read from an elevated stage, *bimah,* in the center of the building; this has remained in traditional Ashkenasic synagogues and has also been called *almemar,* a Sefardic term derived from Al-mimbar, the Arabic term for the reader's chancel in the mosque. In Sefardic synagogues the bimah has been moved to the western wall. In ancient synagogues, women attended worship, and we have no evidence that they sat in a gallery set aside from the men.

THE SYNAGOGUE COMPLEX AT WORMS— A MEDIEVAL SYNAGOGUE

The ancient synagogue of the Rhenish city of Worms (see the photo on p.124) gives us a picture of the changes in synagogues that resulted from forces inside and outside of Judaism. The building stood until 1938 in the old ghetto and was about 900 years old, a monument to German civilization. The German government has rebuilt a replica, unfortunately mainly as a museum, while it waits for the return of Jews to Worms. The modest complex of buildings still has an atmosphere of sanctity and was one of the great sanctuaries of Jewry, a place hallowed by masters, graced by students, sanctified by martyrdom.

A small synagogue, the building measures 50 feet by 50 feet. On the outside it looks like a simple house, for the Christian rulers did not allow synagogues to be visible as such. It is distinguished merely by an iron rod surmounted by a Magen David, to give it height. By Christian rule, the roof of synagogues could not rise above the other buildings in town, and so the Talmud's requirement of height had to be interpreted symbolically. Built in the Romanesque and early Gothic styles of the time, it may even have been planned by the same architect and built by the same masons who erected the famous cathedral in whose shadow it nestles.

As the worshiper enters the rounded gate, he or she can see, at the righthand post, a deep depression in the stone where pious worshipers had touched it lovingly to carry their fingers reverently to their lips. Steps lead down to the sanctuary, in conformity, it was claimed, with the word: "Out of the depths I call You, O Lord" (Ps. 130:1). The actual reason was to give the interior greater height by placing the floor below street level.

In the front of the room, on the east wall, is the Aron Hakodesh, with steps leading up to it and an Eternal Light over it. Near the front wall stands the great Hanukkah menorah. At the foot of the steps, facing the Ark, is the reading desk of the cantor, who brought the prayers of the congregation to God. His position was not elevated, for as messenger of the congregation, he spoke out of the midst of the people. In the center of the building stands the bimah, an elevated reading platform from which the Torah is read. The people gathered around, as their ancestors had done at Mount Sinai and as the people had surrounded Ezra as he read the Torah to them from a tower, committing them to the covenant (Neh. 8:4). When the worshiper faced the Ark, he faced east, toward Jerusalem.

At the left, toward the front, was a transept, the women's section, entered by a separate gate. A wall completely hid the women from the men, and a small window in it allowed one woman to follow the service and lead her sisters in prayer. The total segregation of women from men through a *mehitzah,* a wall of separation, and their removal to a gallery, had by then been ordained and is still followed in Orthodox synagogues.

Next to the synagogue is the entrance to the Bet Midrash, the room of study. It has been called Rashi chapel, for Rashi, the great commentator, was once (mistakenly) thought to have taught there. It is a small room, too, perhaps 20 by 15 feet; one wall is straight, the other slightly circular and broken by windows. Stone benches surround the walls, surmounted by a great elevated stone chair with armrests cut out of the wall; we also find a lamp, a table of later date, and books.

Stepping out of the synagogue and Bet Midrash into the courtyard, we find the entrance to the *mikveh,* the ritual bath, used by pious women to purify themselves every month before

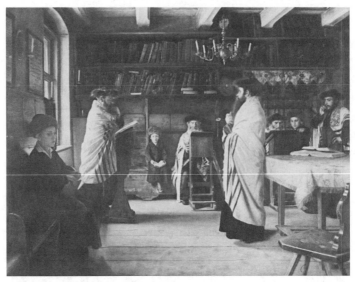

Lively discussion is commonplace when Jews gather to study, as at this Eastern European Bet Midrash.

returning to their husbands' love and embrace. Cut deep in the rock, it reaches to the level of the nearby Rhine, so that "living waters" from the river might form the basin of its font. A small niche in the wall offered a place to undress. These were heroic women, who braved cold and darkness and damp murkiness to fulfill the law of marital purity.

Modern Synagogues

In the nineteenth and twentieth centuries, Jews built magnificent synagogues, at times of daring conception and frequently designed by leading architects. The buildings came to express the security Jews had acquired in their environment. In Germany they were mistaken in this belief, and the synagogues were burned down, regardless of their beauty or historic value. American synagogues proclaim the faith of the Jews in democracy, where Jews as truly equal citizens claim their right to be respected for their faith.

Modern synagogues vary greatly. Some of them originated

in a Jewish desire to adapt synagogues to the plan of Protestant churches, although when a pulpit is added for the preacher, it is secondary to the pulpit for the Torah. The bimah has frequently been moved to the front and the cantor faces the people from an elevated chancel in order to be heard better. This arrangement provides space for more worshipers and permits the multi-purpose use of the room, when the Ark is hidden by a folding wall. A few synagogues have steps leading down into the sanctuary. Conservative and Reform synagogues permit mixed seating to keep the families together; their galleries hold the overflow. Sefardic synagogues seat the worshipers facing each other across a center aisle, rather than directing them toward the Ark.

Synagogues face east. The holy Ark may be veiled by a curtain, as in Worms, or not, as in Sefardic synagogues. All have *Ner tamid*, the "Eternal Light"; many also have a memorial light to the martyrs of the Holocaust. Additional symbols have frequently been added: the Magen David; the Lion of Judah (from Gen. 49:9); the seven-branched candlestick, which was an early symbol

Built in 1732, this simple synagogue in Mainz thrived as a house of worship and house of study. Destroyed by the Nazis, the synagogue was rededicated by the author in 1996.

Large or small, ancient or ultramodern, the synagogue shows the dedication of the congregation that saw to its building and nourished its growth. Synagogues have been built all over the world in every country where Jews have lived, in every age since ancient times, in the styles admired by the congregations responsible for building them. The synagogues pictured in this chapter, as well as the synagogues in Worms (p.126), Venice (p. 121), and Newport, Rhode Island (p. 216), give but a few examples of how Jews have expressed their needs and hopes for a sacred place of worship, study, and congregational meeting.

of Judaism found in the Temple of old facing the holy of holies and is today the coat of arms of the State of Israel. Two tablets serve as reminder that once the Ark contained the holy tablets of the Ten Commandments. Over the Ark we frequently find inscribed: *Da lifne mee attah omed,* "Know before Whom you are standing" (B.T. Berakhot 28b).

Every synagogue has meeting and dining rooms and kitchens. Above all it has its school, and, in modern congregations, the school plant is larger than the sanctuary, for the study of Torah is the safeguard of survival. Regardless of specific plan, in every synagogue Torah is always and everywhere the center of worship.

This 1781 synagogue in Wolpa, Poland, protected the Jewish community within its fortress-like wooden structure. Synagogues, especially in Eastern Europe, were at times built like citadels, offering protection in times of pogroms, while rural synagogues often exhibited beautiful wall paintings. Only a few escaped destruction by the Nazis.

Mirroring the architecture of its time, the gothic Altneuschul was the center of Jewish life in Prague.

Baron von Rothschild helped to finance the Friedberger Anlage synagogue, built in 1907 to hold the growing Jewish population of Frankfurt.

Chapter 22

TORAH

Torah is the foundation of Jewish life and the guarantor of its survival. The Jewish people would not exist without Torah. It has been the companion of the Jews throughout history and has given the Jews the will to survive and the hope of eventual redemption. Rabbenu Gershom put it in these words: "From exile to exile has all of Judah been banished, living in constant agony, and no one . . . comforts him. . . . Nothing is left us but this Torah. Mighty Redeemer for your sake deliver us . . ." (S'lihot for Yom Kippur).

The term *Torah*, meaning the "instruction," has acquired different connotations, depending on the context in which it is used:

1. In its narrowest sense, Torah denotes the Book of the Torah, the *parchment scroll* upon which the Five Books of Moses, the Pentateuch, are written. From such a scroll the prophet Ezra read at the people's convocation that he called in 445 B.C.E.

When ancient Torah scrolls became too worn to use, they were placed in a "hiding place," *genizah*, usually the attic or cellar of the synagogue. The oldest and largest collection of such documents is the *genizah* of the Ezra Synagogue in Cairo, Egypt.

(Neh. 8:1). Still today each congregation must have at least one scroll for public reading. Possessing a Torah scroll and reading from it, all Jewish congregations, regardless of denomination, form a united community.

2. Since Ezra, the Torah has been read from the scroll in public worship at appointed times for the instruction of the congregation. Torah in this sense denotes the *content* of the scroll and of all holy books.

3. But Torah, more than the *written* word, also includes the *Oral Torah* that has accompanied the written word from the beginning. This twofold Torah is the source of the 613 mitzvot that form the action-centered heart of Judaism. Judaism is a religion of spirituality unfolding through laws that are divine commandments, mitzvot. As we discuss the mitzvot we shall refer to their source in Torah, both Written and Oral.

4. At Ezra's convocation the Levites interpreted the text so the people could understand it (Neh. 8:9). This also is Torah, meaning *interpretations* of Scripture. In this sense, Torah stands for all commentaries on Scripture, including, for example, the insights that came out of the Jewish mystics' specific reading of Torah. When contemporary Jewish women seek new interpretations that strengthen the position of women under halakhah, Jewish law, that is part of Torah.

5. All commentaries and interpretations grow from the experiences of the Jewish people—their encounters with history and their way of life throughout the centuries. Life itself is an interpretation of our relationship to God. Jewish theologians throughout history have developed their thinking by confronting the life and ideas of the world from the context of the eternal Torah. Torah in this fullest meaning is synonymous with *Jewish heritage.*

6. In its ultimate sense, Torah stands for the *Spirit of Judaism,* the essence of Judaism. Jews are the people of Torah.

THE CANONIZATION OF THE TANAKH

For Ezra and the people gathered about him, Torah was literally the word of God. Orthodox Jewry regards it as such to this day. A great number of books existed, however, that had spiritual value but lacked divine inspiration. A careful selection among many worthy books had to be undertaken, so that only the writings that were truly God's utterances would be admitted to the *canon*, the authoritative list, of Holy Scriptures.

The final editing and canonization of the Tanakh fell to the Sages, who were fully aware that the task was momentous. The Word of God was being preserved for eternity. This Word could never be changed, revised, or altered. As it stood, it had been spoken by God and was therefore immutable for all the world, for all generations. Unless the Rabbis were certain that a book had been written under the guidance of the "Holy Spirit," they omitted it from the canon.

They considered the merits of every one of the books, and their interpretation of a book could affect whether or not it was included in the canon. For example, should a love song like the Song of Songs be included? Rabbi Akiba insisted that "If all the songs are holy, Solomon's Song of Songs is the holiest of them all." He strictly forbade, however, any interpretation of the Song as simply a love poem; it is, rather, an allegory of God's love for Israel.

The Rabbis' views on the authorship of the biblical books frequently contrast with modern criticism. They ascribed the authorship of Judges, Samuel 1 and 2, and Ruth to the prophet Samuel; Jeremiah was considered editor of Kings 1 and 2, Jeremiah, and Lamentations. King Hezekiah headed a group who published Isaiah, Proverbs, Song of Songs, and Ecclesiastes. The men of the Great Assembly were regarded as the editors of Ezekiel, the Twelve Minor Prophets, Daniel, and Esther. Ezra wrote the book bearing his name, as well as Nehemiah and Chronicles. David edited the Psalms, which had been composed by himself and many others. Moses composed the Pentateuch and Job. Some Rabbis held that Moses could not have written the last verses of the Pentateuch, which deal with his death and burial; others disagreed, claiming that God dictated the final words to the prophet before his death.

THE APOCRYPHA. The Rabbis excluded some books from the biblical canon because they repeated messages already contained in others, or because they might confuse the reader, or simply because they were composed too late. Since these works had already been translated into Greek before they were taken out of circulation, we still have them. These works were not to be used in public worship, lest the worshiper be confused and consider them holy. They could, however, be used for private inspirational reading. They are called the "hidden books" or *Apocrypha*. Among them are the Books of ben Sirah, Esdras, Tobit, Judith, the Story of Susannah. The Books of the Maccabees, excluded from the canon simply because they were written too late, are nevertheless the source of the festival of Hanukkah.

Here we find the tedious work of the Masoretes. Their transmission has guided thousands of scribes as they have copied the Tanakh.

HOW THE TANAKH WAS TRANSMITTED: THE MASORAH

After the canon had been established, the rabbis were concerned that the Word of God be transmitted without change or error. In the period between the sixth and tenth centuries C.E., a number of scholars recorded the exact number of letters, words, and paragraphs found in the books of the Tanakh. They counted how many times a word occurred. They indicated where the middle of a book could be found, by word count, by letter count, or by verse count. They added paragraphs, vowel signs, and cantillation marks for the readings. They made a list of traditional deviations. Even spelling errors in the originals were retained; rather than create confusion among copyists, the Rabbis made a note of the errors and advised readers to substitute the correct reading. This tedious work was undertaken by the Masoretes, the humble men of *masorah*, the "transmission," or the "counting." Guided by these notes, thousands of scribes have copied tens of thousands of scrolls, and all the scrolls are alike. Recently discovered texts have shown our modern versions of the Tanakh to be generally identical and accurate.

THE ORIGINS OF THE TANAKH ACCORDING TO MODERN CRITICISM

Before the Rabbis started their work of editing and correcting, a great many versions of the Tanakh had already come into existence. With them had appeared spelling errors, some of which escaped the Masoretes and were discovered by modern scholars in the process of providing critical editions. The philological work of these scholars in correcting errors in the text is called "lower biblical criticism."

"Higher biblical criticism" went to the subject matter itself. This form of critical Bible study reached its height in the middle of the nineteenth century. Central to their argument was the critics' recognition that in the Book of Genesis God is referred to in different terms. The story of creation uses the term *Elohim*; later we find two terms, *YHVH* and *Elohim*, being joined; eventually, we have only one word or the other.

Modern critics, analyzing the Bible as a secular text, have held, on the basis of style and vocabulary, that the different terms for God indicate different authors. They have concluded that the first author, who lived in Judah during the ninth century B.C.E., molded and shaped written documents and oral traditions into

Recent biblical criticism emphasizes the text itself, its impact on its time of origin, its internal connections, and its influence upon the spiritual, literary, and aesthetic values of Western tradition.

◆

The Rabbis, too, noted the differences in terms referring to God and explained them by saying that God had originally intended to govern the world by stern justice (Elohim also means "judge"). Recognizing that the world could not endure if governed by justice alone, God added the attribute of mercy, expressed in the tetragrammaton, YHVH. Even this was too stern an approach, and God decided to govern the world by mercy (YHVH) alone.

one great work. The critics called this the "J" Document, after the German spelling of the first letter of the tetragrammaton. A century later, another author wrote a second account, with a different emphasis. It was referred to as the "E" Document, after the first letter of *Elohim*. An editor wove together the two source books. One hundred years later, a third great work was produced, Deuteronomy—"D"—which stressed the covenant of Sinai as the central event in the history of Israel; the same author also revised the books from Joshua through 2 Kings. Eventually, a fourth work was written, by a group of priests— therefore "P"—in the sixth century, after the Babylonian Exile; "P" is an account of the religious development of Israel, emphasizing cult and ritual. A redactor, "R," combined the various documents and edited the entire work. Thus the whole Scripture forms a lacework of interwoven parts.

THE BIBLE IN TRANSLATION

The power of the biblical style can be felt even in translation and has influenced the speech of many countries and civilizations. Luther did not merely establish the Reformation on the basis of his translation of the Bible: he actually created a unifying German language, without which Germany would have fallen apart into numerous different dialects. The British King James version strengthened the English language; Winston Churchill used it to rally his people during the Battle of Britain in World War II. The Bible in translation deeply influenced the Puritans, even as its laws shaped the character of New England Puritan society; it has remained a root and source of American language, custom, and law. Throughout history, great translations of the Tanakh have injected new vigor into the societies from which the translations emerged, but they have also reflected the theological outlook of the translators.

The Septuagint translated Torah as nomos, "law." This has created misunderstandings. Torah means "instruction." Although it contains many laws, it is not only law.

Historically speaking, the earliest translation of the Bible was into Greek. A document possibly written around 200 B.C.E. reports that the Greek translation of the Torah had been ordered by the Egyptian King Ptolemy II (283 B.C.E.–247 B.C.E.). The king's great library held all the works of the world's wisdom except those of the Jews, without which it was incomplete. On the king's request, the high priest Eleazar of Jerusalem sent him seventy-two Jewish scholars, who translated the Hebrew Bible into Greek. Using a round number, posterity has called it *Septuagint*, the translation of the "Seventy." Fortunately, the Septuagint was completed before the rabbis canonized the books of Scripture, and it contains the "hidden books," or Apocrypha.

New Bible translations become necessary whenever the Bible must be brought closer to the people and as meanings of the Bible are elucidated by archaeology and our knowledge of other ancient texts.

The translation of the Septuagint does not always strictly conform with the masoretic text. Sometimes the translators paraphrased, rather than translating with exactitude. This shortcoming was remedied in a new translation by Aquila, a convert to Judaism who lived during the life of Rabbi AKIBA BEN JOSEPH (c. 45 C.E.–135 C.E.). At the time of the Masters of the Mishnah, called Tannaim (whose period of teaching falls between 20 C.E. and 200 C.E.), the Bible was translated into Aramaic, the language spoken by the common people. The SAADIA GAON (882 C.E.–942 C.E.) translated it into Arabic. In the fourth century, St. Jerome translated the Septuagint into Latin. It was called the Vulgate, and all Catholic translations are based on it.

The translation used in this book is *Tanakh: A New Translation of the Holy Scriptures According to the Traditional Hebrew Text*, issued in Philadelphia by the Jewish Publication Society in 1985.

Women in the Bible

The writing of biblical history was the work of men and, as modern feminists maintain, minimized, demeaned, and even omitted the role of women. To offer but a few examples: Woman, originally equal to man (Gen 1:27), becomes an appendage to him, cut from his rib (Gen. 2:22–23). The influence of Sarah,

Rebecca, Leah, and Rachel on the lives of the patriarchs has to be inferred from the few remarks about them that we find in the text. When the prophet Miriam and the high priest Aaron suggested that their revelations from God might be equal to God's revelations to Moses, Miriam was rebuked and severely punished while Aaron was merely rebuked (Num. 12). Deborah, prophet and head of the people, served so valiantly as the military leader and judge of the people that she could not be overlooked (Judg. 4:4–5:31), but she knew her contribution would be discounted because the Lord would be delivering the enemy "into the hands of a woman" (Judg. 4:9). We read little of Hannah, mother of the prophet Samuel, who established prayer in a silent outpouring of the heart as a true approach to God (1 Sam. 9–19). Only in passing do we hear of the prophet Huldah, yet she must have been of paramount importance because King Josiah turned to her regarding the divinity of a book found in the Temple (Deuteronomy); she certified it as God's word and inspired the king's religious reforms (2 Kings 22:14 ff.).

Since the 1970s Jewish feminists have been studying biblical and other sources to reveal the unique contributions of Jewish women. Until their work is better known, our knowledge and understanding of biblical history is incomplete and misleading.

WRITTEN TORAH AND ORAL TORAH

As the word of God, the written text of the Torah precisely conveys the divine will and intent. Every word and every letter has a meaning and contains a divine message. According to tradition, however, Moses received not only written but also oral instructions from God, which were transmitted by word of mouth, or referred to by subtle hints in the written text, or arrived at by logical deduction from the text or interpretations of it. This was Oral Torah.

Oral Torah transmits, augments, interprets, and frequently gives the full meaning of a passage of the written word. From the very beginning we have therefore two sources of authority, and it is essential for our understanding of Judaism to keep in mind that the religion is based on both *Torah shebikhtav*, Written Torah, and *Torah shebe'al peh*, Oral Torah. For many centuries all oral traditions and the interpretations deduced from Written Torah were transmitted by word of mouth alone. Later they were written down in a work called the Talmud, which we shall discuss in the next chapter.

Exploring both Written and Oral Torah, the Sages investigated and interpreted the Torah very much as a court of law interprets the meaning of the words of the Constitution. In applying the principles of law to practical situations, the Rabbis added new understanding to the words of Written Torah and established precedents. The weight of an interpretation or precedent depended both on the soundness of the argument and on the authority of the interpreter. A ruling ascribed to Moses, for example, would have an authority almost equal to the Written Torah itself, since Moses received his instructions directly "from Sinai," that is, from God. Through Oral Torah the meaning of the fixed Written Torah evolves. Judaism has therefore—within the laws of Torah—grown and adjusted to change and yet steadfastly remained the religion of Torah, just as Jews have faithfully remained the people of the Torah covenant even as their religion has evolved.

THE RABBIS. Just as the Constitution remains incomplete without the decisions of the courts to explain and enlarge it, so does Written Torah remain incomplete without Oral Torah to explain and develop it. Similarly, the American judge who interprets the Constitution and law must be absolutely loyal to the Constitution and have a thorough knowledge of law combined with the power of clear and critical thinking. The same requirements apply to the interpreter of Torah, the rabbi. As supported by the Written Torah, ordination confers the authority to render decisions (Deut. 17:8–11). The decisions must be based on a thorough knowledge of the sources, result from critical thinking, and above all be rooted in full allegiance to Judaism and its tradition. While modern rabbis have functions in many other fields, the traditional rabbi is also a judge, an interpreter of traditional law to meet practical situations. The rabbi decides individual cases on the basis of Written and Oral Torah, codes, precedents, the rulings of earlier authorities, and, in difficult situations, the advice of distinguished talmudists. The official rabbinate in the State of Israel has been primarily devoted to this task.

Chapter 23

ORAL TORAH

The Oral Torah grew from Jewish teachers expounding the Written Torah. The Mishnah collected and summarized in written form this vast range of laws, interpretations, and teachings that had evolved and been handed down orally from the time of Ezra in the fifth century B.C.E. until its codification around 220 C.E. In the third through fifth centuries, scholars examined the Mishnah in great detail and their discussions and decisions were recorded. The Mishnah combined with this set of commentaries on it forms the Talmud. The rich history of the compilation and study of Oral Law shows its constant growth and development.

THE MASTERS AND RABBIS OF THE MISHNAH

The Pharisees were fully conscious that the Torah was the Word of the living God, the heritage of the people and binding on all Jews. The Rabbis of the Talmud were the Pharisees' spiritual successors. They believed themselves charged with preserving and interpreting the Torah and entrusted with supervising its practical application. They were deeply aware of the people's needs in changing times and conditions and were prepared to meet new situations in the spirit of an evolving Torah.

Conscious that they were not simply philosophers, "lovers

of wisdom," but the spiritual "fathers" of their people, the Rabbis fashioned the Jews into the People of the Book. They collected the masters' ethical maxims into a small book called "Chapters of the Fathers," *Pirke Avot*, which is part of the Mishnah. The text shows how seriously the teachers took their duty as role models to the people, for they were exceptionally strict in their performance of the mitzvot. Revered by the people for their obedience to God's word, their warmth, love of humanity, and high ideals, the Pharisees and Rabbis succeeded in implanting and developing the strict laws of Torah in Jewish society.

The Jewish term for the master, "Father" shows the responsibility that attaches to knowledge. The teacher becomes a spiritual father to the students, whose mind and moral character he is to mold. Generally the designation "father" is reserved in the Tanakh for biological sons or descendants. But Elisha calls Elijah, with whom he was not biologically related, "my father" (2 Kings 2:12). The idea of the teacher being the students' "father" was widespread in Judaism (see B.T. Sanhedrin 19b). Judaism calls its masters "Fathers" but has also had "Mothers" to guide the people. The Rabbis could not see that. They excluded women from study, denied them the right to participate in the development of halakhah, and excluded them from power and authority.

Pharisaic Leadership during the Time of the Temple

During the time of the Temple, the Pharisees prepared the people against despair should the Temple fall. They saw themselves as divinely appointed bearers of a tradition that Moses had received on Sinai, that had been passed on through the generations to their own time, and that would continue into the future. The "Chapters of the Fathers" lists this line of descent (M. Avot 1:1–18).

SIMEON THE RIGHTEOUS is the first mentioned by name. He is said to have been the high priest who appeared before Alexander the Great and moved the king to mercy when he took Jerusalem in 382 B.C.E. Simeon's words are the legacy for the future: "On three things stands the world: On Torah, on Worship, on Acts of Kindness" (Avot 1:2).

His disciple, ANTIGONOS OF SOKHO, touched a theme that has been repeated with variations throughout Jewish religion: the service of love. The sole guiding force in the service of God should not be the expectation of reward, or the hope of a reward in the hereafter, or the fear of future punishment, but, rather, the love of God.

As we follow the generations, we come to SIMEON BEN SHETAH. He is said to have been the brother of Salome Alexandra, the only reigning queen of the House of the Hasmoneans. Simeon opened the Sanhedrin, the Supreme Court, to the Pharisees and established their spiritual and political power. He established the ideal of justice as the Pharisees understood it: Neither personal nor political considerations may color judgment in a court of law. Mercy, however, should prevail. This basic principle has prevailed from Simeon's days to modern times.

JOSHUA BEN PERAHYAH carried Simeon's injunctions into the sphere of daily living: "Get yourself a teacher, acquire a friend, judge everyone in his favor" (Avot 1:8). Study, fellowship, and charity in judgment make life distinguished.

When the leadership passed to SHEMAYA and AVTALYON, a new precedent was established, for the two men were not of Jewish descent. Avtalyon emphasized the grave responsibility of the teacher, whose every word can have unforeseen consequences. Familiar with the pleasures of non-Jewish culture, especially of philosophy, he sternly warned the teachers against the province of error.

True Pharisees were known for their poverty and piety, patience and honesty, charity and consideration for others, love of learning and strength of self-analysis, deep humility and modesty, profound love of wife and family. These were the qualities which made the Pharisees great. Thus they became the eternal teachers of Judaism. The greatest of them, during the time of the Temple, was HILLEL (end of the first century B.C.E. to the early first century C.E.).

Some men joined the Pharisees because they were prestigious and influential, from self-interest and the desire for self-aggrandizement. The rabbis called these men "painted ones," whose piety was but painted on, a varnish designed to hide a heart of selfishness. It is a tragedy that the "painted ones" came to represent all Pharisees in the common usage of the term. This does an injustice to one of the great ethical movements in civilization.

Hillel

During the reign of Herod, Hillel came to Jerusalem to study with

Shemaya and Avtalyon. He was a descendant of the House of David, born and reared in Babylonia.

Hillel was very poor. A story is told of him:

> Every day he would hire himself out for two small pieces of silver. Half of his earnings he gave to the doorkeeper at the academy for admission, the other half he used for the upkeep of his family and himself. One day he earned nothing, and the doorkeeper would not let him enter. So he climbed unto the roof, that through the skylight he might hear the words of the Living God revealed by the mouth of Shemaya and Avtalyon. . . . It was on the eve of the Sabbath, deep winter, and snow fell on Hillel and covered him. In the morning Shemaya said to Avtalyon, "Brother Avtalyon, this house . . . is very dark today. . . ." They looked up, saw the shape of a man on top of the skylight, went up and found Hillel covered by three feet of snow. They removed the snow, took him down, washed him, rubbed him, sat him near a fire. . . . "This man deserves that the Sabbath be profaned in his behalf." (M. Yoma 35b)

Hillel learned from his masters that the Sabbath may be profaned for the sake of a human life. This principle has remained fundamental but Jews have always used this discretionary power with extreme caution, making certain that violation of the law of Torah is the only way of saving a life.

Knowing the worth of every human being entails love, Hillel admonished: "Be of the disciples of Aaron, loving peace and pursuing peace; loving all beings and leading them to Torah" (M. Avot 1:12). As love leads to Torah, so too does Torah lead to love:

> The more Torah, the more life,
> the more discussion, the more wisdom,
> the more counsel, the more understanding,
> the more charity, the more peace. (M. Avot 2:8)

Hillel's philosophy of life won him friends, not only among his people, but among non-Jews as well. Once a heathen came to the other great teacher of Hillel's day, SHAMMAI (50 B.C.E.–30 C.E.) and said to him: "You may convert me if you can teach me the Torah while I am standing on one foot." Shammai threw him out and the heathen came to Hillel, who converted him by saying: "Do not do to your neighbor what would *In Hillel's honor, Jewish student organizations at modern universities bear the name Hillel Foundations.* be hateful to you were it done to you. This is the whole Torah, all else is commentary. Now go and study it" (B. Shabbat 31a). This is the golden rule, as Hillel formulated it. Hillel addressed a man who had not yet learned the Jewish way of love: Let him start by refraining from doing harm to others and in time, as he immerses himself in the study of Torah, he will advance to where he will do good for his fellow human beings.

Hillel, the spiritual antagonist of Herod, became the patriarch, Nasi, of the pharisaic community, acknowledged for his intellectual greatness and ethical stature. He drew many disciples and was loved for the simplicity of his life, his friendliness to Jews and non-Jews alike, his love, and his patience. Becoming ground rules for Jewish living, Hillel's ideas speak through the words of subsequent sages.

HILLEL AND SHAMMAI. When Hillel opened his academy at Jerusalem, called Bet Hillel, House of Hillel, another famous rabbi, Shammai, headed another academy, Bet Shammai, House of Shammai. The two schools became friendly rivals. Hillel realized that the Torah is for humans, not humans for the Torah. His decisions always considered the needs of the people and their circumstances; he tried not to burden them too heavily. Shammai, on the other hand, followed strictly the letter of the law. In the face of bitter controversies, their friendship nevertheless endured. It is said that a voice was heard from heaven:

> Both the words of the House of Hillel and the words of the House of Shammai are the words of the living God. The decision, however, is to be according to the House of Hillel . . . because they were friendly and humble, and considered the views of the House of Shammai like their own, citing these even before their own. (B.T. Eruvin 13b)

Judaism grants freedom of opinion as long as the differences are based on sincerity in the search for truth. But love of humans determines the decision to be followed. The halakhah follows the School of Hillel because of his understanding of the people and his love for them.

The Sages: Leaders after the Fall of the Temple

With the fall of the Temple, different sects of Judaism disappeared, except for the Pharisees, who became the people's rabbis. To comfort the despondent who feared that, with the fall of the Temple, God's Presence, Shekhinah, had departed from the Jewish people, these new leaders, later known as the Sages, gave them the assurance that God was and would always be in their midst.

> As two sit together and the words of Torah are the subject of their talk, Shekhinah, the divine Presence rests in their midst—even when one sits in occupation with Torah, God appoints unto him a reward. . . . When three eat at a table, speaking words of Torah it is as if they partake of God's own table. (M. Avot 3:3–4)

Rabban JOHANAN BEN ZAKKAI, one of Hillel's disciples, was leader of the transition. Rabban GAMALIEL II was Rabban Johanan's successor and the first Nasi recognized by the Romans as head of the autonomous Jewish community in the Land of Israel. He was convinced that only strong leadership and uniformity in Jewish observance could keep the people together now that the Temple had fallen. He made Yavneh the universally recognized center of world Jewry and permitted free debate among the scholars, but he insisted that he alone had the authority to render decisions.

He codified the order of the obligatory prayers and endorsed the continued celebration of the Pesah Seder, which every family was to observe even in the absence of the sacrificial lamb of Temple time. The redemption of the Land from alien ownership was also made a religious duty. All existing bonds with Christianity were broken, in order to shield the Jews from the influence of the new religion. A special invocation against sectarians, including the Christians but not exclusively directed at them, was introduced.

In reprisal for the failed Bar Kokhba rebellion, the Roman emperor Hadrian prohibited the study and practice of Torah. Rabbi AKIBA BEN JOSEPH continued to teach the people, unmindful of danger. Asked why he did not give up, he replied with a homely parable:

> A fox once called out to the fishes in the brook: "Come ashore and escape the dangers of being caught by the big fish of prey." "No," they replied, "water is the element of our life. If we leave it we perish. If we stay, some will die, but the rest will live."

"Torah is our element of life," Rabbi Akiba concluded, "some of us may perish in the trials of these days; but as long as there is Torah, the people will live." Rabbi Akiba was among those who gave their lives. They tore off his flesh with red hot pincers. His disciples wept, but Rabbi Akiba smiled: "Does it not say, 'You shall love the Lord your God with all your heart and all your soul and all your might?' The soul, that means my life, should I not smile, now that I may serve God with all my life?"

Those who have given their lives for God and Torah are remembered as *Kedoshim,* holy ones, "saints." By their lives they have preserved Israel, by their death they have sealed the covenant.

MISHNAH AND TANNAIM

"At the time of Rabbi Akiba's death, Rabbi [Judah the Prince] was born" (B. T. Kiddushin 72b). Before the sun of Akiba had set, the sun of Judah had risen.

Rabbi Akiba's martyrdom overshadowed the life of Rabbi JUDAH HA-NASI (c. 135–210) and his generation. Concerned that Oral Torah might not survive another purge of its masters, Rabbi Judah concluded that the ever-growing body of rules and ordinances could no longer be transmitted orally, even during periods of undisturbed study.

Rabbi Judah decided to edit in written form the oral tradition of the past. In order that such a code might not prevent the organic growth of a growing, changing, ever-evolving Torah, he set down only the basic ideas. He prepared a brief, concise text that could become the source for further discussion. He also included the views of opposing schools and scholars of his own time, as well as of the past, such as Hillel and Shammai, for minority opinion some day might become majority decision.

The work was made easier because the "lecture notes" of older masters could be used. Rabbi Akiba had already removed the prohibition against written records and he had admonished his disciples, especially Rabbi Meir, to collect and write down decisions, views, and opinions. This work was now arranged systematically, enlarged, and clarified.

Halakhah and Aggadah

The Mishnah ("Instruction")—the codified Oral Torah—includes *takkanot,* "ordinances," which form the "fence around the Torah," that is, injunctions that may not be violated. Some of these takkanot might be for a specific period only, while others are permanent. Together with the word of Torah they form the *halakhah,* literally, "the way (of life)," the body of norms and mitzvot that is derived from Written and Oral Torah and that directs religious practice, which in turn permeates the life of the Jew. An individual ordinance in specific cases is equally called halakhah, "You shall kindle no fire throughout your habitations on the Sabbath day" is a halakhah, directly based on Written Torah (Exod. 35:3). The weight of a halakhah varies, depending on whether it is *mi-d'Oraita,* explicitly found in Torah itself; or *halakhah l'Mosheh mi-Sinai,* a law given by God to Moses at Sinai; or *mi-d'Rabbanan,* an injunction enacted by the Rabbis on the foundation of Sinaitic law and in its protection.

Another body of instruction called *aggadah,* "narration," was paired with the halakhah to give direction and show the underlying principles of practical observance, explaining the spirit of the law. These ideas and ideals were taught by maxim and parable, preaching and wise counsel, and like the halakhah were based on interpretations of Torah. We find aggadah in the body of the Mishnah, in Gemara (see below), and in the Midrash ("Search for Meaning"), a separate commentary to the Scripture, following its text. Divided into halakhic midrash and a large body of aggadic midrash, the Midrash evolved over a period of many centuries, even after the completion of the Talmud. Halakhah and aggadah are closely related: one directs actions and the other shows their purpose—to bring the person to God. The following aggadah may serve as an example:

> Rabbi Simlai lectured: 613 commandments were handed down to Moses; 365 of them are prohibitions, corresponding to the days of the year; 248 of them are laws of action, corresponding to the bones and human limbs.
> Rabbi Hamnuna said: When David came, he reduced the commandments to eleven, for we read: A Psalm of David; Lord, who may sojourn in Your tent;
> who may dwell on Your holy mountain?
> He that *lives without blame* and *does what is right* 2
> and *in his heart acknowledges the truth* 3
> whose *tongue is not given to evil* 4
> who *has never done harm to his fellow* 5
> nor *borne reproach for acts against his neighbor* 6
> for whom *a contemptible man is abhorrent* 7
> but who *honors those that fear the Lord* 8
> who *stands by his oath even to his hurt* 9
> who *has never lent money on interest* 10
> or *accepted a bribe against the innocent* 11
> He that doeth these things shall never be moved (Ps. 15).
> When Isaiah came, he reduced the commandments to six; for it is said:
> He who *walks in righteousness, speaks uprightly* 2
> *spurns profit from fraudulent dealings* 3
> *waves away a bribe instead of grasping it* 4
> *stops his ears against listening to infamy* 5
> *shuts his eyes against looking at evil* 6
> such a one shall dwell in lofty security (Isa. 33:15).
> When Micah came, he reduced the commandments to three; as it is said:
> He has told you, O man, what is good and what the Lord requires of you:
> only to *do justice* 1
> and to *love goodness,* 2
> and *walk humbly with your God* (Micah 6:8). 3
> Then Isaiah came again, reducing them to two, as is said:

Thus said the Lord:
Observe what is right and *do what is just* 2
for soon My salvation shall come, and My deliverance be revealed
(Isa. 56:1).
Then came Amos and reduced them to one:
Thus said the Lord to the House of Israel: *Seek Me* and you will
live (Amos 5:4)
(B.T. Makkot 236–24a)

These interpretations may seem playful and arbitrary, for they appear to have no regard for the historical sequence of the prophets. But let us look more closely: Rabbi Simlai wishes to teach that we must keep away from evil every day of the year (hence 365 prohibitions that keep the Jew) but serve God with every fiber and limb in our body (hence 248 ordained actions that enable the Jew). Rabbi Hamnuna makes it clear that there must be a divine rationale behind the commandments. The religious life must be a search for God through justice, mercy, and humility that finds realization in the 613 mitzvot that Torah ordains. Thus halakhah and aggadah do not contradict each other, although halakhah constitutes the main body of the Mishnah.

The Organization of the Mishnah

The Mishnah is organized in six Sedarim (Orders). Each Seder is in turn subdivided in Masekhtot (tractates, books), then into Perakim and Mishnayot (chapters and paragraphs).

1. ZERAIM (Seeds), the first Order, deals with the laws of agriculture. Its first book is *Berakhot,* Blessings. Since nature and its rewards depend on God, our relationship to God forms the first subject. The order of the service is explained, the rules for daily benedictions are laid down, and instructions are given on how to say grace and how to give thanks for God's special favors. Here we find the blueprint for Jewish worship. The other books deal with tithing and charity, which became duties as soon as the harvest was gathered.

2. MOED (Appointed Days), the second Order, contains a

series of books explaining the rules for the festivals. The first and second books—*Shabbat* and *Eruvin*—deal with the laws of the Sabbath (Shabbat), the first giving the details of work prohibition, the second providing the rules against moving goods in workaday toil. The Sabbath, as observed according to these laws, becomes a day of otherworldliness.

Pesahim, the third book, treats the celebration of the feast of Passover and includes the sacrifice once offered in Temple courts. In this book we also find the outline of hymns, songs, and the story for the celebration of the first night of the festival, the Seder, which rehearses the story of the Jews' deliverance from Egypt. The family Seder of today still follows the ritual laid down in the Mishnah.

Shekalim speaks of the offering of the Half-Shekel. Ordained in Scripture (Exod. 30:11–16), the Shekel became a freewill offering of world Jewry for the upkeep of the Temple and of the schools.

Yoma (the Day), discusses the great and awesome Day of Atonement. On this day Jews throughout the ages have approached God in penitence, to confess their shortcomings and their sins, and to ask for forgiveness and guidance throughout the year to come. The service, as once performed in the Temple, is outlined here in the Mishnah, and the road to spiritual renewal is described.

Sukkah (Booth) speaks of the festival of Booths. It sets the rules for the Sukkah, the booth in which the people are to spend their days or at least take their meals on the festival of Sukkot. It also deals with the four kinds of plants—palm branches, myrtles, willows, and citron—that make up the bouquet to be used in worship. The book tells of the joyful exuberance during the feast, when rabbis danced before God, Giver of all good things.

Yom Tov (Holiday) is often called *Betzah* (Egg), after its first word, which refers to an egg laid on the holiday; this section gives the rules applying to all holy days.

Rosh Hashanah (New Year) lays down the regulations and liturgy for the New Year's Day and the rules for the sounding of the shofar, the ram's horn, on this day. The book also tells us about the calculations of the calendar, the monthly determination and announcement of the beginnings of the months, and the appointment of the leap years by the rabbis.

Taanit (Fast Day) deals with days of fasting.

Megillah (Scroll) details the regulations pertaining to the reading of the Scroll of Esther on Purim and matters relating to holy objects.

Moed Katan (Minor Holy Days) discusses the observance of minor holy days, the period between the first and the last days of Passover and the Festival of Booths. Only the first and last days are major holidays; those in between are minor, with limited observance of special rules.

Hagigah (The Festival Sacrifice) lays down the rules for the holiday pilgrimages to Jerusalem which were once obligatory and deals with individual sacrifices and other regulations of ancient festival observance.

3. NASHIM (Women), the third Order, contains marriage and divorce laws. Among its books are *Kiddushin* (Sanctification of Marriages); *Ketuvot*, dealing with civil laws of marriage; *Gitin* (Divorce), and others. The Jewish marriage ritual is based on these books, as are the laws of religious divorce proceedings observed to this day.

4. NEZIKIN (Damages) forms the Code of Civil and Criminal Law, which was public law in ancient Israel. The civil law section (including *Baba Kamma, Baba Metzia, Baba Batra*) deals with ownership, damages, trade, commerce, and liabilities, as well as detailing the laws against idolatry (*Avodah Zarah*). The section on criminal law (including *Sanhedrin, Makkot*) sets down the ground rules for courts from the time of the Sanhedrin on and includes the laws of evidence, trial procedures, and penalties. The code goes into detail about civil litigation and, even more so, capital punishment. The Rabbis bent every effort to avoid inflicting the death penalty. The laws of evidence and the court proceedings established in the Oral Law made it almost impossible, but the rabbis still considered capital punishment, for it was mentioned in Torah. God had, however, surrounded the

death penalty with so many hedges that the Rabbis seem to have come to the conclusion that God did not really wish any human being to die by execution. As they pointed out in their exhortation of the witnesses, "he who destroys a single soul is deemed by Scripture as having destroyed a world, and he who keeps alive a single soul ... as having sustained a whole world." For all practical purposes the Rabbis opposed and eliminated the death penalty as contrary to the spirit of Torah.

At the end of this Order we find Avot, the "Sayings of the Fathers," which we have discussed above. This is the only book dealing exclusively with ethics, as if to say: ethics is superior to formalized law; it prevents where the law punishes; it is spiritual, not simply physical; it is the foundation of all law. Procedure and the letter of the law are important, but the spirit alone will give them true meaning.

> It is not [necessarily] your duty to complete the work; neither are you free to desist from it (Rabbi Tarphon, M. Avot 2:21).

5. KODASHIM (Holy Things) deals with the laws of Temple sacrifices. The book *Hulin* lays down the dietary rules that have been so important in Jewish life.

6. TOHAROT (Purifications) states the laws of ritual purity and impurities, of immersion required for Temple service, and how these are to be performed.

The last two orders and some of the individual tractates give an idealized picture of Temple worship and reveal the Rabbis' expectations to return to their Land and to the Temple, whose order of service is therefore discussed in detail.

The Masters of the Mishnah

The masters of Oral Law who appear in the Mishnah are called *Tannaim*, the "Teachers." There were over two hundred Tannaim in Palestine from the death of Hillel until the Mishnah was codified around 220 C.E.

The ordained rabbis among the Tannaim bear the designation Rabbi. They were not rabbis in the modern sense. Although ordained, they were not "professionals," and did not

The early recorded masters, who spoke in the Mishnah, lived in Temple times. They were so great that they needed no rabbinic titles, their names alone sufficed. Among them were Hillel and Shammai. Their successors living after the Temple's fall were given the title Rabbi. *Collectively, the teachers of the Mishnah are known as* Tannaim *(Teachers). Rabbi Judah, the editor of Mishnah, is a Tanna. The Mishnah evolves in the Gemara. The masters who spoke in it held the title* Rav *and are collectively known as* Amoraim *(Speakers). Rav Ashee was an Amora teaching in Babylonia. The greatest of the masters were simply known by their title: Rabbi Judah the Patriarch was simply* Rabbi. *Rabbi Abba Arikha's wisdom, knowledge, and influence were so great that he became known simply as* Rav *(he and Samuel became the first heads of the two leading Babylonian academies).*

make a living from the study and teaching of Torah. In a largely agricultural community, many were farmers or day laborers; others were cobblers, blacksmiths, or carpenters. Even the poorest among them were agreed that "one may not make the Torah a spade to dig with" (that is, a source of income), nor a crown for self-glorification, for "he who takes profit from the words of the Torah displaces his life" (M. Avot 4:7).

The work of these teachers continued, and new questions arose. The Mishnah called for new interpretations. Out of the teachers' discussions grew another work, the Jerusalem Talmud. Its significance was dwarfed, however, because the center of Jewish life and learning had passed to Babylonia.

TALMUD AND GAONIM

"A person's most valuable quality is foresight" (M. Avot 2:13). Conditions in Palestine were unsettled, and two of Rabbi Judah's great disciples felt that the time had come to give new strength to the Babylonian centers for the study of Torah. Thus ABBA ARIKHA, Abba the Tall, a giant of a man both physically and intellectually, moved to Babylonia and was joined by Samuel, a brilliant colleague.

Background of the Babylonian Talmud

Several million Babylonian Jews enjoyed freedom and prosperity in the lands of the Tigris and Euphrates. Within the kingdom of Persia and, later, under the Caliphs, they formed an autonomous state almost comparable to one of the states in the U.S. At the head of the Jewish community stood the Exilarch, descendant of the House of David. He was governor in the full political sense of the word. The central government expected him to collect the taxes that his people had to pay; otherwise, he had a free hand.

THE GAONIM. Although the Exilarch might be a man of learning, this was not always so. The rabbis therefore reduced his authority and in return expanded the magnificence of his court, surrounding him with elaborate ceremony. He depended upon the Gaonim—the heads of the two great academies at Sura and Nehardea—for guidance, assistance, and halakhic decisions. The Gaonim were the chief justices and the spiritual heads of the community, and the importance of their offices was reflected in their title, "Head of the Yeshiva of the Excellence of Israel," or briefly, *Gaon,* which means "Excellency."

THE GREAT SANHEDRIN. In the yeshiva, the academy for Torah study, the Gaon, usually a member of the hereditary aristocracy, sat on a dais, flanked by his deputy and the head of the rabbinical court, facing seven rows of ten scholars, each with his own rank and title. This hierarchical assembly was referred to as the Great Sanhedrin. Admission to it was granted only after extensive preparation in the various grades of lower yeshivot.

Twice a year, in spring and fall, thousands of scholars from all parts of the country convened at the two main centers for one month. These meetings were called *Kallah,* "Assembly." At each assembly the scholars were given assignments for individual study to be followed by general review at the next meeting. This is how the Babylonian Talmud emerged.

Gemara: The Talmud

Under the leadership of Rav and Samuel and their successors, the text of the Mishnah was examined, almost word by word and sentence by sentence. The discussions in the Great Sanhedrin and the meetings of the Kallah were taken down in writing. The decisions, proclaimed by the Gaon and Exilarch, became halakhah. This is the *Gemara,* "Body of Instruction

We would not fully understand the Talmud today had it not been for a great medieval commentator, Rashi, who wrote a running commentary to every sentence and word. It is printed at the margin of every Talmud edition.

Based on Tradition."[1] Exploring Written Torah in the light of Oral Torah, Mishnah and Gemara combined are called *Talmud,* the "Compendium of Study." Eventually, the accumulated material was twice revised and edited under the direction of Rav ASHEE (c. 335–c. 427), the head of the academy of Sura for close to fifty years. He was assisted by his disciple Ravina. The work was completed around 500 C.E., although some of the tractates of the Mishnah remain without Gemara. We call this work *Talmud Bavlee,* the Babylonian Talmud.

The Babylonian Talmud follows the orders of the Mishnah and its subdivisions. Each Mishnah is quoted verbatim and four orders (plus two tractates from the other two orders) are followed by Gemara, the debate and explanation. It would be difficult to find one's place in the Talmud, which consists of many heavy folio tomes, were it not for a truly ingenious arrangement. In all editions of the Talmud, the paging is the same. If we are referred, for instance, to "B.T. Baba Kamma 83b," we know that the text can be found in the Babylonian Talmud, Tractate Baba Kamma (in the Order of Damages dealing with civil law) on page 83b (on the back of leaf 83).

The Talmud is not a dead compendium of conclusions, for it

Showing the interaction of some of the principal sources of Judaism, this page from the Babylonia Talmud, Sanhedrin, chapter 3, draws a picture of the study of a passage from the Mishnah: Mishnah and Gemara (center); Rashi's commentary (right); the Tosafot (left); textual notes by Elijah, Gaon of Vilna (1720–1797) (far right); citations of where to find pertinent material in the main codes of law, the commentary of the tenth-century North African Rabbi Hannuel, and annotations of Rabbi Sirkes (1561–1640) of Poland (far left).

1. Originally, Jews spoke simply of Mishnah and Talmud. During the Middle Ages, when Talmud was maligned by Christians, and Jews were persecuted on account of its "blasphemies," Jews used the term *Gemara,* hoping to be left in peace.

breathes the living spirit of the debates and discussions that gave rise to it—questions and answers, bonmot and jest, to the point and rambling. Everything is in it, halakhah and aggadah, discussions encompassing every field of human knowledge from law to medicine, biology to geology to astronomy. Life in its entirety passes in review.

Talmudic exchanges of thought can still make for difficult reading, especially due to the Rabbis' frequent free association of one subject with another. The Talmud must be studied rather than merely read. Even in English translation, some parts may be fairly easy reading while others call for guidance by an experienced tutor. In this sense, the compendium of interpretation and guidance has remained Oral Torah: it can still be mastered only through discussion and personal instruction.

> *Rabbi Eleazar ben Azariah said: A Sanhedrin that put a man to death even once every 70 years was considered bloodthirsty. Rabbi Tarphon and Rabbi Akiba said: had we been members of the Sanhedrin no one would ever have been executed (Mishnah Makkot 1:10).*

The elaborate arguments of the Talmud should not deceive us. According to the Rabbis, the Torah, given by God, was perfect and unchangeable law, and every nuance of it had to be examined. The Gemara does not hold with a theory of historical evolution, so if the word of Torah did not agree with ideas of justice as the Rabbis held them, then the fault lay not with the Torah but with human error in re-interpretation. For example, if Judaism had outgrown the literal interpretation of the scriptural verse "an eye for an eye," the Gemara points out that the practice could never have been Jewish justice as intended by God—the Torah must be interpreted in order to establish the true intent of the law in line with its divine spirit of justice and of love. Although an interpretation may seem tortuous, it is simply the effort to adjust law without abolishing the word of Torah.

Babylonian Jewry after the Completion of the Talmud

The completion of the Talmud around 500 C.E. came none too soon. Persecutions were taking place in Persia. Islam, the religion of Mohammed, had begun to spread all over the Middle East and lands around the Mediteranean. The year of

Mohammed's death, 632, saw the transition of Babylonia from Persian to Islamic rule. The relationship which developed between the two religions was good, for Mohammed himself had learned much from the Jews in Arabia. Exilarchs and Gaonim continued in their positions and the yeshivot flourished for several hundred years.

As Islam conquered country after country, cultures were fused. Persian ideas became accessible, arts and sciences flourished. In addition, the works of the Greek philosophers became widely known, and many Jews were greatly attracted by Greek philosophy with its compelling logic. Jews in general viewed their faith from within; they lived inside Judaism, and it never occurred to them to step outside—as the philosopher must—to view it from without and to talk *about* it. Meeting with Aristotle's arguments led to the development of Jewish philosophy. At the same time, dissension within Judaism arose in the eighth century C.E. as the Jewish sect of the *Karaites,* Scripturalists, emerged, recognizing only the Written Torah and rejecting the Oral Torah, embodied in the Talmud.

The man who addressed himself to all of these issues was SAADIA GAON. His appointment as Gaon was an exception among the Gaonim; he hailed from Egypt and came from a humble family. He was appointed only due to his superior knowledge.

Saadia wrote in Arabic, the language that the Babylonian Jews knew best. He translated the Bible into Arabic, a translation still used by Jews in the Middle East. He wrote commentaries to a number of the books of the Torah, made a Hebrew dictionary, and compiled a Hebrew grammar. He edited the prayer book and wrote original prayers.

Uncompromising in his decisions, Saadia was a man capable of engaging all opponents. His life was therefore stormy. As a philosopher, he could meet the arguments of the Greek philosophers (see ch. 33).

As new centers of learning developed in diaspora communities in Spain, Italy, and Germany, the Gaonim hoped to make the Babylonian Talmud the authoritative foundation of halakhah and themselves the exclusive halakhic authorities for all of Jewry (as against the Jerusalem Talmud and the decisions of the Palestinian Jewish authorities). They succeeded. They sent their Talmud to the communities of the diaspora, dispatched emissaries to all diaspora communities, and issued *teshuvot*, formal responses, to their questions. The Babylonian Talmud became *the* source of halakhah.

Chapter 24

PRAYER AND THE PRAYER BOOK

The Hebrew term for prayer is *tefillah*, from the root *pll*, which means praying, evaluating, meditating, anticipating, pleading before the Judge, praising, and giving thanks to God. Prayer combines respect with love, reverence with intimacy. Another term for prayer, *avodah*, originally applied to the sacrificial service in the Temple but was used later by the Sages to emphasize that the people's prayers, offered with devotion, rank equally with the sacrificial service. Prayer is "service of the heart" (B.T. Taanit 2a). Supplication, thanksgiving, intercession—all of this is prayer, speaking with God. Reflecting on the spiritual meaning and purpose of life can also become prayer. And the study of Written or Oral Torah is prayer too—in a very real sense, for it is communion with God.

Offered with *kavvanah*, "attunement of heart," prayer brings us into an absolute intimacy with God in which the world, with all its pain and sorrow, is removed. Prayer is thus one of Judaism's healing gifts, even if God does not answer as we wish.

BIBLICAL PRAYER

Jewish prayer is as old as Judaism. Prayer runs through the pages of Torah like a silken thread, holding together its history and people and linking God's children to God, whom they affirm and praise by pouring out their needs and offering their thanks. The thread links biblical and post-biblical times. For instance, we find in the Book of Ben Sirah, which belongs to the Apocrypha, a prayer that is a model for the Amidah, the core of daily worship as established by the Sages.

The Sages ascribed the initiation of the three daily prayers to the patriarchs: Abraham inaugurated the morning prayer, *Shaharit*, as he set out to sacrifice his son Isaac in obedience to God's command; Isaac initiated the afternoon prayer, *Minhah*, when he meditated in the afternoon in expectation of the wife God would send to him; and Jacob began the evening prayer, *Ma'ariv*, when he, fleeing from the wrath of his brother Esau, sought a night's rest in the wilderness, asking for divine shelter (B.T. Berakhot 26b).

Prayer in the Torah teaches us how to converse with God. Based on an intimacy with God, prayer dares to ask and to challenge, as when Abraham pleaded with God for the preservation of the wicked city of Sodom, should God find but ten good people in it: "Far be it from You . . . to bring death upon the innocent as well as the guilty. . . . Shall not the Judge of all the earth deal justly?" (Gen. 18:25). Abraham's words show great respect, trust, and affirmation, and out of these qualities grew his challenge. In the same spirit, Moses appealed to God's mercy on behalf of the people who had made an idol (Exod. 32:9–14), and further pleaded that God personally guide the people to their land.

God's divine attributes, revealed to Moses, guide every person to enter into prayerful dialogue.

> The Lord! the Lord! a God compassionate and gracious, slow to anger, abounding in kindness and faithfulness, extending kindness to the thousandth generation, forgiving iniquity, transgression, and sin . . . (Exod. 34:6–7)

Those who pray know to Whom they pray. When Hannah, mother of Samuel, prayed for the child so far denied her, she "was praying in her heart; only her lips moved, but her voice

could not be heard" (1 Sam. 1:13). Always near, God simply is—
in glory, power, majesty, love, and infinite mercy. Solomon's
Temple was dedicated to prayer—the simple, heartfelt outpouring of those who came to worship, not only Jews but all peoples
(1 Kings 8:27–43).

On the Early Evolution of Formal Prayer

During the period of the Second Commonwealth, the
Temple was Judaism's religious center, and priests conducted its
sacrificial service. The priests, who lived throughout the land,
were divided into twenty–four watches and took turns "going
up" to Jerusalem to conduct the sacrificial service. Eventually,
the people desired to be represented as well, and a delegation of
distinguished laymen from the hometowns of the priests—the
Anshe Maamad—"Bystanders"—joined each watch to offer
prayers in the Temple. The people in the Bystanders' home
communities conducted simultaneous services in their synagogues, and weekday services became common.

The morning service, *Shaharit,* which coincided with the
morning sacrifices, reviewed the world's and Israel's walk
through time and history, from creation through revelation to
redemption. The Bystanders gave thanks for the new day, an
ever-new creation; then they expressed gratitude for the Torah
and read the Ten Commandments and the Sh'ma, which are
God's revelation; then they affirmed God's grace in redeeming
Israel from its oppressors in the past, which gives assurance of
Israel's ultimate redemption. Each day they read the appropriate
passage from the creation story, offered psalms and petitions,
and may have concluded with the majestic Alenu hymn.

In early afternoon they offered an additional prayer, *Mussaf,*
with special pleas for those in danger and distress. Later, coin-
ciding with the afternoon sacrifices, they rendered an afternoon
prayer, *Minhah.* At the time of the closing of the Temple gates,
they presented a closing prayer, *N'ilah.*

The fall of the Temple in 70 c.e. was a shattering experience. Some rabbis were despondent that "the gates of heaven

henceforth are closed" (B.T. Berakhot 32b). Rebukingly they were told, "The gates of heaven are never closed, God is always near to those who call" (Deut. Rabba 2:12). The synagogues became the centers of communal prayer. Some of the Temple rites were transferred to the synagogue, for example, the sounding of the shofar on Rosh Hashanah, the festive bouquet of Sukkot, the processions and prostrations (reserved for the High Holy Days), and the priestly benediction; other rites, especially the sacrifices, were abolished. The people were assured that God's presence dwelt in every synagogue:

> How do we know that God's presence is found in every synagogue? Because it is said, "God stands in the divine assembly" (Ps. 82:1). (B.T. Berakhot 6a)

Rabban Gamaliel II, the first Nasi after the fall of the Temple, understood the people's need for prayer after the terrible tragedy that had befallen them. Under his guidance the order and content of the obligatory prayers were reformulated and their sequence and content were laid down. Their wording, however, continued to be left to the *shaliah tzibbur,* the congregation's "messenger," any gifted Jew of high character possessing the skill to frame and render the prayers who was invited by the assembly to lead the congregation in prayer. All prayers had to be framed in the plural, for the messenger spoke for all those who had honored him as their speaker. The members of the congregation stood listening in reverent silence and identified with each prayer by responding, at the end, *Amen,* "So may it be."

Many centuries passed before the text of the prayers was canonized. The first prayer book originated with the Gaon Rav AMRAM (810–875). Responding to an inquiry of the congregation in Barcelona, Spain, he sent them his *seder* (order). He thereby canonized the text of the prayer book, from which all others derived. A single authorized text could adequately express the yearnings of the heart whereas the average person alone might not find the words. Above all, a single, uniform text would unite the Jewish people throughout the world.

THE MAIN PRAYERS OF THE DAILY SERVICES

The prayers offered in the Temple and in subsequent synagogue services set the pattern for Jewish daily services: *Shaharit* (morning prayer), *Minhah* (afternoon prayer), and *Ma'ariv* (evening prayer), plus *Mussaf* on Sabbath and holy days and *N'ilah* on Yom Kippur. All of the services contain a number of blessings (berakhot), and the day is bracketed at morning and evening by Judaism's central affirmation, Sh'ma. Kaddish, the Amidah, and Alenu are recited at every service.

Aware of the danger that formal prayer can become a matter of routine, or words spoken thoughtlessly, the Rabbis emphasized that prayer must be an outpouring of the heart. Body and soul must be filled with kavvanah, holy attunement to God. The form of the prayers is to be the vessel into which the spontaneity of the human heart is to be poured.

Berakhah: The Blessing

To foster the awareness of God's presence, the rabbis surrounded the entire life of the Jew with prayer. For this purpose they devised a basic, formulaic unit of prayer, the *berakhah* (blessing), which begins "Blessed are You, Lord, our God, Ruler of the universe...." Of biblical origin, the prayer was used by the Psalmist, "Blessed are You, O Lord; train me in Your laws" (Ps. 119:12). Eventually, every occasion came to be hallowed by blessing:

> Over fruit growing on trees one says: "Blessed are You, Lord, our God, Ruler of the Universe, who creates the fruit of the tree"...
> Over wine one says: "Blessed... who creates the fruit of the vine"
> ...Over fruits of the ground one speaks: "Blessed... who creates the fruit of the ground." Over bread one pronounces: "Blessed ...who brings forth bread from the earth." Over anything which does not grow from the earth one says: "Blessed... by whose word all was created." After a meal everyone shall say grace. (Mishnah Berakhot 6:1, 3, 6)

We offer blessings "over comets, earthquakes, thunder, storm and lightnings, over mountains, hills, oceans, rivers and deserts; ... over rain and on getting happy news ... on receiving evil tidings." On happy events, on the annual return of the festivals, or if we build a house or buy new clothes, we speak the berakhah: "Blessed are you, Lord, Our God, Ruler of the universe, who has kept us alive, hast sustained us and has brought us to this time" (Mishnah Berakhot 9:2, 3, 5).

Berakhot serve a crucial function in all communal synagogue prayer and are recited privately to accompany every facet of an individual's life as well. The blessings reveal Judaism's existential theology: the Jew's thoughts constantly revolve around God as Creator and Sustainer of the world, and the enjoyment of this world makes us realize that everything really belongs to God. We may have grown our food or bought it, but we request God's permission to use it. Contemplating nature and history, we recognize God's sovereignty and our stewardship. Mourners at the moment of their bitter grief, the moment of parting from a dear one, praise the Judge, whose judgment is truth.

Sh'ma

The Sh'ma affirms God's covenant with the Jews as one people linked to the One God. Jewish being and survival rest on the love of God, and this love commits the Jews to love God in return. Jews express their commitment in the great affirmation of faith from Deuteronomy 6:4–9, known as the Sh'ma from its opening words *Sh'ma Yisrael*, "Hear, O Israel."

The Sh'ma accompanies Jews throughout life, giving form and unity to their existence. The prayer is learned by Jewish children when they begin to speak and is uttered by Jews with their last breath. Every Jew in every land knows the Sh'ma. Countless generations have recited it aloud.

The Sh'ma
Hear, O Israel! The Lord is our God, the Lord is One.

[Congregation adds in affirmation (not in Bible): *Blessed be the Name of God's glorious kingdom for ever and ever.*]

You shall love the Lord your God with all your heart and with all your soul and with all your might. Take to heart these instructions with which I charge you this day. Impress them upon your children. Recite them when you stay at home and when you are away, when you lie down and when you get up. Bind them as a sign on your hand and let them serve as a symbol on your forehead [literally, between your eyes]; inscribe them on the doorposts of your house and on your gates. (See Deut. 6:4–9)

Amidah: Petition

The Amidah—meaning "standing," which the worshiper does when reciting it—consists of a series of short petitions, each a berakhah. Originally, the version offered on weekdays contained eighteen berakhot, hence another name for prayer: *Shemone Esre*, the "Eighteen." A nineteenth berakhah was added, directed against apostates, during the early years of Christianity. At morning prayer (*Shaharit*), afternoon prayer (*Minhah*), and *Mussaf* service the Amidah is first spoken silently by each worshiper and then repeated out loud by the cantor; at evening prayer (*Ma'aviv*) it is recited silently but not repeated aloud.

The Amidah has three sections treating (1) contemplation of God (three berakhot); (2) our needs (three sets of three berakhot and one set of four); (3) our most precious goods (three berakhot). On Shabbat and the festivals, the second section is replaced by one berakhah of homage and thanksgiving.

The nineteenth berakhah, in the middle section, was added after the name "Eighteen Prayer" had already taken hold. The Nasi Rabban Gamaliel introduced the berakhah around the fall of the Second Temple, when members of splinter groups within Judaism, including the Christians, used the occasion of

OUTLINE OF THE AMIDAH

Section 1. Contemplation of God
1. The Redeemer
2. The Sustainer of the living and the dead
3. The Holy One

Section 2. Statement of our needs
A. *SPIRITUAL NEEDS*
4. *wisdom and understanding*
5. *return to Torah, service, and repentance*
6. *acknowledgment and plea for forgiveness of sins*
B. *PHYSICAL NEEDS*
7. *conciliation of conflict*
8. *healing*
9. *sustenance*
C. *ISRAEL'S NEEDS*
10. *redemption, ingathering, freedom*
11. *justice under God's rule*
[19.] *abolition of evil, frustrating the hopes of evildoers [added petition]*
12. *vindication and mercy for the just and pious, leaders, scholars, faithful converts, all the people*
D. *THE WORLD'S NEEDS*
13. *redemption and the rebuilding of Jerusalem*
14. *the Messiah*
15. *acceptance of prayer in loving divine response*

Section 3. Our most precious goods
16. *divine acceptance of our worship*
17. *gratitude to God and the wondrous gifts that surround us*
18. *peace*

PRAYER AND THE PRAYER BOOK   353

regular synagogue worship to make converts to their sect. Seeing in this missionary activity a danger to the purity of Judaism, the berakhah against sectarians, the *Birkat ha–Minim,* was added to the Amidah. Members of the sects could not respond with "Amen" to the berakhah, which implores God to bring the activities of the sectarians to nothing; they were thereby recognized and no longer admitted to services. Later the Church accused the Jews of having added the benediction specifically against the Christians, and under the pressure of Christian censorship it had to be revised. The berakhah following *Birkat ha–Minim* includes a plea for the vindication of faithful converts of Judaism whom the Church claimed would be damned.

Peace is the most sublime of all gifts. With this prayer the Amidah reaches its climax and its conclusion:

The Kaddish

Reader: *Magnified and sanctified be His Great Name throughout the world which He has created according to His will. May He establish His kingdom during your life, your days, and during the life of all the House of Israel. To this say: Amen*
People: *Amen. May His great Name be blessed for ever and ever.*
Reader: *Blessed and lauded, glorified and lifted up and exalted and enhanced and elevated and praised be the Name of the Holy One, Blessed be He, although He is high above all blessings, hymns and lauds and uplifts that can be voiced in the world. To this say Amen.*
People: *Amen.*
Reader: *May there be abundant peace from Heaven, and life for us all and for all Israel. To this say Amen.*
People: *Amen*
Reader: *May He who establishes peace in His universe, make peace for us also and for all Israel. To this say Amen.*
People: *Amen.*

Grant peace to the world ... with grace, love and mercy for us and all Your people Israel. Bless us, our Father ... one and all with the light of Your Face, for by that light of Your face have you given us the Torah of life and love of kindness, and justice, blessing, mercy, life and peace.

The Kaddish: Sanctification

The opening words of the Kaddish are based on a prophecy by Ezekiel: "I will magnify Myself and sanctify Myself and make Myself known in the sight of many nations. And they shall know that I am the Lord" (see Ezek. 38:23). Ezekiel tells of conflicts in times to come, when the whole world will be drawn into battle. Out of it, God will emerge in glory, and the divine majesty be vindicated. The Jew, not waiting for the end of days, glorifies God now.

A very old prayer, the Kaddish was written partly in Aramaic, the vernacular of the people, long before the fall of the Temple. The prayer was recited at the end of rabbinical lectures in the Bet Midrash, the house of study, and may still be recited after a talmudic lecture. Today the Kaddish is used widely. It serves as a call to worship for *Mussaf* and *Minhah*, as part of the closing section of all of the daily prayers, and as a concluding proclamation marking the sections of public worship. Its central affirmation is the unison testimony of the congregation: "May God's great Name be blessed for ever and ever." It has been given many different musical settings for various holy days. Kaddish is also recited by mourners as evidence of their faith in God even in moments of supreme agony. The Kaddish shows parallels to the Christian prayer, the Lord's Prayer, indicating one of the ways that Christian liturgy developed from Jewish sources.

Alenu: Adoration

Public worship originally concluded with the Kaddish. There is a magnificent hymn, however, whose first section was probably recited by the *Anshe Maamad* in the Temple to conclude their daily services, called Alenu. It reflects the task, the dedication, and the hope of every Jew. This prayer opens with a call to Israel to bend the knee to God, if need be alone in a heathenish world, and ends with assurance that the day will surely come when all humanity will worship God. The hymn was incorporated into the *Mussaf* of New Year's Day, but its vision of the future is so beautiful, its outlook so universal, and its language so poetic that it was ultimately also included in the three daily services, as their fitting conclusion.

The hymn was held by the Church to contain a slur against Jesus. This contrived accusation was totally without substance, but persecution and censorship forced the Jews to eliminate the passage. So severe were the persecutions that in the ancient Jewish community of Mainz, Alenu was no longer recited as public prayer.

Alenu

[The Task:] *Unto us [Alenu] the duty is given to praise the Lord of All, to give greatness to the Creator of the world. For He has fashioned us unlike other people of the many lands, situated us unlike the families on earth, assigned us a lot unlike theirs and a destiny unlike their throng.*

[The Dedication:] *Therefore we bend the knee and bow down to render homage unto the King of the king of kings, the Holy One blessed be He. He stretched forth the heavens and established the foundations of the earth. The seat of His glory is in the heavens above, the majesty of His power in the loftiest heights. He is our God, there is none else.*

[The Hope:] *We therefore put our hope in You, O Lord our God, that we may soon behold the glory of Your might, when You will remove idolatry from the earth and all false gods will wholly be wiped out, and the world be set aright under the Kingdom of the Almighty, and all humanity will call upon Your name. When You will help the wicked of the earth to turn to You. May all the inhabitants of the earth become aware and understand, that unto You alone every knee must bend and every tongue pledge allegiance. Before You may they bend the knee, giving glory to Your Name. May they all accept the yoke of Your Kingdom, and You rule over them forever. For the Kingdom is Yours, and to all eternity You will reign in glory, as is written in Your Torah: "The Lord shall reign forever and ever." And it is said: "The Lord shall be King over all the earth. On that day the Lord shall be One and His Name shall be One."*

THE STRUCTURE OF THE DAILY SERVICES

> You shall love the Lord your God with all your heart and with all your soul and with all your might. Take to heart these instructions with which I charge you this day. Impress them upon your children. Recite them when you stay at home and when you are away, when you lie down and when you get up. (Deut. 6:5–7)

The morning and evening prayers have their foundation in these words of Torah. Twice a day these words must be rehearsed: in the morning, as guidepost of the day; in the evening, as a yardstick to review the day's accomplishments. The afternoon prayer lets us pause to reflect in the midst of our work: How well have we done so far? What must we yet do to give the day true meaning? Thus we have three daily prayers: *Shaharit*, the morning prayer; *Minhah*, the afternoon prayer; and *Ma'ariv*, the evening prayer.

All the daily services share a very similar structure. The

congregation recites Psalms in order to enter into a spirit of *reflection*. The public service commences with the prayer leader's *call to worship*, "Bless God . . .," and the congregation's response; Kaddish opens worship in the afternoon and at *Mussaf*. This is followed morning and evening by *affirmation* (Sh'ma), and then *petition* or *homage* (Amidah). The service concludes with the *sanctification* of God's name (Kaddish), adoration (Alenu), and the repetition of the Kaddish. The basic structure adjusts to the time of the day, day of the week, Shabbat, and festivals, so that each service has a particular character.

The order of Jewish worship closely follows the structure of Psalm19:
  God is Creator of nature: "The heavens recount the glory of God."
  God is the loving Giver of Torah: "The Torah of the Lord is perfect, restoring the soul."
  Humans petition God: "Errors, who can discern them; cleanse me from hidden ones."
  Plea: "May the words of my mouth and the meditations of my heart find grace before you."
  Adoration: "You, O Lord, are my Rock and my Redeemer."

MORNING PRAYER. Even before *Shaharit*, morning prayer begins with berakhot giving thanks for the new day and preparing us for the day ahead. *Shaharit* includes three berakhot, after the call to worship, that affirm God as (1) Lord of nature; (2) the loving Giver of Torah (followed by the Sh'ma); and (3) Lord of History. Then the Amidah is recited. On weekdays, individual penitence follows the Amidah; on festivals, the recitation of Psalms 113–18, Hallel, the Psalms of Praise. The congregation receives the Word of God as read from Torah on Monday, Thursday, fast days, festivals, and Shabbat.

On Sabbath and holy days, special additional sacrifices were offered in the Temple of old; after its fall, the *Mussaf* came to be assigned only to these special days and combined commemoration of the ancient sacrifices with the plea for restoration of the Temple. Similarly today, the *Mussaf* is offered following the Torah reading of the day on Sabbaths, festivals, and Rosh Hodesh (New Moon).

AFTERNOON PRAYER. The significance of afternoon prayer, *Minhah*, lies in the Jew finding a moment in the midst of the day to put his or her worldly pursuits aside, commune with God, and renew the knowledge that all success depends on divine

Poets and Poetry

Throughout the Middle Ages, rabbis and cantors were often their own lyricists, writing poems for special occasions and inserting them in various sections of the obligatory prayers. These poems are called Piyyutim from the Greek poietes. Their creators are called Payyetanim, "poets." For a while, some of the Gaonim opposed the insertion of extraneous poetry in the obligatory prayers. Their opposition was of no avail, and soon we find great rabbis, for instance Saadia Gaon, writing Piyyutim for special services. Some of these Piyyutim were of lasting literary value, others were not. Individual congregations created their own liturgical customs by adopting or rejecting certain Piyyutim.

The printing press brought an end to the free creation of Piyyutim and, at the same time, contributed to the length of the service. In order to insure wide acceptance of their books, printers published all of the Piyyutim that were in vogue among a variety of congregations. This "canonized" the poems in popular use at the time regardless of their artistic merit, prevented new ones from being composed, and led worshipers to think that all of the prayers in the book had to be read or sung.

mercy. Afternoon prayer invites individual penitence on weekdays and includes a Torah reading on Shabbat and fast days.

EVENING PRAYER. In the time of the First and Second Temple, evening prayer, *Ma'ariv*, was not related to any sacrificial offerings. Reciting the Sh'ma has always been obligatory but the rest of the service was not. Eventually, evening prayer obtained the same structure as morning prayer (with the exception of the repetition of the Amidah), and the two prayers frame the day. As morning prayer opens with berakhot of preparation, evening prayer includes a prayer for protection during the night:

Grant us, O Lord our God, to lie down in peace, and raise us up again, O our Ruler unto life. Spread over us the tent of Your peace. Direct us aright through Your good counsel; help us for Your Name's sake. Be a shield about us. Keep away from us every enemy, pestilence, sword, famine, and sorrow. Protect us from evil desires that may confront us or follow us, but shelter us in the shadow of Your wings. For You, O God, are our Protector and Deliverer. Guard our going out and our coming in unto life and peace, from now on and for evermore. Blessed are You, O God, who guards Your people Israel for ever.

N'ilah, the prayer when the Temple gates were closed each day, became a metaphor for the closing of the gates of heaven. Thus we say it, with deep fervor, only at the end of Yom Kippur, the Day of Atonement, when the prayer brings the day to its climactic conclusion.

These Palestinian Jews wear tallitot and tefillin as they pray together at the morning service.

WORSHIP AND THE JEWISH PERSONALITY

Jewish worship in content and form, poetry and chant, mirrors the Jewish character. The Jew is realistically optimistic and loves life regardless of the many scars it inflicts on Jewish bodies and souls. Beginning everyday with a song, the Jewish person is decently aware of the body, neither considering it deserving of neglect nor regarding it as a source of sinfulness. Belief in immortality entails the conviction that the soul is precious, the gift of God that came pure to all humans; there is no original sin. Human beings are free to work out their individual destinies and with the help of God can become the co-workers of the Eternal One. The worshiper is aware of the frailty of all human beings but also of the abundance of God's mercy. Being both mortal and co-worker with God, the Jew humbly rejoices in the task God has given humans in the world, and finds happiness in the intimacy which binds the Covenant people directly to the Absolutely One God. God the Eternal is approached by each individual person directly without intermediary, and grants the human being the consciousness of assured

Jewish Liturgical Music

Prayer is not simply read, it is chanted. Readings from the Torah and the Prophets are recited to the congregation in a chant based on short melodic figures used in various combinations that follow the natural speech rhythm of the words; the Gregorian chant of the Catholic Church was profoundly influenced by it. Annotations for the cantillation of Torah are found in the printed Hebrew Bible but not in the scroll from which it must be recited. The reader must know the chant by heart, and so the recitation of Torah is an art which can be learned only through long study.

Similar groups of melodic patterns—called modes—are used for the prayer chants, some of which, like the Torah recitatives, are very ancient. The basic building blocks of Jewish chant, the modes were given names. A very old mode, for instance, has the title Me-Sinai, "from Sinai"—as if to say, this melody was given at Mount Sinai.

Beyond these basic melodic gestures, Jewish music shows the influences of many ages, many lands, and varied conditions. German Jewish liturgical music, for examples, contains the trills and embellishments of the medieval troubadour, the swirls of the Baroque, the majestic hymns of German choral music, the harmonic structures of Western music. In Eastern European Jewish music, we recognize the introspective minor keys of Slavonic song. Israeli music resonates with the shepherd's plaintive voice and the Yemenite camel driver's desert litany. Thus a superstructure was built on the basic modes that varied from country to country, bearing the marks of Jewish dispersion. Since most Jews in America, Europe, South Africa, and Israel trace their origins to Eastern Europe, the mood of Slavonic melancholy can be found in much of Jewish liturgical music today. The joyful exuberance of the Klezmer (Yiddish from the Hebrew k'lei zemer) musicians who played at weddings and other joyful occasions in the shtetl, has entered the concert halls of America, sometimes combined with jazz elements.

---

redemption. While the Deist says that God no longer regulates the world, the Jew knows that God is here—in nature, in Torah, in mitzvot, and in history. With God revered as ruler of history, vision becomes worldwide; the Jew's prayer becomes one for all humanity, for the redemption of the world and for universal peace. In action or, if need be, in suffering, the Jew hopes to bring closer this future under God. Jewish prayer expresses gratitude, readiness for service, and hope for peace.

Knowing of God's everlasting concern for every individual, the Jewish congregation is a society of equals, a democracy without priest or intermediary, and—ideally—without class distinctions. Every individual is indispensable for the formation of the minyan—the ten people required for formal liturgical prayer—but is incomplete without the other nine, and he or she feels certain that under God all of society will someday become such a congregation, if only humans persevere in toiling for a united humanity.

At the same time, Jewish worship reveals an ideology that has come under challenge. Traditional Judaism presumes the worshiper to be male, for only the man is commanded to study Torah and put on tallit and tefillin. God is "our Father in heaven," the father is head of the household, loving and stern, gracious but entrusted with authority. His wife is his helpmate, "a royal princess" but her glory is within the house (Ps. 45:14). Women did not function in worship, and were relegated to the gallery veiled from the men's synagogue below. All prayers were composed in the masculine, and the women, frequently poorly educated, used their own additional prayer book, the *Techines* (Yiddish for "Supplications"), containing prayers in Yiddish.

Modern women, out of the very spirit of Judaism, have challenged this outlook and practice for two reasons: (1) all Jews must be treated as equals; and (2) excluding half of the Jewish people from making this full contribution to the intellectual and spiritual growth of Jews and Judaism is a waste of great resources. Jewish worship thus mirrors the evolution of Judaism itself as it meets ever-new exigencies to preserve its eternal spirit.

The Jewish tradition of chanting prayer has given us the cantor. Great cantors can truly move multitudes. Many have also composed special theme songs for every festival, giving each holy day a musical theme by which it can be recognized. Cantors trained their successors for many years until they had mastered the craft. Eventually, cantors also obtained conservatory training and learned to write down the music that they created. Modern cantors receive religious and musical training in the cantorial schools of rabbinical seminaries. In addition, recent composers of first rank, among them Ernest Bloch, Darius Milhaud, and Leonard Bernstein, have written music for Jewish worship and incorporated Jewish musical themes into their general works. There are hopeful signs of a revival of Jewish music that fuses traditional Jewish music and modern aesthetic forms.

Dressing for Prayer

Words have a deeper impact when they are reinforced by concrete reminders—outward signs—of their meaning. Jews wear several such reminders as objects of worship: the prayer shawl, phylacteries, and skull cap. By dressing for prayer in a special way, Jews put on tangible symbols of their belief. They show their respect for God and at the same time "wear" their identity in an intimate way.

Tallit

The Lord said to Moses as follows: Speak to the Israelite people and instruct them to make for themselves fringes on the corners of their garments throughout the ages; let them attach a cord of blue to the fringe at each corner . . . ; look at it and recall all the commandments of the Lord and observe them. (Num. 15:37–41)

Jews in antiquity commonly wore a four-cornered robe, as do the Bedouins to this day. The fringe, which by Jewish law had to be attached to it, was a constant reminder to stay within the bounds of decency, morality, and ethics. We no longer wear four-cornered robes, but we make a special four-cornered garment to wear during worship—the *tallit*. Young people begin wearing the tallit when they reach the age of bat mitzvah or bar mitzvah. In the past, women did not wear the tallit, but many do today. It can be long and wide, permitting the worshiper to wrap the body in it or draw it over the head to exclude the world while in communion with God; it may be a smaller "prayer shawl." It is worn in daytime only—when one can "look at it" and see it by the natural light of God's sun—but the leader of worship wears it even at night. Putting it on, the Jew is always careful to have the ribbon at the top and facing outward, for the tallit must not be worn upside down. The tallit clothes the worshiper in responsibility and at the same time wraps him or her in the warmth and comfort of God's presence.

The tallit can be of any color, which has inspired modern weavers to fashion talliot of artistic designs and colors. The fringes at the corner, *tzitzit*, must be white and consist of four cords knotted by hand in a prescribed manner. The cord of blue is no longer included, since we do not know which hue of blue the Torah had in mind. From the original combination of white and blue the colors of the State of Israel have been derived, thereby symbolizing the roots of the modern state in the eternal Torah.

What Is a Congregation?

Whenever ten are gathered together, they can form a minyan, a quorum for the purpose of public worship. Among the Orthodox, only men may be counted; in most non-Orthodox congregations, women are recognized as equal to men and perform all of the functions in public worship; they are counted in the minyan, lead the service, are called to speak the blessing of the Torah, read from the Torah, preach, and are ordained as rabbis and cantors. The congregation represents the Household of Israel.

Tefillin

> Hear, O Israel! The Lord is our God, the Lord is One. You shall love the Lord your God with all your heart and with all your soul and with all your might. Take to heart these instructions.... Bind them as a sign on your hand and let them serve as a symbol on your forehead; inscribe them on the doorposts of your house and on your gates. (See Deut. 6:4–9)

The phrases, bind them upon your hand, have them between your eyes, may be meant figuratively: Let God guide the work of your hand and give you vision. The commandment was, however, interpreted literally as well, as an order to have visual reminders of these spiritual rules. These visual reminders are the *tefillin*: the words about the love of God, written on small parchment scrolls, are encased in a small black parchment cube attached to a leather strap, and one of the straps is wound down the arm to the hand. Thus—visually—the hand is placed under God's command and

Why ten for a minyan? *As the Rabbis point out, the term* congregation *is used in the Bible in connection with a group of ten: Of the twelve scouts Moses sent to Canaan to explore the enemy's strength, ten came back to report: "We cannot conquer our enemy even with God's help." God called out: "How much longer shall that wicked congregation keep muttering against Me?" (see Num. 14:26). In this typical example of rabbinical interpretation of a Torah text (Mishnah Sanhedrin 1:6), the biblical congregation of scouts who defeated God's plan is replaced by the true congregation of worshipers who promote God's plan.*

the arm with its strength submits to God's rule; placed on the left arm, the commandment faces the heart, directing its desires creatively. A similar phylactery with the same words in it is attached to a strap and placed high on the forehead between the eyes, thus encircling the Jew's mind by the commandment of love and directing the vision of our eyes. Tefillin are worn during morning worship on weekdays; Shabbat surrounds the Jew with an atmosphere of holiness, so no other reminder is needed on that day.

The passage in Deuteronomy that commands the use of the tefillin led to the creation of another visual reminder, the *mezuzah*, literally, "doorpost," from the text "inscribe them on the doorposts of your house and on your gates." A small scroll including the Torah words of the Sh'ma is encased in a container and affixed at the right hand doorpost (as one enters), slanting inward toward the inside of the house or room. Taken figuratively, the command in Deuteronomy bids us to make the love of God and the teaching of Torah our motto, so that our home may become a sanctuary. A visual reminder, the mezuzah invites those who enter to bring with them the spirit of love, in order that the home may remain a sanctuary of God; it admonishes those who go out into the world to carry the spirit of love into their work and dealings with others. It is like tefillin for the house, binding all who enter.

Kippah

Orthodox Jewish men keep their heads covered at all times, wearing a skull cap, or *kippah* (a Yiddish word for the cap is *yarmulka*). Although some Jews do not wear kippot at all, most non-Orthodox Jews wear them at prayer, in the synagogue, or

when they study the Bible and Tal-
mud. The head covering may be used
to proclaim that the human being is
subject to God, as did Rabbi Huna,
who "never walked four cubits with
uncovered head, for he used to say:
the Shekhina, God's Presence, resides
above my head" (Kiddushin 31a).
The head covering has become a
symbol of Jewish self-affirmation in
society.

No Jewish custom is more difficult to explain than the
wearing of the hat in the synagogue. The Torah has no ruling
about it. The Talmud observes simply: "Men sometimes have
their heads covered, and sometimes go bareheaded; women always cover their heads; children always go bareheaded" (B.T.
Nedarim 30b). This pointed to complete freedom of choice as
far as men were concerned.

Male head covering may perhaps have become fixed in deliberate opposition to Christianity. Paul rebuked those who
kept their heads covered in prayer (1 Corinthians 11:2–5). In
pronounced contrast, Jews insisted that the men wear hats
when praying or reading from the Torah.

In the Shulhan Arukh, Jewish code of law, we find three
rulings that were gathered in from ordinances issued at various
times. Each is more restrictive than the one preceding, indicating a process of evolution, and, perhaps, mirroring the increasing outside pressure upon the Jews. In viewing these laws, we
conclude that the law and custom had remained fluid until very
late in Jewish history, hardening at a period when external oppression, internal strictness, and literal interpretation reached
their height.

Another explanation may be suggested. In the Middle Ages
the king, as the Head of the State, kept his head covered while
his courtiers bared theirs as a sign of humility. In the same
manner, the Torah reader, as spokesman for God, was to have
his head covered, symbolically expressing the majesty of God,

the Head, whose word he proclaimed. Further, to the medieval Jew, the Jew-hat was a mark of humiliation imposed by the Christian community. He may have responded by making it a badge of honor. Forced upon him as a sign of shame, it became for him an emblem of proud self-identification. In the synagogue, where he was free to develop his own pattern of conduct, he insisted on the hat, as if to say: You force us to wear a hat in the street in distinction from you. We choose to wear it in the House of God, where you remove it, for we deem ourselves royal princes rather than outcasts, and may keep our heads covered in the presence of the King of Kings. Thus the hat of humiliation was transformed into a crown of distinction, a token of self-identification, the symbol of Jewish pride and self-respect.

This emotional attachment may explain why Jews have held on to the wearing of the hat with such tenacity. As a custom, anchored in the emotions of the people, the covering of the head has exerted a greater power than many a well-established law that has been modified or abolished. No change in Jewish practice has met with greater resistance than the rule of American Reform Judaism permitting worship with uncovered heads. In many Reform congregations, rabbis and cantors again wear kippot and their use is growing among the members—men and women alike.

These women wear talliot and kippot as they pray together at the morning service.

THE STRUCTURE OF WORSHIP

	Morning	[Mussaf]	Afternoon	Evening
	Berakhot on arising			
Reflection	Psalms	Psalm	Psalm 145	Psalms
Call to Worship	Call to worship	Kaddish	Kaddish as call to worship and affirmation	Call to worship
Affirmations	Creator of Nature Giver of Torah Sh'ma Sovereign of History			Creator of Nature Giver of Torah Sh'ma Sovereign of History Prayer for protection Paraphrase of Amidah (weekdays only)
Petitions	Amidah Repetition of Amidah Individual penitence (weekdays only) Festive Psalms, Ps. 113-118 (on festivals only)	Amidah Repetition of Amidah	Amidah Repetition of Amidah Individual penitence (weekdays only)	Amidah (no repetition)
Torah reading	(Mon., Thurs., Shabbat, festivals, and fast days)		(Shabbat and fast days)	
Sanctification	Kaddish Alenu Kaddish	Kaddish Alenu Kaddish	Kaddish Alenu Kaddish	Kaddish Alenu Kaddish

Chapter 25

THE JEWISH CALENDAR

The Jewish calendar is developed from a lunar calendar that is adjusted to the solar year. To count the months, Jews follow the phases of the moon; holidays coincide with the seasons as well, so the months must also be adjusted to the cycle of the sun.

In ancient days, making this adjustment was simple because every new month was officially pronounced by the Sanhedrin. Witnesses who had observed the first emerging sickle of the new moon appeared before the court and were examined; upon their evidence the court declared the first day of the new month, *Rosh Hodesh.* Messengers were sent throughout the land to spread the news. Depending on the moon, or on the arrival of the witnesses, a month might have twenty-nine or thirty days. This information was extremely important, for the exact date of the holidays was counted from the date of the new moon. If spring was slow in coming and the grain not yet ripe, the Sanhedrin would declare a leap year, which meant adding one complete month. Thus the lunar year was adjusted to the cycle of the seasons by actually observing nature itself. The calendar was balanced through astronomical calculations as well.

Under order of the Christian emperor Constantius (337–361), the Jewish court was no longer permitted to determine the calendar and announce it. The measure was one of numer-

The messengers who carried the news of the beginning of the month were only able to cover the territory of Palestine in the time between the first of the month and the holidays. For this reason, Jews in the diaspora were sometimes late in getting the news and were never quite certain about the length of the preceding month. To be sure that they observed the holiday on the appointed date, they celebrated for two days. Thus it came that holy days were observed for one day in Israel and for two days among traditional Jews elsewhere throughout the world.

Today, the dates of holy days are exactly fixed, but many Jews in the diaspora still observe two days where Israelis observe only one. There is actually no reason for the observance of a second day, since we know the exact date, and so Reform Jews have eliminated the observance of the second day, while others have retained it in deference to tradition and custom. Conservative Judaism left its observance to congregational option.

ous decrees against the Jews, designed to disrupt their way of life. The grave danger that this posed for Jewish life motivated Patriarch Hillel II in the year 358 C.E. to work out a permanent, fixed calendar and send it throughout the entire Jewish world. Hillel's calendar, with minor corrections in the tenth century, still works today.

Hillel's task was not easy. He had to adjust the lunar year of 354 days with the solar year of 365 days, an annual difference of 11 days. Then he had to ensure that certain holy days would not fall on certain weekdays. The Day of Atonement, for example, could not fall on Friday or Sunday, for the day of fasting and complete work prohibition would interfere with preparations for Shabbat, or Shabbat would interfere with preparations for the fast.

To achieve the proper balance, the Jewish calendar includes seven leap years in nineteen years. Each leap year has one additional month. Solar year and lunar year are equalized over a period of nineteen years:

19 *solar* years of 365 days equals	6935	days

19 *lunar* years of 354 days equals	6726	days
plus 7 leap months of 30 days equals	210	days
	6936	days

Within the nineteen solar years, there are a number of leap years with 366 days. These, and other slight differences, were taken care of by varying the length of the years. Some regular Jewish years have 354 days, some have 353 days, and some have

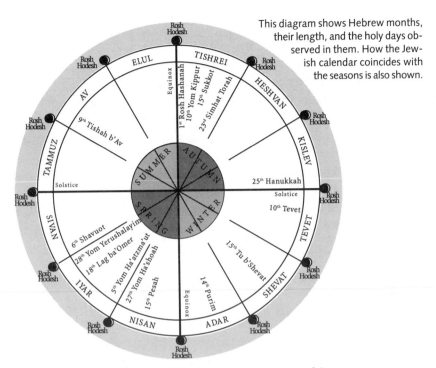

This diagram shows Hebrew months, their length, and the holy days observed in them. How the Jewish calendar coincides with the seasons is also shown.

355 days. Leap years have 30 days more than these. In this way, all of the differences between solar years and lunar years are equalized, and the holy days fall on the right days of the week. With the leap months, the date of a Jewish holy day moves back and forth within a span of 30 days.

The Jewish year has twelve months: Nisan, Iyar, Sivan, Tammuz, Av, Elul, Tishrei, Heshvan, Kislev, Tevet, Shevat, and Adar. In leap years an extra month is added at the end of the year, called Adar Rishon (First Adar); the regular Adar becomes Adar Sheni (Second Adar). Some months are 29 days long, and others 30. Because the beginning of the month corresponds to the beginning of a lunar cycle, the date on which a feast falls is also linked to a particular phase of the moon. Pesah and Sukkot, marking the transition from winter to spring and from summer to fall, occur on a full moon; Rosh Hashanah, on the new moon.

The year has more than one "new year": Torah designates Nisan as the first month, with Pesah coming mid-month; Jews celebrate the new year as a feast on Rosh Hashana, in the seventh month—Tishrei. Nisan and Tishrei, with Pesah, the Days of Awe, and Sukkot, are the pillars of the Jewish year; they mark the spring harvest and fall harvest and coincide with vernal and autumnal equinoxes (except in leap years).

Years are counted from the "creation of the world." Using the genealogy in Genesis, the generations are added up to provide the total number of years since Adam. Hallowed by tradition, this system has never been changed, irrespective of scientific discoveries. In writing the year, the thousands may sometimes be omitted. The plaque commemorating the death of the martyrs in Worms, for example, reads 856 but means 4856 (1096 C.E.).

SHABBAT AND HOLIDAYS

The seventh day of each week—Shabbat, the Sabbath—marks a day of rest in accordance with Torah: "God blessed the seventh day and declared it holy, because on it God ceased from all the work of creation" (Gen. 2:3). The celebration of Shabbat, the "Queen of Days," permeates the life of the Jews and guides the observance of the other holidays of the year, which are also days of rest.

Jewish holidays are natural pauses for reflection through the year. Their dates follow the calendar as the calendar follows the seasons. There are three types of festivals:

1. *Shalosh regalim*, the Pilgrimage Festivals—Pesah, Shavuot and Sukkot—celebrate events in nature and in Jewish history, as does Simhat Torah.

2. *Yamim Noraim*, Days of Awe or High Holy Days—Rosh Hashanah and Yom Kippur—have less contact with nature and place the Jew "outside" the world in communication with God.

3. The minor festivals—Hanukkah, Tu b'Shevat, Purim, Lag ba'Omer, Yom Ha'atzma'ut, and Yom Yerushalayim—celebrate events in nature or moments of redemption in Jewish history. Fast days, above all Tishah b'Av, commemorate tragic events. (Yom Ha'atzma'ut, Yom Yerushalayim, and Yom Hashoah are of recent origin.)

Chapter 26

SHABBAT, THE SABBATH

Shabbat—the Sabbath—is the heartbeat of history. It restores strength to the weary and brings hope to the disheartened. Shabbat resonates in the daily life of the Jew. It makes humanity human and is the foundation of social justice; all other social legislation is based on it. Shabbat—the right to rest for all—was a revolutionary innovation and constitutes one of Judaism's greatest contributions.

Counting the days of a week was established by the Semites, who, early on, studied astronomical phenomena. While counting the days grew naturally from the observation of nature as the farmer divided the moon's cycle into its four phases, the Jews gave the last day, the Sabbath, a new and twofold meaning: it became a day of universal rest, making real the universal equality of master and slave, employer and employee, lord and servant, humans and beasts; in addition, it became a time of spiritual recreation and restoration.

Judaism considers Shabbat the holiest of holy days. It is the only holy day enjoined in the Ten Commandments, which give two versions of the Shabbat ordinance:

Remember the sabbath day and keep it holy.... For in six days the Lord made heaven and earth and sea, and all that is in them, and

He rested on the seventh day; therefore the Lord blessed the sabbath day and hallowed it. (Exod. 20:8–11)

Observe the sabbath day and keep it holy . . . that your male and female servants may rest as you do. (Deut. 5:12)

Remember the Sabbath, Torah says: Remember that God is the Creator of the universe to whom all of creation is dear, who is close to all humanity, and who has appointed humankind to act as stewards of the divine creation and in kinship to each other as children of God. At the behest of the Creator of all, you and all who work for you must lay down all work. *Observe the Sabbath,* the Torah adds: Your divine Employer requires that you grant rest equal to your own to those who work for you. "Remember and observe were spoken in one divine breath," the Rabbis stated: *remembering* charges us to celebrate the spiritual character of Shabbat, while *observing* translates it into social action (B.T. Shevuot 20b). The two cannot be separated, and without social justice during the week, Shabbat is without meaning as well (Isa. 1:13–14).

To Jews, Shabbat is the supreme comforter in trouble. They count the days of the week in relation to it: first of Shabbat (Sunday), second of Shabbat (Monday), and so on. I learned this as an inmate of the Sachsenhausen concentration camp. The denial of Shabbat was one of the ways that the Nazis dehumanized their captives. By taking it away they tried to deprive us of hope, for the days were to flow in the endless monotony of slave labor. But even though we could not enjoy the blessed presence of Shabbat, we knew it was there, and, dishonored as we were, we did not lose our dignity.

Shabbat is a sign of the Covenant between God and Israel (Exod. 31:12–17). Prophets emphasized that Shabbat guarantees Israel's eternity and binds the people together in indestructible unity (Isa. 56:1–7, Jer. 17:21–27). Restoration of Shabbat in purity was central to Nehemiah's work of religious and physical renewal (Neh. 13:15–22). The Rabbis of old remarked: "As Israel has kept Shabbat so did Shabbat keep Israel alive."

WORK PROHIBITION

Rest and the cessation of work had to be defined. Left to individual interpretation, the spirit of the command might be violated; the master might decide that his servant's tasks were not really "work." This must not be, for all must be treated alike. Written Torah states that God rested from all work (Gen. 2:2), but human beings cannot rest from every last bit of work and survive. As its starting point in elucidating the work prohibition, Oral Torah began with the fact that the world is God's sanctuary (see Isa. 66:1). Therefore all work once connected with the sanctuary that Israel built for God—the Tent of Meeting in the desert—shall cease. Israel's rest will then correspond to God's rest and both will rest from all tasks linked to the making of the sanctuary: God in the creation of the world, Israel in the building of the Tent of Meeting. According to the Mishnah (Shabbat), this led to the prohibition of thirty-nine basic kinds of work:

1. The growing and preparation of food: plowing, sowing, harvesting, and so forth; baking, cooking, broiling: 11 prohibitions.
2. Clothing: shearing, washing, bleaching, spinning, weaving, sewing, and similar work: 13 prohibitions.
3. Leather work and writing: catching animals, slaughter, skinning, tanning, preparation of furs, preparation of parchment, writing, erasing, and so on: 9 prohibitions.
4. Shelter: building or demolition for the purpose of re-building: 2 prohibitions.
5. Fire: kindling and extinguishing: 2 prohibitions.
6. Work completion: the final hammer stroke and touch: 1 prohibition.
7. Transportation: Moving objects from one private domain to another, or into public domain, or within public domain, or from public to private domain: 1 prohibition.

To these basic prohibitions, the Rabbis added secondary ones. In order to prevent preparation for future work, which would cancel out the idea of Shabbat rest, the handling of tools, the implements of work, and raw materials was prohibited. With regard to travel, a city surrounded by a wall may constitute a single dwelling and all people may move within its confines; walking 2,000 cubits (about three-fourths of a mile) beyond a city's limit is travel, however, and is prohibited. The use of vehicles violates the rest of animals. The use of the automobile or turning on electricity calls for the creative act of producing fire, and these actions are prohibited according to the traditional interpretation of the law. The intent of the prohibitions is basic: Physical effort as such need not constitute labor, regardless of how strenuous it may be; creative effort, however, is indeed work, regardless of how small the physical effort involved.

Under these conditions rest is complete, and the spirit of Shabbat takes over. But Shabbat is not a day of gloom and joyless worship; it has no Puritan harshness. Of all festivals, the Talmud states: "Half is for God, half is for you" (B.T. Betzah 15 b). Food, drink, song, the afternoon nap, the leisurely walk in the fields or on riverbanks are all part of the traditional Shabbat. Many a boy and girl can find each other during an afternoon stroll on this day. Consummation of married union is part of the holy day's joys.

Modern life and conditions have changed Shabbat observance. Some changes have occurred as Reform and Conservative Jews have interpreted and reinterpreted halakhah. Like other aspects of Judaism, the details of Shabbat observance might grow and develop. We must take extreme care, however, that the restlessness of our age not erode the sanctification of the day as we *remember* and *observe* it. A Jew who has not fully tasted Shabbat will never know how great is its loss; and those who brush it aside in hasty living miss out on one of the great joys in life.

TRADITIONAL SHABBAT OBSERVANCE

Every day starts with the night preceding it. "And there was evening and there was morning" says Torah (Gen. 1:5), putting night before day. All days, including Shabbat and all holy days, begin on the preceding evening. Thus Friday night is one of the highlights of the week: the beginning of Shabbat.

Friday

Traditionally, the whole day Friday was devoted to Shabbat preparations. The house was cleaned and food prepared. In the afternoon, the women took their main dish for the next day to the baker in whose great oven it would cook overnight, or they might place it in their own oven. Three meals were ordained for the day, and they were the best the household could provide. A Jew might starve during the week, but the Shabbat meals had splendor.

The people dress in their best Shabbat clothes. A white tablecloth, carefully guarded during the week, covers the table. Candlesticks gleam, and a goblet and decanter of wine stand next to the plate of the head of the house. Next to the wine are set two loaves of twisted bread, symbolizing the twofold measure of manna that God gave to the Israelites in the desert on Friday to last them through the Sabbath; the loaves are covered by an embroidered cloth, as dew once covered the manna (Exod. 16:14–27). The loaf is called *hallah*. Wine and bread are the most perfect gifts of food and drink, an equal blend of God's bounty and human ingenuity. They are perfect symbols for giving thanks.

As dusk falls all is ready; now is the moment to relax. I have seen people in the poorest sections of Jerusalem at this hour, their houses gleaming, their faces radiant, their children around them, and the greeting on their lips: *Shabbat shalom,* "the peace of Shabbat be with you."

Traditionally, the male members of the family go to the synagogue.

Fish is a traditional Shabbat dish. Eastern European Jews invented gefillte fish. The fish were split open and the meat removed, leaving the skin intact. Then the meat was chopped up, mixed with bread and spices, and replaced in the fish. The fish was "filled." Gefillte fish has remained a favorite and famous Jewish dish, although prepared more simply today in the form of fish balls.

Even the poorest Jew is bidden to have Shabbat lights and Shabbat bread. A pauper may have to beg for it, borrow it, or starve for it during the week, but Shabbat must be honored. There is only one exception. If, in providing for Shabbat, a person would lose human dignity, then, as Rabbi Akiba says: "Treat your Shabbat as a weekday" (B. T. Shabbat 118a).

Blessing the Shabbat candles on Friday evening: At dusk, the mother lights and then blesses the candles. As a rule, a berakhah must precede a mitzvah, but this is not possible at this time, for as soon as the mother speaks the blessing, her Shabbat begins and the kindling of lights is forbidden. She therefore lights the candles first, then speaks the blessing, shielding her eyes from the light to enjoy it only after the blessing. On festivals, when the kindling of lights is permitted, the blessing precedes the lighting of the candles.

✦

According to legend, when the men return home from the synagogue Friday evening, two angels go with them, a good one and a destructive one. If the home is filled with Shabbat spirit, the good angel blesses: "May it be thus next week also." But if there is no Shabbat spirit, the destructive angel says: "May it be likewise next week." Each angel always has to respond to the other angel, against his will, "Amen," so be it. Thus did the rabbis recognize the psychological significance of habit on a person's ability to worship. The family welcomes the Shabbat angels: Shalom Aleikhem, "Peace be with you," may your coming, your blessing, and your going be unto peace. The hymn has become universally popular. In the author's childhood, the family would hold hands and march around the room while singing.

The mother, mistress of the home, lights the candles. There are at least two, a double portion of light compared to the one portion of the week. Spreading her hands, she speaks the blessing: "Blessed are You, O Lord our God, Ruler of the world, Who has sanctified us ... by commanding us to kindle the Shabbat lamp." Standing in front of the candles she asks God's blessing upon her home, her husband, her children, and her dear ones. Shabbat has arrived.

When the men return from the synagogue, the parents lay their hands upon their children in blessing: saying for boys, as Jacob had taught, "God make you like Ephraim and Manasseh" (Gen. 48:20), and for girls, "God make you like Sarah, Rebecca, Rachel, and Leah." Then, "The Lord bless you and keep you..." (see Num. 6:24–26). In verses from Proverbs, gratitude is expressed to the mistress of the house, source of all its blessings: "What a rare find is a capable wife! ... Extol her for the fruit of her hand, and let her works praise her in the gates" (Prov. 31:10–31).

The members of the family wash their hands and gather around the table. The head of the house raises the cup. (Cup, *kos*, derives from the word *kosas*, "that which is measured out by God"—it symbolizes our destiny.) The *Kiddush*—Hebrew for "sanctification"—is sung. This traditional prayer over the wine that ushers in

Shabbat begins with the scriptural story of the first Sabbath, when the heaven and the earth were finished and God rested from all His work and blessed the seventh day (Gen. 1:31; 2:3). The berakhah over the wine follows. Then God is praised for the gift of Shabbat: God has sanctified us by the commandments and in love and favor has given us holy Shabbat as a heritage, "Blessed are You, Who sanctifies the Sabbath." The celebrant of the Kiddush drinks from the cup and passes it to the members of the family. Then the family speaks the berakhah over the bread, it is broken,

Gathered around the table as the Sabbath meal begins, the family shares wine from the Kiddush cup.

and a portion is passed to each member of the household. The meal begins. When the meal is completed, Shabbat hymns (Z'mirot) are sung, the Torah portion of the week might be discussed, grace is offered, and then the family retires.

Friday evening services in the synagogue traditionally begin at sundown. In years past, only the men would attend the service while the women ushered in Shabbat at home. The Shabbat meal would follow the men's return from the synagogue. Now many communities hold the service later, after families have finished their Shabbat meal.

Worship opens with *Kabbalat Shabbat*, the "Reception of Shabbat" with psalms (Ps. 95–99 and 29) and hymns. The mystics of Palestine had a custom of going out into the fields in solemn procession to welcome the Shabbat Bride as she entered the town. Solomon Alkabetz (c. 1505–84), a member of the Safed circle of mystics, wrote the poem, "Lekhah Dodi," and it became one of the most popular hymns of the

Kiddush must always be linked to the meal. On Friday nights and most holy days (with the exception of Pesah), Kiddush is also recited in the synagogue. Originally, this was on behalf of wayfarers, who were then fed in the synagogue annex. Today, reciting Kiddush in the synagogue has become a public proclamation of Shabbat and the holidays.

synagogue: "Come my friend the Bride to meet; the Sabbath in person we will greet." As the hymn reaches the last verse, the whole congregation turns around and faces the door in greeting, as if Shabbat were entering:

Come then in peace, crown of your spouse,
come also in joy to jubilant applause,
amidst your faithful, God's very own tribe
come you, O Bride, come you, O Bride.

With a courtly bow the congregation receives her. Shabbat has come.

Psalms 92 and 93 are sung. Psalm 92, connected with the Sabbath in Scripture, opens with thanksgiving, then turns to reflection. Humans cannot understand God fully. Wickedness and injustice succeed and flourish; how can that be? Shabbat gives the answer. Evil triumphs but for a moment; the work of evildoers has no future, but the righteous will flourish forever and declare "that the Lord is upright, my Rock, there is no flaw in Him." Psalm 93 acknowledges God as ruler, robed in grandeur and firmly enthroned from eternity; the world cannot be shaken and God's decrees will endure forever. "Holiness befits Your house, O God, for all times." Reviewing life in the light of Shabbat, the Jew finds it good, both in general and in personal terms, for God rules. The evening prayer follows.

Late Friday night services, introduced in many congregations to serve those unable to attend either earlier services or Shabbat morning worship, are worthwhile in giving the congregation an hour of fellowship with blessings, food, and song. But their deeper value has lately been questioned. Many Jews feel that the people should be guided to find their way back to the beauty of the family celebration and the inspiration of Shabbat morning worship when Torah is read.

Shabbat Day

Worship, attended by the whole family, fills the morning. The Torah is read, a different portion every week. As the family returns home, Kiddush is again recited over the cup of wine and the fourth commandment, the ordination of Shabbat, is repeated. After a brief meal, family members visit friends, the newly wed, or the sick, or those in mourning. Early afternoon brings the main meal with table hymns and grace. An afternoon "nap" becomes a "delight," as the rabbis held. This is typical of Judaism's earthiness—its realism and its ability to give enjoyment a spiritual dimension. Judaism has never been ascetic; it hallows decent earthly pleasures and has thereby survived.

Saturday is a traditional time for the study of Torah and Talmud. *Minhah* is recited in the synagogue, then the family takes a walk. Return-

At the Havdalah ceremony with his family, this little boy smells the sweetness of Shabbat.

ing home just before dusk, they gather for the third meal. Jewish mysticism developed this hour into a time of mystical union. As night shadows slowly rose, disciples used to share a morsel of the food their rabbi had tasted and listen to him as he pierced the gathering darkness with visions of eternity.

The End of Shabbat: Havdalah

Three stars in the sky proclaim the end of the day. Once again the people assemble for worship, and in Psalms 144 and 67 they express their faith and their hope as they face the burden of the week: "Blessed is the Lord, my rock, who trains my hands for battle, my fingers for warfare [the battles of life]" (Ps. 144:1); "May God be gracious to us and bless us" (Ps. 67:2).

After the evening prayer has been completed a last farewell is offered to Shabbat in the synagogue and at home. Light and the cup, which have welcomed the day, gently usher it out in a

Once a special Shabbat lamp graced every home. It hung from the ceiling and could be raised and lowered. In its star-shaped bowl, oil was poured on Friday evening to give light during the Sabbath meal. At the end of Shabbat, the lamp was raised up to the ceiling for another week, and the medieval Jew said: "As the lamp comes down, sorrow goes up to vanish; as it goes up again, sorrow comes down once more." But as the lamp went up the Jew began to count: "This is the first day toward the next Shabbat." This hope upheld him, this forward look kept him alive and proud.

ceremony called *Havdalah,* meaning "Separation." Havdalah is surrounded by prayers and biblical quotations invoking God's help during the forthcoming week. The cup is filled. A box of spices—*besamim*—is on the table; the spice box is frequently in the shape of a tower, for God is the Tower of Salvation. A twisted candle, like a torch, is lighted and held by one of the children. This begins the first day of the week, when God created light and blessed it. The prayer of Havdalah begins with words of confidence:

Behold the God who gives me triumph!
I am confident, unafraid;
For Yah the Lord is my strength and might,
and He has been my deliverance. (Isa. 12:2)
I raise the cup of deliverance and invoke the name of the Lord. (Ps. 116:13)

The berakhot blessing the wine and the spices follow. The leader waits as the spice box is passed around, giving the family a last breath of the sweet scent of Shabbat. Then the leader takes the candle from the hand of the child who has held it and speaks: "Blessed are You, God . . . who creates the illumination of fire." Slowly the leader passes his or her hands beneath the flame, watching the play of lights and shadows. The reader takes the cup again and completes Havdalah:

Blessed are You, O Lord our God . . . who did make distinction between holy and secular time, between light and darkness, between Israel and other people, between the seventh day and the six days of work. Blessed are You, God, who makes distinction between holy and secular time.

The candle is extinguished in a drop of wine poured from the cup. The wine is consumed; Shabbat has ended. The people who have greeted each other on Friday evening with *Shabbat shalom* (or, in Yiddish "gut Shabbes") now wish each other *Shavua tov* (in Yiddish, "gut Woch"), a "good week." It is held that the prophet Elijah, Israel's guardian, is present at this juncture of sacred and ordinary time, and many families sing a popular traditional hymn to him, *Eliyahu ha-Navee,* expressing their hope with the words, "May he come and bring the Messiah."

Chapter 27

PILGRIMAGE FESTIVALS AND SIMHAT TORAH

According to Torah, Jewish families were expected to travel to Jerusalem to celebrate three feasts in the year:

> Three times a year—on the Feast of Unleavened Bread, on the Feast of Weeks, and on the Feast of Booths—all your males shall appear before the Lord your God in the place that He will choose [during the period of the Temple, Jerusalem]. They shall not appear before the Lord empty-handed, but each with his own gift, according to the blessing that the Lord your God has bestowed upon you. (Deut. 16:16–17)

Because of the requirement to go to Jerusalem, these three feasts are known as the *shalosh regalim,* "three pilgrimage festivals." Pesah (Passover, the Feast of Unleavened Bread) is celebrated in the middle of the first month (Nisan), with Shavuot (the Feast of Weeks) coming seven weeks later. Sukkot (The Feast of Booths) begins on the 15th of Tishrei, the seventh month, following the Days of Awe (the High Holy Days); adding a ninth day to the celebration of Sukkot brings another festival, Simhat Torah.

The three pilgrimage festivals are connected both with the cycle of nature (its awakening in spring, flowering in summer, and maturing in fall) and equally with pivotal events in Jewish history (the Jewish people's birth in the Exodus, development in the giving of the Ten Commandments, and maturing under God in the journey through the wilderness).

The great modern Jewish thinker Franz Rosenzweig saw the road of history rehearsed in the liturgical year through these three festivals: Pesah, telling of the liberation of the Jews, celebrates the *creation* of Israel; Shavuot, commemorating the giving of the Ten Commandments, celebrates divine *revelation*; Sukkot, celebrating divine protection, forecasts *redemption*. Many Jews of the diaspora, especially those in the ghettos, came to lay greater emphasis on the religious background of the festivals than on their seasonal character, but they never totally lost sight of the festivals' character as holidays of nature. In modern Israel, the twofold character of the holidays has recovered its full expression.

PESAH (PASSOVER), THE FEAST OF UNLEAVENED BREAD: REBIRTH IN FREEDOM

With the Exodus the Jews gained their freedom and obtained their inalienable rights to life, liberty, and the pursuit of duty with which the Creator has endowed all human beings. Pesah is the Independence Day of the Jewish people. Pesah is also the festival of Spring, of sprouting grain, which marks the onset of the harvest in the Holy Land; the first barley was cut after Pesah and offered in the Temple. Both aspects of Pesah—freedom and spring—are mentioned in Torah:

> In the first month, on the fourteenth day of the month, at twilight, there shall be a passover offering to the Lord, and on the fifteenth day of that month the Lord's Feast of Unleavened Bread. You shall eat unleavened bread for seven days. On the first day you shall celebrate a sacred occasion: you shall not work at your occupations.... The seventh day shall be a sacred occasion. (Lev. 23:5–8; also Exod. 13:4; 23:15; 34:18)

> Observe the month of Abib [the "Month of the Green Corn"] and offer a passover sacrifice to the Lord your God, for it was in the month of Abib, at night, that the Lord your God freed you from Egypt. You shall slaughter the passover sacrifice for the Lord your God, from the flock and the herd, in the place where the Lord will

choose to establish His name. You shall not eat anything leavened with it; for seven days thereafter you shall eat unleavened bread, bread of distress—for you departed from the land of Egypt hurriedly—so that you may remember the day of your departure from the land of Egypt as long as you live. For seven days no leaven shall be found with you in all your territory. (Deut. 16:1–4)

At the onset of the renewal of nature in spring, Judaism celebrates Pesah, the rebirth of the community. The Jews were redeemed from Egypt and freed from bondage so that they might form a community proclaiming "release throughout the land for all its inhabitants" (Lev. 25:10). Having been slaves and having felt the bitterness of oppression firsthand, Jews acquired empathy with the oppressed. Jews have never hidden the fact that they were slaves in Egypt. To be a slave is no reason for shame; it is only shame to enslave others.

Unleavened bread, *matzah*, symbolizes both slavery and freedom. In Egypt, the Jews had little time to bake real bread, so matzah had to do; it was the bread of affliction. At the moment of their redemption, they again had too little time to bake leavened bread for the journey, "since they had been driven out of Egypt and could not delay" (Exod. 12:39); matzah in this con-

---

Not only must matzah *be eaten but also anything containing* hametz, *"leaven," may neither be consumed nor stored ("no leaven shall be found with you in all your territory"). This calls for a great spring housecleaning preceding Pesah. Everything made with starch or through the fermentation of grain has to be removed from the house; even the last crumb of bread has to go. Leaven is used in a great variety of items: bread and pastry, alcohol made of grain, tablets made with starchy binders, medicines containing grain spirit, and so forth. On the night before the holiday, the family searches the house for the last remnants of leaven: "One must search for the hametz by the flame of a light" (Mishnah Pesahim 1:1). The candlelight march through cellars, rooms, and attic becomes a joyful event for the children, who gather crumbs (left on purpose) to be burned the next morning in a bonfire. The injunction against hametz also forbids the use of dishes and cooking utensils that have come in touch with hametz during the year, so special Passover dishes are used for the feast. As people cast out the leaven of time and habit, they are reborn and their spirit is renewed.*

text represents freedom. Unleavened bread is to be eaten for seven days because on the seventh day after having fled Egypt, the Israelites crossed the Red Sea, finally free from their enslavers. This explains the length of the festival, seven days (eight in most communities in the diaspora). The first days, the departure from Egypt, are full holidays; the middle days, the period of marching, are intermediate holidays, *hol hamoed*; the last days, Israel's liberation, are again full holidays.

In the courtyard of the Baghdadi Synagogue in Bombay, India, a woman prepares matzah. The unleavened bread, matzah, consists of only flour—guarded throughout the year against fermentation—and water. Quick kneading and baking prevents rising. No other ingredients may be added. It is flat and thin, for heat has to penetrate it quickly to bake it to a crisp.

The Seder

The Passover sacrifice ceased with the end of the Temple in Jerusalem; none of the ancient sacrificial services have been performed for almost 2,000 years, prayer taking their place. But the story of freedom is still told on the eve of the festival in a family rite of great beauty, warmth, and inspiration. It is called the *Seder* and is observed even by Jews who are otherwise lax in religious observance.

Seder means "order," for the celebration follows a definite order based on the guide of the *Haggadah,* the "Story" (or literally, the "Telling"). Traversing Jewish history from its beginning to its eventual culmination in universal, messianic peace, the Haggadah tells the story of the Exodus and includes many elements (prayers, stories, songs, poems). The Haggadah existed in the time of the Temple, and is outlined in chapter 10 of the tractate of Mishnah dealing with Pesah. The service revolves around the meal, which is truly a Holy Supper.

THE CUPS. At each place at the table there is a copy of a Haggadah and a cup. Each cup will be filled with wine four times,

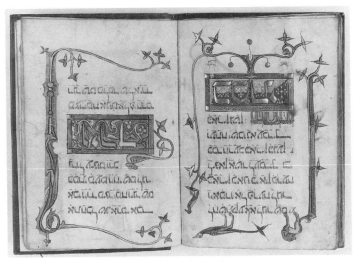

The family's celebration of Pesah is guided by the Haggadah.

and four times it will be emptied. This corresponds to four promises God made to Israel, all of which have been fulfilled:

> I will free you from the labors of the Egyptians and [I will] deliver you from their bondage.
> I will redeem you with an outstretched arm and through extraordinary chastisement.
> And I will take you to be My people, and I will be your God.
> (Exod. 6:6–7)

According to rabbinic interpretation, the fifth promise—"I will bring you into the land"—speaks of ultimate redemption, the messianic time. Security for Israel and for humanity as a whole is still far-off but will surely be reached with the help of God, our work for it, and our hope. According to the prophet Malachi (Mal. 3:23), the messenger of the end of days is Elijah the prophet. He is envisioned as present at the transition from enslavement (in any form) to complete liberation. For him, another cup is placed in the center of the table. No one drinks from it, but everyone is aware that the salvation of humanity can become a reality, today or tomorrow, if we hold out the cup of Elijah.

THE MATZOT AND SYMBOLIC FOODS. In the center of the

The Seder meal contains three matzot and six foods that symbolize both hardship and the joy of freedom.

table, near the seat of the head of the house, is the Seder Plate. It contains three matzot, the bread for which God is to be blessed, which will be broken and shared; the three matzot stand for the three family groups in Israel—the Priests, the Levites, and the Israelites, all of whom were redeemed and led to freedom. Six symbolic foods are arranged on the table. Two items— *a roasted shankbone,* reminder of the Passover lamb, and an *egg,* ancient symbol of spring and a reminder of Temple offerings— are not eaten. The other foods on the plate are used in the service: sprigs of *parsley,* used in times of old and a symbol of the new, green growth of spring, as appetizer; *salt water* in which the parsley is dipped, reminder of the bitter, salty tears shed by the slaves in Egypt, and reminder as well of the salty Red Sea, which opened up to form a highway to freedom; *maror,* bitter herbs— lettuce or horseradish— reminder of the bitter life in Egypt; h*aroset,* a mixture of apples, nuts, cinnamon, and wine, brownish in looks, like the mortar that the Israelites had to prepare, and in which the bitter herbs are dipped.

Like the symbols on the table, the service alternates between memories of hardship and joy in freedom. The participants recline in cushioned chairs, as free persons. Mother speaks the blessing and lights the festive candles. Each person raises a cup, reciting the Kiddush, and everyone partakes of the wine. This is the first cup.

The leader of the Seder pours water from a pitcher over his or her hands to clean them before dipping the parsley in the salt water and distributing the sprigs so that all may partake. Hope in new life mingles with the tears of slaves.

All participants in the celebration remember that there is poverty in the world today as there was in the past. The leader breaks the middle matzah into two unequal parts, like a poor man who has only one piece of bread and breaks it to keep something for the future. The big piece is wrapped in a cloth for later use and put away. The small piece is shown to all: "This is the bread of affliction which our fathers had to eat in the land of Egypt." Those who are poor and homeless are invited in: "May all who are in need come and celebrate with us." Memories of slavery and want engender immediate action. Now the story turns to the past.

THE PAST. The Seder is keyed to the children. By telling the story of the Exodus—the central event in the distant past—the family encourages the children to carry on the Jewish ideals that the celebration calls to life and to understand the meaning and obligation of freedom. The youngest child asks four questions:

1. Why does this night differ from all other nights?
   Why tonight do we eat no bread, only matzah?
2. Why tonight do we eat bitter herbs?
3. Why tonight also, do we twice dip our herbs in condiments?
4. Why tonight do we lean comfortably [in cushioned chairs]?

The leader answers: "We were slaves and God made us free." People can be oppressed by two kinds of slavery: physical slavery and, for those who do not know God, spiritual slavery. Israel has suffered from both, and has been freed by divine grace. Jews must constantly review the message of Pesah; the ancient Rabbis, learned as they were, never ceased to study it. The Rabbis found four versions of the command that requires that the story of Exodus be told to the children. To the Rabbis, this showed that there are four types of children, each of whom approaches his or her Jewish heritage in a different way. All of them—the wise, the irreverent, the average, and the simple—must be taught in their own way to understand the meaning of freedom.

The leader tells the story of Israel's road from spiritual and physical enslavement to freedom and dignity, stressing that persecution and godlessness are not events of the past; they happen every day, and every day God helps those who are strong in trust.

> The divine promise given our ancestors abides for us also, for not merely one enemy rose against us to destroy us, in every generation did enemies rise to annihilate us, and The Holy One Blessed be He has delivered us from their hands. (Haggadah)

The Holocaust rises before the family's eyes; almost every Jew has an ancestor or relative among the six million who perished, but the Jewish people has survived. In persecution, extermination, and deliverance, Jews have become conscious that they are one mystical body. The liberation from Egypt is their own liberation:

> In every generation, each person has to feel as though he or she had personally gone forth from Egypt, as is written, You shall explain to your child on that day [the Seder], it is because of what the Eternal did for *me*, when I, myself, went forth from Egypt. (Haggadah)

In gratitude to Israel's Redeemer in all ages, the story of the Ten Plagues is recited. As each plague is mentioned, each person dips a finger into the cup and lets a drop fall onto the plate, indicating that the suffering of the enemy diminishes our joy. Then the whole family joins in the lively song *Dayyenu*. Had God done less for us, *dayyenu*, "It would have been enough for us," but the All-merciful has given us an abundance of blessings. The leader explains the meaning of Pesah, of the ancient Temple sacrifice, of matzah, and of maror, and then all sing the first psalms of the Psalms of Praise, the Hallel (Ps. 113–114), lift the cup, recite the berakhah, "Blessed are You, God, Who has redeemed Israel," and partake of the wine. This is the second cup.

THE PRESENT. From the past, the Seder now moves into the present. All wash their hands. The matzot are broken, and, with a blessing to God "who has commanded us to eat matzah," everyone eats a portion. The

Where is the afikomen? The little children, too small to understand even the simple words of the Seder, have been encouraged to "steal" the matzah. This is a way of entertaining them, of giving them something to remember for next year when they may be able to understand more. Perhaps it will teach them not to wait for the old generation to relinquish religious leadership to them but to "steal" it early. The leader of the Seder ransoms the piece of matzah with a little gift to the child.

bitter herbs are dipped in the haroset; after blessing God, "who has commanded us to eat maror" the family consumes them. The leader makes a sandwich from horseradish and matzah in memory of Hillel, the great spiritual leader of the first century B.C.E., who used to eat in this manner; the remembrance is apt because of Hillel's deep love of humanity.

A big banquet follows. Jewish law ordained that even the poor who had but little food had to provide a Seder meal of at least two hot dishes. They served boiled eggs, dipped in salt water, and the family does the same at the beginning of the dinner as a reminder to sustain those in need. The meal will be concluded by consuming the piece of matzah previously put aside; the family shares it, the most essential part of the meal, in remembrance of the ancient Passover offering and as a substitute for the Pesah lamb. This matzah is called *afikomen,* a term of unclear Greek origin. All eat a bit of the afikomen, and the dinner is concluded; no food may be eaten afterwards. Grace is recited by the family, and the third cup is emptied in gratitude for the gifts of the present.

THE FUTURE. The celebration turns to the future, the expected coming of the Kingdom of God. A child opens the door to welcome Elijah. By this time, tired and a little drowsy, the child may actually feel Elijah entering and taking a drop of the wine from his cup; did you not notice the ripples? The door is closed again, and the rest of Hallel (Ps.115–118) is sung, followed by additional psalms and hymns: "Praise God, Who is good, Whose goodness abides forever."

The family chants the anthem whose tune became the theme for Pesah:

God of Might promptly rebuild Your Temple
Do it soon, do it soon, in our days and promptly
God, o build, God, o build
build Your Temple promptly!

The family raises the cup for the fourth time, a toast of faith to the future.

The hour is late and the children sleepy. A game adapted from German folk songs of the fifteenth and sixteenth centuries keeps them awake a little longer: Who is One? God is One. What is two? Two is for the two tablets of the Ten Commandments. What is three? Three stands for the three patriarchs. And so on.

And then the final song, telling in childlike words of God's ultimate triumph in a world of injustice: My father had a little kid—but the cat ate the kid—the dog killed the cat—the stick beat the dog—the fire burnt the stick—the water quenched the fire—the ox drank the water—the butcher killed the ox—death claimed the butcher— but God wiped out death. The death of the little kid led to God's defeat of death itself. When you must suffer, little Jewish child, don't lose your faith in God. God's design has meaning, life will triumph over death.

With the wish *L'shanah ha-bah b'Jerushalaim*, "Next year in Jerusalem," the Seder ends. Bedtime prayers are omitted on the Seder night, for this night celebrates protection.

The Days of Pesah

Public worship during the Pesah festival follows the regular order of the service for festivals. The Torah reading tells the story of the Exodus. On the first day of the festival, the congregation includes a prayer for life-preserving dew, praying that the water granted us be for blessing, life, and plenty.

Beginning with the third day of the festival, part of the

Hallel Psalms of praise are omitted. Jubilation has to be curbed, for Israel's liberation caused the death of Egyptians, also God's children. In the words of the ancient Rabbis, God rebuked the angels who rejoiced at Egypt's destruction: "The works of My hands are drowned in the sea, and you want to sing?" (B.T. Sanhedrin 39b). Compassion with every human being and every creature, even the enemy, is the hallmark of freedom. This, too, is a lesson of Pesah.

The Road from Liberation to Revelation: The Counting

On the evening of the first day of Pesah, sheaves of barley were cut in the field and the measure of one *omer* (about two pints) was presented the next day at the Temple. From the second night of Pesah, the days and weeks are counted, leading to the festival of Shavuot, which falls seven weeks later and thus has the name Festival of Weeks.

> And from the day on which you bring the sheaf of elevation offering—the day after the sabbath [the festival]—you shall count off seven weeks. They must be complete: you must count until the day after the seventh week—fifty days; then you shall bring an offering of new grain to the Lord. . . . On that same day you shall hold a celebration; it shall be a sacred occasion for you; you shall not work at your occupations. This is a law for all times in all your settlements, throughout the ages. (Lev. 23:15–21)

The counting, called the "counting of the omer," links the festival of physical liberation, Pesah, and the day of spiritual liberation, when the Ten Commandments were given.

SHAVUOT, THE FEAST OF WEEKS: LIFE IN TORAH

Freedom from slavery leads to the freedom to work willingly at the tasks that God has set for us.

> On the third new moon after the Israelites had gone forth from the land of Egypt, on that very day, they entered the wilderness of Sinai. . . . Israel encamped there in front of the mountain, and

---

Moses went up to God. The Lord called to him from the mountain.... God spoke all these words, saying: I the Lord am your God who brought you out of the land of Egypt, the house of bondage: You shall have no other gods besides Me. (Exod. 19:1–20:3)

Shavuot is the feast of revelation, the giving of the Ten Commandments. It also celebrates the wonders of nature as the spring harvest is in progress. God's spiritual and physical blessings are revealed.

In the days of the Temple, bread made of new wheat was offered, and thankful farmers, their animals decorated with wreaths and garlands, would ascend to the Temple in procession and place the best of their first fruit before the altar. On Shavuot today, Jews celebrate the beginning of summer. Synagogues are adorned with flowers, the Torah scrolls bear wreaths. The Ten Commandments are read, the nonscriptural text preceding the reading of God's word: The text is a poem of deep appreciation for the gift of Torah composed by Rabbi Meir ben Isaac, a renowned talmudist, rabbi, and cantor at the Rhenish city of Worms in Rashi's time:

Jews celebrating Shavuot continue the tradition of giving thanks both for Torah–the revelation at Sinai that took place on this day–and for God's gifts in nature.

Before I shall read the [Ten] words
I plead for permission
  in two, three sentences and with trepida-
  tion
to laud the Eternal, who sustains His
  creation.
His power is timeless, all description defies,
though of parchment were made all the
  skies
all the forests' trees transformed into quills
all the world's wide seas filled with ink
and all humans on earth were scribes of skill
they would still be incapable
to relate the story
of God, the Lord's, unfathomable glory.

On Shavuot, Jews read the Book of Ruth. The story is appropriate not only because it takes place at the time of the summer harvest but also because it tells of a person's decision to choose Judaism as a way of life. At the climax of the story, Ruth, a non-Jew by birth, elects to stay with her Jewish mother-in-law, promising her, "wherever you go, I will go; wherever you lodge, I will lodge; your people shall be my people, and your God my God" (Ruth 1:16). In this way Ruth entered Jewish history as one of its "mothers"; she is the great-grandmother of King David.

The "ten words" he was to read were, of course, the Ten Commandments.

Many congregations have introduced a confirmation service on Shavuot. Young people who have completed their basic religious education, usually through junior high school years, pledge their allegiance to God and Torah on this Day of Revelation. The form of the service varies from congregation to congregation, depending on the size of the confirmation class and the character of the congregation.

SUKKOT, THE FEAST OF BOOTHS: THANKSGIVING AND JOY IN REDEMPTION

On the 15th of Tishrei, Jews observe the festival of Sukkot. Just as Pesah celebrates the spring harvest, six months later Sukkot celebrates the fall harvest. The name of the festival comes from *sukkot* (singular, *sukkah*), "booths," the make-shift huts in which the Israelites camped during their forty years' wandering in the wilderness of Sinai and that farmers in ancient Israel erected in their fields to live in during harvest time.

On the fifteenth day of this seventh month there shall be the Feast of Booths to the Lord, [to last] seven days. The first day shall be a sacred occasion: you shall not work at your occupations; ... On the first day you shall take the product of *hadar* trees, branches of palm trees, boughs of leafy trees, and willows of the brook, and you shall rejoice before the Lord your God seven days; you shall observe it . . . as a law for all time, throughout the ages. You shall live in booths seven days; . . . in order that future generations may know that I made the Israelite people live in booths when I brought them out of the land of Egypt, I, the Lord your God. (Lev. 23:34–43)

The harvest calls for thanks to God for all material blessings and for the protection of divine Providence that allows human beings to enjoy these blessings in peace. Gratitude for divine blessings is expressed symbolically by the festive offering of plants; gratitude for God's protection is expressed by the *sukkah*, the festive booth.

Sukkot is the origin of American Thanksgiving—when the Pilgrims wished to set aside a day to give thanks for the foods they had and for divine guidance to the new land, they imitated the Feast of Booths.

The sukkah is a small hut covered by branches instead of a firm roof and decorated with fruits, flowers, and wall coverings. In ancient Israel, the harvest celebration in the fields was held in such huts. In European villages, the small Jewish houses had special gables whose shingles could be replaced by a roof of branches, forming a sukkah. Many Jewish families have a sukkah, and the children visit them joyously during the holiday. Members of the family "live in it" by taking their meals there, except in rainy weather. Placing themselves beneath the starry sky, they express their faith in divine protection. Jewish congregations of every denomination have at least one sukkah, at the synagogue, in which the congregation assembles to break bread and give thanks.

Jews build sukkot in the fall, when people with summer homes seek shelter in sturdy winter houses. Jews enter the sukkah in obedience to God. This shows their trust. Throughout history, Jews have repeatedly been made homeless by their persecutors, who dwelt in comfort. The sukkah symbolizes for Jews, even in times of terror and expulsions, the assurance of God's providence and the anticipation of the day of redemption when Israel and all humanity will dwell "in the sukkah of peace" (evening prayer), protected by God.

בסכת תשבו שבעת ימים

Affirming their connection with history and nature, Polish Jews prepare to celebrate Sukkot.

ARBA'AH MINIM, THE FOUR KINDS OF PLANTS. Thanksgiving for divine protection is accompanied by gratitude for divine blessings. This is expressed in the cluster of four special plants brought to the Temple: "the fruit of hadar trees," a citron, called *etrog*; a branch of the date palm, called *lulav*; boughs of leafy trees, myrtles, called *hadassim*; and willows of the brook, called *aravot.* These plants represent all the types of vegetation brought forth by the earth. The etrog has beauty, smell, and taste; dates have no special smell but a sweet taste; myrtles no remarkable taste but a pleasant smell; willows of the brook have no striking taste or smell, and yet, like many plants, their leaves give shelter and they are essential on earth. The Rabbis saw in the four plants a parallel to human society: some people are full of wisdom and helpfulness; others may have knowledge but lack human understanding;

The lulav and etrog decorate a coin struck in 132–135 C.E.

others may be kind, yet lack great intellectual gifts; still others have no distinguished traits and are just simple human beings. All of them form one great human family in which all are essential, none expendable.

At morning prayer, *Shaharit,* Jews wave the festive bouquet—one lulav, one etrog, three hadassim, and two aravot—while reciting the Hallel, the Psalms of thanksgiving (Ps. 113–118). "Praise the Eternal who is good, whose mercy endures for ever": As each word is recited, the branches are waved in a different direction—north, east, south, west, upward, downward. God's blessings come from the four corners of the earth, from heaven above, and from the earth beneath. The divine Sustainer is everywhere and is to be thanked in every direction.

After the *Mussaf* service, which follows morning prayer, thanksgiving is once again expressed, this time by a solemn procession with the branches around the synagogue, just as in the days of the Temple when the people marched around the great altar. Taken from the Ark, the Torah leads the procession; behind it walk the members of the congregation, palms in hand. Humanity walks before God. I remember it from my childhood—every member had a palm, forming a waving forest of branches during the Psalm and a grand procession behind the Torah. As the procession advances, the reader begins to chant, and the congregation responds:

Reader (plea)	*Congregation* (response)
Hoshanah. Save us, God, we beseech You	Hoshanah
For Your sake, O our God	Hoshanah
For Your sake, O our Creator	Hoshanah
For Your sake, O our Redeemer	Hoshanah
For Your sake, You who seek us	Hoshanah

On the first and last days of the festival, which are full holidays, all work except the preparation of food is prohibited. The intermediate days, *hol ha-moed,* are secular work days of feasting, observed in worship by holding the four plants and at home by eating in the sukkah, but there is no work prohibition.

In Temple times, the end of the first day was a time of merrymaking. All of Jerusalem was wrapped in joyful abandon. Dignified rabbis danced and sang and played. Rabban Simeon ben Gamaliel juggled eight burning torches (M. Sukkah 5:1 ff.; B.T. Sukkah 53a). "You shall rejoice," Torah ordains. Pleasure is woven into the fabric of Judaism. By hallowing it, Jews eliminate the excesses which might otherwise result from too much denial or too little regulation. This balance shapes the character of the Jew.

From gaiety, Jews turn to more serious business and give thanks for the blessing of water. The last day of Sukkot is regarded as a day of judgment, namely, the amount of rain to be allocated by God. Because the procession with the plant bouquets winds around the synagogue seven times, the day is called *Hoshanah rabba,* "the day of many Hoshanah processions"; willows of the brook are held over the ground, like a divining rod. Officially, summer is over. On *Shemini Atzeret,* the eighth and concluding day of the feast, Jews leave the sukkah. Prayer for rain is offered, as prayer for dew was offered on Pesah.

SIMHAT TORAH

Diaspora Jewry celebrates Sukkot for a ninth day, called Simhat Torah, "Joy of Torah." On this day the annual cycle of Torah reading is completed and begun over again. In observing the feast, many modern Jews have recovered some of the abandon of the Rabbis' Sukkot celebrations. All of the scrolls are taken from the Ark

Dancing with their congregation's scrolls, women rejoice in the completion of the annual cycle of Torah reading and the beginning of the new cycle.

and carried around the synagogue in joyful procession, escorted by children. One of the elders of the congregation is honored by being made *Hatan Torah* (Bridegroom of the Torah); he recites the blessings over the Torah and witnesses the reading of the concluding paragraphs of the Torah. The Torah itself is the Spouse. A young member is honored as *Hatan Bereshit* (Bridegroom of the Beginning) to whom are read the first verses of the new cycle, *Bereshit*... (the opening of the Book of Genesis, "In the beginning God created...") ; in this case, the witness to the reading of the Beginning is the spouse of creation. In Conservative and Reform synagogues, women are also called upon for these honors and are called the Bride of Torah and Bride of the Beginning. After the reading, old and young dance joyfully with the Torah scrolls in their arms.

In rejoicing with the Torah, the long season that started in penitence with the Days of Awe at the beginning of the seventh month ends. Torah in hand, thanksgiving in the heart, certain of God's protection and willing to witness it, the Jew dances into the dark winter months of the year, knowing that with God's help winter's long night will lead to a new spring.

Chapter 28

YAMIM NORAIM, THE DAYS OF AWE

In the fall, after the harvest, the farmer reviews his successes and failures and plans how to remedy mistakes he may have made—a new year begins for him. We may also say that the farmer, having completed the chores of the summer, turns his creative thought toward the year to come. His "new year" is thus a moment of rest, change, and creation.

Jews, too, observe their main New Year in autumn. The Jewish New Year also honors the creation of the world, which is said to have taken place at this time. The New Year's season is a period of accounting for the spiritual harvest; it calls for an evaluation before God of one's life and work: It is a time of repentance. Each New Year opens with *aseret yeme teshuvah*, "ten days of repentance," which include Rosh Hashanah, followed by seven days that culminate in Yom Kippur. Rosh Hashanah and Yom Kippur are *Yamim Noraim*, "Days of Awe." They immediately precede Sukkot, the feast of thanksgiving for the good harvest; thanksgiving acquires meaning through previous *teshuvah*. *Teshuvah*, the Hebrew term for "repentance," literally means "return." During the Days of Awe we return to God and the right way of life by calling to mind God's greatness, love, and mercy.

TESHUVAH, REPENTANCE

In the period of repentance beginning the Days of Awe, a young boy thinks of others as he shares what he has in *tzedakah*.

Moses Maimonides, the Jewish philosopher who in 1180 formulated the general religious code of law, Mishneh Torah, described *teshuvah*, repentance, as a "way," a path towards God and humanity, in which "the sinner parts from his sins, banishing them from his thoughts, pledging in his heart never to commit them again." She or he must "speak out," Maimonides says, sincerely "revealing the innermost feelings in tearful prayer to God." A crucial aspect of *teshuvah* is performing acts of compassion, kindness, helpfulness, and support to others—*tzedakah*—"to the very limit of strength, ability, and means" (Maimonides, Mishneh Torah: Hilkhot Teshuvah 2:2–5).

Every person must enter into an honest self-examination, searching out even the kind of lapses in integrity, honor, and kindness that people easily rationalize. Maimonides gave five examples of sins that a person might try to explain away:

> (1) A person who accepts an invitation to dinner from a host who has not enough to feed his own family commits a sin but rationalizes that, after all, it was an invitation. (2) A person who uses a tool given as bond for a poor person's loan commits a sin but likes to believe that use never harms a tool. (3) A man who looks with desire at another's wife, excusing himself that he has, after all, not touched her—he is committing a sin. (4) A person who tries to rise to honor by defaming a neighbor commits a sin but stills the pangs of conscience by claiming that the other was not around to hear it and that the neighbor's conduct was used only as a frame of comparison to demonstrate the speaker's own achievements. It is a sin. (5) A person who holds the innocent in suspicion, becalming the inner voice of truth by claiming that "mere" suspicion is no injury, this person has sinned. (Mishneh Torah: Hilkhot Teshuvah 4:4)

In addition, everyone must beware of habits that can become traits of character and then be particularly difficult to throw off: defamation of others, gossip, irascibility, evil thoughts, and keeping bad company. Indeed, continues Maimonides,

> Do not think that teshuvah is required only for grievous acts of commission, such as adultery, robbery, or theft. We must equally examine ourselves and cast away evil traits of character: wrath, hatred, envy, cynicism, greed for wealth, craving for honors, and similar ones. If we find them in us we must repent them; and this may be very hard indeed. (Mishneh Torah: Hilkhot Teshuvah 7:3)

Teshuvah also requires a life within and for the Jewish community. "A person who withdraws" from it—

> even if that person commits no sins, and merely stands apart from the community of Israel, does not perform the mitzvot in common with the community, does not share its distress or that of its members . . . but goes his own way as if he were not one of them and instead lives as if he belonged only to the general society of the world—

commits a grievous offense (Mishneh Torah: Hilkhot Teshuvah 3:11). Identification with the Jewish people and the Jewish community in both thought and in action is fundamental to *teshuvah*.

Teshuvah is renewal of the heart expressed in action. Sins against God will find ready mercy as the penitent, in utter privacy and complete sincerity, pours out his or her soul to God and to God alone; God, who knows the emotions of the heart, forgives. Sins against fellow humans are not so readily obliterated. God forgives them only insofar as we have first sought and obtained reconciliation with those against whom we have transgressed. The sinner must spare no effort of appeasement, but the one to whom the appeal is made must be considerate too and may not cruelly turn down an earnest plea for forgiveness. A person's conduct from then on is the final proof of *teshuvah,* and conduct alone brings ultimate pardon.

Days of Repentance: Preparation

Repentance is a daily duty, for God is always near. Every day we are reminded of this as we say the Amidah, with its plea, "Forgive us, O our Father, for we have sinned." The Days of Awe, however, put the utmost emphasis on the task of *teshuvah*. Beginning with the month of Elul, the *shofar*, ram's horn, is sounded every weekday at the end of public worship, to call all worshipers to *teshuvah*. The preparation intensifies the week before Rosh Hashanah. The congregation recites *S'lihot*, penitential prayers, from before dawn until sunrise, the hour of morning worship.

At the center of all the pleas voiced by the congregation stands the repeated recital of God's "Thirteen Attributes":

> The Lord! The Lord! A God compassionate and gracious, slow to anger, abounding in kindness and faithfulness, extending kindness to the thousandth generation, forgiving iniquity, transgression, and sin ... (Exod. 34: 6–7)

According to the Sages, God, revealing these divine attributes to Moses, also revealed to him,

> Whenever the people Israel have sinned, may they [offer penitence] following this order [in prayer], and I shall pardon them, ... [for the two identical opening words of the Attributes,] "God, God" [mean] that I am full of grace before the human being has sinned, and after the person has sinned and done teshuvah. ... It is enshrined in the Covenant that the [recital of] the Thirteen Attributes [in prayer] will not remain without response. (B. T. Rosh Hashanah 17b)

With this as a core, poets have woven S'lihot of great beauty and deep feeling.

Rosh Hashanah

Rosh Hashanah affirms God, before whom we have sinned by failing to apply the divine yardsticks in our life. But sin is hardly mentioned, and confessions are not yet heard, for only the greatness of God is rehearsed, and divine love and mercy are held out to us.

The Eve

The service on the eve of Rosh Hashanah is of utter simplicity, a regular evening service followed by the Kiddush. Many pious Jews used to fast on this day. At home, the table is set as for Shabbat; the candles are lit and berakhah recited, the children are blessed, Kiddush recited, and bread broken. The loaf of bread, often shaped in the form of a wheel, reminds us that "a wheel goes through the world"; those on top now may find themselves at the bottom a year hence, those who eat their bread in tears this year may enjoy it in ease a year from now. The hope that the year be sweet is expressed symbolically by dipping bread and sweet apple in honey and then passing them to the people around the table with the prayer "May it be Your will, O God, to renew the year unto us as a good year, full of sweetness."

> *Jews express their hope for their family and friends on Rosh Hashanah eve, saying to them, "May you be inscribed by God unto a good year." God inscribes the verdict for the coming year on Rosh Hashanah and seals it on Yom Kippur. The blessing thus expresses our desire that God will write our friends and family down for a good year.*

The Day

On Rosh Hashanah the synagogue is draped in white, the color of purity. The mantles of the Torah scrolls, the curtain of the ark, the cover of the pulpit—all are white. In some congregations, men wear the white robes in which they will some day be buried. These are reminders of death, but also of life beyond death and of life on earth as well, when equality will rule and all will be dressed alike in the garments of purity and of love. Jews celebrate creation and express their longing for the coming of God's reign on earth, the basic theme of the high holy days, in the Amidah for these days:

> Eternal our God, implant the awe of You in all Your creatures, reverence for You in all of Your creation. That all those You

have fashioned may stand in awe before You and all creatures bow to You. May they all form one communion to do Your will with a perfect heart. We know, O Eternal our God, that You hold sovereignty, in Your hand is strength, in Your right hand might, and that Your Name is awesome in all that You have created . . .

Therefore, O God our God, grant honor to Your people, glory to those that revere You, hope to those that seek You, confidence to those that wait for You; joy to Your land, gladness to Your city, the emergence of the radiance of Your servant David and the rise of the light of Jesse's son our Messiah, speedily in our days.

Then will the just behold and be happy, the upright exult, the pious rejoice in song; iniquity will be silenced and all wickedness be consumed like smoke when You remove the tyranny of arrogance from the earth.

Then You alone, O God, will rule over all Your creation.

THE MORNING SERVICE. *Shaharit* of Rosh Hashanah follows the regular pattern, but is embellished with poetry invoking God as *Melekh,* compassionate king, instead of, as during the year, *El,* God who judges. After the Amidah, a special petition is offered in the form of a litany, confessing that we have sinned, affirming that we have no ruler but God, and pleading for a good year, a year free from war, sickness, and evil, a year of forgiveness and peaceful living. The prayer, Avinu Malkenu, ends with the plea, "be gracious to us and answer us for we have no deeds to entreat for us. Grant us Your mercy and loving kindness and save us."

The Torah reading tells the story of Abraham. In complete submission to a divine command, Abraham was ready to sacrifice his own son Isaac. But God does not want sacrifices that diminish human life and extinguish it. Rather, the All-merciful calls for sacrifices that enrich life by adding to it new dimensions of service.

THE SHOFAR AND THE *MUSSAF* SERVICE. Following the reading from the prophets, the shofar, the ram's horn, is sounded in accord with Torah: "In the seventh month, on the first day of the month, you shall observe complete rest, a sacred occasion commemorated with loud blasts" (Lev. 23:24). The natural voice of the horn is weird, primitive, produced without concern for key and harmony, the very voice of nature and creation. When the

Jewish people wandered in the desert following the Exodus, the shofar's signals called them together when they were to hear the word of God. At Sinai it heralded God's voice at the revelation of the Ten Commandments (Exod. 19:36).

The Amidah in the *Mussaf* service, following the blasts of the shofar, has three special benedictions used only on Rosh Hashanah: God is affirmed as King of the universe; is praised as supreme Judge, Who remembers all creatures for good; and is glorified as the world's Redeemer, sounding the shofar of redemption. After each benediction the shofar is sounded in God's honor.

The universalistic concept of Rosh Hashanah as judgment day for all the world is expressed in the liturgical poem, "Unetane tokef." The hymn originated in the seventh century in Palestine, then part of the Byzantine Empire; later, Rabbi Amnon of Mainz, a martyr during the Crusades, gave it the poetic setting that has been adopted worldwide. The poem deals with contrasts: The days of judgment are days of pardon. God is judge, the divine quality is mercy. The shofar of judgment meets the still small voice of love. Human beings are decreed their destiny but can efface its severity by *teshuvah*. God is the living God, human life is fleeting. God is truth, humans are full of pretensions. God the

When this girl hears the sounding of the shofar during the Days of Awe, she will recall Rabbi Borowitz (see chapter 35) telling her how the instrument called the people to repentance even as they wandered with Moses.

Three different types of blasts sound forth from the shofar when it speaks during the Rosh Hashanah service: *Tekiah*, ——, long and straight; *Shevarim*, VVV, three strong broken; *Teruah*, vvvvvvvvv, whimpering, a sound of nine broken notes; then follows *Tekiah* again. They are sounded in the order:

    Tekiah–Shevarim–Teruah–Tekiah (X3)
        ——VVVvvvvvvvvv——
    Tekiah–Shevarim–Tekiah (X3):
        ——VVV——
    Tekiah–Teruah–Tekiah gedolah (X3):
        ——vvvvvvvvv——

the last *Tekiah* being long *(Tekiah gedolah)*.

Rabbi Samson Raphael Hirsch explains: In the desert days of wandering, *Tekiah* called the people to attention; *Shevarim* and *Teruah* were the signals to break camp and to prepare for departure; *Tekiah* again was the signal to march in a new direction. Similarly for us today: *Tekiah* is the signal awakening the complacent from routine living; *Shevarim* the command to break with the past in a spirit of brokenhearted sorrow; *Teruah* symbolizes the response of a penitent people weeping at their sins; the final *Tekiah* proclaims victory over sin and temptation, the resolve to move in the new direction of the right road.

Creator understands the creatures' weaknesses. The sinner, through *teshuvah,* finds acquittal.

> Let us tell of the great holiness of this day for it is truly a day of awe and dread. On it . . . Your throne is established in mercy, and You sit upon it in truth. In truth You are judge, prosecutor, and all knowing witness. . . . You remember all that we forgot. You open the Book of Remembrances, and each deed speaks out by itself, for it is signed by each person's own hand. The great shofar is sounded; a still, small voice is heard. The angels even are terrified. . . . You bring every living soul before You, . . . and You determine the limit to every creature's life, and set down its destiny.
>
> On Rosh Hashanah it is written, on Yom Kippur it is sealed: how many shall pass away and how many shall be born; who shall live and who shall die . . . who shall have ease and who shall be afflicted, . . .
>
> But repentance, and prayer, and works of goodness are the severity of the decree.
>
> For as Your Name so is Your grandeur: slow to anger, easy to appease. You do not desire the death of the guilty. . . . To the very day of his death You wait for him. If he returns You will immediately receive him. You are their Creator, You know their cravings, that they are but flesh and blood. The earthlings' origin is dust and his end is dust. He earns his bread at the hazard of his life. He is like withering grass, like a passing shadow, . . . a vanishing dream.
>
> But you are King, the living and everlasting God.

"Unetane tokef" speaks to the living for whom the "day of awe and dread" can become, through *teshuvah,* "a day of mercy."

TASHLIKH. In the afternoon, the people go to the banks of rivers and streams. Watching the waves hurrying down to the sea, they recite the last verses from the Book of Micah:

> Who is a God like You,
> Forgiving iniquity
> And remitting transgression;
> Who has not maintained His wrath forever
> Against the remnant of His own people,
> Because He loves graciousness!
> He will take us back in love;
> He will cover up our iniquities,
> You will hurl [*ve-tashlikh*] all our sins

into the depth of the sea.
You will keep faith with Jacob,
Loyalty to Abraham,
As You promised on oath to our fathers
In days gone by. (Micah 7:18–20)

Ve-tashlikh, "you will hurl," has given the prayer its name.

This ritual probably stems from a medieval German custom that found its way into Jewish observance. The Italian poet and traveler Petrarch (1304–1374) reports having watched crowds of people at the bank of the Rhine in Cologne on New Year's Day, strewing herbs and flowers on the river in silent prayer. They told the poet that with these herbs, they cast all the misfortunes in store for them in the coming year into the waves. Rabbi Jacob Moellin, "Maharil" (died 1427), rabbi of the Rhenish city of Mainz and a collector of Jewish customs, *minhagim,* is the first to mention Jews reciting the prayer from Micah and casting their sins away, a custom that has since become worldwide. This *minhag* is an example of how Jews have transformed suitable non-Jewish customs, making them "Jewish."

BETWEEN ROSH HASHANAH AND YOM KIPPUR. Good resolutions in a new life can be implemented in the week between Rosh Hashanah and Yom Kippur. During the week worshipers continue to rise early for S'lihot and one day of fasting, the Fast of Gedaliah, is included. The Fast of Gedaliah commemorates the assassination by Jewish fanatics of Gedaliah, the benevolent Jewish governor installed by the Babylonian king, Nebuchadnezzar, after the fall of the First Temple (Jer. 40; 2 Kings 25:22–25).

YOM KIPPUR, DAY OF ATONEMENT

The Lord spoke to Moses, saying: Mark, the tenth day of this seventh month is the Day of Atonement. It shall be a sacred occasion for you: you shall practice self-denial, . . . you shall do no work throughout that day. For it is a Day of Atonement, on which expiation is made on your behalf before the Lord, your God. . . . It shall be a sabbath of complete rest [Sabbath of Sabbaths] for you, and you shall practice self-denial; on the ninth day of the month at evening, from evening to evening, you shall observe this your sabbath. (Lev. 23:26–32)

Sabbath of Sabbaths, this day is called. For twenty-four hours, neither food nor drink touch the lips of the Jew, who spends the day away from the world, in the house of God engaging in no other task but *teshuvah.*

The Eve

The preceding day is given over to preparation. As the afternoon advances, people recite their confession of sins, then eat a festive meal that is considered as much a duty as the fast to follow; Jewish law wants to prevent people from being more pious than the biblical command demands so no one is permitted to fast for an additional day. The candles are lit, and, with them, a light to burn through the twenty-four hours of the fast. Parents bless their children with a special blessing. Friends greet each other, *Gemar hatimah tova,* "may a good verdict be confirmed by [divine] seal." In conformity with the call for self-denial, people wear soft non-leather shoes, which increase discomfort by their lack of support. Many dress in the white robes of eternity. Memorial lights for the departed burn throughout the night and day.

THE EVENING SERVICE—KOL NIDRE. The evening service has received its name from the prayer "Kol Nidre," with which the service opens. The song is a declaration of dispensation from ascetic vows taken as special acts of piety and then neglected. In a haunting melody that expresses the longing of the soul for God, the song reflects on sorrow and hardship and soars in its final passage to triumph and faith.

The "Kol Nidre" is immediately followed by the motto of the day: "The Lord spoke: I pardon, as you have asked" (Num. 14:20). Forgiveness is God's response to our confession, offered in each Amidah during the evening service and throughout the day. After *Ma'ariv,* evening prayer, S'lihot are offered, giving a "program" of the whole day's course: May our entreaty rise at evening, our plea at morning, and our elation at the next evening. The service ends with Avinu Malkenu, Alenu, and Kaddish, although some worshipers remain to recite the entire Book of Psalms.

CONFESSION OF SINS. Confession is first spoken silently, giving the penitent an opportunity to add his or her personal concerns or transgressions against God, that need be confessed only to God. It is repeated publicly as expression of mutual responsibility, and only the transgressions against humans are mentioned. The core of all confessions is the testimony:

> Our God and God of our ancestors, may our prayer come before You; hide not from our plea, for we are not so arrogant and stiff-necked to say before You, O God our God and God of our ancestors, that we are righteous and without sin, for indeed, we *have* sinned.

This is the gist of all repentance, and the evening service's detailed enumeration of sins is rooted in it. All confessions are framed in the plural: *we* have sinned. Everyone is responsible for his or her fellow human beings—to set the right example, to give guidance and support, and to offer counsel and admonition to the best of his or her ability. Failure makes the other's sin to some degree our own.

The Day

THE MORNING SERVICE. The theme of *Shaharit is s'lihah,* the plea for forgiveness. Penitential prayers, S'lihot, are a part of every Yom Kippur service and have a prominent place in *Shaharit.* Solomon ibn Gabirol (1020–1050), philosopher and poet, has stated the motto of *Shaharit* in a S'lihah: May our prayers take the place of the ancient morning offerings of the Temple.

In the reading from the Prophets that follows the Torah reading, Isaiah's call to social justice shows the true meaning of the Yom Kippur fast:

This is the fast I desire to loose the fetters of wickedness, to untie the cords of the yoke, to let the oppressed go free, and that you break off every yoke . . . it is to share your bread with the hungry, and to take the wretched the poor into your home, when you see the naked to clothe him, and not to ignore your own kin. (Isa. 58:5–7)

THE *MUSSAF* SERVICE. In the Amidah of the *Mussaf* service following morning prayer, the ritual of Yom Kippur in the ancient Temple is recapitulated. Yom Kippur was the only day of the year when the high priest was permitted to enter the holy of holies; he made confession for all, invoking the awesome Name of God, and when the congregation heard the Name they fell on their knees and prostrated themselves.

Jews today kneel at the same moment as once their ancestors did in the Temple. On Yom Kippur, removed from the world and experiencing in his or her heart a foretaste of the time when all humanity, bending its knee, will invoke God's Name—only then may the Jew kneel down. Kneeling in adoration, the Jew proclaims: "Blessed be The Name, Whose glorious kingdom is for ever and ever." Past, present, and future merge as modern Jews remember the Temple and anticipate the end of days.

THE AFTERNOON SERVICE. The theme of *Minhah* is the sanctification of God's Name through martyrdom. The martyrs' surrender of their lives is evoked, from the ten Rabbis who were tortured and murdered under the Emperor Hadrian to the six million who were slaughtered by the Nazis. Their faithfulness teaches the meaning of devotion to God. The commemoration of the dead is celebrated following *Minhah,* it is thus linked to the commemoration of the martyrs. Worshipers remember their own departed; each one suffered a bit of martyrdom for the sake of Judaism. May God grant them honored rest in eternity and may their lives be models to their kin, guiding them to work as faithful Jews for humanity's future under God's reign.

The afternoon Torah reading is followed by the Book of Jonah, the reading from the Prophets for that day. Jonah was the prophet who tried to run away from his God-given duty but could never escape. He was also the prophet who had to learn the lesson that all people, even Israel's enemies, the people of Niniveh, are God's children, for whom God cares.

> And should not I care about Niniveh, that great city, in which there are more than a hundred and twenty thousand persons who do not yet know their right hand from their left, and many beasts as well! (Jonah 4:11)

The reading calls for justice and invites us to have compassion for our enemies.

THE CONCLUDING SERVICE. The theme of *N'ilah* is the plea of the penitents to be accepted in God's grace before the sun sets and the gates of heaven are closed. As shadows lengthen, *N'ilah*, the concluding prayer offered only on the Day of Atonement, begins. Worshipers offer a last plea for mercy, a renewed expression of repentance:

> Open unto us the gate, at the time that the gate is being closed, as day has almost waned. The day is waning, the sun is waning fast, let us enter Your gates!

For the last time Avinu Malkenu is recited; the plea to God to "*inscribe* us in the Book of Life," is changed to "*seal* us in the Book of Life."

The stars have risen in the sky, flames flicker in candles burned low. The Ark is opened. The congregation stands in awed silence. This is the moment of affirmation, of the vision of God's Kingdom. Slowly, word by word, the people recite in unison: "Hear, O Israel, the Lord our God the Lord is One."

The shofar is sounded at nightfall as Yom Kippur ends.

Blessed be God's Name, the glory of God's Kingdom is forever" (three times). "Adonai . . . the Eternal is God!" (seven times). The Shofar is sounded, onward into life! The day is done.

The mystics have held that, at this time of nightfall, after the congregation has affirmed its allegiance to God in the words of the Sh'ma, the Shekhinah, God's indwelling presence, departs. The Shekhinah returns from earth through ten spheres (*sefirot*) to the divine abode and is given a tenfold farewell in the ten proclamations that follow the Sh'ma.

Yom Kippur releases the worshipers, weak from fasting but filled with a deep spiritual joy. The people greet each other, not wishing one another a good week, but *hag sameah,* or in Yiddish *Gut yontef,* "Happy festival."

Chapter 29

MINOR FEASTS AND FASTS

We shall follow the minor feasts and fasts in sequence from Rosh Hashanah. The Fast of Gedaliah between Rosh Hashanah and Yom Kippur has already been mentioned.

LIGHTS IN WINTER'S NIGHT: HANUKKAH

Hanukkah begins on the 25th day of Kislev. Historians and the Rabbis have different perspectives on what Hanukkah is and why it is celebrated. The name of the festival means "Dedication," and it is observed to commemorate the victory of the Maccabees over the Syrians, in 165 B.C.E., and the rededication of the Temple, which had been desecrated by the enemy. The Talmud tells the story:

> What is Hanukkah? The Rabbis teach: On the twenty-fifth day of Kislev the days of the Feast of Hanukkah begin. There are eight of them, days on which there may be no public mourning nor fasting. When the Greeks [Hellenist Syrians] entered the Temple they desecrated all the oil in the Temple. After the leaders of the House of the Hasmoneans had overcome and defeated them, they searched all over and finally found just one little cruse of oil still bearing the seal of the high priest; just enough oil to last for one day [in the holy menorah of the Temple]. But a miracle happened,

the oil lasted for eight days [until new oil could be prepared]. The following year it was ordained that these days be observed with songs of praise and thanksgiving. (B.T. Shabbat 21b)

The menorah, the seven-branched candelabrum of the Temple, became the coat of arms of the Jews. It is the symbol of Judaism, found on the ancient synagogue in Capernaum, on Jewish graves in the Jewish catacombs of Rome and Bet Shearim, and on the Great Seal of the State of Israel. The symbol tells of an eternal light of divine origin that is tended by humans: "Not by might but by My spirit will you prevail."

Thus the Rabbis transformed Hanukkah, emphasizing its spiritual meaning. Hanukkah celebrates a divine miracle, not a human victory. Courage, determination, and military skill have long been characteristic of the Jew. Joshua and Gideon, Deborah, Saul at his prime, and David were supreme strategists as well as daring and fearless soldiers. The Maccabees outfought a powerful enemy through good strategy, fearless courage, and supreme mastery of the art of war.

The Rabbis of old knew of Jewish courage, but they wished to stress the source from which this strength comes. The courage of the Maccabees came from the light of God in their hearts, which they rekindled in the Temple. The flame that burned in the Temple for eight days symbolized the flame of faith that wrought the miracle of Jewish survival. The motto of Hanukkah is expressed in the passage from the Prophets that is read during the festival: "Not by might, nor by power, but by My spirit [will you prevail]—said the Lord of Hosts" (Zech. 4:6).

Hanukkah is a minor holiday, with no work prohibition. At night the lights are kindled on a nine-branched candelabrum, correctly called a *hanukkiah* (in contrast to the seven-branched menorah). Before it is lit, the blessings are recited:

> Blessed are You, Eternal . . . who has sanctified us by Your commandments by commanding us to kindle the Hanukkah light.
> Blessed are You, Eternal . . . who has wrought miracles for our ancestors in ancient days at this season.

One light of the *hanukkiah* is the serving candle, whose flame touches the others, calling them to life. Beginning with one candle the first night, an additional flame is added every evening until the number reaches eight, for the miracle increased with every day. Every member of the household must light the candle. If a person has to borrow money to buy the candles, he or she must borrow; even those on public welfare must kindle it, for it is truly the lamp of Jewish survival. The Hanukkah lights may not be used for practical purposes, for reading or for work; they are holy. By injunction of the Sages, the light is to be made visible to the outside world, that the miracle of God's redemptive action be proclaimed far and wide.

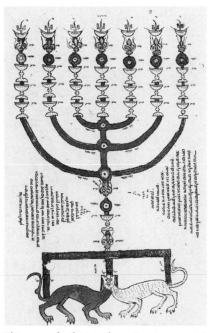

This page of a thirteenth-century manuscript of the Mishneh Torah illustrates Maimonides' summary of laws concerning the menorah.

After the candles are lit, a hymn, "Maoz Tzur," is sung. It speaks of various times when the Jewish people and the Jewish faith were in danger of extinction by foreign powers but were rescued through divine intervention.

HANUKKAH AND CHRISTMAS. Hanukkah and Christmas have both entered the Jewish experience, one from within Judaism, the other from without. Both are observed at the same period of the year. Both are spiritual holidays that have added secular elements. By tradition, Hanukkah is a minor holiday, but it has become among many Jews one of the most widely celebrated "major" festivals—Jewish life can transform Jewish law. Christmas has always been a major holiday. Hanukkah is an affirmation of Jewish identity; Christmas is an affirmation of Christian identity.

The author of the text of "Maos Tzur" is unknown, although it may date to the thirteenth century. Its tune is a strange mixture of a soldiers' song from the Thirty Years' War in Germany (1618–1648) and a Lutheran chorale; nevertheless, the hymn is an integral part of Jewish observance.

On the inspiration of Rabbi Menachem M. Schneersohn, who was the Rebbe of the Lubavitcher Hasidim, giant hanukkiot have been erected in central public squares of great cities from Moscow to Melbourne, San Francisco, New York, Paris, and elsewhere. The lights are kindled every night, while the chant of the berakhot, amplified by loudspeakers, floats over the entire neighborhood.

But Christmas has become so universal a holiday, surrounded by trees, decorations, carols and lavish gifts, that it had to touch Jewish life, and Jewish parents and children have had to cope. They do not wish to be excluded from the festivities, but spiritually they do not participate in the universal celebration of the birth of Christ.

A personal recollection from my childhood offers perspective. When beautiful Christmas carols floated around us, my father would say: "I rejoice with our Christian friends, who can sing the beautiful Christmas songs tonight. But I am also proud that we can sing, not once a year, but every week. We have our beautiful Sabbath songs, Z'mirot, every Friday night of the year." I believe I understand what he meant. Jews should rejoice that precious gifts are granted to others without wishing to partake of them. There is no prohibition against Jews accepting invitations from their Christian friends at this season, or extending invitations to them for the celebration of Hanukkah, or sending them Seasons Greetings. But Christmas belongs to the

Dreidel is a game played by children on Hanukkah. The term *dreidel* is Yiddish, from the German *drehen,* "to spin." A spinning top has four sides, each inscribed with a Hebrew letter, corresponding to *N–G–H–S.* The letters are the initials of a Hebrew sentence: *Nes gadol haya sham,* "a great miracle happened there." To the child, *N* stands for *nothing* to be gotten out of the kitty; *G* means *getting* it all; *H* gives *half*; *S* means *set* or put one in. In order to play, the children receive some candies or nuts as chips and a few pennies of *Hanukkah gelt,* money; this is traditionally the extent of Hanukkah gift giving.

Christians, while Jews remember the beauty of lived Jewish life on Shabbat—when Jews celebrate the coming of God's indwelling presence—and on Jewish festivals, with their songs and joy.

BETWEEN HANUKKAH AND PURIM

THE FAST OF THE 10TH OF TEVET. Following directly after Hanukkah, this fast commemorates the siege of Jerusalem by the Babylonians, but it actually counsels: You have been celebrating; perhaps you have overdone it. Stop for a moment and reflect.

TU B'SHEVAT. Tu b'Shevat, the 15th Day of Shevat, the "New Year's

Jewish children hope to grow as strong as the trees they plant on the 15th of Shevat.

Day of Trees" (M. Rosh Hashanah 1:1), celebrates the beginning of the planting season in Israel and invites a brief celebration of spring. The children are given fruit, especially the kinds for which the Holy Land is distinguished (Deut. 8:8). Many communities plant the types of trees that are grown in Israel, and over the years the children watch them grow. With the planting of the trees comes the hope that the children's development will keep step with the trees' growth and that each child will reach fullness of body, mind, and spirit, and produce fruit that will nourish others.

THE FAST OF ESTHER. On the day before Purim, the Fast of Esther is observed, although Esther did not fast on this day. The fast may remind the Jew to retain a sense of balance even during Purim: Like Carnival, from which Purim has adopted many features, the festival offers escape, but the Jew must always return to daily observance.

THE MERRY FEAST OF PURIM

The feast of Purim, celebrated on the 14th day of Adar, is based on the story of the Book of Esther. On the eve of the feast, after evening prayer, *Ma'ariv*, the Book of Esther, is publicly recited from a handwritten scroll, the *Megillah*. It will be repeated the following morning. Children turn rattles when hearing the name of the wicked villain of the story, Haman.

Women take great pride in Esther. Originally exempt from hearing the Megillah, women opted from the outset to perform this mitzvah. They now take part in all of the rituals of the festival.

In the morning, friends send gifts to each other and to the poor, as Esther commanded. This shows the spirit of Jewish *tzedakah*, charity. No one need feel embarrassed because he or she is poor, for the giver means: I am sending you this gift not because you are poor but because you are my friend.

At noon, merrymaking takes over. Masquerades were introduced in the spirit of Carnival, which is celebrated around the same time. A festive meal is taken in the afternoon, and drinking is a duty, "until one does not know the difference between 'blessed Mordecai' and 'cursed Haman.'" The Talmud relates this story:

> Raba and Rav Zera celebrated the Purim feast together; and when they were all drunk, Raba got up and chopped off Rav Zera's head. The next day he pleaded with God for mercy, and God revived Rav Zera. The following year Raba said to Rav Zera: Would the master please come that we may celebrate the Purim feast together. But Rav Zera declined and said: Miracles do not happen every time. (B.T. Megillah 7b)

In Judaism, there is a time even for getting drunk; habitual excess is curbed by permitting it for a moment, in the name of God. The Shulhan Arukh (code of religious practice) ordains drinking on Purim until sensibility is lost, but Rabbi Moses Isserles (1525 or 1530–1572), in the sober mood of Ashkenasic Jewry, added:

In Israel, Purim is observed with carnival parades and great exuberance.

> He need not drink that much; just a little more than usual. Then he will fall asleep and no longer know the difference between "cursed" and "blessed." He who does much and he who does little are equally right, provided that everyone's intention be for the sake of Heaven.

DAYS OF MOURNING

FAST OF THE 17TH OF TAMMUZ AND TISHAH B'AV. A three-week mourning period occurs during the summer. It opens with the Fast of the 17th of Tammuz, which commemorates the day when the walls of Jerusalem were breached and the daily Temple sacrifices came to an end. It leads up to the darkest day of the Jewish year, Tishah b'Av, the 9th of Av, the day when both the First and the Second Temple were destroyed (in 586 B.C.E. and 70 C.E., respectively).

On Tishah b'Av, for twenty-four hours the people fast. The congregation sits on low stools. The curtain of the Ark has been removed and the lights are dim. In the evening, the Book of Lamentations is recited. In the morning, dirges are sung, composed

King Ahasuerus of Persia chose Esther as his queen, not knowing that she was a Jew and the ward of the wise Mordecai, who remained her advisor. Mordecai secretly told Esther that he had overheard a plot to assassinate the king. The culprits were hanged and the event was duly reported in the royal chronicle. The king's vizier, Haman, commanded everyone to prostrate themselves before him, but Mordecai refused, for he would bow down only to God. Haman plotted revenge on Mordecai and on all the Jews, convincing the king that they were subversive and needed to be wiped out. The thirteenth day of Adar was chosen by lot to be the day of their extermination (the term for "lot" is pur, hence Purim, the Feast of Lots).

Mordecai asked Esther to speak with the king. To enter the king's chambers without being summoned may have meant death, but to save her people Esther was willing to risk her life. The king received her graciously and promised to fulfill her wish. Prudently, she merely asked him to dine with her that evening and to bring Haman with him. At the dinner, the king asked her once again to express a wish. She simply asked him to dine with her again the next night and again to bring Haman.

After the first dinner, the king could not sleep, and so, as was his custom, he had an attendant read to him from the royal chronicle. The king learned that it had been Mordecai who had saved his life but that Mordecai had received no reward. In the morning, when Haman approached the king to obtain permission to hang his enemy, the king asked Haman how to honor a man to whom the king was indebted. Haman, certain that he was to be honored, was horrified to learn that the man was Mordecai, and, rather than hanging him, Haman had to lead Esther's advisor through the city, proclaiming Mordecai's fame to all.

Hardly back home, Haman was summoned to the second dinner. This time Esther revealed Haman's plot to murder the Jews and told the king that she, too, was Jewish. Haman was hanged, Mordecai made vizier, the Jews saved. Esther, assisted by Mordecai, then enjoined the Jews to celebrate the days of deliverance: "They were to observe them as days of feasting and merrymaking, and as an occasion for sending gifts to one another and presents to the poor." (Esther 9:22)

by various poets and reflecting on Israel's tragic fate through the ages. Jews mourn not only the fall of the Temple but all Israel's agonies throughout the centuries. The great poet Judah Halevi clearly expresses the theme of the day:

> Zion, wilt thou not ask if peace's wing
> shadows the captives that ensue thy peace
> left lonely from thine ancient shepherding?
> Lo, west and east and north and south—worldwide
> all those from far and near, without surcease
> salute thee: Peace and peace from every side.
> To weep thy woe my cry is waxen strong;—
> but dreaming of thine own restored anew
> I am a harp to sound for thee thy song.
> Thy God desired thee for a dwelling place;
> and happy is the man whom He shall choose,
> and draw him nigh to rest within thy space.
>
> (Translation by Emma Lazarus)

But no Jewish worship service ever releases the people in despair, for hope is the lifeblood of the Jew. There is a saying, "on the 9th day of Av, the Messiah will be born." Out of agony, redemption will come. The sufferings of the ages are the birth pangs of the world of the Messiah—if we but understand this. Three weeks after Tishah b'Av, the month of Elul comes again, and the shofar is once more sounded, announcing another year with new hopes, new opportunities, new trials, and new rewards.

DAYS OF RENEWAL

ROSH HODESH. Rosh Hodesh, "Beginning of the Month," refers to the emergence of the new moon at the beginning of each month of the Jewish calendar. In antiquity, the Sanhedrin announced the appearance of the new moon with great solemnity, as the new moon fixed the calendar. Today, Rosh Hodesh is celebrated as a minor holy day, announced in the service of the preceding Sabbath, which includes a plea for a blessed month. Several evenings after the appearance of the new moon, as the moon waxes, observant Jews may gather outdoors to give thanks: "Blessed are You, Adonai our God, . . . who has told the moon to renew itself."

Tradition has regarded Rosh Hodesh as a monthly "mother's day," honoring women for their superior piety by which the Jewish people is eternally re-created (Rashi and the Tossafot to Megillah 22b). Jewish feminists have helped to renew the observance of the holy day in our time. It would be both beautiful and Jewishly meaningful were men to express their gratitude to wives, mothers, sisters, daughters, and female friends by some token of appreciation each Rosh Hodesh.

"And let us hallow the
Rosh Hodesh festival,
weaving new threads
into the tapestry of tradition."

. . . . . .

The moon "renews its light
for those just beginning,
who will one day find
their own renewal."

From Marcia Falk, *The Book of Blessings: New Jewish Prayers for Daily Life, the Sabbath, and the New Moon Festival* (Boston: Beacon Press, 1996), pp. 398 and 412.

MODERN DAYS OF COMMEMORATION

Since the re-establishment of the State of Israel, new days of commemoration and celebration have been adopted that have begun to take root in the Jewish community. Since the new holidays have no foundation in Torah, they have no work prohibition, and the liturgy for the days, still in evolution, varies from congregation to congregation and denomination to denomination. If a holiday falls on a Sabbath, it is observed on the preceding Thursday.

YOM HASHOAH. Yom Hashoah, Day of Catastrophe, observed on the 27th day of Nissan, commemorates the Holocaust and the fighters fallen in Israel's war of liberation. In Israel, all movement and all traffic come to a complete standstill while the heroes and martyrs are silently remembered. In some synagogues, a liturgy, featuring new prayers, has been created, generally adapted from the liturgy of Tishah b'Av.

YOM HA'ATZMA'UT. Yom Ha'atzma'ut, Israel's Independence Day, is observed on the 5th of Iyar. In many synagogues, when the Amidah is recited a thanksgiving prayer, *Al Hanissim*, is inserted: "We offer thanks for the miracles God has wrought." It follows the pattern of the similar thanksgiving prayers on Hanukkah and Purim. Hallel, the Psalms of Praise (Ps. 113–118), is sung and the Torah is read (Deut. 7:12–8:18); the Haftarah is from Isaiah 10:32–12:6.

YOM YERUSHALAYIM. Celebrated on the 28th of Iyar, Yom Yerushalayim commemorates the re-unification of Jerusalem and its designation once again as Israel's capital. Three thousand years ago King David made Jerusalem Israel's capital. In 1996, the three thousandth anniversary of the city as capital of Israel was observed with special celebrations.

Chapter 30

THE ROAD OF LIFE

The celebration of rituals surrounding birth, adolescence, marriage, and death sanctifies the human life cycle. The rituals recognize, develop, and extend the individual Jew's bond to God and to the Jewish community of the past, present, and future. The marking of life's major stages is part of the richness of the Jew's everyday life, of which prayer and the observance of dietary laws may be a binding force.

BIRTH: INITIATION INTO THE COVENANT

Children are the Jews' greatest treasure and blessing. They guarantee both the physical and spiritual survival of Judaism. Rabbi Meir once said: When Israel approached God to receive the Torah, God demanded guarantors from them that they would observe it. God turned down the patriarchs, offered by the people as role models of observance, and rejected the prophets, who had shortcomings. But when the people of Israel said: "Our children will guarantee observance of the Torah through eternity," God accepted the guarantee and gave them the Torah (Shir Hashirim Rabba 1:4).

The birth of a child brings great rejoicing within the family and the family's congregation. After the child's birth, the

Traditionally and for synagogue use, a person bears a Hebrew given name together with the name of the child's father: Isaac son of Abraham, or, in Hebrew, Yitzhak ben Avraham; Miriam daughter of Amram, Miriam bat Amram. Lately, both the father's and the mother's name are being used in many circles, Yitshak ben Avraham ve-Sarah, Miriam bat Amram ve-Yohebed.

The child's name is bestowed at circumcision, initiation, or in the synagogue. The naming is frequently surrounded by ceremony and forms part of Sabbath worship.

By this name the Jew is called to the Torah; prayers are offered for him or her in sickness and distress; memorial prayers are spoken after the person's death. This name is inscribed on documents such as the ketubah and on the tombstone.

father is called to the Torah the next time that it is read; he offers a special blessing for the child and the speedy recovery of the mother. Traditionally, boys are solemnly initiated into the Covenant of Abraham. Among the Orthodox, girls are welcomed with little ceremony; when her father is called to Torah she receives her Hebrew name and her initiation is complete. More recently, however, many Jewish communities have developed rituals of initiation for girls, based on the ritual for boys.

BOYS. According to Torah, Abraham received the commandment regulating the initiation of boys through circumcision: "You shall circumcise the flesh of your foreskin. . . . And throughout the generations, every male among you shall be circumcised at the age of eight days" (Gen. 17:11–12; Lev. 12:3). Circumcision became the seal of God's covenant with Abraham (Genesis 17), and from the time of the patriarch all Jewish male children are circumcised. The rite is so important that it must be performed on the eighth day, as Torah ordains, even if the day falls on a Sabbath or on Yom Kippur, when work is otherwise strictly forbidden; the rite may be postponed only if the baby is ill.

The ritual of circumcision (*B'rit Milah*) is performed by a mohel, a pious person specially trained in both the techniques of the operation and the religious laws pertaining to the B'rit. During the Middle Ages and in Eastern Europe, the rite was often performed in the synagogue; today it is performed in the home. Tradition calls for a minyan to be present. Two chairs are arranged in front of the mohel, one for a relative, who holds the child during the operation; he becomes the *sandek*, the child's godfather. The other chair remains empty; it is—symbolically—

the chair of the prophet Elijah, guardian of Israel's eternal covenant with God and present at this moment in the child's life.

A grandmother or aunt brings in the child, an act which makes her his godmother. All rise to greet the child: "Blessed be he that comes in the Name of God." The mohel offers a prayer for divine assistance in the operation, then recites the berakhah: "Blessed are You, O God ... who has sanctified us by His mitzvot and given us the mitzvah of circumcision." The father of the child adds his blessing before the mohel performs the operation: "Blessed are You, O God ... who has sanctified us by His mitzvot, commanding us to enter him in the covenant of our father Abraham." The mohel joins with the assembly in response to the father's berakhah: "As he has entered the covenant, so may he come to enter the realm of Torah, of marriage and of good deeds. Amen."

The Jew's civic given name is chosen in conjunction with his or her Hebrew name by a number of methods. The simplest way is to use a Hebrew name both in the synagogue and outside: Abraham, Sarah, Rebecca, Jacob, Rachel, Miriam, Joseph, and so on. English versions of Hebrew names may also be used: Johanan and John are the same name, so are Miriam and Mary, and Hannah and Anne. Names may be translated from the Hebrew: Simhah becomes Joy, for example. The meaning of a Hebrew name may be sought and then an English name looked for that has the same meaning. For example, in the Book of Genesis, Judah is compared to a "lion's whelp" (Gen. 49:9); if Judah stands for Lion, then Leo might be used as a corresponding English name. The most commonly used method is to choose an English name beginning with the same letter as the Hebrew name: Maurice to correspond with Moses, for example.

The mohel raises a cup of wine and with his blessing gives the child his name. "Our God and God of our ancestors: preserve this child unto his father and mother; and may his name be called in Israel ———." A drop touches the baby's lips; the mother drinks the rest. The cup used at circumcision is frequently the gift of the godfather to the child. A treasured heirloom, a link in the chain of generations, it will be used on other occasions in the child's life, including his wedding. The Rabbis ordained a mitzvah meal to follow.

GIRLS. In the conviction that Jewish daughters are entitled to a formal initiation equal to that of Jewish sons, a ceremony—naturally without an operation—has been instituted. No definite

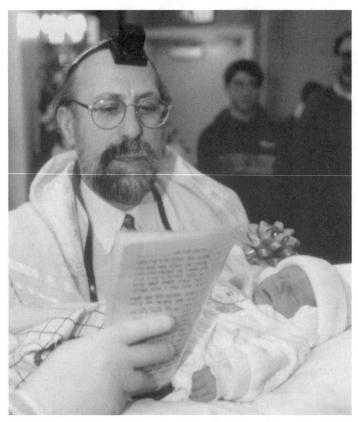

To be a mohel is an honor and a great distinction. His or her reward is bringing a child into the fold of Judaism. Some mohelim perform the B'rit strictly as an act of mitzvah, without taking any fee. The Conservative and Reform movements have established institutes for the training and certification of pious men and women, mainly physicians, as mohelim, in order that they be cognizant of the halakhic requirements of circumcision.

rituals have been generally adopted, except for Reform Judaism, which includes a ceremony in its *Shaarei Ha-Bayit/Gates of the House: A New Union Home Prayer Book.*

Actually, the traditional ceremony surrounding the B'rit lends itself well to adaptation and merely requires a change in the text from masculine to feminine. Thus, the baby girl is brought in and welcomed by the assembled guests, "Blessed be she that comes in the Name of God." Having placed her in the arms of the godparent, who is seated next to the chair of Elijah, the parents speak the berakhah, "Blessed are you, O God . . . who has sanctified us by Your mitzvot, commanding us to enter her in the covenant of our people Israel." The child is blessed over the cup of wine, given her Hebrew name, and a festive meal follows.

BAR MITZVAH AND BAT MITZVAH: EDUCATION

When children begin to speak, they are taught to pray. Informal education begins in earliest infancy. Children learn the Sh'ma, berakhot, and selected maxims from the Torah—Moses charged us with the Teaching [Torah] as the heritage of the congregation of Israel (Deut. 33:4), for example. As children grow older, formal study expands their learning of the Torah.

Originally, the formal education of his sons rested on the father. When many fathers were no longer capable of providing adequate instruction to the older sons, Simeon ben Shetah, a Pharisee and great teacher of the first century B.C.E., ordained that a school for boys sixteen to seventeen years of age be established in every principal town (B.T. Baba Batra 21a). Eventually, fathers were no longer able to teach even the younger boys. The high priest Joshua ben Gamla (first century C.E.) therefore decreed that every town must appoint schoolteachers for the smaller children.

During the Middle Ages, Jews were the only population that was generally literate, and even the most hard-pressed Jewish communities maintained communally supported schools, where boys studied from the age of five to at least thirteen, in some communities up to fifteen. Study was generally confined to Torah. Although the Talmud rules that every father must teach his son an honest trade, there was little to teach children in the medieval ghetto, and most trades and skilled crafts were

When a boy was one year old he was brought to the synagogue by his father for a brief moment after the Torah had been read and he offered a small gift to the Torah. The swaddling cloth used at the boy's circumcision had been made into a wrapper for the Torah scroll, called a wimpel, to be wound around the parchment. It was cut into long bands, embroidered with the child's name, birth date, and the wish that he grow up to Torah, marriage, and good deeds. From then on the boy's name was symbolically woven around the Torah.

Family names had to be universally adopted by the Jews, on Napoleon's order, a law followed by other states. Some Jews chose their name from the caste to which they belonged. Priest in Hebrew is cohen. *From this are derived Kahn, Kohn, Cohn, Cohen, Kaplan, Katz. Others took the name of their place of origin: Oppenheimer, from the Rhenish city of Oppenheim. A characteristic of their house might be selected: Rothschild, a house with a red shield; Trepp, a house reached by stairs (trepp). Or they adopted beautiful names: Rosenthal, a valley of roses, or Morgenroth, the red glow of dawn.*

closed to Jews. For many, Talmud study became a full-time, lifelong occupation. Girls received some informal schooling at home, where they were mainly trained by their mothers in keeping a kosher house.

BAR MITZVAH/BAT MITZVAH. From the age of thirteen—the onset of puberty—the boy is responsible for his religious acts; until then, responsibility rests with the father. Girls, maturing earlier, are responsible from the age of twelve. At thirteen the boy is *bar mitzvah,* "son of the commandment"; at twelve the girl is *bat mitzvah,* "daughter of the commandment." Bar/Bat Mitzvah is a state of responsibility into which a Jew enters automatically. No ceremony is required. The emphasis on ceremonial celebration of a boy's Bar Mitzvah is of later origin, and Bat Mitzvah celebrations are a recent innovation.

A boy of thirteen can be counted among the ten making up the quorum for public worship. For the first time in his life he is therefore called to offer blessing for the Torah and read from it in public. His father gives thanks to God for having brought his boy that far. A good talmudic student might show his potential as a scholar by expounding on a talmudic subject he had carefully prepared with a teacher. In this simple manner, boys were introduced to their duties.

In modern practice, the Bar Mitzvah speaks the blessings of the Torah and reads part of the section from the Torah and the portion from the Prophets for the Sabbath of his celebration, using the traditional chant of the synagogue. He may present a short address, an adaptation of the talmudic discourse, or offer a prayer. His parents may publicly thank God and have words of encouragement for their son. He may listen to a charge by the rabbi and receive the rabbi's blessing. He may even be permitted to lead portions of the service. These practices vary with

The cantor helps a young woman prepare to recite her portion of Torah on her Bat Mitzvah.

different congregations. At the celebration that follows he will receive gifts.

In the past, girls grew into their responsibilities without ceremony. In our day, however, with an ever-growing recognition of equality between the sexes, Bat Mitzvah ceremonies are evolving and becoming prevalent in all types of congregations. The services vary with the religious traditions of the individual communities; in some congregations, Bat Mitzvah is identical to Bar Mitzvah, in others a minor celebration, separate from the traditional liturgy.

The ceremonies of Bar Mitzvah and Bat Mitzvah are valuable for several reasons. First, they are rites of passage that give clear distinction to the young person, who, in puberty, may be confused about being regarded as an adult or as a child; the young Jew knows that parents and elders will henceforth increasingly regard him or her as an adult with growing adult rights and responsibilities. Second, the ceremonies are linked to Jewish learning. Many congregations demand several years of religious education and participation in worship as prerequisites and expect the young person's religious education to continue.

CONFIRMATION. The Confirmation of groups of fifteen- or

sixteen-year-old boys and girls was instituted in the nineteenth century by Reform Jews as an adaptation of the Protestant practice. Designed as a substitute for Bar or Bat Mitzvah, it has not replaced the traditional individual observance. As an additional rite, Confirmation has been retained to motivate young Jews to continue their religious education for several additional years.

MARRIAGE

Jews used to marry young. The Talmud suggests the age of eighteen. Rather than postpone marriage until the young man was able to support a family, the girl's father might support the new family for a while, especially when the young man was a promising talmudic scholar. Frequently, however, the new husband was so completely immersed in Talmud that it fell to his wife to provide the family's livelihood.

The Rabbis reveal two aspects of marriage:

> As husband and wife are worthy, God's Glory dwells in their midst. (B.T. Sota 17a)

> A wife may be acquired in three ways; and gains her freedom in two ways: She is acquired by silver, through contract, and through marital cohabitation. She gains her freedom through a Bill of Divorcement and by the death of her husband. (Mishnah Kiddushin 1:1)

Marriage is thus a legal contract, as two people assume certain obligations. But, more than that, it is a union that partakes of the divine and in which God's glory resides. Jewish wedding rites reflect both of these aspects.

In ancient Israel, betrothal and marriage were celebrated about one year apart. As time went on, it was found that to be bound to each other without being married was a hardship for both groom and bride, and so the two acts were united in one ceremony. The Jewish wedding rite now comprises both the ancient act of betrothal and the vows of marriage. Non-Orthodox Jews no longer hold the view of the Mishnah that the man *acquires* a wife. Marriage is a union of equals.

The Rites

The Jewish marriage ceremony includes all three of the actions that the Mishnah mentions as making a marriage legal; as a legal procedure, the ceremony also requires two witnesses not related to the couple or to each other.

1. Two people may become husband and wife by living together and building a home. This is symbolized by the *huppah*, wedding canopy.
2. A man may "acquire" a wife by "silver"—by handing her something of value and declaring that he wishes to marry her by this gift. As she accepts it she becomes his wife. Early in history this gift was presented in the form of a ring; thus the practice has remained and it has become established in other faiths.
3. Contract legalizes marriage. This is the *ketubah*, marriage contract, in which the husband promises to honor and cherish his wife, to support her in decency, to love her in truth, to take care of all her needs "down to the shirt off his back," to provide for her in case of his death or in the event of a divorce. In some modern ketubot, the wife, in turn, equally promises to fulfill her duties in sincerity and truth.

To prepare for the wedding, the bride goes to the *mikveh*, the women's ritual pool. If any of the couple's parents have died, groom or bride visit the graves. On the wedding day, just as on Yom Kippur, groom and bride fast and confess their sins before taking their solemn vows.

Before the wedding ceremony begins, the couple, their parents, immediate family, and the witnesses gather with the celebrant in a room apart from the other guests. The

In contrast to the traditional text of the ketubah, which gives the man the active role of "acquiring" the woman and making the pledge, and the woman the passive role of accepting it, modern egalitarian ketubot give both the man and the woman the same status as equal partners and require identical pledges. Many highly artistic ketubot have been created in recent years.

Artistically rendered, the ketubah is a marriage contract that tells of the obligations of the wife and husband to each other. A symbol of the couple's commitment to each other, the ketubah often hangs in a prominent place in their home.

witnesses sign the ketubah. Looking at his bride, the groom places the veil over her face (Ketubot 2:1) while the rabbi speaks: "Our sister, may you grow into thousands of myriads [Gen. 24:60]. May God make you like Sarah, Rebecca, Rachel and Leah."

The wedding procession enters where guests have gathered. Traditionally, the parents of the groom escort him under the huppah and the parents of the bride escort her.

The rabbi, flanked by the witnesses and standing before the bride and groom, makes certain that they truly wish to join their lives together and that they are doing so by their own free will and consent. Having received this affirmation, the rabbi celebrates the betrothal (*erusin*). Raising a cup of wine, the rabbi blesses God, by whose word betrothal and marriage have come into being, and the couple share the cup. The betrothal ceremony is ended; it leads directly into the marriage rites *(nisuin)*.

The groom places the ring on the index finger of his bride's right hand and solemnly speaks the words: "Be you consecrated unto me [as my wife] by this ring according to the law of Moses and Israel." The bride accepts the ring and the two are married. She may wish to give the groom a ring, an act which has no legal significance under traditional Jewish law but is significant as a recognition of the equality of the sexes. Now the rabbi reads the ketubah. The three legal acts that unite a man and a woman have been performed.

Next, God's blessing is invoked. A second cup is raised as the rabbi recites the sevenfold blessing:

Mouryey Gottlieb (1856–1879) artfully portrays the three acts validating marriage: the reading of the marriage contract, exchange of property, and dwelling together, as symbolized by standing under the huppah.

Blessed be You, O God . . . who creates the fruit of the vine.

Blessed be You, O God . . . who creates all to Your glory.

Blessed be You, O God . . . Creator of the human being.

Blessed be You, O God . . . who has created the human being in Your image and likeness and given it the capacity for eternal self-perpetuation. Blessed be You, O God, Creator of the human being.

May Zion, childless now, rejoice, when her children are gathered in her midst in joy. Blessed be You, O God, who gives joy to Zion through her children.

Make these beloved mates to rejoice in great joy, as once You gave joy to Your creatures in the Garden of Eden. Blessed be You, O God . . . who makes groom and bride to rejoice.

Blessed be You, O God . . . who has created joy and gladness, groom and bride, jubilation and exultation, delight and satisfaction, love and brotherhood, peace and friendship. O God, our God, may soon be heard in the cities of Judah and in the streets of Jerusalem, the voice of cheer and the voice of happiness, the voice of groom and the voice of bride, jubilantly cheering from their huppah . . . Blessed be You, O God who makes the groom rejoice with his bride.

The cup is handed to the bride and groom. They share it as they will share the cup of life throughout the years to come. May God reside in their home, and may their "cup," their measured fate, always be a blessed one. The rabbi pronounces them husband and wife in accordance with civil law and Jewish law. By custom, the groom smashes a glass and the whole company bursts forth in "Mazel tov."

At some point in the ceremony, the rabbi may address the couple and bless them with the blessing of the Torah: "God bless you and keep you . . ." (Num. 6:24–26). Traditionally, the couple are led to the privacy of a room together. Groom and bride are now really alone, in *yihud,* union, while being guarded by the witnesses outside the door. The third of the three knots has been tied, not only symbolically but in reality.

Married Life

In order to fulfill the first injunction of Torah—"Be fertile and increase, fill the earth and master it" (Gen. 1:28)— every family was to have at least two children (Mishnah Yevamot 6:6). If God were gracious they would be granted a son and a daughter. But procreation is not the sole justification for sex. Every husband and every wife has a right to ask sex of the spouse as a pleasure to be enjoyed. God rejoices at the union of human beings for it mirrors the divine union with God's children. As the Sabbath is a sign of this union, intercourse on this day becomes a special mitzvah. Denial of sex is a cause for divorce.

The joys of sex are strictly limited to a married couple. Yet for almost two weeks out of every month, husband and wife are forbidden even to touch each other; during the woman's menstrual period and seven days thereafter they were to be apart. Only after the wife had immersed herself in the mikveh were they to come to each other again. Husbands did not tire of wives they could not approach half of the time. Wives could turn

The breaking of the glass was introduced by Rav Ashi at the wedding of his son to curb excessive merrymaking (B.T. Berakhot 31a). It has come to be so deeply rooted that it its regarded by many as indispensable. As in this illustration, many ancient synagogues had a special plaque in the interior or exterior wall of the building against which the glass was hurled by the groom. The breaking gives symbolic recognition of the sorrows of Israel since the time of the destruction of the Temple. It reminds the couple that even in moments of supreme happiness Jews may not think of themselves alone: their hearts must always turn to the community of Israel and to all those who may be burdened.

down husbands at given times. Orthodox Jews still abide strictly by this law of Torah (Lev. 15:19 ff.).

BIRTH CONTROL. Judaism has always considered the gifts of the body to be good. The Talmud does not advocate abstinence in marriage; it tolerates contraceptives under certain conditions. Three situations are mentioned in particular: "a minor, a pregnant woman, and a woman breast-nursing her child" (B.T. Yevamot 12b). The minor is granted this permission because she might die from a pregnancy; the pregnant woman since it was believed that additional semen might harm her embryo; and the nursing mother since she might be forced to wean her child too early, which might endanger the child's life. Later generations ruled against contraceptives with greater severity. In using contraceptives, including the birth control pill, a woman should be guided by her conscience, religious community, husband, and physician.

ABORTION. Abortion is an ethical and religious issue. So is the determination of when life begins. The Jewish position is, at times, quite different from that of many Christian churches. In Judaism, the decision lies with the woman, her physician, her rabbi, and the father.

Judaism forbids abortion for the sake of convenience. In case of a danger to the mother's life, Judaism speaks categorically, making abortion mandatory, even at the ultimate stages of pregnancy. Rashi explains (B.T. Sanhedrin 72b) that as long as the fetus has not emerged into the world, it is not a human being (*nefesh*, literally "soul"), and it is in our power to kill it, in order to save its mother, but once it has emerged, as far as the forehead (M. Niddah 3:5), we may not touch it to kill it, for then it is regarded as born and we may not give preference of one life over another, as the Mishnah clearly points out (M. Oholot 7:6).

But the qualification, "danger to the mother's life," need not be restricted to the mother's risk of death in childbirth. It can be given an extended meaning. In his *Guide to Religious Practice*, Rabbi Isaac Klein has listed the relevant decisions and their sources: During the early stages of pregnancy the fetus is regarded by the Rabbis as part of the mother's body, by some, "as merely water." Abortion is therefore permitted, if a mother's physical or mental health is in danger, which would include psychological damage and mental anguish resulting from the birth of a genetically damaged or malformed child, and the dishonor of having a child as a consequence of incest or rape.[1]

There is disagreement as to the duration of this early stage; some limit it to the first forty days, others extend it to the first three months of pregnancy.

DIVORCE. Torah permits divorce and remarriage (Deut. 24:1–4). Although lately divorce has increased, it used to be rare and was decried: "When a man sends away his wife, even the altar sheds tears . . . this man is hated by God" (B.T. Gitin 90b). When there was no hope, when living together became impossible, divorce could be obtained, but only by the man. No "guilt"

1. Isaac Klein, *A Guide to Religious Practice* (New York: Jewish Theological Seminary, 1979), pp. 415–17.

had to be proven. It was easy for a man, who could get a divorce for any reason; it was expected of him if his wife bore him no children for ten years. It was harder for the wife, but she could ask the court to force her husband to divorce her, for instance when his conduct or type of work made it impossible for her to live with him. According to the tenth-century ordinances of Rabbenu Gershom, however, a man was not allowed to divorce his wife against her will.

According to Jewish law, there has to be a Jewish religious divorce, performed before a religious court of three rabbis with two witnesses present. A decree obtained in civil court is not sufficient to dissolve a marriage. A bill of divorcement, a *get,* is made out on request of the husband; the document must be written in conformity with exact and detailed regulations. As the wife accepts the document which the husband places publicly into her hands, she is divorced and may remarry after ninety days. She may remarry her husband, but only if she has not married another after her divorce.

The divorce laws have many disadvantages for women. If a husband has vanished, she cannot remarry as long as his death has not been ascertained by witnesses; he may still be alive and he has not given her a *get.* She becomes *agunah,* "tied down." Or the husband may use extortion in return for granting her a *get;* or he may refuse simply out of spite; or he may not believe in the necessity of a *get,* especially as he himself may remarry without one—the prohibition of polygamy was pronounced by Rabbenu Gershom in the tenth century but is not found in Torah.

Conservative Judaism has instituted various prenuptial agreements between the partners in order to decrease the likelihood of divorce; as a last resort a central rabbinical court has the authority to declare the marriage void. The court has this authority because all marriages are entered according to the sense of the rabbis, who therefore acquire the authority to annul them. Reconstructionists have created a double *get;* the man can give one to his wife, and the wife to her husband. Reform Judaism regards the civil divorce as sufficient, holding that the *get* was originally ordained by Torah so that a man might not simply throw out his wife, a condition fulfilled through the courts of the state. Reform Judaism has, however, introduced a Ritual of Release and a Document of Separation. Since it is a binding principle in Judaism that "the law of the land is *the* law" (B.T. Baba Kamma 113a)—that is, that civil law is religiously binding—no Jewish divorce may be granted in the United States and Western Europe without a preceding civil divorce.

SICKNESS AND DEATH

SICKNESS. "One may not live in a town without a physician" (P. T. Kiddushin 4:12). To get competent medical help is a duty, for life is everyone's most precious gift. In this spirit, Jews have always seen in the art of healing a divine calling.

Everyone must do his or her utmost to keep the body in good condition and to find competent medical help to restore it to health and strength. Everyone must also assist their neighbor in times of sickness. All those who visit the sick take a portion of the sufferer's ills away by bringing hope and courage to their friend. But human resources are limited; healing comes from God, who is the "physician of all flesh" to whom we pray, and prayer may spell the difference between life and death, or between a quick recovery and a lingering illness. When reciting the Amidah silently during daily prayer, we may add personal petitions for friends and dear ones to the plea for the general health of humankind. When a person falls seriously ill and life is in danger, friends may offer a special benediction after the reading of the Torah, or they may assemble to recite Psalms in supplication for the sick person's speedy return to well being.

AS DEATH APPROACHES. A Jew nearing the end of life should not be alone but be surrounded by family and friends—even if he or she is no longer capable of recognizing them. This is a source of comfort throughout life, for no one need fear facing eternity alone; all know that companions in life will offer escort and prayer, at least to the portals of life everlasting.

Among all Jewish communal organizations, none has traditionally enjoyed greater prestige than Hevrah Kadisha, the "Holy Fellowship," men and women of proven worth and piety who hold the privilege of attending to the dying and the dead. There is no greater love than the love extended to those who cannot say "thank you" any more.

The Jew's last words are to be the affirmation of faith: *Sh'ma Yisrael*... "Hear, O Israel, the Lord our God the Lord is One." As a person reaches the end, the men or women of the Hevrah take turns staying with the dying. They spend the time in prayer and make a confession of sins with or for the dying person. They repeat the Sh'ma, during the final moments, in order that the Jew's last breath pronounce the affirmation *Ehad*—"God is One!"

When death is imminent, the person is not to be needlessly touched or moved, for any manipulation may hasten death and it is not for any mortal to shorten another's span of life even by a hair's breadth; God alone determines the length of the human being's days and years. Judaism categorically forbids active euthanasia. The life of the sufferer need not, however, be prolonged by heroic means; a living will stating that no such measures be initiated is permitted. The issue of "pulling the plug" has been debated by various rabbinic authorities, and the family of the dying person needs to consult their rabbi.

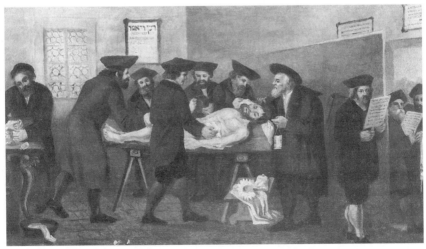

Members of the Hevrah Kadisha are honored to prepare the body of a member of their congregation for burial, as in this depiction from Prague, c. 1780.

PREPARING THE DEAD FOR BURIAL. Death in traditional Judaism is ascertained by the cessation of the heart's beating and of breathing. The issue of "brain death" has not been cleared halakhically. After ascertaining that death has come, it is then permitted to remove organs that the departed may have donated to save the life or sight of another human being.

The attendants close the departed's eyes and take the body off of the bed and unto the dust whence mortals have come. Members of the Hevrah Kadisha then obtain the coffin, of simple rough wood. Embalming is forbidden, for all that has come from the dust is to return to it.

They wash the body and cleanse it, then pour water over the covered body, reciting the words spoken by Ezekiel, in sympathy with God, "I will sprinkle clean water upon you and you shall be clean; I will cleanse you from all your uncleanness and all your blemishes" (Ezek. 36:25). They dry the body and clothe it in the simplest of white linen garments. The tallit is placed around the shoulders, and the body wrapped in a white shroud. Thus robed in purity, the departed is laid in the coffin. Earth from Eretz Yisrael is sprinkled on it. The custom of equal robes and equal coffins developed in ancient Israel as a result of a rabbinical ordinance. Previously, the poor frequently denuded themselves in an effort to give lavish funerals to their dear ones; now all are equal, and the dead do not impose unduly on the living.

It is considered an honor for the dead to be returned to the earth, the final resting place of all mortals, as quickly as possible; thus funerals were often held on the very day of death. They may not be conducted on the Sabbath but are permitted on the second day of holidays.

BURIAL. As the body is taken to its resting place, friends and the members of the congregation join the procession. A eulogy may be offered, except on holy days. At the moment of their most bitter grief, the mourners put a tear in their garment; on the left—over the heart—for father and mother; on the right for other relatives. At the same time they bless God, "the Judge of Truth." The body is lowered into the grave, also prepared by loving hands, and the children put the first shovels of earth upon the coffin. It is the last token of respect and of love; children are returning the mortal remains of their parents to the earth whence God has formed us. Then they stand to recite the Kaddish: "Magnified and sanctified be the Name of God." By glorifying God in the hour of their bereavement, they give testimony to the piety of their dear ones and witness to their teachings. Passing through two rows of friends, the mourners return home. "May God comfort you among those who mourn for Zion and for Jerusalem" is the parting greeting of the assembly.

The custom of placing a stone on the tombstone originated in ancient days when stone heaps marked the graves. Each visitor added to the upkeep of the grave by placing a stone on it. Today it marks the visits and visitors. The basic Hebrew inscriptions on Jewish tombstones are: At the top: the letters P.N., poh nikbar, "here is buried"; or P.T., poh tamun, "here is concealed." On the bottom the letters T.N.Tz.B.H., Tehi nafsho (nfashah) tzerurah bitzror ha-hayim, "may his (her) soul be bound up in the bond of [eternal] life."

THE PERIOD OF MOURNING. Once home, the mourners take off their shoes and sit on low stools for seven days. A memorial light is lit in the home that will burn throughout the week. The first meal is brought by friends, lest the mourners forget to eat. Morning and evening worship are conducted in the home; the families of the community come to visit. Only on the Sabbath may the mourners leave their home. As the Sabbath is ushered in they enter the synagogue, are met by the rabbi at the door and escorted to their seats with the words: "May God comfort you ..."

Shivah, the seven days of mourning, is ordained for father and mother, son and daughter, brother and sister, husband and wife. During this period the thoughts of the bereaved dwell upon their dear ones. They may read from the Book of Job. Friends speak to them of their departed and of death as an act of grace.

> Two vessels are sailing the seas; one setting out from sheltered harbor to unknown destination; the other returning from strenuous voyage with precious cargo. As the ship comes home the people rejoice. Even so is life. Yet we rejoice when birth sends out the child on the uncertain voyage of life, should we not find comfort when the ship finally reaches the sheltered harbor of God's peace? (Shemot Rabba 48:1)

For three days the mourners may surrender to full expression of grief; from the fourth day, restraint is in order. After thirty days life must return to normal; mourning comes to an end, except for the death of father or mother, who are remembered for a full year. By tradition, the souls of average human beings may undergo divine punishment for a year. Every day, morning and night, the children say Kaddish in the synagogue, up to the end of the eleventh month. Jewish mourning rites and customs show deep insight into the needs of the bereaved.

After one year the tombstone is unveiled and dedicated. Until then the mourners are not to visit the grave, in order to give healing a chance. The anniversary of death, called *Yahrzeit* (from the German *Jahr,* "year," and *Zeit,* "time," meaning anniversary), is observed in all homes. A light burns from evening to evening. This custom, probably taken from the Catholic church, was at first assailed by the Rabbis but is now firmly established. The Kaddish is recited by the children on the day itself and on the preceding Sabbath. The study of Torah, giving charity, and perhaps fasting as a call to repentance, set the day apart. If possible, children visit the graves of their dear ones, placing a little stone on the tombstone.

On Yom Kippur, on the last day of Pesah and Shavuot, and on the eighth day of Sukkot, the names of the departed are remembered in memorial services. Some congregations have memorial plaques on which children may have the names of their parents inscribed. A light will be kindled on the plaque, near the name, to burn on Yahrzeit and during memorial services on the Sabbath preceding it.

DAILY DISCIPLINE: DIETARY LAWS

Jewish festivals and rites of passage attain their full force when they are rooted in an all-encompassing life of daily discipline. Jewish dietary laws have played a major roll in creating, maintaining, and safeguarding the distinctive character of the Jewish community. A great deal has been said about the background and purpose of these laws. They have been traced back to taboos existing even before the emergence of the Jewish people, and they have been regarded as health laws. There is truth in both of these explanations. Jews have always insisted on strict rules of food preparation, on certain forms of meat inspection, and on the purity of foods. The prohibition of certain kinds of seafood, such as shellfish, turned out to be a sound measure, especially in Palestine, where heat could lead to immediate spoilage. To the Jew, however, these laws have had a different meaning. A Jew has three basic motivations for observing dietary laws: (1) They are the laws of God, who knows their purpose, even though mortals may not be able to grasp it; they are to be observed in obedience to the divine will, in affirmation of God's sovereignty. (2) They are considered a means of preserving the uniqueness of the Jewish community; unable to share their neighbor's table, Jews were tied to one another in closer communion, retaining their identity, and perpetuating their heritage. (3) They might be regarded as symbolic acts, expressing belonging to a group; dietary laws have the power to bind the members of the community in close fellowship to one another, to their history, and their tradition. Of these three, the first is the most important; the others emerge from it.

Jewish dietary laws center around a number of basic regulations and prohibitions that form the fabric of observance and of practice. There is no prohibition of any vegetable food. Regarding foods of animal origin, the Torah sets definite rules in Leviticus 11 and Deuteronomy 14. It is permitted to eat "Any animal that has true hoofs, with clefts through the hoofs, and that chews the cud" (Lev. 11:3), for example, cattle, ox, sheep, deer. Animals which have only one of these characteristics are excluded: the camel and the hare, having no parted hoofs; the pig which does not chew the cud. Anything "in the seas or in the streams, that has fins and scales" (Lev. 11:9 and Deut. 14:9) may be eaten. This eliminates all shellfish (no fins) and eel (no scales). Torah gives a list of forbidden birds, mostly birds of prey; since the exact meaning of the Hebrew terms for these birds has become obscured, only those birds are permitted that have always been regarded as "clean," such as chicken, geese, ducks, pigeons, and turkeys. "All winged swarming things that walk on fours shall be an abomination for you" (Lev. 11:20-23);

locusts and grasshoppers, etc. are regarded as prohibited. "The things that swarm on earth" are similarly prohibited (moles, mice, lizards) (Lev. 11:29–31).

In general, we find that all animals that live by the destruction of other lives, be they wild beasts or birds, are prohibited. The law implies a call to peace and peaceful living.

Even the permitted animals may be consumed only under certain conditions. The following are prohibited: animals that have died on their own (Deut. 14:21; see also Lev. 11:39); animals that have been torn by others (Exod. 22:30); all blood (Lev. 7:26); certain animal fats (Lev. 3:17); certain sinews (Gen. 32:33).

Preparation of Meat

Animals and birds must be killed by cutting through the arteries, veins, and windpipe at the neck. The knife must be sharp, without the smallest nick in it. The severing must be performed in one continuous stroke, without interruption, without downward pressure, and without meeting any obstacles in the animal's throat. If any of these conditions is not met, the animal may not be eaten. Lungs and other organs are then examined. The communal official, the *shohet,* who performs the slaughter and inspection must have both technical knowledge and learning in halakhah, as well as a special certification from the rabbi.

Rapid drainage of blood makes the meat better fit for longer preservation; the elimination of blood falls on the consumer. The meat is soaked in water for about one half hour; then covered with salt on all sides and left for about one hour. After the salt has been washed off, the meat can be prepared for consumption. When the entire process is completed, the meat is fully *kasher,* which means "all right." Care for the elimination of blood requires that meat be soaked within three days, otherwise the blood congeals and the meat cannot be eaten. For the same reason, liver must be broiled over an open fire in order that the blood may flow out freely.

All kitchen utensils that have been used in connection with forbidden foods cannot be used in a "kosher" household. This includes knives, pots, pans, bowls, and plates. Kosher dishes cannot be washed with soap that contains animal fats.

The prohibition, "You shall not boil a kid in its mother's milk" (Exod. 23:19; Exod. 34:25; Deut. 14:21), appears three times in Torah, which was interpreted as conveying three different messages: you shall not eat meat and milk products together; you shall not cook those products together; you shall not use any mixture of them. There is to be no butter at a meat dinner, no ice cream to follow it. A waiting period has to be allowed between the consumption of meat and milk dishes. The law goes further. As meat is cooked, its juices penetrate the pores of the pots; as it is cut, they enter the knife; as it is served, they seep into the chinaware. The same applies to milk. The kosher household, therefore, has two complete sets of dishes, from cooking pots to spoons, that are never used together or washed together. Only glass, which has no pores, can be used either way. A third, additional set of dishes may be reserved for neutral, *pareve*, foods in neither category, such as fruit. In addition, a kosher kitchen has to have complete duplicate sets for Passover, when the year-round dishes cannot be used because they have been permeated by grain products.

The dietary laws impose such a regimen of observance and self-discipline so that members of the community can never forget their identity. In addition, the observance of dietary laws has shown the people the power of Torah, its authority, and its eternally binding force. Some non-Orthodox Jews, however, no longer feel bound by the laws of *kashrut*, the Jewish dietary laws. Others wish to maintain it in their homes as a symbol of Jewish belongingness; among them are those who will obey some of the rules without accepting all of them. These people will eat some or all regular foods when they are away from home. Others will simply deny themselves some particular foods, such as pork, as a matter of religious discipline. But there are a great many Jews who obey the dietary laws without compromise and who find happiness in doing so. To them, the technical problems of having a kosher home have become routines of life and present no major obstacles.

Chapter 31

WOMEN AND RELIGIOUS LAW

The progress achieved by women in their struggle for equal rights in the political life of America and in Israel made the restricted position of the Jewish woman in the religious sphere incongruous. Golda Meir, prime minister of Israel, had to sit in the women's gallery of the synagogue. Jewish women representing Judaism in literature and arts remained unrepresented in public worship. The recognition of Judaism which, as Jews, they fought for in public was withheld from them, as women, among their own.

Jews were denied equality throughout the centuries on account of their faith, but they denied equality to women within their faith. Jews had fallen behind the secular world where women were concerned, even though, through the millennia, Judaism had been the advocate of social justice for all.

WOMAN'S POSITION IN TRADITION

Many of the great works of Judaism—the Bible, Mishnah, Talmud, codes of law—were written by men and reflect a male point of view. Talmudic law was framed at a period in history when women throughout the world were not held as equal to men. Even so, Judaism was then ahead of the world in giving women certain rights and, above all, great dignity.

The woman's traditional position in the Jewish home was one of dignity and power. She was endowed with the privilege of kindling the lights of the Sabbath, for to her belonged the authority in the home. The education of the small children lay in her hands. Her husband, who greeted her every Friday night with the Hymn of Praise from Proverbs, knew how much she meant to him. Many a talmudic scholar found in his wife the support of his family while he gave his life to study. They found food for their families and gave courage to their husbands. The Talmud speaks of all Jewish women throughout history when it points out that "for the sake of the pious women were our fathers redeemed from Egypt" (Shemot Rabba 1).

The eminence of Jewish women and the respect in which they were held can be recognized in the Bible. Miriam was explicitly recognized as "prophetess" (Exod.15:20); the prophet Deborah led Israel as general and judge (Judges 4:4–5:32); Hannah revealed the efficacy of silent prayer (1 Samuel 1:12–17); the prophet Huldah confirmed the divine character of the Book of Deuteronomy (2 Kings 22:14 ff.); Esther, a supremely gifted diplomat, saved the Jews of her country from extermination.

Legally, however, the position of women was inferior from the beginning. When the daughters of Zelophehad, who had no son, claimed their inheritance, they were entitled to their father's claim only because there were no sons (Num. 27:1–11). At the behest of a jealous husband accusing her of adultery, a woman had to undergo a public ordeal of drinking "bitter waters" to determine her guilt; if she was guilty, the water's "spell" would distend her belly, make her barren, and render her "a curse among her people"(Num. 5:11–31).

In antiquity, women could and did hold public positions of power and even acted as presidents and leaders of synagogue congregations. Under the law, however, they were subject to their husbands, and the woman was confined to the house and its duties. From the day she entered her husband's home, her hair was veiled, sometimes even cut; her beauty was not for the world to see. She was ex-

In Germany Bertha Pappenheim (1859–1936), founder in 1904 of the Association of Jewish Women (Jüdischer Frauenbund), sharply criticized the patriarchal character of Judaism.

pected not to leave the house except on essential errands. She could not talk to anyone of whom her husband disapproved (M. Sota 1:2). Her education was inferior, confined to the basics needed to teach her infants and keep a kosher house. She could not get a divorce against her husband's will. If her husband disappeared leaving no trace she could remarry only after his death had been certified by witnesses; otherwise she became *agunah*, "tied down," never permitted to remarry.

Daily, each man thanked God, "who has not made me a woman." The birth of a boy was the fulfillment of his parents' hopes. The story is told of Rashi, who was grieved, for he had no son, until God appeared unto him in a dream to promise him that his daughters' husbands and children would bring him glory. Women held onto the task that was theirs uncontested: to be the builders of the generations of the Jewish people. They raised their children in the fear of God, in respect for their elders, and in love of Torah.

WOMEN AND RELIGIOUS DUTIES

Release from Duties of Time

According to Jewish law, "women are released from all mitzvot of performance that are linked to a specific time" (M. Kiddushin 1:7), that is, all duties that require a person to do something at a specific time. Among such mitzvot are wearing the tallit and tefillin, hearing the shofar, dwelling in the sukkah, shaking the lulav on Sukkot, hearing the Book of Esther on Purim. Women were also released from the study of Torah, even though it was not linked to a specific time (see B.T. Kiddushin 34a–35a). The recital of the Sh'ma, being ordained evenings and mornings, was not obligatory. The dispensation recognizes women's special conditions. In times of pregnancies or nursing, a woman's duties could conflict with the times of the performance of the mitzvah, and so the woman was released from performing these mitzvot.

This implied, however, that women were free to perform these mitzvot if they so chose. It appears that in talmudic times, when women wished to take upon themselves mitzvot from

Henrietta Szold (1860–1945), whom we have met in chapter 16 as the founder of Hadassah, the Women's Zionist Organization of America, and the savior of thousands of Jewish children, steadfastly stood by her right to fulfill her religious duties. In a letter to a friend, who offered to say Kaddish for her mother on her behalf, as there were no boys in the family and the recitation of the mourner's Kaddish is a mitzvah of time, Szold wrote, expressing her thanks but graciously declining his offer:

The Kaddish means to me the survivor publicly and markedly manifests his wish and intention to assume the relation to the Jewish community which his parent had, and that so the chain of tradition remains unbroken from generation to generation. You can do that for the generations of your family, I must do that for the generations of my family.

I believe that the elimination of women from such duties was never intended by our law and custom—women were freed from positive duties when they could not perform them, but not when they could. It was never intended that, if they could perform them, their performance of them should not be considered as valuable and valid as when one of the male sex performed them. And of the Kaddish I feel sure this is particularly true....When my father died, my mother would not permit others to take her daughters' place in saying the Kaddish, and so I am sure I am acting in her spirit when I am moved to decline your offer.

Quoted in Ellen M. Umansky and Diane Aston, eds., *Four Centuries of Jewish Women's Spirituality: A Sourcebook* (Boston: Beacon Press, 1992), pp. 164–65.

which they were exempt, the rabbis acceded and ruled that they could perform them. Women took upon themselves the hearing of the shofar, the hearing of the *Megillah* on Purim, and the weaving of the festive bouquet on Sukkot (see B.T. Rosh Hashanah 33a). Some women in antiquity wore tallit and tefillin. The Talmud reports that Michal, King Saul's daughter, wore tefillin and the Rabbis did not object (B. T. Eruvin 96a). Rashi (c. 1040–1105) who had no sons, is said to have permitted his daughters to put on tallit and tefillin, an exception in his time. Eventually, however, women were forbidden to opt for these mitzvot. When women came to be forbidden to opt voluntarily for the performance of these mitzvot, in which the study of Torah was included, they were relegated to an inferior status. In a society in which Torah study was a sign of distinction, this enforced dispensation alone branded women as inferior in the minds of many.

Exclusion from Religious Functions

The recitation of the Amidah was obligatory, as it was petition (B.T. Berakhot 20b) rather than a mitzvah linked to time. This would qualify a woman to lead the congregation in prayer, since a person who is obligated to pray can lead others. She was empowered to read the Torah in public. But this right, too, was denied her. The reason was found in a rabbinic ruling that states:

> The Rabbanan taught: Any one is allowed to be among the seven [who step up to the Torah on the Sabbath and read one section] including a minor and a woman; but—said the Sages—a woman should not be permitted to read from the Torah out of respect for the dignity of the congregation. (B.T. Megillah 23a)

Correspondingly, the Shulhan Arukh, the code of law compiled in the sixteenth century, rules:

> All may go up to the Torah on the Sabbath, up to a total number of seven to be called; even a woman and a child who knows to Whom we pray, may go. The Rabbis have said however: a woman should not be called out of respect for the congregation. (Orah Hayim 282, 283)

A woman reading from the Torah might embarrass men who were illiterate, so she therefore had to be excluded. *Congregation* meant a congregation of men. Women could not be counted for the minyan.

The Mehitzah

In the Temple, men and women mingled freely in the "Women's Court," and women entered the inner courts when

---

offering sacrifices. Only for the merriment on Sukkot were they eventually placed on a balcony and screened off. This separation came to be applied generally, and the women's gallery was hidden from the view of the men by a *mehitzah*, a lattice or screen.

Seated in the gallery, women could barely hear the voices of prayer from below. Being called to the Torah was out of the question. But the women were free to sing among themselves, following their "fore-singer" and free to develop their own prayers as adjuncts to the mandatory ones to which halakhah committed them. These have come to be known as *Techines*, supplications. They reveal a certain independence. Deeply personal, frequently in the singular (in contrast to the plural form of the obligatory prayers), they call, not on the fathers of Israel, as do the ordained prayers, but on the mothers—Sarah, Rebecca, Rachel, and Leah, and also Miriam, Deborah, and others—to intercede. For example, a *techine*, speaking of the Mothers in paradise, ends with the appeal:

> Now, dear women, when the souls are together in paradise, how much joy there is! Therefore I pray you to praise God with great devotion, and to say your prayers, that you may be worthy to be there with our Mothers.[1]

Denied the study of Torah, the women found instruction in the *Zene Rene* (Yiddish after: *T'ze-enah ur-enah*, "Go out and behold, daughters of Israel," Song of Songs 3:11), a commentary to the weekly Torah portion, written in Yiddish, with parables and midrashic legends.

JEWISH WOMEN TODAY

Jewish women have given their gifts to the reconstruction of Judaism. In the early seventies, groups like Ezrat Nashim (the Women's Court, named after the area in the Temple mentioned above) were organized for the purpose of raising consciousness.

1. Ellen M. Umansky and Diane Ashton, eds., *Four Centuries of Jewish Women's Spirituality: A Sourcebook* (Boston: Beacon Press, 1992), p. 55.

Orthodox women of today pray as these women did, in a separate gallery of the synagogue.

Rosh Hodesh, the day the new moon appears each month, re-garded by Rabbi Meir of Rothenburg as a special holy day for women, came to be observed by them in gatherings and celebrations. Women began to study Torah and attend seminary. This movement encompasses women of all religious groups within Judaism. Within the Jewish women's movement, various groups have emerged, calling for reevaluation of tradition and for action. They have expressed themselves in general activities, such as the creation of organizations, the publication of books and magazines, lectures and discussions; activities within Orthodoxy, designed to abide strictly by halakhah; activities within Conservatism, designed to reinterpret halakhah; activities within Reform and Reconstructionism, resting essentially on the ethical principles and needs of our time and prepared to overrule existing halakhah and establish new ones.

Orthodox women have had great difficulties. Nevertheless, they have established prayer meetings strictly for women, from which men are excluded and which do not claim to be public worship, which means that all those prayers requiring a minyan are omitted. The Torah is read but only for learning purposes. Bat Mitzvah can be celebrated in this environment. These

Amy Eilberg, the first woman rabbi of the Conservative movement, attends a study session prior to her ordination.

women's groups have organized a network of mutual encouragement and created new rituals. The movement is growing.

There is a precedent in halakhah for these gatherings: When a person has survived a life-threatening experience, a prayer of thanksgiving to God is to be offered in the presence of a minyan. In the strictly Orthodox congregation of Mainz and in accordance with halakhah, women, especially after childbirth, spoke the prayer in the presence of a female minyan. At this moment *congregation* stood no longer for men, but for women. The women's prayer meetings serve this purpose among Orthodox women, giving them a sense of belonging, and of being a part of publicly active Jewish life. The project has found approval among some rabbis but has also been attacked by others.

Conservative Judaism has had to wrestle with women's issues. It had long permitted mixed seating and abolished the mehitzah. After long debates and in consultation with all member congregations, the Conservative rabbinate has granted full

Ray Frank (1865–1948), a newspaper reporter in Spokane, Washington, was able to persuade the city's Jewish community to establish a Jewish congregation. She preached to them during the Days of Awe and outlined the challenge to the Jewish community in general and the Jewish woman in particular—as rabbi and mother— to mend Jewish life as men have not so far been able to do.

rights to women: They may wear kippot, tallit, and tefillin; be counted among the minyan; be called to the Torah; be ordained as rabbis and invested as cantors. Local implementation rests on the decision of the congregation, and within the Rabbinical Assembly—the organization of Conservative rabbis—a faction rejects the innovations.

Lily H. Montague (1873–1963), founder of the liberal Jewish movement in Britain and of the World Union of Progressive Judaism, saw a special spiritual function for women as contributors to the revival of Judaism, which entailed equal rights for women. She helped to reveal the bond between women in the struggle for women's equality both in general and among Jews.

Reform Judaism was the first denomination to ordain women, but women rabbis had to overcome considerable resistance on the part of congregations, who were used to men. The Reconstructionists would have been the first to ordain women, but the Reconstructionist Rabbinical College had not yet reached the point of ordaining rabbis at all. Its founder, Mordecai M. Kaplan, a strong believer in women's equality, was the first to introduce Bat Mitzvah.

Beyond Equal Rights

The issue of women's equality transcends the granting of equal rights to women in the synagogue. It affects the liturgy and reaches to the interpretation of Torah itself. Reconstructionists, Reform Jews, and Conservative Jews are in the process of creating gender-inclusive prayer books. In biblical interpretation, the role and the influence of women and the spirituality of women call for greater emphasis and reevaluation. Halakhah has to be reexamined as well.

The search for the expression of female spirituality in Jewish literature, for instance in Kabbalah, has continued. Women seek recognition, not simply as being equal to men, but for having something specific to offer in terms of their own sexuality, spirituality, sensitivity, and outlook on family life and communal obligations.

So far, Jewish women have been given the right to participate in a religious life that has remained essentially male-centered in content. Jewish feminists such as JUDITH PLASKOW (born 1947) call for a restructuring of Judaism, a new confrontation with Sinai, as the title of her book, *Standing Again at Sinai* indicates. Assessing the current situation of women being counted in the minyan, being called to the Torah, serving as rabbis and cantors, Plaskow finds it still wanting:

> We become full members of a tradition that women played only a secondary role in shaping and creating. We appear to be equals, but we leave intact the history, structures, images and texts that exclude and testify against us.... Feminism, I believe, aims at the liberation of all women and all people, and is thus not a movement for individual equality, but for the creation of a society that no longer construes difference in terms of superiority and subordination. The project of creating a feminist Judaism fits into a larger project of creating a world in which all women, and all people, have both the basic resources they need to survive, and the opportunity to name and shape the structures of meaning that give substance to their lives. In the Jewish context, this means reforming every aspect of tradition so that it incorporates women's experience. Only when those who have had the power of naming stolen from us find our voices and begin to speak will Judaism become a religion that includes all Jews—will it truly be a Judaism of women and men.[2]

Having made great strides, especially in non-Orthodox Jewry, the women's movement is still confronted with opposition based on tradition and habit. In its history, Judaism has been renewed through movements emerging from hitherto neglected elements. The emergence of the Pharisees, the influence of Eastern European Jewry, and the rise of Zionism, for example, transformed the Jewish people. Jewish women have been powerful molders of the Jewish spirit, even while being excluded. As contributors to its transformation they are leading the Jewish spirit to unfold in as-yet-unknown ways.

2. Judith Plaskow, *Standing Again at Sinai: Judaism from a Feminist Perspective* (San Francisco: Harper, 1990), pp. xvi–xvii.

Chapter 32

THROUGH THE EYES OF THE JEWISH MYSTICS

Jewish mysticism, like other forms of mysticism, deals with the possibility of achieving direct communion with God. Mystical experiences are overpowering, immediate, personal encounters with the divine. Mystical knowledge consists of intuitions that transcend ordinary comprehension, such as insights into the deepest meaning of the words of Torah. Mystics center their lives and teachings around these experiences and insights. They often gain their wisdom by penetrating the secrets behind the written word, through contemplation, or in spiritual ecstasy.

Jewish mystics seek insights into the nature of God, the creation of the universe, the destiny of human beings, the nature of evil, and the ultimate meaning of Torah. The words of the Jewish mystics are often obscure, and their teachings sometimes diverge from the conclusions that can be derived from Torah by reason, and from those that the Rabbis have drawn from the Written Torah. To many of the Rabbis, this posed a danger to Torah and faith. Jewish scholars of the nineteenth century brushed mysticism aside as superstition, feeling that Judaism could find recognition in the world only as a religion of reason. The mystics were frequently opposed both by Jewish rationalists and by rabbis. Many also understood, however, that the mystics by their special knowledge might have acquired mastery over creation, the power to perform miracles, and the authority to create new rituals or fill old ones with new meaning.

Jewish mysticism has had the greatest following during times of crisis and sorrow. Becoming an antidote to despair, it took hold in Germany after the Crusades, in Palestine among those exiled from Spain, and in Poland after the Chmielnicki massacres and the collapse of messianic expectations. Its appeal to contemporary Jews may be an effect of the Holocaust.

FROM THE BEGINNINGS TO THE ZOHAR

Mysticism in Torah and Talmud

Mystical experiences are woven into the fabric of Judaism. Abraham was granted a mystical vision at a moment of despair: In a deep trance, he saw a flaming torch pass between the pieces of the sacrifice he had lined up, consuming them, and God appeared to him, making a covenant with him (Gen. 15:12–21). The revelation at Sinai, the great turning point in Israel's history, was also linked to mystical vision, for the leaders "saw the God of Israel: under His feet there was the likeness of a pavement of sapphire, like the very sky for purity" (Exod. 24:9–10).

The Kedushah, the sanctification of God that is recited in daily congregational prayer, was revealed to Isaiah in a mystical experience:

> I beheld my Lord seated on a high and lofty throne; and the skirts of His robe filled the Temple. Seraphs stood in attendance on Him. Each of them had six wings: with two he covered his face, with two he covered his legs, and with two he would fly.
> And one would call to the other,
> "Holy, holy, holy!
> The Lord of Hosts!
> His presence fills all the earth!" (Isa. 6:1–3)

Some of the basic ideas regarding the character of Jewish mysticism have come from the opening of the Book of Ezekiel.

When Ezekiel was among the disheartened "community of exiles" in Babylon, "the heavens opened" and he saw "visions of God" (Ezek. 1:1). The prophet tells of *Maaseh Merkabah,* the "Event of the Chariot," the heavenly throne surrounded by the chariots of heaven. Initiates have been given their mystical experiences after a preparation of fasting, meditation, and separation from the world. The divine revelation has not been the property of the recipient, however, but *universal* revelation to be made public to all. Above all, the Jewish mystic has never dissolved his personality in God; the separation between the divine and the human is never obscured.

Many of the Sages were mystics, and the daily recital of the Kedushah was introduced in talmudic times. Nevertheless, the Sages advised great caution regarding the study of mysticism, warning that speculation may lead the seeker out of Judaism or destroy his life. Only the initiated were given mystical instruction, and, they, in turn, transmitted it only to a small group of the select. "The mysteries of creation, *Maaseh Bereshit,*" for example, "may be taught not even to two students at a time. *Maaseh Merkabah,* the mysteries of the heavenly chariot, not even to one student, except he be a sage and grasp it out of his own understanding" (M. Hagigah 2:1). The content of this transmission to the initiates was later called *Kabbalah,* "special transference."

Hekhalot *and* Merkabah *Literature*

The thoughts of the mystically initiated talmudic Rabbis have come down to us only in fragments but have nevertheless had great influence on later kabbalistic thinking. These fragments form the *Hekhalot* and *Merkabah* literature, focusing on Ezekiel's vision of the heavenly chariot (*Merkabah*) and the Song of Songs, telling us of the ascent of the mystic, Rabbi ISHMAEL (second century C.E.), through the seven heavens or temples (*Hekhalot*) to the throne of God, where the mystic perceives the "Great Glory," surrounded by the court of Heaven.

This literature, showing the influence of non-Jewish gnostic teachings, shocked many of the Sages, and while the "Great

Glory" is not identical with God's essence but only emanates from it, the anthropomorphisms were regarded as heretical. Nevertheless it opened new approaches to God. Manuscripts were produced in Italy, Spain, France, and Germany, and the angelic hymns composed by the mystics found wide use.

Sefer Yetzirah: *The Book of Creation*

Sefer Yetzirah, the Book of Creation, composed sometime between the second and sixth centuries, existed in the talmudic period and was held in such veneration that pious minds attributed its authorship to the patriarch Abraham. This small book introduces the elements on which future kabbalists based their concepts, above all the term *sefirot* and the concept of the creative power of the letters of the Hebrew alphabet.

The universe was created by God through the power God implanted in letters. The Hebrew alphabet has twenty-two letters. To ten of these letters God assigned a special additional function; together with the twenty-two letters of the alphabet they form a total of thirty-two. Each Hebrew letter has a numerical value. The term used for "number" is *sefirah*, plural *sefirot*; the book of creation gives the first ten special letters the designation *sefirot*. With these God created all the elements of which the cosmos is composed. As elements of creation, the letters have creative powers. The Talmud tells of two rabbis who were able to master these and create a calf that they ate on the Sabbath (B.T. Sanhedrin 65b and 67b).

Sefer Bahir: *The Book of Light*

Written in its present form during the twelfth century, the *Sefer Bahir*, the Book of Light, is the first truly kabbalistic work. Its original sources are older, the text is scrambled, the language is often confused, and parts are missing. Written in the form of the Midrash, an interpretation of biblical verses containing mystical parables, it shows the influence of the earlier Mishnaic writings and of the *Sefer Yetzirah*. Several of its ideas became important in the future

Mystics often gave their books titles associated with light: Sefer Bahir, Book of Light; Zohar, Book of Radiance.

development of Jewish mysticism, including the contemporary movement of the Lubavicher and other groups of Hasidim. Differing in many ways from the traditional interpretation of Torah, these teachings rest on mystical meditation and unique exegesis of Torah verses.

TORAH. The mystics, reading and interpreting the sacred scripture in their own way to find new meanings and new associations, used a passage from Proverbs to explain the true nature of Torah and its significance. In Proverbs we read:

> It is Wisdom calling.... The Lord created me at the beginning of His course.... In the distant past I was fashioned, at the beginning, at the origin of the earth.... I was with Him as a confidant, a source of delight every day, rejoicing before Him at all times. (Prov. 8:1, 22–30)

The mystics interpret the text to mean that Wisdom, which is Torah, speaks, revealing that she is God's confidant and constant companion. Torah is, therefore, not merely a sacred book, she is alive. God delights in her, his abiding counselor, and consults her in creating and maintaining the universe.

THE COSMIC TREE. Guided by Torah, God created the universe by releasing the divine powers within himself to fashion the cosmos (Isa. 44:24 in the mystics' reading). God fills the universe, is its fullness, is creator and sustainer of the cosmos. In a mystical reading of Deuteronomy 33:23, the *Bahir* understands God as a pool whose water nourishes the universe. In this pool of the divine, God has planted a cosmic tree, composed of His divine powers. Its roots reach upward. Planting the cosmic tree was God's first act—from it the world and all that is in it proceeds and develops. This cosmic tree is perpetually watered from the source, the pool (God), and continually bears fruit.

The tree's root, which extends into the pool, is the Hebrew letter

On tefillin, the capsule for the head has the letter shin *sculpted on both sides. On one side the letter has three strokes, on the other side four. To the mystics the* shin *on one side indicates the present limitation of life and the incompleteness of the Torah—only three streams flow down from the divine "pool." The* shin *on the other side, with its four strokes, points to the time of redemption—when the letter is complete, as will be Torah.*

shin, which looks like a root. The tree is watered by divine wisdom, *hokhmah*—Torah—and extends to earth. The tree's flourishing depends on the deeds of Israel. Some modern synagogues therefore have an Eternal Light in the form of a *shin.*

THE UNFATHOMABLE GOD. All mystics affirm that God is absolutely unfathomable and wholly removed from our contemplation and any definition. Only through the powers, attributes, that God released from himself to create the world does God become accessible to human thought. Why God released these powers and how God did so will be forever hidden from us and are wholly outside of the ability to speculate. We must understand that these powers remain within God and are not separated from God.

THE *SEFIROT.* Internally, God unfolds by ten attributes and powers, the *sefirot.* This internal movement is the source of all creation and the entire unfolding of the cosmos. Of them the cosmic tree is composed. The term *sefirot,* taken from *Sefer Yetzirah,* no longer means numbers but God's internal powers. The number ten is derived from the Mishnah, "Through ten words the world was created" (M. Avot 5:1). We shall discuss the *sefirot* below, in regard to the great work on mysticism called the *Zohar.*

According to the *Bahir,* prayer is concentration on the unity of the *sefirot,* the powers of God. *Kavvanat ha-lev* meant "mystical concentration of the heart" on the *sefirot; kavvanah* in prayer must include all the ten *sefirot* as the way to the unfathomable One God of the Sh'ma—"Hear, O Israel, the Lord our God, the Lord is One" (Deut. 6:4).

TRANSMIGRATION OF SOULS. "One generation goes, another comes" (Eccles. 1:4) means in the *Bahir* that a generation comes that has already gone, that is, has been there before. If Israel is good then God will take new seed (a new soul) from the Sabbath, the divine storage place of the seeds (souls), and implant it in new bodies; if Israel fails then God will take from the seed that was already in the world, had come once before, and bring it back. Only when all the souls have completed their wanderings and been purified, will the Messiah come. The migration is only from human to human, not to any other creature. This idea of transmigration and reincarnation has been rejected by Jewish tradition.

Medieval Mysticism in Germany, France, and Spain

During the twelfth century, centers of Jewish mysticism were established in Germany, in Worms and Regensburg, and also in Provence, in cities like Marseilles, Lunel, Beziers, Narbonne, Perpignan, Carcassonne, and Toulouse. Jewish life and scholarship flourished in both areas, and ancient traditions were still known. The leaders of the mystical movement were also outstanding talmudic scholars. In Germany, Rabbi Judah he-Hasid was central to the mystical movement (see chapter 9). In Provence, Rabbi ABRAHAM IBN DAVID OF POSQUIÈRES (c. 1125–1198) was a commentator on the Talmud, a halakhist, and a mystic, who in spite of his great wealth lived an ascetic life dedicated to inward communion with God.

GERMANY. Seared by Jewish martyrdom during the Crusades, the Hasidei Ashkenas, the Pious Men of Germany, had a deeply pessimistic outlook and members of the group were harshly ascetic (see chapter 9). They believed that God created the world as a place of tests and trials. In addition, every joy contained an element of sin, except marital relations, which are ordained in Torah and are a symbol of union with God.

The Hasidei Ashkenas understood that the world had been created through the letters of the Hebrew alphabet and would be redeemed through *kavvanah,* attunement to God in prayer. Torah and the prayer book were, they believed, divinely revealed. They therefore saw significance in every word, and even every letter, and tried to evoke the power contained in the letters of the alphabet. In prayer they drew out every word in song and opposed every change in the text. They counted the letters in a word or sentence for their numerical value, *gematria,* or understood them as abbreviations of whole sentences, *notarikon,* and exchanged them to gain new meanings out of them. The hidden meanings of the word conveyed more than knowledge, giving power over the forces in the world, including demons and evil spirits. This power was granted above all to the Zaddik; he understood the very deepest meaning of the word and had the Godlike power to shape and affect events. He could successfully intercede for others. Like God, he had to be entirely unselfish.

PROVENCE.ISAAC THE BLIND, son of Abraham ibn David of Posquières, was accorded the honorary title of a "Father of the Kabbalah." Many called him Isaac he-Hasid. He had inner intuition, could feel the aura of a person approaching him and sense whether his visitor's soul had gone through transmigration. It was claimed that his prayers for the sick were always answered, for he was a "master of prayer" in the mystical sense. He wrote a commentary to *Sefer Yetzirah.*

Isaac left behind instructions about the specific *kavvanah* that should accompany each prayer. The worshiper must leave his body and all its needs behind and enter the deepest communion, *devekut,* with God. Since the destruction of the Temple, prayer, the service of the heart, has replaced the sacrifices. It must specifically correspond to *olah*—"the rising up" of the Temple sacrifice that was fully consumed on the altar—by the personal sacrifice of elevation, through meditation and prayer. The same *kavvanah* must equally undergird the performance of every mitzvah. After a life filled with such prayer and mitzvot, the Jew may become fully worthy to be "bound up in the bundle of life"—the hereafter—and to attain a high place at the time of resurrection. The petition "may his [her] soul be bound up in the bundle of life" (after 1 Sam. 25:29) has since come to be inscribed on every Jewish tombstone.

Isaac coined the name *Kabbalah* as the specific term for esoteric, mystical tradition. He initiated the term *En Sof,* the Boundless, for the absolute, one, and wholly unfathomable God who is unreachable and beyond all thought and contemplation. This term was to be used by all future kabbalists. Isaac also introduced new names for the seven lower *sefirot* that henceforth were to be generally used. He based them on the verse : "Yours, God, are greatness (*gedullah*), might (*gevurah*), splendor (*tiferet*), triumph (*netzah*), and majesty (*hod*)—yes, all (*khol*) that is in heaven and earth: to You, God, belong kingship (*mamlakhah*) and preeminence above all" (1 Chron. 29:11). For the first three *sefirot* he retained the names given them in the *Bahir*.

GERONA. The kabbalistic movement in Spain had a center in Gerona, not far from the Provence. There a "holy company" of mystics gathered, in which Nahmanides, the defender of the Talmud at the disputation at Barcelona (see chapter 7), played a leading role.

The group followed Isaac the Blind's teachings on prayer and mitzvot. Every Jew must live an active life in Torah and mitzvot, in strict obedience to halakah. In prayer, he should strive completely to surrender his own will to God's. These mystics were apprehensive, however, that Kabbalah, if spread beyond the circle of the initiates, might lead simple Jews into error. It might distract them from mitzvot and make them believe that prayer to God had to go through various divine "agents." The teaching of Kabbalah became restricted.

The kabbalists of Gerona gave detailed formulations to the mystical concept of God. They also described Torah as God's companion, as *Sefer Bahir* had pointed out. Nahmanides, echoing *Sefer Yetzirah*, explains that creation can exist only as the name of God is engraved on it. This engraving is Torah. The ten *sefirot* are contained within the depth of the letters of Torah. Torah is the heart of creation. According to Nahmanides, the entire Torah consists of the names of God. The whole Torah is a configuration of God's name, the tetragrammaton YHVH. Out of this name the living fabric of the universe has been shaped. The Torah woven of holy names is a living organism. Therefore God looked into the Torah when he created the world.

But this is not the Torah as the Jews read it. Rather, it is *Torah kedumah*, primordial Torah. Its letters were not divided into words: This was the Torah handed to Moses, but before the people received it, the letters

The words of the kabbalists throw into focus what Torah means to Jews. A special reverence for Torah fills every Jew, be she or he bound to tradition or not; the Torah's message, God's inspired word, evokes honor and respect. But, in the spirit of the mystics, Torah, beyond its understandable message, also holds in every single letter, word, sentence, and even the division of its paragraphs, a divinity unknown to human beings. Torah is not merely a book of divine origin, it is a live organism. Its words, as the words of the living God, are creative and redemptive.

were scrambled, divided into words, sequences of events, imparting God's mitzvot. Had God given the Torah in its original form it would have enabled its readers to perform miracles and raise the dead. The Jewish reader therefore does not know the importance of the letters, words, and sections in the Torah that Israel possesses. Sections that appear as insignificant may be of great importance in their hidden meaning. Even the spaces between letters and paragraphs are letters in the primordial Torah.

Zohar: The Book of Radiance

Zohar, the Book of Radiance, became the textbook of the mystics and, beyond that, almost a second Torah for large segments of the Jewish people. When the Yemenite Jews were rescued and evacuated to Israel they took, next to the Torah, the

This devout family reverences the tomb of Rabbi Simeon bar Yohai (at Meron), believed by many to be the author of the *Zohar.*

THROUGH THE EYES OF THE JEWISH MYSTICS

Zohar in their arms with them. The book's main author was
MOSES DE LEON (c. 1240–1305), a member of the kabbalistic circle
of thirteenth-century Spain; he ascribed its authorship to Rabbi
SIMEON BAR-YOHAI (second century C.E.), a pupil of Akiba, in order
to give the work greater prestige. Rabbi Simeon had been an
outspoken critic of the Roman occupation in Palestine and
therefore had to flee. Legend has it that he spent thirteen years
in a cave in the Judaean mountains, miraculously supplied with
food and water. He devoted his time to mystical speculations,
which he laid down in the *Zohar*. The work is written in the
form of a midrash to the Torah, giving a verse by verse exegesis. It is in Aramaic, in an exalted style, and shows the influence
of earlier works, such as *Sefer Bahir*.

The Sefirot

The *Zohar* is concerned with the inner life of God. Its ideas
rest on those of earlier mystics, which are summarized and
given comprehensive expression, especially the theory of *Sefer
Yetzirah*, that God "engraved" the world, and the doctrine of the
sefirot as started in *Sefer Bahir* and further developed by Isaac
the Blind. The *sefirot*, which are in God, constitute the inner
movement of God and represent contradictory elements—
good and evil—in the divine organism. They are also in the
world because all that exists is engraved by God—has some of
the *sefirot* in it. The *sefirot* exist, above all, in the human being,
who is created in the image of God. The *sefirot* are located in the
mind, trunk, and limbs of the body. In addition, since the concept of the human being, as bearer of the *sefirot*, can be applied
to God, God can be understood an-
thropomorphically. Finally, the
sefirot can also be imaged as a tree
formed by the layers of the divine
powers. God's mystical tree, with
roots, trunk, and limbs, is configured
similarly to the human body.

In the commentary to Genesis,
the *Zohar* explains that God is

*As the Torah is taken from the Ark, a
prayer from the Zohar is recited in
many congregations. It opens with
the words, "Blessed be the Name of
the Lord of the World." Before the
scroll is returned to the Ark after the
appointed reading, the congregation
affirms: "She is a tree of life to those
who grasp her" (Prov. 3:18).*

In mystic prayer, all ten of the *sefirot* are kept in mind at the same time. As the man in this sixteenth-century drawing prays, the roots of the tree reach to heaven and the Shekhinah (below his hand) is on the earth.

absolutely one but can nevertheless be found in various grades or degrees of divine creatorship that follow each other in descending and ascending order. The first three of these degrees emerged before creation, the remaining seven during the seven days of creation. These degrees correspond to the *sefirot* already postulated by previous kabbalists. The *sefirot* are now the mind and limbs of God, who is understood in human form (see the illustrations).

EN SOF. God as En Sof, the Boundless, is hidden and wholly inaccessible to us.

KETER ELYON, THE SUPREME CROWN OF GOD. By a mysterious will and act, En Sof turns outward from concealment to reveal itself, to create, to let its light shine upon the world. This is a breakthrough, wrenching the introspective En Sof from its fullness of repose. Keter Elyon, the first emanation, is the point where En Sof discloses itself. Keter Elyon is intimately bound to En Sof. The only difference between them is that Keter turns to what is below. Having no features, no individuality, Keter is simply boundary, the ultimate point to which human thought can penetrate in its quest for the perception of God. Keter Elyon has no beginning; from it the other *sefirot* emerge.

HOKHMAH, WISDOM. When the *sefirah* Hokhmah, Wisdom, emerged from Keter Elyon, this was the primordial beginning of creation. Hokhmah is the womb of creation, the *Beginning*. It is the first point at which the divine *will* can be detected. It is the active male element within God, the Upper Father.

BINAH, INTELLIGENCE. From Binah, Intelligence, the actual building of the world begins. Binah is the feminine element within God. She receives her seed from Hokhmah and is Upper Mother. From her womb all of creation emerges, both in the "upper world," that is, the other seven *sefirot*, and in our world below. Binah means both intelligence and "that which divides between things"; through Binah, all that was undifferentiated in God is given individuation.

Throughout the centuries, Christians have shown great interest in Kabbalah, perceiving in it parallels to their own faith. For instance, they saw the three upper sefirot as a representation of the Holy Trinity.

Keter Elyon, Hokhmah, and Binah constitute the head. The remaining seven *sefirot* are the trunk and limbs.

HESED, MERCY, AND GEVURAH (OR DIN), POWER, JUDGMENT. Hesed and Din, the arms, emerge from Binah. Hesed, on God's right, is unrestrained divine love pouring out blessing and abundance. Hesed must be balanced by Gevurah, Din—judgment—on God's left; both are absolutely necessary for the existence of the world. As long as they are balanced, equilibrium is maintained. If the balance is upset—as by human sinfulness—Din pours forth without restraint and actually becomes evil. The kabbalists thereby place a source of evil in God.

TIFERET, SPLENDOR (OR RAHAMIM, COMPASSION). Tiferet mediates between Hesed and Din, because the world could not exist if governed by either one alone. Tiferet is part of the trunk of the body, in direct line beneath Keter Elyon. The kabbalists emphasize that Tiferet is a "son" of Hokhmah and Binah. He is the embodiment of God as Person, filled with compassion, as Judaism has generally understood God. To him

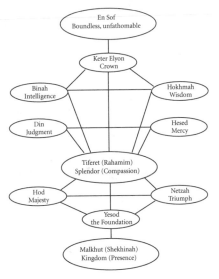

The *Sefirot*.

are applied the names by which God is widely called in prayer and discourse, such as "the Holy One, blessed be He."

NETZAH, TRIUMPH, ENDURANCE, AND HOD, MAJESTY. Netzah and Hod, on the right and left, reflect God's reign, either as compassionate ruler or in stern majesty. The sources of prophecy, they are the legs.

The Zaddik, an unconditionally righteous person wholly committed to God and Torah, is not merely a role model on earth but a cosmic force reaching up to heaven, the embodiment of the commandments, establishing peace and stability in the world.

YESOD, THE FOUNDATION. In Yesod, the Foundation, all the generative forces in God, all *sefirot,* are gathered and together flow into the last *sefirah,* Malkhut. Yesod is the place of the phallus, or procreation. The Zaddik is seen as the embodiment of Yesod (Prov. 10:25: "the righteous *[Zaddik]* is an everlasting foundation *[Yesod]*"). The Zaddik holds his generative powers under the control of Torah and pours out God's powers on the people.

MALKHUT, KINGDOM (SHEKHINAH). Malkhut, Kingdom, is equated with the Shekhinah. In rabbinic writing, *Shekhinah* simply refers to God's indwelling presence in Israel and the world. In the Kabbalah, Shekhinah is the tenth *sefirah.* In contrast to the other nine, she has no power of her own but, rather, receives the outpouring of the others and is the vessel and conduit through which these forces flow into the world. Shekhinah is the moon that reflects light but has none of its own. Other names given her include Lower Mother, Rachel, Earth, Queen, Bride. She is the female element. The kabbalists emphasize that she is Binah's daughter, and "all women are contained in her mystery." She is the lover of Tiferet, but this union is filled with tension. When their union is consummated, it spells cosmic unity; separation means the Shekhinah's exile. From her union with Tiferet during the night of the Sabbath, the souls of Israel emerge. She is therefore Israel's mother and guardian. As the community of Israel is identified with her, it becomes an element in God.

The kabbalists speak of a Shekhinah above, closely linked with Binah, and a Shekhinah below, closely linked to the world. Using a text from the Talmud—"God's *Shekhinah* [divine presence] went with Israel into all its exiles" (B.T. Megillah 29a)—the kabbalists explain that in the Shekhinah, a part of God is exiled from God and is with Israel in exile. The Shekhinah, the most precious part of God's divinity, was given to Israel in pledge that God will never desert or abandon the people, even if they fall into sin. The Shekhinah below brings the needs and supplications of Israel and human-kind to her upper embodiment. The task of uniting Shekhinah with God, the ultimate goal in history, is given to Israel, the Jewish people, the bearer of Torah. The comfort of these words helps us to understand the *Zohar*'s impact on the Jewish people.

Those trying to find peace in our hectic times may find the teachings of Abraham Abulafia (1240–after 1291) intriguing. He strove to find a wholly intimate union with God. To achieve it, he used meditation methods—including practicing body postures and breathing techniques similar to yoga—that are widely recommended for overcoming stress, creating calm, and promoting enlightenment. He lived in Spain and wrote a number of handbooks around the same time as the Zohar.

Implications of the Sefirot

DESCENT AND ASCENT. The divine descends through the *sefirot*, and the mystic ascends in prayer to *devekut*. The ascent begins with the Shekhinah, who is the gate into God's realm. Humans become aware of God's presence. From here they progress as far as they can go.

SEXUAL IMAGERY AND SYMBOLISM. The representations of the *sefirot* in the image of a human body means that all the *sefirot* interact organically, for they connect in the same way as do the organs in human beings. This leads the *Zohar* to sexual imagery. For example, Shekhinah is the female element in God, the vessel that receives and brings forth the fruit; God in the *sefirah* Tiferet and the Shekhinah are described as celestial groom and bride joining in sacred union. On earth, the bliss of absolute union is felt in sexual intercourse, in which all separateness vanishes, and creation is its blessed fruit. God rejoices. Sexual union on the Sabbath enhances the day's expression of the union of God and Israel. The act should be performed in joyful surrender and in God's presence.

EVIL AND ITS CAUSE. The *sefirot* constitute an organic whole within God and produce harmony in the world. A sinful person who breaks this organic unity destroys this union and creates the false world of evil. There exists also a domain of darkness independent of human sinfulness. As the *Bahir* had already stated, Din, strict Justice, is also the source of evil in the world. It is balanced by Hesed, Mercy. When Din breaks loose from Hesed, however, it breaks wholly away from God and is

The elaborate ornamentation of the *Zohar* illustrates the reverence with which
Moses de Leon's book was held.

transformed into radical evil. According to the *Bahir,* God has an attribute called *Evil;* this destructive force, one of the powers by which God acts, is called *Satan,* which means "he who pitches downward, pitching the world into guilt" (from the root *satah*). The many messengers of this force, called "Evil, Evil," lead people to sin, are the source of every evil urge, and plunge the world into guilt, that is, *tohu,* the "unformed" (Gen. 1:1).

THE SOUL. Based on medieval philosophy, including Maimonides, the *Zohar* teaches that there are three "souls": *nefesh* is life; *ruah* is spirit; *neshamah* is the true, holy soul. According to the *Zohar,* all souls were formed by God at creation. In God's treasure house, a celestial paradise, they await the time when they will be put into bodies, which results from the union of God with the Shekhinah. While in the body, the soul weaves the garment it is to wear upon its return to its origin, the mystical paradise. The mitzvot are the threads from which the garments are woven. When they appear before God's court, the souls that have few mitzvot or have sinned are naked or their garments are full of holes; they are sent to purgatory in the fiery stream of Gehennah, or, if they have been wholly evil, they are burned.

RABBI ISAAC LURIA, THE ARI

The expulsion of the Jews from Spain in 1492 was a catastrophe that brought a crisis in Jewish life. The Kabbalah had to adjust to it and find new directions. Up to this time, it had been concerned with the ultimate root of creation; now it had to direct its attention to the expectation of redemption and had to explain the tragedy of exile. Was the death of a glorious community a result of the corruption of the world, a punishment for the sins of the past and present, or did exile mean the birth pangs of the Messiah? Whatever the explanation, *teshuvah,* repentance, was called for, to bring about the rebirth of the people and the world. *Teshuvah* included acceptance of sufferings and called for prayer with *kavvanah.* It further entailed spreading the message of Kabbalah among the people, whose collective action was needed to accelerate the coming of the Messiah. The kabbalists settled in Eretz Yisrael, the Land where the messianic hope would be realized. They established a new center at Safed and stepped out of their splendid isolation to be close to the people. The charismatic personality who inspired his followers to take up the ideas of mysticism was Isaac Luria (1534–1572), who came to be seen as the leader of the Safed movement and to be regarded as a "saint" by his disciples and their successors. His disciples called him *Ari* ("lion"), the initials of his name: Ashkenasi Rabbi Isaac. To his followers he was the "Sacred Lion." The Ari was a visionary, seeing souls in everything, even stones. He made frequent pilgrimages to the nearby tomb of Rabbi Simeon ben Yohai, then regarded as the author of the *Zohar*. In the Safed circle we find Rabbi Joseph Karo (1488–1575), author of the Shulhan Arukh, the authoritative halakhic guide for traditional Jewry all over the world.

Dying young, after having lived at Safed for only three years, the Ari left very few writings behind, but his disciples spread his teachings. In his commentary to a section of the *Zohar*, inspired by the prophet Elijah, whom he claimed to have appeared to him, the Ari developed highly independent ideas.

TZIMTZUM. According to the Ari, in order to make room for the world that God was about to create, God retreated and abandoned a part of the divine omnipresence. This act of withdrawal, called *tzimtzum*, preceded creation; in a sense, God went into exile in order to make room for creation. Then God created the world out of the void, reentering it through creation and revelation. At creation, the divine light flowed into the *tzimtzum*. The first configuration is *Adam Kadmon*, primordial man, wholly spiritual, first and highest form of the manifestation of En Sof. Divine light from Adam Kadmon flowed into the *sefirot*. Since finite beings were to be created in accordance with the *sefirot*, the *sefirot* needed bowls, vessels, to hold the light. The first three *sefirot* could hold the light, but when it broke upon the seven lower *sefirot*,

In traditional prayer books, we find meditations preceding the performance of mitzvot, such as entering the sukkah or shaking of the lulav, with kavvanot that include the words, "it is my intention to promote the unification of Your Name."

they could not hold the light and the vessels broke. The broken shells, *kelipot*, to which some of the holy sparks adhered, sank into the uttermost regions of primordial space, the abyss, where the spirit of evil dwells. Through the breaking of the vessels the union of the universe within itself and with God was torn apart, and the universe and the human world were torn in catastrophic conflict; the unity of God in the world had been broken. The Shekhinah fell when the vessels broke and, as the last *sefirah*, is in exile.

Tikkun, given a modern meaning as the call to promote unity and justice throughout the world, is perceived by modern Jews as a paramount task, challenging both Jews and non-Jews alike. A Jewish periodical bears this name.

TIKKUN. The powers of evil must be transformed into powers of love, the world must be mended, and the manifestation of God be restored to unity. This is the work of *tikkun*, restoration. With the beginning of *tikkun*, the Shekhinah acquired new strength. Placed in the hands of humanity, *tikkun* is advanced in the process of history, and the Jew has a special function in bringing it about; the Jew's *kavvanah* must be directed toward this goal. The divine sparks are scattered throughout the entire world, and Israel, like the Shekhinah, is called to go into exile to the very ends of the world to gather them.

THE IMPACT OF ISAAC LURIA AND KABBALAH ON JEWISH PRACTICE

Luria's teachings have had a deep and lasting influence upon the Jewish people. To his contemporaries, the Ari revealed the meaning of their exile from Spain and gave hope that every person could be an instrument of redemption. In the terror of the Holocaust, his message also brought comfort and resolve. Many of the customs and practices that he and his followers instituted have had an abiding impact on all of Jewry.

According to Isaac Luria, the Jew must strive for devekut and every prayer must be filled with kavvanah, the mystical intention to bring about the unification of God's Name. Every act, even menial labor, serves this goal and can lead to the eternal Sabbath; every act vitally affects both God and humans. Filling both personal prayer and the prayers of the liturgy with kavvanah, the Jew ascends to God and advances tikkun.

The mystical movement of Hasidism flowered in Poland and Russia beginning with the eighteenth century. Rooted in the traditions of Jewish mysticism, above all those of Isaac Luria, Hasidism emphasizes the power of every individual Jew to promote tikkun *through* kavvanah *in prayer and in daily work. The Rebbe is the Zaddik, who embodies Torah and has direct access to the divine.*

THE SABBATH. *Kabbalat Shabbat,* the service welcoming the Sabbath, originated in the Lurianic community of Safed and has been universally adopted. Part of this service, the hymn "Lekhah Dodi," "Come beloved, to meet the Bride," was written by Solomon Alkabetz, one of Luria's disciples. On Friday at dusk, the Ari and his followers went out into the fields, closed their eyes, sang, and, after the entrance of the "Bride," the Shekhinah embodied in the Sabbath, reopened them. For on the Sabbath the Shekhinah is temporarily removed from exile, is united with Israel, which is equally released momentarily from exile. Today the congregation turns toward the entrance door of the synagogue while singing the last verse of "Lekhah Dodi," as if the "Bride" were indeed making her entrance.

Returning home, Luria's company would walk around the Sabbath table, welcoming the Shekhinah in song. Today, the hymn "Shalom Aleikhem" is sung by many families as, holding hands, they march around the table before Kiddush. The hymn welcomes the angels who, according to the Talmud (B.T. Shabbat 119a) accompany the Jew from the house of God to his home. The custom of singing the verses praising the virtuous wife (Prov. 31:10–31) on Friday night in honor of the mother of the house was introduced by the kabbalists to honor the Shekhinah, the heavenly wife.

THE FESTIVALS. As the Torah is taken out of the Ark, God's thirteen attributes of mercy are recited followed by a prayer for divine help, containing mystical *kavvanot.* This was introduced by the school of Luria, first only for the month of Elul and the Yamim Noraim, then extended to all festivals.

On Rosh Hashanah the sounding of the shofar is preceded by a meditation by the person who will sound it. Earlier versions contained mystical names of God that are now omitted. After each of the three sections of sound, meditations are offered as well.

Two vigils are held during the year, namely, the night of Hoshanah Rabbah and of Shavuot. The text for the celebration, denoting its character, is called *Tikkun*. Hoshanah Rabbah, the last half-holiday of Sukkot, was transformed by the kabbalists from a day of joy to a day of penitence, akin to Yom Kippur; they stayed awake in prayer and penitence during the night. The celebration is still observed—usually with coffee and cake; the Book of Deuteronomy is read, followed by the Book of Psalms and selections from the *Zohar*.

The kabbalists saw in the revelation at Sinai that took place on Shavuot the sacred marriage between the Shekhinah and Israel. The preceding night served as preparation for the "bride." On the Shavuot vigil the first and last paragraphs of the books of the Tanakh and of the tractates of the Mishnah are read, followed by excerpts from *Sefer Yetzirah*. The concluding prayer for both vigils condenses the teachings of Lurian Kabbalah.

In many traditional congregations, Yom Kippur Katan, a "little Yom Kippur," is observed during *Minhah*, afternoon prayer, on the eve of a new month. It includes penitential prayers, and the affirmation of faith, during which "Sh'ma Yisrael . . ." (Hear O Israel) is recited once, "Barukh Shem . . ." (Blessed be His glorious kingdom) is recited three times, and "Ad'nai Hu ha-Elohim" (God He is God) is repeated seven times. The affirmation of God's unity is thus followed by ten pronouncements, corresponding to the ten *sefirot*. This moment of the hidden (new) moon was to the kabbalists a special time of *teshuvah* and *kavvanah*. The moon represented the Shekhinah; its restoration to light, her restoration to full radiance.

THE MEZUZAH. Under the influence of kabbalistic thought, the mezuzah became more than a reminder of God's presence and a call to love. The divine name *Shaddai* (Exod. 3:6) was to be inscribed on the back of the text and was to be visible on the outside. It came to be seen as an abbreviation of *Shomer delatot Yisrael*, "guardian of the doors of Israel." The mezuzah thus acquired the character of an amulet.

Chapter 33

ANCIENT AND MEDIEVAL THOUGHT

Philosophy, as the German philosopher Immanuel Kant (1724–1804) has pointed out, addresses the questions, What do I know? What must I do? What is my ultimate hope? In this sense, everyone has a philosophy that guides her or his life and actions. The philosopher addresses all or some of these questions systematically, using reason. Theology is the "science of God," out of which a philosophy of life emerges. Theology may lack the independence of philosophy, for a theologian who believes in God takes belief and tradition into account, as well as more purely philosophical speculation. Philosophy and theology do not exist in a vacuum. They are bound to the historical conditions out of which they arise and in some way constitute the autobiography of their creators.

In Torah and Talmud we find a theology and philosophy of life. It is expounded, not in written philosophical works, but in the works of mitzvot, which God has given Israel as an act of divine favor, and in which Israel immerses its mind. The Jewish philosophy of life clearly enunciates, what we know is what Torah tells us of the world's beginning and existence; what we must do is lead a life of mitzvot, which are lived ethics; what our ultimate hope is, is to be blessed by God in this life and in the world to come and to witness the coming of the

---

Messiah. Judaism does not rest entirely on the process of a freely creating reasoning mind, as does the philosophy of Plato and Aristotle. Instead, Jewish philosophy has reacted to the ideas of the great philosophers. This response can be compared to a musical theme with variations in music: the theme is established by the principles of Judaism, the variations are necessitated by changing times and changes in general thought.

THE IMPACT OF HELLENISM: PHILO OF ALEXANDRIA

Philo of Alexandria's variation to Judaism's perennial theme, called forth by the impact of Hellenism, resulted in a variation that ultimately moved away from Judaism—the theology of Paul. Philo (20 B.C.E.–50 C.E.) was a man of wide knowledge who wished to show that Hellenism and Judaism could be merged; he hoped to inspire seekers of wisdom to join the Jewish faith. He became a channel through which Greek and Jewish ideas flowed and partially merged, but never completely mixed.

Philo led a private and simple life devoted to thought and study. Called to the defense of his people, however, he overcame his aversion to public life. During the reign of the Roman emperor Caligula, Alexandrian Jewry came under vicious attacks spearheaded by Apion, an influential author and adamant Jew hater who incited the population to violent massacres. Philo headed a delegation of Jews seeking redress at Rome.

Living in two worlds, the world of Jewish thought and practice and the world of Greek philosophy, Philo hoped to show that the two messages were compatible. Plato was the great master he followed, and the School of the Stoics influenced him deeply. Plato taught that our world has no reality and is but a transitory copy of reality that exists in the higher realm of the Forms. The highest of these is the Form of the Good, which brings all other Forms into being and sustains them. To those who have been guided by reason to the realm of the Forms, the Good is revealed in a flash of intuitive enlightenment. Far removed and seen only with the inner eye by those who are immersed in contemplation, this Good may be identified with God. Philo has the same understanding of God. God is all spirit and is found through the spirit, while the body and physical things have no reality. Body and soul contrast to each other: the body is temporary, holding us down; the soul is eternal, lifting us up.

Like the Stoics, Philo also thinks that God pervades the universe, a whole governed by reason. To assume our fitting place in this world, we must follow reason exclusively and cast aside all passions and emotions. Guided by reason, we will know and do our duty, which alone makes us human. From this perspective, Torah is the book in which divine Wisdom instructs human beings in virtue and makes its adherents true servants of God. The personalities in Torah are allegories, presented for our guidance. For example, Abraham represents the person who wishes to go beyond self-knowledge to the vision of God, who is beyond human understanding. The patriarch's response to divine grace was faith (Gen. 15:6); no longer ensnared by the world, his reward was joy.

Philo thus explains the commandments as a visible way to convey ethical lessons. The Sabbath teaches the power of God, who created all; circumcision portrays the "excision of pleasure and all passions."[1] Unless we grasp the inner meaning of the commandments, their observance is without meaning, for the practice is like the body and the meaning like the soul. But, Philo warns, people should never abandon the commandments but, rather, strive to keep their meaning in mind; the commandments must be observed, but divine grace alone—not obedience to the commandments—allows us to rise to God.

Philo did not find it reasonable that God—so supreme, so far removed, so perfect and imperceptible—reached down from divine remoteness to make the physical universe. According to Torah, God created the world by the divine Word, or *Logos*, to use the Greek term. Logos, to Philo, is the sum of God's thought, wisdom, and power, out of which the world was created. Finding

1. Philo, "Soul and Body of the Divine Laws," in *Three Jewish Philosophers* (New York: Harper Torchbooks, 1965), part 1, pp. 40–41.

further meaning in the term Logos, Philo interprets a verse in the Book of Proverbs that speaks of Wisdom as God's first creation—"The Lord created me at the beginning of His course as the first of His works of old" (Prov. 8:22)— to mean that God released an angel or creative agent who built the world according to God's plan. The angel is called Logos, the Word, and this is what is meant by Logos. Logos is a part of God; Logos is also apart from God, God's messenger, God's son.[2]

As the first Jewish philosopher, Philo saw Judaism from a vantage point outside of it. At the same time, he was the first to make philosophy the handmaiden of revelation. Philo's impact upon Jewish thinking has been minor, although Jewish mysticism mirrors some of his ideas. Christian theology, on the other hand, shows Philo's influence to a greater degree. Basic Christian concepts—the dualism of body and soul, the fundamental importance of faith against actions, and above all the idea of the Word, Logos, of God being "in the beginning" (John 1:1), expanded to the Logos assuming bodily form, as the Son of God—can be traced to Philo. Even though Philo did not understand these terms as Christians later interpreted them, Hermann Cohen nevertheless said of him, "Had Philo not formed the notion of the Logos, no Jew would ever have fallen into doubt."[3]

THE IMPACT OF GREEK THOUGHT AND COMPETING RELIGIONS: SAADIA GAON

Tenth-century Baghdad, a dazzling city of beauty, splendor, and luxury, was a great center of learning and religious and intellectual disputes. Greek thought clashed with religious traditions, and the religions—Judaism, Christianity, Islam, Zoroastrianism, Manichaeism—vied with each other. Judaism was assaulted on many points: Islam taught that the Torah had been superseded by the Koran, Christianity advocated the principle of the Trinity, Zoroastrianism and Manichaeism saw the

2. Philo, "The Lord Shepherds Me," in *Three Jewish Philosophers*, part 1, p. 30.
3. Reported by Franz Rosenzweig. See Hermann Cohen, *Jüdische Schriften* (Berlin: Schwetschke, 1924), p. liii.

world torn by two equally powerful forces of good and evil, light and darkness, God and the devil. Within Judaism, the Karaites denied the validity of Oral Torah, accepting only Written Torah as binding. In this world of turmoil, Saadia ben-Yosef (892–942) felt obliged to give guidance to his people.

According to Saadia, God, as creator, possesses life, power, and wisdom, for without these, God could not create. We must not think of them as three different attributes, however, but as part of the divine Oneness. Our language is incapable of expressing them in one single word, so we use three terms in expressing what is really one.

Saadia asks, How can we accept tradition as true? How do we know that the Torah is really God's word? We must, he answers, put faith in reliable tradition. After all, our entire life rests on faith in the truth of other peoples' words. Without such faith we could not transact business, trust another's word, enact the affairs of state. Our knowledge comes from four roots: sense perception, reason, knowledge by inference as we draw conclusions from given premises, and, especially for "believers in the unity of God," reliable tradition. The revelation at Mount Sinai took place in front of an entire people; it was public, excluding any possibility of deception, and therefore we must accept the report as reliable, as true. Similarly, Oral Torah comprises a body of reliable tradition.

Saadia's position in his work, *The Book of Doctrines and Beliefs*,[4] is very simple and at the same time startling: Judaism teaches nothing contrary to reason or closed to reason. The truth, transmitted through revelation, can also be found through reason. Revelation gives us the truth in advance that we may be guided by it, helping us to perform the rules of religion and to lead the right kind of life. Without revelation, it might take us too long to find truth, or we might lack the perseverance to arrive at it, and in the meanwhile we would flounder, being without guidance. Ultimately, however, approval of all things God has commanded us, and disapproval of all things God has prohibited us, God has implanted in our reason.[5]

4. The translation of the title of Saadia's work follows Alexander Altmann's. See "Saadya Gaon: Book of Doctrines and Beliefs," ed. and trans. Alexander Altmann, in *Three Jewish Philosophers* (New York: Harper Torchbooks, 1965), part 2, pp. 9–190.
5. Saadia, *Book of Doctrines and Beliefs*, part 2, p. 97.

God has given us two types of commandments and they are intended for our good. Some, by the guidance of our reason, we all readily understand, such as truth and honesty. By obeying them everyone gains ethical stature and society improves. These commandments were therefore merely restated and amplified in revelation. The revealed religious commandments help us in ways not yet known to us; by obeying them we store up rewards in heaven. Rewards and punishments equally serve our own good; the consequences of obedience or disobedience, they are divine means to return us to loyalty.

The final goal of every human being is to be worthy of redemption. If a person has followed the commandments, the soul will depart in purity. Separated in death from the body, the soul will be reunited with it on the day of resurrection. Then body and soul will be judged. After the resurrection will come the day of the Messiah, and all humanity will witness the restoration of Israel.

Saadia's conclusions are those of Bible and Talmud. To him, the tradition of Judaism—Oral Torah as well as Written Torah—is holy and true, and reason is the supreme yardstick. At some future time, reason will arrive at the same truths. In the meanwhile, we follow the law of God and gain happiness. Saadia proclaims Judaism as the religion of reason. This idea has remained one of Judaism's claims to distinction.

In Defense of a Despised Religion: Judah Halevi

Judah Halevi (c. 1075–1141) witnessed the plight of the Spanish Jews as they were caught between the Muslim and Christian conquests in the eleventh century. He felt challenged to save his people's honor and undertook to prove that Judaism, the despised religion, was in fact the foundation of both Christianity and Islam and the bearer of the highest—the absolute—religious truth. A philosopher and a Jew, Judah knew that Torah and reason could not disagree.

Judah's philosophy unfolds in the frame of a story that

reflects the style of a Platonic dialogue. The central character is Bulan, king of the Chazars, the Kuzari. Bulan seeks the right faith after having been told by an angel that his "intentions are acceptable to the Creator, but not the actions."

Dissatisfied by what he learned from his conversations with a philosopher, a Christian, and a Muslin, Bulan learns from a Jew that Israel's God is the living God of history, who, at Sinai in public revelation, called Israel to action, charging it to lift up humanity to the divine. God can be found, the king realizes, in response to the divine appeal, in fulfillment of the divine commandments, and in yearning for the Holy One with heart and soul—but not through intellectual activity alone.

For Judah, the God of Israel and the Torah of Israel are the one and only source of absolute truth. All other religions are manmade. But why did Israel alone receive the truth? Judah's answer, which is the core of his thought, is the answer of the heart, which needs no philosophical proofs. Israel is a special work of creation, which makes the faith of Israel different in quality from any other:

> For me it is sufficient that God chose them as His community and people from all the nations of the world; that the Divine power descended upon the whole people, so that they all became worthy to be addressed by Him. This power even swayed to their women, among whom were prophetesses.[6]

Judah maintains that divine chosenness began with Adam and was inherited through the generations, but only by one distinguished son, until at Sinai a whole people, Israel, was chosen. It alone has the true religion. Therefore it was given God's most precious land, the Holy Land. But even away from its land Israel has a function: it is the heart of humanity. Israel beats for humanity, bears the afflictions of the world. Israel's distress reveals "diseases" that eventually will bring deep distress to all of humanity, and Israel gives humanity the capacity to throw off such diseases before they become deadly. As healers

6. Judah Halevi, *Kuzari*, ed. and trans. Isaak Heinemann, in *Three Jewish Philosophers* (New York: Harper Torchbooks, 1965), part 3, p.45.

of humanity, Jews have to lift up humanity to the divine. They have given the recognition of one God to Christianity and Islam. Jews should cling to Torah and mitzvot, in joy and in gratitude to the Creator, trusting in messianic redemption, when all humanity will truly understand God.

THE IMPACT OF ARISTOTELIAN PHILOSOPHY: MOSES MAIMONIDES

In the panorama of western civilization a few personalities tower above the rest by being universal minds who encompassed the totality of knowledge available to their period, evaluated it

critically, and carried it beyond the frontiers of their time. Among this select group we may count Aristotle, Thomas Aquinas, Leonardo da Vinci, Goethe—and Moses Maimonides, 1135–1204. He was philosopher, physician, biologist, codifier, and commentator. He was an ardent disciple of Aristotle, and he affirmed Torah as the lodestar of his life. Reason, Maimonides argued, is the human's greatest endowment, and Torah, divine and infallible, is reason; Aristotle's philosophy, also based on reason, is only human. When Aristotle disagrees with Torah, we must show where his human error lay; and when the words of Torah seem to conflict with reason, philosophy can shed new light upon their deeper meaning and resolve the conflict.

Talmudic scholar and Aristotelian, Maimonides had a profound influence on western philosophy and Jewish theology.

Out of these convictions, Maimonides wrote his *Guide for the Perplexed*. He wrote the book, not for the instruction of the masses, nor as a beginners' text in philosophy, but for the religious thinker, well schooled in Torah and philosophy, who was confused and inclined to feel that if he is guided by reason, he may have to reject some terms [of Torah] as he understands them, and may think that he has rejected the foundations of Torah. Yet ... in refusing to follow reason and by turning his back to it, he discovers that he has acted against his intellectual integrity.[7]

Like Aristotle, Maimonides maintains that reason is the great distinction of humans over all the other creatures, and its pursuit gives us greatest happiness. Unlike Aristotle, he is convinced that reason gives fulfillment to human life only if it leads to knowledge of God. Following Torah and Talmud he affirms, "The fear of the Lord is the beginning of knowledge" (Prov. 1:7); obedience to God's commandments is a first essential step on the road to God and must lead to a study of tradition, to studies in Judaism. Beyond that, Maimonides envisions a higher level: philosophy leads to theology and culminates in a direct intellectual conversation with God as far as human limitations will permit it. This is prophecy.

God

All we know about God, Maimonides holds, is *that* God is, we cannot know *what* God is. Our thoughts cannot comprehend God, nor have we words to express God. Whatever we say about God is inaccurate. For example, if we say, "The man exists," we actually say three things: (1) there is such a thing as a man; (2) he exists; (3) more than one man may exist. But we cannot make the same statements about God, for God is one, no other exists, God is outside the category of number. God's essence and existence are the same. God's Oneness is absolute and unlike any oneness we can understand, God's existence unlike any existence we can grasp. Similarly, when Torah speaks of God in anthropological expressions, such as God's "eyes," or God's "voice," or "God is merciful," these terms are used only to bring God closer to the understanding of average people. We

7. Moses Maimonides, *Guide for the Perplexed*, trans. M. Friedlander (London: Tuebner, 1885), introduction. For another translation, see Isadore Twersky, *A Maimonides Reader* (Springfield, N.J.: Behrman House, Inc., 1972), pp. 236 ff.

feel an *effect* of God watching over us, speaking to us, having mercy on us. The acts of the One God have numerous effects on us, but there is just one source—God, whose character we do not know.[8] Our statements about God can only be negative statements: God is *not* like anything we understand. We call this *negative theology*. This does not mean that we deny God's existence; we simply state that we have no comprehension of God and nothing compares to God. We cannot give God any positive attributes.[9]

Creation

For Maimonides, creation is an incontestable fact and can be proved philosophically. But philosophy alone cannot explain creation out of nothing, hence we must abide by the reliable report of Torah. For Jews its testimony is proof: God created. Since Torah has given us an explanation of the world's beginning we can philosophize freely and need not worry that immediate experience distorts our philosophical conclusions.[10]

Why did God create the world? We don't know, for the will of God is inscrutable, but the purpose of the world surely is to perform God's will.[11] Torah tells us that God created the world because God found it good to do so. Upon us rests the duty to give meaning and purpose to our lives, to gain understanding in order to become worthy of communion with God in the life of immortality. What is this life of immortality? God, whom we cannot describe, has prepared for us a life which is equally beyond our description. But life in the world to come must not be mistaken for the messianic age here on earth, when Israel will be restored and, through it, all of humanity.[12]

The Meaning of the Commandments

Maimonides explains the social function of the commandments. In many cases, this is easy; the Sabbath law, for instance,

8. Maimonides, *Guide* 1, ch. 26, 35, 50.
9. Maimonides, *Guide* 1, ch. 50.
10. Maimonides, *Guide* 2, ch. 17.
11. Maimonides, *Guide* 3, ch. 13 and ch. 25.
12. Maimonides, Mishneh Torah, Hilkhot Teshuvah ch. 8–9.

can easily be explained in a rational way—it provides rest for everyone. Other laws, however, do not yield to explanation so easily. Here Maimonides occasionally uses a thoroughly modern approach; he explains them scientifically. The most striking example occurs in connection with the laws of animal sacrifices, which he explains psychologically: When Israel was delivered from Egyptian bondage, all the nations of the world offered animal sacrifices to their gods. God realized that it would be asking too much of the people to make them change their form of worship completely. Change had to come gradually. Therefore God permitted Israel to offer animal sacrifices, and even taught how to offer them, in order that the people would not follow the crude customs of the heathens, and that their hearts would be directed to God. Yet God always had in mind to lead Israel to true worship, namely, through prayer. God therefore appointed but one exclusive place where animal sacrifices were permitted, the Temple. Prayer and supplication—true worship—may be offered at any place and time.[13]

Maimonides may have given Thomas Aquinas the idea to combine and harmonize Aristotle's work with the principles of faith. Aquinas's method and conclusions frequently follow Maimonides' reasoning; Christian scholasticism and many philosophers throughout the ages have been influenced by Maimonides, both directly and through Aquinas's works.

Maimonides under Critical Attack

Soon after his death, Maimonides' philosophy became controversial. Some opponents asked if the great thinker's mind was split—the Maimonides who authored the Mishneh Torah, the code of mitzvot, being a faithful Jew, and the one who wrote the *Guide for the Perplexed* being an Aristotelian. Asheknasic Jewry especially could see philosophy as a danger to faith: After the massacres of the Crusades these Jews had deliberately withdrawn from general culture to immerse themselves in the realm of the Talmud. Occupation with philosophy and science, tending to draw Jews away from the study of Torah and Talmud, could endanger Jewish steadfastness.

13. Maimonides, *Guide* 3, ch. 32.

Some of Maimonides' specific assertions were also subjected to criticism. He had, for instance, declared that any person ascribing a body to God was a heretic (Hilkhot Teshuvah 3:7). Abraham ibn David of Posquières, "Rabad" (c. 1125–1198), who himself held that God has no body, took issue with Maimonides' view as much too harsh. A person, especially a Kabbalist, who believed that God could be imagined in an anthropomorphic way, was certainly no heretic.

Hasdai Crescas (c. 1340–1412), the chief rabbi of Aragon, had been a victim of the pogroms of 1391, in which his only son was murdered. In light of the trials God had imposed on him, he turned to a loving God directly in communion with humanity. He did not oppose philosophy but took issue with the power that Aristotelianism held over many minds, and he disagreed with Maimonides on several basic issues.

Hasdai, like Maimonides, maintains that the essence of God is beyond human understanding. In contrast to Maimonides, Hasdai did not object to ascribing positive attributes to God, above all divine goodness reaching out to all. His ultimate conclusion is that God positively loves humanity and especially Israel. Crescas's thoughts gave strength and hope to the afflicted, whose suffering made them all equal and who looked to God for loving, providential care, whether they were intellectuals or simple people.

Chapter 34

LIVING IN TWO CULTURES

German Jewish Thought

Following the Emancipation, German Jewry was immersed in the culture of Germany as well as the traditions of Judaism. Jews found their model and guide in Moses Mendelssohn, a wholly committed Jew who was acclaimed as "a philosopher of the German nation and language." His own prototype was Maimonides, the universal scholar and dedicated Jew. As Mendelssohn's ideas entered Jewish thought, they had an impact even on the uncompromisingly Orthodox Samson Raphael Hirsch, who called for *Torah im Derekh Eretz*—Torah combined with worldly culture—and saw the ideal Jew as immersed in state, society, and secular culture, together with equal unyielding steadfastness to halakhah.

German Jewry equipped itself for this synthesis by sending many of its children to the university. University educated rabbinical leadership emerged, and a tight regional organization of congregations under rabbinical supervision developed. Assisted by the state, Jewish elementary schools were established in many communities. Schools for teachers were created; graduates held public teaching credentials and were equally equipped to serve as religious functionaries in their congregations. At the same time, instruction in Jewish religion was compulsory in all public schools, and Jewish children acquired a basic knowledge of

Judaism there. Although blending German culture and Jewish tradition sometimes led to the erosion of Jewishness, especially when family life lost its Jewish character due to the influences of the surrounding society, the results of such an education could be significant. My father, for example, was a profoundly religious Orthodox Jew. He introduced me to the study of the Talmud, analyzed Schiller's and Shakespeare's plays for me, tutored me in Latin, gave me an appreciation of art by explaining the works of the great masters throughout the ages, and initiated me in the beauties of music, especially opera, which he loved. And he was just a businessman, as his father, who wrote poetry, had been before him.

German Jews shared with other educated Germans a certain liking for philosophical questions. Above all, German Jews had developed a philosophy; in 1929, just before the advent of Hitler, they celebrated the bicentennial of Moses Mendelssohn's birth. This is one of the reasons that German Jews played a key role in the development of faith and tradition throughout western Judaism. The majority of French Jews, living in the Alsace, the southern part of the Rhineland, were German in culture. English Jewry chose German-trained men for its first two Chief Rabbis. American Jewry called German-educated rabbis to lead it and to found and direct its seminaries.

Hermann Cohen and Franz Rosenzweig were products of this environment.

THE IMPACT OF KANT: HERMANN COHEN AND JUDAISM AS THE RELIGION OF REASON

Hermann Cohen (1842–1918) has influenced all Jewish theologians who have come after him. As the founder of the neo-Kantian school at the University of Marburg, he reinterpreted Kant and became the teacher of a generation of philosophers. Cohen was one of the leading German philosophers of his time, and his life was shaped by his Jewishness. He developed a theology of Judaism and supported his coreligionists when they needed a spokesman. He unmasked the pseudo-science of his antisemitic opponents, powerful as they were in the academy and in general society.

Cohen, a Kantian, based his philosophy on reason, and Maimonides, a philosopher of reason, was, next to Kant, Cohen's great master. Rabbi Jacob Jehiel Weinberg, one of the great talmudists of the twentieth century, spoke of Hermann Cohen as Maimonides' true successor and intellectual equal. For Cohen as for Maimonides, reason was illuminated by love. To both, Judaism was the quintessential religion of reason. The last of Cohen's works sums it up, even in its title: *Religion of Reason from the Sources of Judaism.*

Hermann Cohen's rational arguments distinguished his theology. He discussed the Jewish community as "God's congregation," unified with all humanity.

Judaism and Christianity

Cohen's *An Affirmation Concerning the Jewish Question* (1880) marks the beginning of his deepened sense of responsibility toward his faith and people. The challenge came from a leading German historian, Heinrich von Treitschke, who had coined the slogan, "The Jews are our misfortune," and sought to give scholarly respectability to his prejudice. Treitschke characterized Judaism as "the national religion of a basically alien tribe."[1] This was a two-pronged assault: the Jews were alien and their religion theirs alone—Jews and Judaism were meaningless to Germans. Cohen's answer proved the contrary.

Cohen explained the meaning of Judaism in the modern world and showed its relationship to Christianity. Judaism has given the world absolute monotheism, a God who is Spirit; Christianity accepts this spiritual God and is therefore the child

1. See Hermann Cohen, *Jüdische Schriften*, 3 vols. (Berlin: C. A. Schwetschke, 1924), vol. 2, p. 73 f. for Cohen's reply to Treitschke.

of Judaism. Further, Judaism proclaims the messianic ideal to humanity, which Christianity also accepts. Christianity, in turn, has taught that God became man. Stressing the divine powers in the human being more strongly than Judaism does, Christianity actually says to the person: By capacity and freedom you are like God. You have the gift of divine reason, which makes you capable of finding the law of ethical conduct within yourself; God and you are free to implement these ethical principles. Cohen concludes that the Christian who accepts the spirituality of God and the messianic ideal is a "Jew" in these beliefs; the Jew who accepts the autonomy of the moral law is a "Christian" on this point. Judaism grants greater freedom to the individual than Christianity does, which distinguishes the two religions.

Judaism and Christianity, far from being alien to one another, actually are closely knit into a fabric of beliefs. Jews must therefore continue to exist and to represent their contribution to humanity while recognizing the importance of Christianity. Christians must recognize that a living Judaism in their midst is essential.

God and the Bond between Ethics and Nature

Cohen did not accept Kant's idea that we shall never know what the world is really like, that the true world, the "thing-in-itself," is always hidden from us. For Cohen, the "thing-in-itself" is the ultimate in knowledge. From the moment we gain some knowledge of nature, new horizons open to us. The more we learn, the greater are the new vistas revealed. We shall never reach the "thing-in-itself," because it is so far removed, but it leads us to deeper and deeper search. The pursuit of knowledge is an eternal challenge.

Our moral growth is equally an eternal challenge. Ethics and nature, two forms of being, must be keyed to each other, which is assured in the *idea* of the One God. Through the One God, as the common origin of both, nature becomes the stage on which we can exercise our moral powers.

Nature and morality are not one and the same; but they demand a single origin. And the oneness of God finds its scientific proof in the fact that it explains the unity of the source of nature and morality, and with it the unity of our view of the world.[2]

Understanding the absolutely One God as grounds for ethics in the natural world, Israel has affirmed, "Hear, O Israel, the Lord our God, the Lord is One."

History and the Messianic Age

Humankind is challenged to apply its moral powers on behalf of making nature better and purer, a challenge that is eternal and unfolds in history. Revealing whether humanity has morally progressed or regressed, history must be directed toward a goal. The idea of a Messiah in the future—one of Judaism's greatest contributions to ethical humanity—established history as goal oriented. With the messianic idea, we have history as a yardstick for our moral conduct. In the messianic age, moral growth will go on but will no longer be impeded by war, hatred, and poverty. The prophets were the first to envision the ultimate future. Through them, the world was given ethical monotheism. God expects humanity as coworkers to bring about the messianic age. Cohen does not believe in a personal Messiah, but a messianic age.

Correlation and the Holy Spirit

Ethics deals in universal generalities, defines human obligations in universal terms, but fails to see the individual human being in his or her unique situation; ethics has neither concern for the needs of the individual nor compassion with the sufferer. Religion, an element of consciousness within the realm of ethics, awakens compassion:

> As much as the prophets demand justice and righteousness and proclaim their God as God of righteousness, this abstraction is not sufficient for them. They address the human heart, which to

2. Cohen, *Jüdische Schriften*, vol. 1, p. 5.

them is the only treasure house of the spirit. Thus they call forth that form of awareness which alone can meet suffering with compassion.[3]

Only compassion, stirred by religion, creates a relationship between human beings; and compassion grows into love. Cohen calls this relationship *correlation*. By correlation, Cohen means the mutual relationship between each human being and God, which leads to an equal relationship of compassion and love between one human being and the other, who is no longer "other" but a fellow human being whose life, especially in suffering, affects me, makes me act.

The link that sanctifies the partners in correlation is created through "the holy spirit," which in Torah really means, as Cohen points out, the spirit of God's holiness. This spirit is in God and in humans, and it is the connecting link that establishes and maintains the correlation.

God, whom ethics postulated as *idea*, becomes in religion a loving person, reaching out in compassion and expecting response from the human partner. God loves the individual person and forgives the sinner, therefore all human beings must love one another. As they love one another, forgiving each other's shortcomings, they come to love God. Religion reveals the nearness of God, articulates human longing to overcome estrangement from God caused by sin, and finds joy before God and the strength to bear suffering.

God remains *other*, unique and impossible to compare to any other being, but God is no longer exclusively transcendent, God is near. All things have their origin in God, who not only once, in the beginning, created the universe, but who also "renews every day the work of creation," as morning prayer proclaims. Therefore correlation must be renewed daily by human beings as well.

The Soul, Sin, and Repentance

Every person has a pure soul, which is unsoiled by original sin, and is capable of perfect love in correlation. Every person

3. Cohen, *Jüdische Schriften*, vol. 1, p. 310.

is endowed with the spirit of holiness. If a person has soiled this soul, purification before God is achieved as the result of correlation. *Teshuvah*, repentance, makes the individual aware of being a self, an *I*; sin is personal. Individually, a person appeals to God for compassion. God responds immediately, demanding only that he or she show compassion. Reconciliation with the self leads to reconciliation with the fellow human being, with God: The correlation is restored. The reconciliation of the individual with God, the redemption from sin, rests upon the concept of the purity of soul and the holiness of the spirit.

The Significance of Judaism

As a committed Jew, Cohen demands faithful adherence to Judaism. The Jew must be true to his religion to exemplify ethics and compassion. By living *for* the neighbor, the Jew stays in direct and immediate correlation with God. In this free and direct approach to God, Cohen sees a major contribution of Jewish religion to the progress of religion in general. Judaism is in the forefront of humanity, leading the way toward the messianic age. Eventually all humanity will be united. Until then, the Jewish congregation is a symbol of God's congregation, which some day will embrace all humanity within its folds: "God's congregation is not a special covenant of the faithful. It is, in the prophetic sense, the unification of all mankind, beyond castes and nations, in a unity of conscience, a unity of ethical humanity."[4]

Hermann Cohen's Impact

Cohen's thought was seminal because he broke through to an existential relationship with God. Martin Buber's ideas of *I and Thou* are close to Cohen's ideas. Franz Rosenzweig elevated Cohen's assertion, that Judaism and Christianity had to learn from each other, into the principle that both were created by God for mutual dependency. Abraham Joshua Heschel centered his thought on *God in Search of Man* and *Man's Quest for God*. Eugene Borowitz calls for *Renewing the Covenant*, the correlation between God and Israel.

4. Cohen, *Jüdische Schriften*, vol. 1, p. 30.

THE IMPACT OF LIFE: FRANZ ROSENZWEIG

In Franz Rosenzweig (1886–1929), Hermann Cohen's great disciple, Jewry found a guiding spirit and a symbol of its own destiny. His spiritual life led from the periphery of Judaism to its very core, and he experienced the triumph of the spirit over the forces of destruction. He gave fortitude to thousands who were made to suffer for their Judaism.

Rosenzweig grew up among highly cultured, liberal thinking Jews who affirmed their faith but found in Judaism neither message nor challenge. On completing his university studies, Rosenzweig not only faced the question of what to do but, more fundamentally, what to believe. In search of the meaning of his life, Rosenzweig was persuaded to become Protestant. His mother pleaded with him at least to wait until after Yom Kippur. He agreed, and in 1913 went to a little synagogue in Berlin to pray for the last time as a Jew. He had a mystical experience. Overwhelmed by the power of the day and its worship, he realized that he could not desert a Judaism he did not even truly know. He had to experience it. To his cousin, now a Protestant theologian, he wrote, conversion "does no longer seem to be necessary, hence in my case no longer possible. I shall remain a Jew."[5]

Rosenzweig met Hermann Cohen in Berlin and became his disciple. Then came the First World War. Serving as an anti-aircraft gunner in the Balkans, he caught severe pneumonia. He recovered and was filled with a unique, creative clarity of mind. In the trenches, on postcards, he wrote his major work, *The Star of Redemption.*

But a philosophy of Judaism is only a gate, it must open into life. In order to know what it means to be a Jew, one must live as a Jew, since Judaism reveals itself existentially. From the front, Rosenzweig developed a program of universal Jewish education for Western Jewry, and after the war he began to translate his educational program into reality. He opened an adult academy at Frankfurt, dedicated to Jewish studies of the highest intellectual standard. Called Freies Jüdisches Lehrhaus, Free Jewish House of Study, it became the model for a whole system of similar institutions that sprang up all over Germany. These schools

5. Franz Rosenzweig, *Briefe* (Berlin: Schocken, 1935), p. 71.

gave guidance and new enthusiasm to people who had stood at the periphery of Judaism but might be brought to its core. Schools need books, so the growth of the educational system brought new life to the Jewish literary scene, and many books on Judaism were published—classical texts, scholarly tomes, pocket books, and Hebrew texts. These years, just before the collapse, witnessed a renaissance of Judaism in Germany.

In 1922, Rosenzweig was diagnosed with what we now call Lou Gehrig's disease. By the end of 1923, the disease had deprived him of all movement and the ability to speak. Able to move only his thumb, his head held by a brace, he continued to write using a special typewriter. Eventually, he could only point to the letters while his wife, Edith Hahn Rosenzweig, with amazing insight, completed the thoughts he indicated. Miraculously, he kept on living beyond any expectation and completed a translation of Judah Halevi's poetry. In 1925, in coopera-tion with Martin Buber, he began a translation of the Bible, which Buber completed. In November of 1929, he completed the translation of Isaiah, and on 9 December he died.

Largely due to Rosenzweig's in-fluence—the impact of his example, his Lehrhaus, where study and prac-tice were given new life, and the sym-bolic influence of his suffering and courage—German Jewry was not tired or weak when it was destroyed.

Thinking Is Speaking

Rosenzweig radically broke with the traditional method of the "old philosophers," the problem being that they do not listen to anyone. Their thinking was monological and Rosenzweig had only scorn for their labors.

Franz Rosenzweig saw the *Star of Redemption* in the six-pointed Star of David. Rosenzweig's "new thinking" was to be the method of teaching at the Lehrhaus. Speech-thinking was in fact *lernen* as found in the yeshivah. The Yiddish term lernen means studying To-rah: it is dialogical, denotes a spiritual as well as intellectual pursuit, seeks answers to the questions and issues of life, guides life. Giving and taking in dialogue, learners progress.

Rosenzweig based his "new thinking" on two basic assumptions. The first is that all thinking must be based on common sense, on "knowing that a chair is a chair" and not something else. The second is that all thinking must be dialogical, thinking in speech with the other—*speech-thinking*. In it, thought unfolds in time, which will lead to wholly different results from the "old thinking." And because speech-thinking requires another person as partner in dialogue, the "other" is equal and actually the teacher. Therefore, other people are essential for all life and creative thought.

Rosenzweig is aware, however, that common sense is prone to error and may differ between groups and with time. He therefore had to define truth in a way that accounts for these differences. Truth is something of absolutely vital importance to a person:

> The new thinking sees in truth not the truth of the philosopher, but something that is so true for a person that this person eventually will stake even his or her life and the life of the generations for it.[6]

This means that human truth remains divided, is relative, and rests on time. The full truth is known only to God, and this means that all the different truths that people claim by staking their lives on them, are true as they find their focus in the hidden God.

While for Cohen, whose thoughts Rosenzweig develops, the *idea* of God guarantees the unity of nature and human ethics, for Rosenzweig, the living God, creator of nature, assures the unity of humanity because God alone is the truth and has the truth; for both thinkers, correlation is the core element, for the new thinking is nothing else but speaking to one another in time. Therefore, life is the test and reveals the truth. The person who "walks humbly with God" partakes of the truth, not as theological conclusions but as life.[7] Life grants the truth, unfolding it to the person on the way. "To walk humbly with

---

6. Franz Rosenzweig, "Das neue Denken," in *Kleinere Schriften* (Berlin: Schocken, 1937), p.387.
7. See Franz Rosenzweig, *Der Stern der Erlösung*, 2d ed. (Frankfurt: J. Kaufman, 1930), part 3, pp. 210–11.

your God" is the abiding duty of human beings, it rests on trust in God, and from this trust faith, hope, and love will grow.

The Star of Redemption

Through the ages, the *Magen David,* David's Shield, the Star of David, has been a symbol of Judaism. Rosenzweig used it as symbol of his new theology, giving the star a modern meaning as *The Star of Redemption.*

True to his "new thinking," he grounds his thought in common sense and dialogical interaction in time. Common sense and experience tell us that in the universe three fundamental elements exist and are separate from each other: *God, world, humanity.* In addition "experience, as it penetrates even to the ultimate, discovers in human beings only human elements, in the world only worldly elements and in God only divine elements."[8] If we wish to know more of these three elements, we must find out how they interact with each other in time: what they did to each other in the past, what they are doing to each other in the present, and what they will do to each other in the future.

There are three basic actions by which *God, world, and humans* constantly interact with each other in time: *creation, revelation, redemption.* God constantly makes the world through creation. God at all times chooses humans through revelation. God, with the help of humanity's creative work in the world, brings about redemption. God has fashioned the world and in revelation chosen humans for a special task: every human being is God's co-worker in the work of creation, and the world is their laboratory; in life, the human being, active in the world, finds God—and God finds world and humanity. This is redemption.

God, world, and humanity form the upper triangle of the star; creation, revelation, and redemption are represented by the lower triangle. The three elements are interwoven with the three actions, and the six-pointed star explains their constant

8. Rosenzweig, "Das neue Denken," in *Kleinere Schriften,* pp. 387–89.

Terra cotta Magen David, c. third century c.e.

Under Hitler, mandatory yellow badges marked "Jew" were used for quick identification.

Through the ages, Magen David, *David's Shield, has been a symbol of Judaism. It has acquired a new meaning in modern Judaism, both tragic and heroic. The Jews under Nazi domination had to wear it by order of their oppressors and exterminators. Intended to be the Jews' badge of shame, the Jews transformed it into a badge of honor and affirmation. It has acquired a new significance and flows proudly as the flag of Israel.*

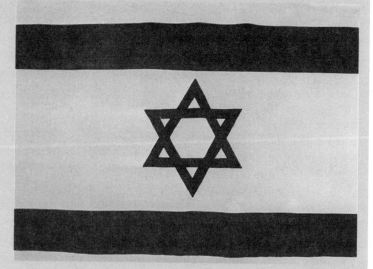

The Star of David shields a new country—a symbol of independence, strength, and reverence for the past.

interaction. Creation, revelation, and redemption are not one-time events but, rather, pose a daily challenge for all human beings on humanity's road through life and history. To the world, the completed star symbolizes a vision toward which humanity is moving, but that has not been fulfilled; the two triangles are not yet interwoven.

Only Israel, the Jewish people, has reached the final goal, and the completed star is therefore its symbol. Israel is with the Father; as a people it has found redemption. This means that Israel has stepped out of history and traverses it only in the liturgical year (as we have seen in chapter 27). It also does so on the Sabbath: Friday evening, the Kiddush celebrates the completion of *creation* (Gen. 2:1–3); the Torah reading of Sabbath morning is *revelation;* the outlook in the late afternoon points to *redemption.*

Judaism and Christianity

Rosenzweig accepts the Christian idea that no one comes to the Father except through the Son (John 14:6) but adds, "except for those already with the Father": Jews, whose Star of Redemption is complete. Rosenzweig concludes that Judaism and Christianity, each in its own way, are essential in God's scheme for the world. Their truth is true for each of them. Christianity is called to bring humanity to the Father through the Son. Judaism, living testimony that it is possible to come to the Father, offers the image of a society that dwells with God and spurs the rest of humanity on its road.

Rosenzweig is the first Jewish thinker who held that Judaism and Christianity are dependent upon each other and that both are necessary under God's plan. Hermann Cohen had explained how Christianity and Judaism needed each other. Rosenzweig elevates this mutual dependency to the level of God's design.

The Road to Mitzvot

The individual Jew must study Judaism and commit himself or herself to the mitzvot. But, admonishing those who, like him, seek the road to return, Rosenzweig advised Jews against a jump into the law as a result of crisis. Rather, the Jew coming from the periphery must purposefully approach each of the mitzvot, until one of them strikes a spark in him or her and the response, "I can" perform it.

More or less small experiences, to be [consciously] awaited will [gradually] actualize by their new biographical energy a new "I can." In this manner, the person of return *[Baal Teshuvah]*, does not, on the road to return, abandon the accustomed— unjewish—pattern of life, and thus remains in life.[9]

Rosenzweig advises "pursuing" a mitzvah until it elicits the response, "I can do it"—because my whole being is in accord with it and urges me to it. Then I will take the leap. Being asked if he put on tefillin, he is said to have replied, "not yet"; the spark had not yet jumped, but it might.

Rosenzweig's Impact

Rosenzweig has had a powerful impact upon Jews and Christians. His existential thinking has deeply influenced contemporary Jewish thinkers and leaders in non-Orthodox Judaism. They have called people back to Torah, and the wellsprings of Judaism, teaching the people Torah and urging them gradually "to return" to the core, bringing with them their secular knowledge. These teachers warn against an emotional leap into the law and have exhorted the people to remain open and permit the spark of mitzvah to strike their souls; teachers encourage the people to reach out until they can accept and perform those mitzvot of which the individual can say, "I can." Rosenzweig has helped make it possible to see Torah existentially as divine, without rejecting the hypotheses of biblical criticism. The Lehrhaus has been transplanted to many communities in the United States.

THE IMPACT OF THE LIFE OF THE DIALOGUE: MARTIN BUBER

Martin Buber (1878–1965) has found worldwide recognition as a teacher of humanity; his sources lie in Judaism. He has

9. Rosenzweig, *Briefe*, p. 508.

become a builder of bridges between Judaism and Christianity, Hasidism and German scholarship, European Judaism and Israel, religion and Zionism, the occidental world and the orient. His hope to forge a link between Jews and Arabs may eventually be fulfilled as well.

As a young man, Buber was drawn to the life of the Hasidim and was inspired to accept their ideas. This is the way Buber understood Hasidism: Every action in life is performed in the presence of God. God speaks to every person, telling her or him individually what to do in every situation, if they only listen. Every act must be a response to a divine instruction, for God has appointed every single person as a partner on earth to work for *tikkun,* the action of restoring the world to unity. Each human being must listen to God, find out what God wants, then carry it out in service to his or her fellow humans. Every person must live in joy and love before God, who has hallowed humankind to be co-workers and has hallowed the world to be God's workshop of salvation.

Buber studied philosophy and the history of art at the universities of Vienna, Leipzig, Berlin, Zurich, and Florence. In 1923, he was called to the University of Frankfurt as professor of religion, the first to occupy, in a German university, a chair established specifically for the teaching of Judaism. With the advent of Hitler, Buber lost his position at the university and assumed the leadership of the great network of Jewish adult education that spread throughout Germany's Jewish congregations and was patterned after Rosenzweig's Lehrhaus. In 1938, he settled in Palestine, teaching at the Hebrew University.

The Life of Dialogue: I and Thou

Buber's concern, like Rosenzweig's and Hasidism's, centered around life and found its marked definition in his work *I and Thou.* Two types of human relationships are possible, *I and Thou,* and *I and It.* Both affect not only the other person but my own being as well. *I and It* makes the other person an object of use to me; if I analyze another person or use him or her, that person is an *It* for me, an object that does not deeply involve me.

Martin Buber integrated hasidic ideas into his philosophy of *I and Thou*. This concept embraces a dialogue of action as well as words.

In *I and Thou,* I face the other person in his or her totality, am influenced by the person's total self, the other becomes a subject, a *Thou.* This happens in true dialogue, which Rosenzweig had called speech-thinking. *I and Thou* is an existential encounter: persons interact in an unfolding process and come to know both each other and themselves. This is the essential correlation between humans. But this dialogue is not a dialogue in words alone; it is a dialogue in action. For instance, if a person in distress calls out to me, at that very moment I am the only one addressed and the only one who can and must respond, giving help.

There is also the *Eternal Thou,* God, who addresses me, the human, individually, calling me and demanding my personal response. What God wants me to do will always be different, and the call is addressed only to me individually. I can find out what my task is by carrying on an unceasing dialogue with God, establishing an *I and Thou* relationship. This is an existential version of what was done among the Hasidim—*kavvanah,* directing of the whole personality to God.

God, the Eternal Thou, enters into every human *I and Thou* relationship. At the moment a person in distress appeals to me for help, God enters, telling me how to respond to the human *Thou.* Every human *I and Thou* relationship is a relationship with the *Eternal Thou;* every relationship with God includes a human one. The direct way from the human to God goes through society, so I must establish a true *I and Thou* relationship with all of my fellow human beings. I must respond with my entire person, not only with my critical faculties of thought:

> The individual answers God when he embraces in human embrace the piece of the world handed to him, and ... with his to-

tal being says "Thou" to all beings that surround him; just as God embraces His creation in divine embrace.[10]

The absence of dialogue, either between humans and God or between humans themselves, is the cause of the breakdown of society and of the human personality. Buber explains that, tragically, this is the condition of our time and society, in which evil has run rampant, for "the I–It relation, gigantically swollen, has usurped, practically uncontested, the mastery and the rule."[11] God has gone into "eclipse," but Buber hopes fervently that humanity will find its way back: "The great dialogue between I and Thou is silent; nothing else exists than his [the human being's] self. That is . . . being untrue. Being true to the being in which and before which I am placed is the one thing that is needful."[12]

The Renewal of Judaism

Buber, who addressed humanity as a whole, nevertheless maintained that a specific dialogue exists between God and Israel, and between Israel and humanity, with God present. Israel is God's people. Israel and God stand in a unique *I and Thou* relationship, because Israel, yearning to prepare a dwelling place for God, is chosen to build the true society. In this light, Judaism must renew and revitalize itself, and every generation must accept its divine challenge. The renewal is threefold:

1. *Judaism must develop the spirit of unity.* Unity can be recaptured in part through study of the past, in the holy works of Scripture and history, which shows us how Israel walked with God through the ages. Study must lead to developing unity among the people living today. In every person there is a divine presence; in the people as a whole it is a fire, sometimes burning low but capable of being fanned to life. The soul's recollection also builds unity as we plumb the depth of our spiritual

10. Martin Buber, *Die Frage an den Einzelnen* (Berlin: Schocken, 1936), p. 42.
11. Martin Buber, *Eclipse of God* (New York: Harper, 1952), p. 129.
12. Martin Buber, *Pointing the Way* (New York: Harper, 1957), p. x.

experiences. The road to a united society must be traveled by every individual alone, but in fellowship with others.[13]

2. *The spirit of unity must lead to action.* Judaism is basically an action program. But ceremonial law with all its detailed prescriptions atomized the program of action. Listening to God and acting in the spirit of the prophets and Jewish tradition, Jesus replaced the observance of details with a great overall program to save humankind in order to establish God's kingdom on earth. In this spirit, Buber wishes to build a bridge between Christianity and Judaism by calling both to joint creative action in the building of God's kingdom of social justice.

3. *The goal is the vision of the future.* The vision of the future must be renewed. "This view," states Buber, "has been the source of messianism. In it the other two tendencies of Judaism, the idea of unity and the idea of action, find the basis for their final and complete fulfillment."[14]

Unity, action, vision of the future: these are the ideals of Judaism. Unity has led to the majestic idea of the One God; action envisions God as world-creating and world-ruling; the vision of the future recognizes God as world-loving and has resulted in the messianic ideal that Judaism has given the world.

Buber's Impact

Buber's philosophy is difficult for average people in everyday living. He rejects mitzvot, the religious duties toward God established by Torah and tradition. To him they are "religion," practices, instead of "religiosity," a response to the immediate voice of God. But mitzvah is a unifying bond of generations. Therefore Franz Rosenzweig rejected Buber's view, and modern Jewish theologians of the existentialist school have stressed mitzvot as a response to the *Metzaveh* (the Commanding God), *commandment* does presuppose a *person* who issues it (God) and a *person* who responds (the Jew). In this manner, mitzvot establish and strengthen the *I and Thou*, and God is experienced existentially.

13. Martin Buber, *Reden an die Jugend* (Berlin: Schocken, 1938).
14. See Will Herberg, *The Writings of Martin Buber* (New York: Meridian Books, 1956), p. 29 f. and notes.

THE IMPACT OF THE HOLOCAUST: LEO BAECK

Rabbi Leo Baeck (1873–1956) became a symbol of Judaism. Born in Lissa in the province Posen, son of a rabbi, he was ordained by the liberal Hochschule but remained personally committed to tradition and its mitzvot. He was scholar, leader, defender of Judaism, and shepherd of his people in their darkest hour.

As a young man he wrote a systematic exposition of Judaism, *The Essence of Judaism*. He was deeply immersed in western culture and investigated Christianity, explaining *The Gospels as Documents of the History of Jewish Faith* and exposing the errors that Christians held regarding *The Pharisees*. His greatest hour came when he accepted the call of German Jewry to be its head and spokesman during the Nazi regime. When his people were taken to the concentration camps and extermination centers, he felt it his duty to join them and their fate. He rejected invitations that came to him from America and England and went to Theresienstadt. Slated for execution, he was miraculously spared. After the war, he settled in England but also taught at the Hebrew Union College in America. Out of his spiritual experience emerged his work *This People Israel: The Meaning of Jewish Existence*, an existential history of the Jewish people.

In his work *The Essence of Judaism*, Baeck stated that "the principle of Judaism in its deepest meaning" is that through action "we shall preach our religion. Our lives shall speak of the greatness of our faith."[15] With the passage of the years, Baeck shifted his emphasis. He no longer spoke of Judaism as a religion, but of Jews as a people, a mystical body, called by God to serve humanity. Israel is "the people I formed for Myself that they might declare My praise" (Isa. 43:21).

For Baeck *covenant* is a central concept. It rests on Cohen's correlation, Buber's *I and Thou*, and Rosenzweig's "new thinking" which places humans, ideas, and events in time. For Baeck as for Cohen, God links nature and ethics—under the covenant. Like Rosenzweig, he sees creation, revelation, and redemption as one and present—in the covenant. Buber's *I and Thou* are

15. Leo Baeck, *Das Wesen des Judentums* (Frankfurt: J. Kaufmann, 1932), p. 304. See *The Essence of Judaism* (New York: Schocken Books, 1948), p. 271.

Leo Baeck tirelessly served his people in Theresienstadt concentration camp. As he describes in *The Essence of Judaism,* the deepest meaning of Judaism is depicted through action.

enshrined—in the covenant. Covenant is expressed in the law, handed to the Jewish people from the *Eternal Thou.* It is an eternal but ever-new law, addressed to the individual and to society. Covenant is identical with the law of nature, which is compelled to obey it, and with the divine summons to humans, who are free to commit themselves to it.

Israel, standing under an everlasting covenant with God, suffers, is creative in spiritual fields of human endeavor, is witness to the eternal covenant of God, and guarantees the oneness of all that human beings are to bring to fruition. Israel has enshrined this awareness of the covenant, given by the prophets, and carried it into the world. Baeck proudly affirms Israel's uniqueness, binding "this people" to humanity as a whole.

Baeck's Impact

Baeck has synthesized and, in a way, unified the thinking of his predecessors. Transmitting Cohen's, Rosenzweig's, and Buber's thoughts, Leo Baeck's ideas have influenced subsequent Jewish thinkers, many of whom he taught. He has been a bridge between the Jewish thinkers of the pre-Holocaust generation and those who followed the Holocaust, between German Jewry and a Jewish people deprived of it. By his life, he was a witness to his thought and faith. Many Jewish institutions bear his name to emphasize for future generations the greatness of his life and work.

Chapter 35

POSTMODERN THOUGHT SINCE THE HOLOCAUST

The Holocaust and the restoration of Israel have raised
questions about God's continuing presence in history, about the
place of Jews in the divine plan, and about how Jews should
respond to these events. Most Jewish thinkers of our time show
the influence of Buber and Rosenzweig.

EMIL FACKENHEIM: A NEW COMMANDMENT

Emil L. Fackenheim (born in 1916) was one of the last students ordained by Leo Baeck at the Hochschule in Berlin. After
the *Kristallnacht*, he was held for some time at the Sachsenhausen
concentration camp, until he found his way to Canada and
served for decades as professor of philosophy at the University
of Toronto. Upon his retirement he settled in Israel, to him the
only place where a Jew could live a fully Jewish life. The Holocaust and the Six Day War of 1967 are central to Fackenheim's
understanding of Judaism and, he believes, to our understanding
of God's presence in history.

In their living dialogue with their past, Jews throughout the
ages have so fully identified with the astonishment of their
ancestors at certain momentous experiences that this astonishment has become real to all generations of Jews, implanted into

their very root and being. Because of the astonishment these experiences evoked, they became *root experiences*. Although history may not verify these events, Jewish consciousness does. For example, the Midrash states that all Jews of all generations were present at Sinai and heard God's commanding voice, which subjected them to the divine will and, at the same time, gave them the freedom to obey or reject it. The truth of these root experiences lies in the fact that we have enshrined them in our prayers and celebrations. The Jew therefore knows that God is all powerful and is involved with the world. Witnessing to this fact, the Jew draws faith and hope.

When disasters struck, such as the destruction of the Second Temple, the rabbis explained that God actually lamented the divine judgment, possibly as a grievous error, and went with the people into exile so that the divine presence and command would always be with them. With God present, the root experiences were carried by the Jews into exile.

But God was absent at Auschwitz, putting the root experiences to their severest test. For over 4,000 years, Jews understood themselves as witnesses to the God of history and staked their collective survival on this concept. Their trust was shattered at Auschwitz. The martyrs in the death camps, however, held fast to God, and the survivors of the Holocaust affirmed God after their liberation. We must not betray them and their conviction that every Jew is called to be God's witness to the world.

Fackenheim is emphatic that Auschwitz defies any explanation. Following Buber, Fackenheim considers the possibility that God went into eclipse. We shall never know why, but we must know that God's commanding voice goes forth from Auschwitz, imposing everlasting sacred duties on the Jews: Jews are commanded to survive as Jews, lest the Jewish people perish; and Jews must remember the victims of Auschwitz, keeping their memory eternally alive. Jews are forbidden to despair of humanity and escape into cynicism or seclusion, lest they abandon the world to new forces of Auschwitz. Above all, Jews are forbidden to despair of the God of Israel, lest Judaism perish and the world lose God's witness. The commandment to survive is the new

614th commandment, added to the 613 of Torah: "Jews are forbidden to hand Hitler posthumous victories."

Israel's Six Day War was for the Jews a new momentous experience, filling them with abiding astonishment. The threat of total annihilation gave way to deliverance. The victory did not explain or adjust Auschwitz, but the Jews' astonishment revealed that God's all-powerful presence had manifested itself again in the history of the Jewish people—calling the Jewish people to respond to the all-powerful presence, giving hope for survival as witness to God, and promising redemption in the coming of the Messiah. The Six Day War made it possible for the Jews to reenact the root experiences of their history, and it calls every Jew to *emunah,* trust, even if God be hidden or in partial eclipse. The Jew must therefore respond existentially to the transcendent, personal God, the *Metzaveh,* "Commander," in mitzvot, as Rosenzweig had taught it. Jewish religion is the commandment of the living God. Jews must listen, obey, and be witnesses.

RICHARD RUBENSTEIN: CYCLICAL RECURRENCE

Richard L. Rubenstein (born 1924) regards the Holocaust as the event that shaped his entire life and thought. Auschwitz has demonstrated that the God who acts in history, and in whom Jews have put their trust throughout the ages, cannot be attested. Instead, Rubenstein goes back to the Kabbalah and affirms God as En Sof, Holy Nothingness, beyond all limitations and relationship to the world. God is the *plenum,* the "fullness." Similar to the mystics, Rubenstein compares God to the ocean, and all existing beings to its waves; as they splash upon the shores they have a brief individual existence, but eventually they all return to the fullness of the ocean.

The Torah cannot be regarded as divine revelation, but, as the "heritage of the congregation of Jacob" (Deut. 33:4), it is sacred on account of the role it has played in Jewish history and it represents the collective wisdom of the Jewish people. Therefore its commandments have a compelling force, but the Jew's response to them is voluntary. The Jew should, however, strive to fulfill as many mitzvot as possible.

Because no divine revelation can be asserted, the Jewish people cannot claim to be a divinely chosen people. As Torah states (Num. 23:9), the Jewish people stand alone in the world, the Jews are strangers wherever they live. The Holocaust proves that Jews were always seen as a foreign and destructive body in Christian society, and the extermination of the Jews by the Nazis revealed the extent to which European civilization was willing to go in order to rid itself of the non-Christian body in its midst.

Rubenstein believes that the aftereffects of the Holocaust are still with the Jews. He finds evidence in the efforts of Jews to escape into the Christian world around them, especially through intermarriage. Within Judaism, conflicts between an increasingly militant Orthodoxy and the other denominations are bound to grow and may lead to a split in Jewry.

Rubenstein also expresses apprehension that Jewish messianism will go hand in hand with a militant Jewish claim to all of the land of Israel, including Islam's holy places in Jerusalem, and will inevitably lead to war with Islam. Nevertheless, the restoration of the State of Israel has fulfilled Jewish eschatological expectations. It allows the Jews to go home, no longer to be strangers, and to be a people like all other peoples. But Jews have to reverse their entire outlook. They are not called to work in history but to stand alone, outside of it. They must become "pagan," which means, living by the cyclical recurrence of nature, away from the projections of history. Their life should revolve around nature, for in nature all that is born returns to the nothingness. The waves return to the ocean. Death is the only Messiah.

Abraham Joshua Heschel: God, World, and Hasidic Tradition

In the video series *Eyes on the Prize*, we can briefly catch sight of Abraham Joshua Heschel (1907–1972) walking next to Dr. Martin Luther King, Jr., in the Civil Rights march to

Montgomery, Alabama. Heschel's involvement in the Civil Rights movement was literally *halakhah*, a "walk" ordained by Torah. In some way it summed up Heschel's life that he joined a segregated, inwardly authentic community fighting for its rights in the name of God, for he had grown up in such a community, the shtetl of Eastern Europe, and remained emotionally deeply attached to its life.

Born in Warsaw, the offspring of a line of renowned hasidic rebbes, Heschel was allowed to study in the West, received his doctorate from the University of Berlin and his ordination from the liberal Hoschschule. His background and evolution resembled Buber's but with the profound difference that while Buber had witnessed the life of Eastern Hasidic Jewry, Heschel had lived it. Buber considered concrete mitzvot a wall between the human *I* and the divine *Thou;* Heschel saw in them a response to the divine *Thou.* Heschel's view harks back to the existential theology of the shtetl, where the life of the pious flowed from their knowledge that God was there.

Firmly rooted in Jewish tradition, Heschel became a builder of bridges between East and West, Orthodox and liberal Judaism, Judaism and Christianity, African Americans and whites. As a representative of world Jewry, he advised the Vatican in the preparation of the resolution on the Jews enacted in the Second Vatican Council. He has been studied by Jews and Christians, particularly by Catholics, and some of his works have become sources for monastic meditation.

Depth Theology

Equally at home in English, German, Hebrew, and Yiddish, Heschel wrote in a circular way. He takes a thought, discusses it, abandons it for another, then returns to it in the light of the new insights gained. Heschel has called his theology *depth theology.* To him, all fundamental insights are *preconceptual,* that is, spring from the depth and precede logical exposition. To find God, the searching person has to plumb the depths.

The search begins with the *radical amazement* to which we must open ourself. Radical amazement refers to all of reality. We are amazed not only by what we see, but that we can see at all, and at ourself as a being who can see. Seeing a flower, we have to go beyond the biologist or painter: we must wonder about its being there, we must wonder in radical astonishment about our being there and our ability to see.

Amazement leads us to the *mystery*. We are aware that the entire universe and all that is in it is God's creation, and God created it out of nothing. This is beyond human comprehension, a mystery. We are struck with awe; we have reached questions that can no longer be answered by human reason but only by God, by religion. Amazement in the face of mystery fills us with awe and leads us to *wisdom*. Wisdom is the ability to look at all things from God's point of view and to identify our will with God's will.[1]

We become aware of the sublime, and have entirely left the level of scientific thinking, as we enter the realm of the ineffable, God. God is in all things and ideas, and God, at the same time, is beyond all things, even beyond the mystery; God fills the world and at the same time is beyond it.

We also become aware that God is active in history. God needs us, has concern for us, has demands on us. God seeks us out for a creative partnership with the divine, in which we affect God. Through this partnership history comes into being. History is covenant with God. We now also understand our own human need to be needed and realize that God, our partner who needs us for divine purposes, may at times say "no" to our concerns. But we are never alone, for God is always there. This is hasidic thinking: whatever is done "below" affects the "above."

The Prophets in Sympathy with God's Pathos

God's call and demand for human response are found in the Bible, specifically in the books of the second section of the Bible, the Prophets. The prophets were normal men and women who were enticed by God, frequently against their will; God reached out to them and they could not escape. They had no theory or

1. Abraham Joshua Heschel, *God in Search of Man* (New York: Farrar, Straus, and Cudahy, 1955), p. 75.

idea of God but, rather, a receptivity to the presence of God. They felt God's anxiety speaking to them out of the events of history. They had an intuitive understanding of God's unspoken message and its hidden meanings.

The prophets were endowed with sympathy, which means that their souls were open to, and in harmony with, God's presence, concerns, and emotions. Because their own feelings were in common with God's, they spoke to God. Called to convey God's emotions, they overflowed with emotional language to arouse the people to action against the miseries of the world, social injustice, or alienation from God.

In the Bible, God is not an abstraction removed from the world, like Aristotle's "unmoved mover." Rather, "the high and lofty One" has *pathos* (from the Greek *pati*, to suffer, meaning to be affected as victim by outside forces)—God cares for all creatures, is involved in human history, and is affected by human acts (see Isa. 57:15). The living God is concerned about the world and its human population because God needs every human being to carry out the divine intent. Every human being is relevant to the living God. Human righteousness and kindness bring joy to God, human callousness grieves God and forces the Eternal to express anger. God delights, not in unleashing anger, but rather in showing affection (Jer. 9:24; 32:41). God delights in doing good to human beings, accepting repentance and letting divine mercy well forth (Ps. 90:3). "In sum," says Heschel,

> the divine pathos is the unity of the eternal and temporal, of meaning and mystery, of the metaphysical and historical. It is the real basis of the relation between God and man, of the correlation of Creator and creation, of the dialogue between the Holy One of Israel and His people. The characteristic of the prophets is not foreknowledge of the future, but insight into the present pathos of God.[2]

Heschel's *The Prophets* reveals that he rejected traditional philosophy and theology, which see in God the object of their in-

---

2. Abraham Joshua Heschel, *The Prophets* (Philadelphia: Jewish Publication Society, 1962), p. 231.

According to Heschel, the Jew must sanctify time—by studying Torah and performing mitzvot—and teach the world the sanctity of time. The Sabbath, embodying the belief in the equality and nobility of all human beings, is holiness in time. The festivals likewise sanctify time. This message is of paramount importance to a world fascinated by space, demonstrated by the emphasis on exploration and on the creation of sacred spaces such as cathedrals.

In spite of his focus on time, however, Heschel sees one sacred space for the people of Israel: the Land assigned even before the people had been created. The universal revival of deep Jewish feeling, when Israel was in mortal danger in 1967, is witness to the Land's sustaining spiritual power. Heschel therefore affirms, "The State of Israel is not the fulfillment of the Messianic promise, but it makes the Messianic promise plausible." *

---

*Abraham Joshua Heschel, *Israel: An Echo of Eternity* (New York: Farrar, Straus, and Giroux, 1969), p. 223.

vestigations, because the Bible contradicts them. For Heschel, "The Bible is not man's theology but God's anthropology."

The Covenant and Special Obligations

The relationship between God and humanity rests, on both sides, on deeds—God's active intervention in the life of every person and the acts of the person in response. "Holy deeds make deeds holy." But Israel, as an outflow of divine pathos, stands under a special covenant with God. Not the same as contract, covenant is rooted in love; the relationship between God and Israel is a personal, loving fellowship. Heschel affirms the chosenness of the Jewish people, a special relationship to God expressing itself in its special obligations toward God:

Israel is a spiritual order in which the human and the ultimate, the natural and the holy enter a lasting covenant, in which kinship with God is not an aspiration but a reality of destiny.... Abandoning Israel, we desert God.[3]

As a member of a "holy people," every Jew must accept the special call of God found in Torah. In order to respond to God, the Jew must make "the leap into the law," namely, halakhah.

Heschel's existentialist approach, based on his premise that religion has the right to criticize philosophy, follows Rosenzweig's "new thinking," Buber's *I and Thou*, and Cohen's concept of

3. Heschel, *God in Search of Man*, p. 423.

correlation. He differs with all of them by taking Torah literally and by insisting on the performance of mitzvot as divine commandments. Heschel did not develop a concrete Holocaust theology, but his whole thought is permeated by its impact.

EMMANUEL LEVINAS: THE DECONSTRUCTION OF PHILOSOPHY UNDER ROSENZWEIG'S IMPACT

Emmanuel Levinas (1906–1995), one of the leading philosophers of France, is gaining recognition throughout the world. As an Orthodox Jew, Levinas found the roots of his ideas in Torah and Judaism, and his thinking was further shaped by the Holocaust. Under the influence of Franz Rosenzweig's "new thinking," he began the "deconstruction" of philosophy. He rejects the philosophy of *being*, pursued by the old, solitary philosopher, which Heidegger represented, for it leads to egoism and self-glorification (and, in Heidegger's case, to rabid antisemitism). Instead, he takes the Midrash as his model, because it "deconstructs" the "old philosophy" in favor of speech-thinking.

The Other

The foundation of Levinas's philosophy is the *other*. Exposure to the other—our first rational act, the condition for all teaching—is pre-original reason and makes the human being a thinking subject before thinking about a theme begins. Awareness of the other makes the person conscious of committing an injustice by being self-centered and therefore forces the person to limit his or her freedom for the sake of the other's freedom. The other is not hostile; the other turns his or her *face*—individual personality, singular humanity—to me, who is the partner in dialogue, claiming his or her God-given rights as a person. I must respond in dialogue and in goodness without expecting any reciprocity. This immediate confrontation summons me to moral action in ethical relation and will bring justice and peace. We must be concerned for the other, although we are always separated from him or her. Being one for another, turning our face to the other, though we are separated beings, is the foundation of ethics, on which all philosophy must rest.

The source of this thinking is Torah. The priests in blessing invoke God to "make His *face* shine upon you" (see Num. 6:22–27). This reveals that God, who is eternally separated from us, is nevertheless concerned and is relating to us. Jews in turn relate to God, not by affirming that they believe in God, but by responding to God, the other, as Abraham responded (Gen. 22:1), "Here I am," translating God's ways into human relations.

The Saying and the Said

Levinas maintains that there is a difference between the *saying* and the said, namely, between the spoken word, the *saying*, which says more than merely its contents, and the *said*, any recorded and analyzed text. This applies to secular language, but is specifically found in the language of the prophets. The prophets spoke at a given moment in time and revealed that there is something more than simply *being*, something that is beyond. If we read the Torah aloud we can recapture traces of the *saying*. We can also transform the *said* into the *saying* by exegesis. Then we encounter the text no longer as a closed *said* but as the voice, the *saying* of the other, immediate, open, vulnerable, and placed in the hands of the interpreter. This is the meaning of the Midrash that states that the Torah was individually given to the six hundred thousand who stood at Sinai: Each person receives the *saying*, brings his or her own interpretation and each interpretation is required to

Levinas has published a series of "Talmudic Readings." He chose to explore the Talmud because, in contrast to the Hebrew Bible, it is not part of the Christian Holy Scriptures and belongs to Judaism alone. As such it reveals the saying in the discussion by the Sages and invites the modern Western Jew to saying, by entering into a living dialogue with Torah, making manifest the unity of Torah that links the generations from Sinai to the present. Levinas also wishes to transform rabbinical discussion into a saying for the contemporary world. In one essay he shows how talmudic discussion arrived at a fully ethical solution to today's issues between management and labor.*

* Annette Aronowitz, ed. and trans., *Nine Talmudic Readings by Emmanuel Levinas* (Bloomington: Indiana University Press, 1991).

bring out the truth. The unity of the word as *saying* stands firm across all time and assures the unity of Israel.

The Jews

For Levinas, Jewish history is sacred history. The patriarchs are alive. The Jews therefore are one body, chosen by God not for privileges but for the duty to be for-the-other. Jews have been given the law to give them distance from the violent flow of history, direct them from the immediate present toward what is to come. As God's gift of grace, the mitzvot give the Jewish people *kedushah,* "holiness," a term that equally means "separation," detachment from the self-centeredness of the world. Obedience to mitzvot brings God's face into the face of the Jew, as he or she faces the human other in ethical relationship, and thereby advances the coming of the Messiah. Standing under the law and anticipating the messianic times, Jews have run counter to general history and its violence.

The messianic time will bring the consummation of history when political violence and social injustice will cease. Basing his ideas on a talmudic discussion (B.T. Sanhedrin 97b–99a), Levinas points to an opinion that the Messiah is found—daily—among the outcasts of "Rome" and reveals himself "when you hearken" to God's "voice," God's *saying,* and in response return to morality and turn your face to the outcasts.

Zionism can therefore be regarded as a form of modern messianism. It rests on the election of Israel and is part of sacred history, not a will to power. The modern Jew has entered political history and taken it seriously. The State of Israel is a political body within history and a spiritual one outside of it.

The Holocaust

Levinas refuses "to make an exhibition of the Passion of Passions"—the Holocaust—though "the world has learned nothing and forgotten everything." He will not talk about the events, they will echo through eternity. He looks instead for a lesson in the unspeakable. Raising the questions, why God did not interfere and what Jews must learn from God remaining hidden, he answers by telling a hasidic story, entitled "I Love the Torah More Than God," which is based on a Midrash in which God says "Would that they forsake Me but kept my Torah."[4]

In this work Levinas concludes that Jewish existence is a particular, essential, and anachronistic category of being. The Jews are outside the world by being committed to Torah-given responsibility for the other, inside the world as the world's monitor. God is preserved in the world because the Jewish people carry forth the moral principles of the Torah. When these principles are violated, God is not there, and the Jews have to suffer and die.

God, even when concealed, calls on all of humanity to carry out its responsibility. Even if God is hidden, the Torah, humanity's link with God, is still there and calls humankind to affirm God in the world by assuming responsibility. When God is hidden and divine assistance withdrawn, the task becomes superhuman, and falls upon the Jews. Thus the modern Jew lives in two worlds. Levinas emphasizes the right and duty of modern Jews to involve themselves in history and politics but warns them not to be swallowed up by them. Judaism is not judged by history—Judaism is called to judge it.

FEMINIST JEWISH THEOLOGY: JUDAISM AND CHANGE

The feminist movement in Judaism grew from the ethical imperatives of our time, given special force by the tragedy of the Holocaust. CYNTHIA OZICK (born 1928) has pointed out that the loss of six million Jews provides a particularly compelling reason not to dispense with the full contribution of half of the Jews—the Jewish women. To her, the loss of Jewish women to

---

4. Emmanuel Levinas, *Difficile Liberté: Essais sur le judaisme*, 3d ed. (Paris: Editions Albin Michel, 1983), pp. 189–93; see Susan A. Handelman, *Fragments of Redemption: Jewish Thoughts & Literary Theory in Benjamin, Scholem, and Levinas* (Bloomington: Indiana University Press, 1991), p. 275–78.

the Jewish people is more severe than the Holocaust itself: the Jews have thereby practiced "cultural self-destruction."[5]

Jewish feminists find that although women have recently been granted fuller participation in the male-oriented world of Judaism, the progress has been inadequate. Reconstruction of Judaism is necessary. Judaism must be founded on the affirmation that the Jewish community encompasses women and men as equals; women must be granted equal rights in its evolution. Aware that this reconstruction will be radical, Jewish feminists have pointed out that an equally radical reformation took place after the destruction of the Second Temple, when Judaism, for the sake of its survival, was given wholly new foundations. This need has arisen again.

Although reconstruction entails creating new concepts of Torah, God, and Israel, feminist theologies remain within the boundaries of Judaism. The divine is experienced within a Jewish framework. Inclusive ethical monotheism remains central. The theologies draw on the ancient texts and sources of Judaism and concern the Jewish community. They assume the observance of the liturgical year, Shabbat, and the festivals, as well as the ritual celebration of life-cycle events.

Jewish feminists share a commitment to the sources of Judaism and call on Jews to expand the interpretive tradition. Ancient texts are being reexamined from the point of view of gender, not only to uncover the hidden voices of women but also to shape how we understand the text. In broadening the ethical terms, a new vision of Jewish religious teaching is evolving. Many women have also contributed to the interpretive tradition through the composition of new, women-oriented midrash, for midrash has always developed and expanded the meaning of Torah. These new interpretations transform how Jews understand the texts. The texts, in turn, shape the self-understanding of the Jew. Seeking to break down the hierarchical thinking that has been a source of injustice, feminist theologians stress that expanding the interpretative tradition builds an ethic of inclusion and equality.

5. Quoted in Naomi Pasachoff, *Great Jewish Thinkers: Their Lives and Work* (Springfield, N.J.: Behrman House, 1992), p. 211.

A crucial issue for many Jewish women is halakhah, which has been male-centered and has degraded women to second-class, peripheral Jews. Feminist Jews have both looked for equality by means of an interpretation of halakhah and have considered a Judaism outside of halakhah. They have inspired new halakhah to be implemented.

Cynthia Ozick and BLU GREENBERG (born 1936), both bound to tradition, believe that halakhah is flexible enough to respond to the demands of Jewish women. Greenberg holds that women should take part in the halakhic process, and Ozick maintains that women can fashion new halakhah of their own, if inclusion can be achieved in no other way. Other feminists have come to stand outside of traditional halakhah.

Rachel Adler

Moving from Reform Judaism to Orthodoxy and then back to Reform, Rachel Adler believed that through interpretation, change was possible within traditional halakhah; she later came to stand outside of traditional halakhah. She points out that traditional halakhah sees women as peripheral Jews, and in Torah, only men represent normative Judaism. Boys and slaves are also peripheral Jews but become normative with age or their freedom—only the position of women remains unchanged. The woman remains an "inferior" Jew. Adler envisions a community of women and men, both standing under the covenant as equals, both covenantally creating a liberal, dynamic halakhah. Jews must create a just society of human beings in ever-changing relationship to each other.

There are problems—political, social, and ethical—in the traditional image of God as exclusively male. Such an image confines our understanding of the One God. In the "exclusively masculine language with which we currently refer to God, … selected metaphors have been taken to represent the totality of the God toward whom they point."[6] Jews must "enrich and diversify the language" of the prayer books and find words and

6. Rachel Adler, *Engendering Judaism: An Inclusive Theology and Ethics* (Philadelphia: The Jewish Publication Society, 1998), p. 66

metaphors for God that include "feminine forms and imagery."[7] Jews must not, however, expunge anthropomorphism because God is a deeply personal Being who commands and reveals and, above all, relates. Thus for Adler, "the most powerful language for God's *engagement* with us is our human language of relationship."[8] For, we

> cannot talk about the God of Israel without talking about the creator, dweller in the thornbush, liberator, covenanter, nursing mother, adversary, voice in the whirlwind, scribe, judge, and exiled Shekhinah.[9]

Marcia Falk

Marcia Falk (born 1946) has become known for the prayers she has written, some of which have been incorporated into non-Orthodox prayer books. Her blessings reveal her theology: God cannot be conceived in anthropocentric terms, either male or female:

> For as long as we image divinity exclusively as a person, whether female or male, we tend to forget that human beings are not the sole, not even the "primary" life-bearing creatures on the planet.... And in doing so, we neglect the real responsibility attendant upon the gift of human consciousness: to care for the earth in ways that respect all human and nonhuman life upon it.[10]

Neither can God be understood as transcendent, for this creates a dualism, such as God and the world or God and human beings, and this dualism leads to the foundation of hierarchy in the human world as well. Instead, God is wholly immanent, permeates the universe, is fully in the world, not above it, and fully within women, men, and all of creation. The

7. Adler, *Engendering Judaism*, pp. 66–67.
8. Adler, *Engendering Judaism*, p. 96.
9. Adler, *Engendering Judaism*, p. 96.
10. Marcia Falk, "Notes on Composing New Blessings: Toward a Feminist-Jewish Reconstruction of Prayer," in *Weaving the Visions: New Patterns in Feminist Spirituality*, ed. Judith Plaskow and Carol P. Christ (San Francisco: Harper, 1989), p.132.

"authentic expression of an authentic monotheism is ... an embracing *unity of a multiplicity of images,* as many as are needed to express and reflect the diversity of our individual lives."[11] Falk has, therefore, explored and extended the full range of biblical metaphors for God—"Rock of Israel," "Tree of Life"—to include metaphors such as "Source of Life," "Breath of All Living Things."

The traditional blessing formula, "Blessed are You, God our God, King of the universe," can be replaced, for example, with "Let us bless," thereby eliminating the problems of male image, hierarchical inequality, anthropocentrism, and transcendence.

Torah is the creation of the Jewish people. Its core teachings—the call to justice and compassion—have inspired and unified the Jewish people. In obedience to these calls, the concept of Israel's chosenness must be eliminated, for it regards non-Jews as not equal. "Rather, than wishing for a world in which all worship as Jews, we might instead strive toward harmony within diversity, toward unity achieved through mutual respect."[12]

Ellen Umansky

Ellen Umansky (born 1950) is in sympathy with Reform Judaism, especially its principles of ethical monotheism, ongoing revelation, and service to God by serving others. Umansky responds to Mordecai Kaplan as he advocates unity in diversity, gives halakhah a voice but no veto, advocates change, and is filled with love for *K'lal Yisrael.*

God is a personal being, commanding and revealing. But the way we imagine God affects our human relationships. Seeing God as king—or queen—creates a hierarchical distinction and leads us to differentiate between races and peoples, women and men, different classes, or ages, or religions. Such thinking "encourages an envisioning of the human–Divine relationship as one of domination and submission" and "establishes this

11. Falk, "Notes," p. 129.
12. Marcia Falk, *The Book of Blessings: New Jewish Prayers for Daily Life, the Sabbath, and the New Moon Festival* (Boston: Beacon Press, 1996), p. 485.

relationship as a model of how things really are."[13] We need instead to create a new image of divinity that will encourage us to "work with God rather than under God's authority."[14] Perceiving God as male *and* female eliminates the distinction between the genders that gives males power and authority, since all humans are created in the divine image.

God is both transcendent and immanent. The existence of evil, injustice, and suffering suggest that God is "neither all-powerful nor all-good." God is so great and so One that God can embrace contradictory or antagonistic attributes and be weak and powerful, evil and good. Umansky explains that "by limiting God, we have in fact limited God's greatness."[15]

We stand under the covenant, which establishes "relation between souls and souls." No self is fully autonomous but depends on the other.

Umansky has created feminist midrashim, for example, her "How did Sarah feel when Abraham took Isaac to be sacrificed?" These feminist midrash focus on women who are mentioned in the Bible but otherwise ignored. The new midrash see women, not as Other, but as normative Jews whose experiences, as we can reconstruct them, transform previously held convictions.

Judith Plaskow

Judith Plaskow (born 1947) is the most radical of the current Jewish feminists. She envisions a feminist society within Judaism. God, Torah, and Israel need to be given new definitions through women's voices. A new midrash is needed in order to make the word of Torah relevant for our times (which was the purpose of the old midrash for its time—in relationship to the male). Torah was written by men and speaks to them; it does not represent the experiences of all Jews. In it women are not normative Jews. Therefore a women's Torah is needed.

13. Ellen Umansky, "Jewish Feminist Theology," in Eugene B. Borowitz, *Choices in Modern Jewish Thought: A Partisan Guide*, 2d ed. (Springfield, N.J.: Behrman House, 1995), p. 337.
14. Umansky, "Jewish Feminist Theology," p. 337.
15. Umansky, "Jewish Feminist Theology," p. 337.

Torah must be read anew to reveal women's voices, lives, and contributions.

The covenant must be affirmed with women and men as equal partners. The concept of Jewish chosenness must, however, be eliminated, as it contains hierarchical distinctions between Jews and other people and among Jews themselves. Israel, too, maintains these hierarchical distinctions among Jews and between Jews and the Palestinians, and Plaskow calls for change. In addition, the validity of halakhah must be rejected because it is law and law is a male form that excludes women. Therefore, all rules must instead be based on women's values—fluidity and relationship—and be made through communal process. The Jews and the people in Israel must, in all institutions, give equality to women and incorporate the women's viewpoint.

God must be redefined. Speaking of a female god retains hierarchical features and is therefore inappropriate: a god-queen is no better than a god-king. God is neither Other nor a separate being. God therefore cannot reveal anything and does not act in history. Rather, God is the energy that permeates the universe, the sustaining ground of the human community, with which we come to be in touch through new interpretations. Changing the social order therefore means, not working with God, but participating in God.

Nevertheless, Plaskow affirms that "the history of the Jewish people is intelligible only as a history of response to the encounter with God in Jewish experience."[16] In understanding God, Plaskow seeks a fully inclusive monotheism, for an

> individual image of God is part of the divine totality that in its totality embraces the diversity of an infinite community. Only when our metaphors for God are sufficiently inclusive that they reflect the multiplicity both of a pluralistic Israel and of a cosmic community will God truly be one—which is to say, all in all.[17]

We note in the work of these feminist theologians the influence of Franz Rosenzweig's *speech-thinking* and Martin Buber's

16. Judith Plaskow, *Standing Again at Sinai: Judaism from a Feminist Perspective* (San Francisco: Harper and Row, 1990), p. xviii.
17. Plaskow, *Standing Again at Sinai,* p. 151.

I and Thou. It may be interesting to explore to what degree inspiration may have come to feminists out of Jewish mysticism. In Kabbalah, we find the utterly transcendent God, who cannot be reached or defined at all and does not allow any anthropomorphism. We also find the God of the *sefirot,* in whom both the masculine and the feminine are found, as well as contradictory attributes. This God is dependent on human beings, especially on the Jews, who, in covenant with the divine, can bring about *tikkun.*

As the dialogue around and about the work of these theologians develops and expands, Judaism and humanity will have a growing body of work to draw and expound upon, enriching the possibilities for discourse.

ELIE WIESEL: MESSENGER OF PEACE

In 1986 Elie Wiesel (born 1928) received the Nobel Peace Prize. The citation reads, "Wiesel is a messenger to humanity. His message is one of peace and atonement and human dignity. The message is in the form of a testimony, repeated and deepened through the works of a great author."

Elie Wiesel earned the Nobel Prize for bringing the Holocaust to the conscience of humanity and at the same time transforming it from a memory into a call for universal peace and justice. He conceived the National Holocaust Museum in Washington, D. C., dedicated in 1993.

Born in Szeged, Transylvania, Wiesel grew up in a traditional Jewish milieu. Still a young boy, he was taken by the Nazis, dragged from one concentration camp to the other. From despair in God he rose to affirmation. Auschwitz thus became for him a new Sinai and, he suggests, should become the same for us.

Rescued and brought to France, he studied under the same teacher as did Levinas, Mordechai Shushani. There are affinities between Wiesel and Levinas: their rootedness in tradition, their affirmation that Jews and Judaism have a unique position in the world and a unique message for it, their basic commitment to the *other.*

Wiesel, in his gripping novels, is a witness to the Holocaust, its external cruelties and the internal life of the condemned

Jews. The Holocaust not only taught him that Jews are bidden to affirm the necessity of their survival as a unique people chosen by God to assume responsibility but also revealed to him anew the beauty and significance of mitzvot. He has called upon Jews to realize that every single Jew is a spokesperson for all Jews and must assume the responsibility to make the world more human.

Wiesel accepted this task as the purpose of his life. Settling in America, holding a distinguished professorship at Boston University, he felt compelled to be witness to the world, admonishing it and pleading with it and judging it by the teachings of Torah. Wiesel, "a messenger to humanity" out of commitment to Torah, has turned his face to the *other.* His prophetic voice is speaking out against all injustice throughout the world.

EUGENE B. BOROWITZ:
POSTMODERNISM AND LIBERAL JUDAISM

Rabbi Eugene B. Borowitz (born 1924), a scholar and teacher, has been Distinguished Professor of Education and Jewish Religious Thought at Hebrew Union College–Jewish Institute of Religion for over thirty years and has also taught at Harvard and other universities. He has examined the Jewish condition and strove to provide contemporary non-Orthodox Jews with guiding principles for an authentic Jewish life. His numerous books combine scholarship with accessibility, and are written for the average intelligent reader. Speaking for Judaism, he has also critically responded to contemporary Christology. In 1970, he founded the biweekly *Sh'ma: A Journal of Jewish Responsibility,* providing critical evaluation of all societal and religious issues out of the resources of Judaism and open to all shades of opinion.

Borowitz wishes to lead non-Orthodox Jews to a renewed affirmation of the Covenant. He wrote his definitive theological work, *Renewing the Covenant: A Theology for the Postmodern Jew,* with this intent. Borowitz analyzes the condition of American Jewry, and provides it with an action program.

The Covenant in Modern History

The Holocaust demolished the modern age, disclosing that reason and science can degenerate into absolute evil. Out of their existential distress, Jews turned once again to the personal transcendent God, their partner in the Covenant. At Auschwitz they tragically discovered the absence of God, but the restoration of the State of Israel and its victory in the Six Day War disclosed the return of the divine presence. Jews stood at the recovered Western Wall, giving tearful thanks to God. The postmodern theologian has the task of calling Jews back to a renewal of the Covenant. Jews need not isolate themselves from world culture and society, and the non-Orthodox must retain their reliance on individual autonomy.

God-Israel-Torah

The Covenant unfolds through the interaction of God, Israel, and Torah. They are one and inseparable: God has an ongoing direct historical relationship with Israel, structured by Torah. This Covenant with Israel, superimposed on a covenant with all humankind, is confirmed in mandates of duty, not theology. Judaism rests on deeds in obedience to the divine command, as disclosed in Torah. Non-Orthodox Judaism affirms that Jewish action is the yardstick of Jewish faith and maintains that living within Judaism means that the Jew is committed to God's demands found in Torah. The traditional conception of Torah is reinterpreted, and with it the absolute authority of halakhah: Jews need the regular performance of mitzvot, knowing that every act expresses duty toward God; rituals and sacred acts bring the divine into commonplace life and express the reality of the Covenant.

Religious practice strengthens the individual's consciousness of God, otherwise obscured by the routine and confusion of daily life, and gives hope amidst disappointments.

Borowitz firmly rejects the traditional representation of God as male, expressed by addressing "him" as the Lord, the King. Faith in the transcendent God may not include any element by which any human would be debased. Feminists are correct, the male hierarchic element must be eliminated.

In the context of the regular performance of mitzvot, a person may even be granted an immediate awareness of the presence and the compassionate help of God. The true ground of being for Jews is the absolute, transcendent God who is One, truly ultimate and without equal. Reversing Isaac Luria's concept that God contracted in order to make room for the universe, Borowitz calls for a human *tzimtzum*: the human being has to retract self-importance to make room for God. At the same time, Borowitz reaffirms the traditional Jewish position that, having entered a Covenant with Israel, God yielded a part of the divine absolute power to humans.

Borowitz concludes that although neither religion nor science can claim a full knowledge of reality and how it works, Jewish belief may return to its traditional affirmations of God to uncover God's relationships to the world, humanity, and Jews. These affirmations tell us what God does, for example,

1. God creates the world. The morning prayer speaks of God renewing daily the work of creation.

2. God everlastingly presents all of humankind with gifts. Usually people appreciate God's gifts only at the emotional high points in life, but Judaism hopes to give its adherents a constant consciousness and thankfulness for the ordinary, daily gifts of God, like the bread God "brings forth from the earth."

3. Revelation, like creation, is for Borowitz, as for Buber and Rosenzweig, a constant living encounter with the living God, the eternal *Thou*, to whom Jews respond in mitzvot. These remain sacred as long as they authentically reflect or renew the individual Jew's relationship with God.

4. God has chosen the people of Israel. Borowitz affirms the chosenness of the Jewish people, which is unique and stands under an exclusive divine command that establishes its particularity.

5. God rewards and punishes. After the Holocaust this has become an especially painful subject. Borowitz affirms that the Jews did not suffer their passion and death because they had in any way sinned. Ultimately, he acknowledges that he has no answer to the questions raised by the Holocaust.

Israel: The People That Creates the Way

Every Jew is intricately bound up with his or her Jewishness. The nation that emerged from the encounter at Sinai bound itself in a relationship with God and one another—the Covenant. We can therefore never separate individual personhood from Jewishness. For Jews to regard themselves as persons-in-general who happen also-to-be-Jews is an error. The Jewish people has a sacred status with special obligations to God, and through that status becomes an instrument of redemption. Jews must shape a sacred society for themselves and all future generations.

Covenantal non-halakhic Jews must fervently seek to serve God as participants in the Jewish people's historic relationship with God, adjusting halakhah as dictated by their faithfulness to the Covenant. The non-Orthodox religious Jew therefore has the burden of determining which mitzvah is demanded of him or her, considering partnership with God in decision making. The binding force of the mitzvot does not reside in the Jewish people and its ways but in God's commanding voice.

The Covenant and the Non-Orthodox Jew

Borowitz points to five basic premises and principles of Jewish duty that must guide the Jew in a life of the Covenant:

1. Jews stand under a special Covenant in addition to the covenant of Noah.
2. Jewish ethnicity is an element of the Covenant. Covenant means Covenant-with-all-other-Jews past and present.
3. The Covenant places the Jew in Jewish history, linking the Jew to the entire history of the Jewish people. Covenant means Covenant-with-prior-Jewish-generations.
4. The Covenant orients the Jew toward the future, ultimately the coming of the Messiah. Covenant means Covenant-with-Jews-yet-to-be especially the Messiah.
5. The ultimate responsibility to decide what God commands lies within the individual. Covenant means Covenant-with-oneself.

Borowitz aims to bring about Jewish unity among the varieties of Jewish belief, all living under the Covenant.

CONCLUSION

Jewish theologians have historically held a unique position. In some ways they were marginal compared to the centrality of the study and practice of Torah and mitzvot. Their thoughts are often "autobiographical," reflecting their individual lives and representing their ideological views. But they also have held a central position. In their works they give a portrayal of the condition of Jewry in different times and within the context of different general cultures.

Viewing the conditions of their time in the light of eternity and committed to offering guidelines for authentic Jewish living and survival amidst the currents of ever-changing situations, they have in their overwhelming majority affirmed all or most of certain basic principles:

1. The Jewish people, the people of the Covenant with God, is of divine election.
2. Response to God in Covenant is by deeds—mitzvot—not theological contemplation or "faith" alone.
3. Immersion in the study of Torah reveals and deepens the Jewish covenantal relationship to God.
4. Jews are a "household," a community that unites all living Jews and all the generations of Jews, past, present, and future.
5. Eretz Yisrael is a religious element in Judaism.
6. The messianic expectation is both a sustaining force and one of the greatest contributions of Judaism to humanity.
7. Jews, under God, therefore function for the future of humanity.

This wide unanimity, in spite of the different shadings, reveals the unity of the Jewish people and the universality of the duties imposed on every Jew. Exactly because these thinkers represent so many different periods, were so deeply involved in the cultures of their surroundings, and reflect such profound differences in ideology, their virtual unanimity on fundamental requirements becomes an affirmation of Jewish unity. Herein lies a challenge to every Jew and an assurance of Jewish eternity and the coming of the messianic age. Returning to these foundations, Jews will be able to transcend their internal differences, overcome external foes, and, standing as witnesses for God, be assured of eternity.

BIBLIOGRAPHY

GENERAL INTEREST

Barnavi, Eli, ed. *A Historical Atlas of the Jewish People from the Time of the Patriarchs to the Present.* New York: Knopf, 1992.
Ben-Sasson, H. H., ed. *A History of the Jewish People.* Cambridge, Mass.: Harvard University Press, 1976.
Encyclopedia Judaica. 16 vols. New York: Macmillan, 1971-1972.
Johnson, Paul. *A History of the Jews.* New York: Harper and Row, 1987.
Seltzer, Robert M. *Jewish People, Jewish Thought: The Jewish Experience in History.* New York: Macmillan, 1980.
Wigoder, Geoffrey, ed. *The Encyclopedia of Judaism.* New York: Macmillan, 1989.

TORAH (CHAPTERS 1–3, 22)

Alter, Robert, and Frank Kermode, eds. *The Literary Guide to the Bible.* Cambridge, Mass.: Harvard University Press, 1987.
Tanakh: A New Translation of the Holy Scriptures According to the Traditional Hebrew Text. Philadelphia: Jewish Publication Society of America, 1985.

ORAL TORAH: MISHNAH, TALMUD, MIDRASH (CHAPTERS 4–5, 23)

Alon, Gedaliah. *The Jews in Their Land in the Talmudic Age, 70–640 C.E.* Jerusalem: Magnes Press, Hebrew University, 1980–1984.
Bialik, Hayim Nahman, and Joshua Chana Ravnitzky, eds. *The Book of Legends, Sefer Ha-Aggadah: Legends of the Talmud and Midrash.* New York: Schocken Books, 1992.
Cohen, A. *Everyman's Talmud.* New York: E. P. Dutton, 1949.
Cohen, Shaye J. D. *From the Maccabees to the Mishnah.* Philadelphia: Westminster Press, 1987.
Goldin, Judah. *The Living Talmud: The Wisdom of the Fathers and Its Classical Commentaries.* Chicago: University of Chicago Press, 1957.

Herford, Robert Travers, ed. *The Ethics of the Talmud: Sayings of the Fathers.* New York: Schocken, 1962.

Holtz, Barry W., ed. *Back to the Sources: Reading the Classic Jewish Texts.* New York: Summit Books, 1984.

Montefiore, C. G., and H. Loewe. *A Rabbinic Anthology.* New York: Meridian Books, 1960.

Neusner, Jacob. *Judaism in the Beginning of Christianity.* Philadelphia: Fortress Press, 1984.

———. *What is Midrash?* Philadelphia: Fortress Press, 1987.

Neusner, Jacob, ed. *The Study of Ancient Judaism.* New York: Ktav, 1981.

———. *A Midrash Reader.* Minneapolis: Fortress Press, 1990.

———. *Scriptures of the Oral Torah, Sanctification and Salvation in the Sacred Books of Judaism: An Anthology.* San Francisco: Harper and Row, 1987.

Neusner, Jacob, trans. *The Mishnah: A New Translation.* New Haven, Conn.: Yale University Press, 1988.

Nickelsburg, George W. E. *Jewish Literature between the Bible and the Mishnah: A Historical and Literary Introduction.* Philadelphia: Fortress Press, 1981.

Strack, Hermann L. Ed. Gunter Stemberger. *Introduction to the Midrash and Talmud.* Edinburgh: Clark, 1991.

JUDAISM AND CHRISTIANITY (CHAPTER 6)

Manuel, Frank. *The Broken Staff: Judaism through Christian Eyes.* Cambridge, Mass.: Harvard University Press, 1992.

ASHKENASIC JEWRY (CHAPTERS 8–9, 12–13)

Gay, Ruth. *The Jews of Germany: A Historical Portrait.* New Haven, Conn.: Yale University Press, 1992.

Richarz, Monika, ed. Trans. Stella P. Rosenfield and Sidney Rosenfield. *Jewish Life in Germany: Memoirs from Three Centuries.* Bloomington, Ind.: Indiana University Press, 1991.

REASON, ENLIGHTENMENT, AND THE JEWS (CHAPTER 12)

Altmann, Alexander. *Moses Mendelssohn: A Biographical Study.* Philadelphia: Jewish Publication Society of America, 1973.

Denominations (Chapters 13, 17)

Gillman, Neil. *Conservative Judaism: The New Century.* Springfield, N.J.: Behrman House, 1993.

Kaplan, Mordecai M. *Judaism as a Civilization: Toward a Reconstruction of American Jewish Life.* Philadelphia: Schocken Books, 1967.

———. *The Meaning of God in Modern Jewish Religion.* New York: Jewish Reconstructionist Foundation, 1947.

Meyer, Michael A. *Response to Modernity: A History of the Reform Movement in Judaism.* New York: Oxford University Press, 1988.

Soloveitchik, Joseph Dov. *The Halakhic Mind: An Essay on Jewish Tradition and Modern Thought.* Ardmore, Pa.: Seth Press, 1986.

Zionism (Chapter 15)

Buber, Martin. *On Zion: The History of an Idea.* New York: Schocken Books, 1973.

Hammer, Reuven, ed. *The Jerusalem Anthology: A Literary Guide.* Philadelphia: Jewish Publication Society of America, 1995.

Hoffman, Lawrence A., ed. *The Land of Israel: Jewish Perspectives.* Notre Dame, Ind.: University of Notre Dame Press, 1986.

Kornberg, Jacques. *Theodor Herzl: From Assimilation to Zionism.* Bloomington, Ind.: Indiana University Press, 1993.

Laqueur, Walter. *A History of Zionism.* New York: Holt, Rhinehart, and Winston, 1972.

Wistrich, Robert S. *Antisemitism: The Longest Hatred.* New York: Pantheon Books, 1991.

America (Chapters 16–17)

Hertzberg, Arthur. *The Jews in America: Four Centuries of an Uneasy Encounter.* New York: Simon and Schuster, 1989.

Howe, Irving. *World of Our Fathers.* New York: Harcourt Brace Jovanovich, 1976.

Karp, Abraham J. *Haven and Home: A History of the Jews in America.* New York: Schocken Books, 1985.

Marcus, Jacob Rader, ed. *The Jew in the American World: A Sourcebook.* Detroit: Wayne State University Press, 1996.

Weinberg, Sydney S. *World of Our Mothers: The Lives of Jewish Immigrant Women.* Chapel Hill, N.C.: University of North Carolina Press, 1988.

THE HOLOCAUST (CHAPTERS 18–19)

Bauer, Yehuda. *A History of the Holocaust.* New York: F. Watts, 1982.

Engelmann, Bernt. *In Hitler's Germany: Daily Life under the Nazis.* New York: Pantheon Books, 1985.

Friedlander, Albert H., ed. *Out of the Whirlwind: A Reader of Holocaust Literature.* New York: Schocken Books, 1976.

Gutan, Yisraek. *Anatomy of Auschwitz.* Bloomington, Ind.: Indiana University Press, 1994.

Hilberg, Raul. *The Destruction of the European Jews.* New York: Harper and Row, 1979.

Langer, Lawrence L. *Holocaust Testimonies: The Ruins of Memory.* New Haven, Conn.: Yale University Press, 1991.

Ringelblum, Emmanuel. *Notes from the Warsaw Ghetto: The Journal of Emmanuel Ringelblum.* New York: Schocken Books, 1974.

Senesh, Hannah. *Her Life and Diary.* New York: Schocken Books, 1972.

Swiebocka, Teresa, ed. *Auschwitz: A History in Photographs.* Bloomington, Ind.: Indiana University Press, 1993.

Volavkova, Hana, ed. *I Never Saw Another Butterfly: Children's Drawings and Poems from Terezin Concentration Camp.* New York: Schocken Books, 1978.

RELIGIOUS OBSERVANCE (CHAPTERS 24–30)

Dorff, Eliott, and Louis E. Newman, eds. *Contemporary Jewish Ethics and Morality: A Reader.* New York: Oxford University Press, 1995.

Falk, Marcia. *The Book of Blessings: New Jewish Prayers for Daily Life, the Sabbath, and the New Moon Festival.* Boston: Beacon Press, 1996.

Greenberg, Irving. *The Jewish Way: Living the Holidays.* New York: Summit Books, 1988.

Hoffman, Lawrence A. *Beyond the Text: A Holistic Approach to Liturgy.* Bloomington, Ind.: Indiana University Press, 1987.

Klein, Isaac. *A Guide to Jewish Religious Practice.* New York: Jewish Theological Seminary of America, 1979.

Saperstein, Marc, ed. *Jewish Preaching 1200–1800: An Anthology.* New Haven, Conn.: Yale University Press, 1989.

Steinsalz, Adin. Ed. and trans. Michael Swirsky. *Teshuvah: A Guide for the Newly Observant Jew.* New York: Free Press, 1987.

Trepp, Leo. *The Complete Book of Jewish Observance.* Springfield, N.J.: Behrman House, 1980.

WOMEN (CHAPTERS 31 AND 35)

Adler, Rachel. *Engendering Judaism: An Inclusive Theology and Ethics.* Philadelphia: The Jewish Publication Society, 1998.

Baskin, Judith R., ed. *Jewish Women in Historical Perspective.* Detroit: Wayne State University Press, 1991.

Biale, Rachel. *Women and Jewish Law: An Exploration of Women's Issues in Halakhic Sources.* New York: Schocken Books, 1984.

Cantor, Aviva. *Jewish Women, Jewish Men: The Legacy of Patriarchy in Jewish Life.* San Francisco: Harper, 1995.

Gluckel of Hameln. Trans. Marvin Lowenthal. *The Memoirs of Gluckel of Hameln.* New York: Schocken, 1977.

Heschel, Susannah, ed. *On Being a Jewish Feminist: A Reader.* New York: Schocken Books, 1983.

Plaskow, Judith. *Standing Again at Sinai: Judaism from a Feminist Perspective.* New York: Harper and Row, 1990.

Umansky, Ellen M., and Dianne Ashton, eds. *Four Centuries of Jewish Women's Spirituality: A Sourcebook.* Boston: Beacon Press, 1992.

MYSTICISM (CHAPTER 32)

Idel, Moshe. *Kabbalah: New Perspectives.* New Haven, Conn.: Yale University Press, 1988.

Matt, Daniel C., ed. *The Essential Kabbalah: The Heart of Jewish Mysticism.* San Francisco: Harper, 1995.

Scholem, Gershom Gerhard. *Major Trends in Jewish Mysticism.* New York: Schocken Books, 1961.

———. *On the Kabbalah and Its Symbolism.* New York: Schocken Books, 1965.

———. *Sabbatai Zevi: The Mystical Messiah.* Princeton, N.J.: Princeton University Press, 1973.

Scholem, Gershom Gerhard, ed. *Zohar: The Book of Splendor.* New York: Schocken, 1974.

Sperling, Harry, and Maurice Simon, trans. *The Zohar.* London: Soncino Press, 1934.

Jewish Thought (chapters 33–35)

Guttmann, Julius. *Philosophies of Judaism: The History of Jewish Philosophy from Biblical Times to Franz Rosenzweig.* New York: Schocken, 1973.

Pasachoff, Naomi. *Great Jewish Thinkers: Their Lives and Work.* Springfield, N.J.: Behrman House, 1992.

Ancient and Medieval Thought (chapter 33)

Husic, Isaac. *A History of Medieval Jewish Philosophy.* Philadelphia: Jewish Publication Society of America, 1941.

Lewy, Hans, Alexander Altmann, and Isaak Heinemann, eds. *Three Jewish Philosophers.* Philo, *Selections,* ed. Hans Lewy. Saadya Goan, *Book of Doctrines and Beliefs,* ed. Alexander Altman. Jehuda Halevi, *Kuzari,* ed. Isaak Heinemann. New York: Harper and Row, 1965.

Twersky, Isadore, ed. *A Maimonides Reader.* Springfield, N.J.: Behrman House, 1972.

Twentieth-Century Thought (chapters 34–35)

Cohen, Steven M. *American Assimilation or Jewish Revival.* Bloomington, Ind.: Indiana University Press, 1988.

Fishman, Hertzel. *The Challenge to Jewish Survival.* Springfield, N.J.: Behrman House, 1993.

Gillman, Neil. *Sacred Fragments: Recovering Theology for the Modern Jew.* Philadelphia: Jewish Publication Society of America, 1990.

Lerner, Michael. *Jewish Renewal: A Path to Healing and Transformation.* New York: Putnam Sons, 1994.

Schweid, Eliezer. *Jewish Thought in the 20th Century: An Introduction.* Atlanta: Scholars Press, 1992.

Franz Rosenzweig (chapter 34)

Glatzer, N. N., ed. *Franz Rosenzweig: His Life and Thought.* Indianapolis, Ind.: Hackett Publishing Co., 1998.

Rosenzweig, Franz. *The Star of Redemption*. New York: Holt, Rhinehart, and Winston, 1971.

Martin Buber (chapter 34)

Buber, Martin. *I and Thou*. Edinburg: T. and T. Clark, 1953.
———. *Legends of the Baal Shem*. New York: Harper, 1955.
———. *On Judaism*. New York: Schocken Books, 1967.
———. *Tales of the Hasidim*. New York: Schocken Books, 1961.

Abraham Joshua Heschel (chapter 35)

Heschel, Abraham Joshua. *God in Search of Man: A Philosophy of Judaism*. New York: Farrar, Straus, and Cudahy, 1955.
———. *Man Is Not Alone: A Philosophy of Judaism*. New York: Farrar, Straus, and Young, 1951.
———. *The Prophets*. New York: Harper and Row, 1962.
Merkle, John C. *The Genesis of Faith: The Depth Theology of Abraham Joshua Heschel*. New York: Macmillan, 1985.
Merkle, John C., ed. *Abraham Joshua Heschel: Exploring His Life and Thought*. New York: Macmillan, 1985.
Rothschild, Fritz. *Between God and Man: An Interpretation of Judaism from the Writings of Abraham Joshua Heschel*. New York: Free Press, 1959.

Emmanuel Levinas (chapter 35)

Levinas, Emmanuel. Ed. and trans. Annette Aronowitz. *Nine Talmudic Readings*. Bloomington, Ind: Indiana University Press, 1990.
Bernasconi, Robert, and Simon Critchley, eds. *Re-Reading Levinas*. Bloomington, Ind.: Indiana University Press, 1991.
Handleman, Susan A. *Fragments of Redemption: Jewish Thought and Literary Theory in Benjamin, Scholem, and Levinas*. Bloomington, Ind.: Indiana University Press, 1991.

Eugene B. Borowitz (chapter 35)

Borowitz, Eugene B. *Choices in Modern Jewish Thought: A Partisan Guide*. 2d ed. Springfield, N.J.: Behrman House, 1995.
———. *Renewing the Covenant: A Theology for the Post-Modern Jew*. Jewish Publication Society of America, 1991.

INDEX

Ten Commandments, 18
  Ark and, 308, 314
  See also Shavuot
teshuvah (teshuvot), 38, 345, 403–406, 410,
    412, 479
  See also Yom Kippur
Thirteen Articles of Faith
    (Maimonides), 118–119
Thirty Years War, 150
Tiberias, 76–77
  center of learning, 90
tikkun, 156, 162, 483
Tishah b'Av, 90, 371–372, 423, 426, 428–429
  See also Five Scrolls; Lamentations,
    Book of
Titus, 80–81
Torah, 3–22, 317–326
  Borowitz, Eugene B., 537–538
  definition, 4, 6–7
  Falk, Marcia, 531–532
  Gaon of Vilna, 165
  Halevi, Judah, 490–492
  Hasidism and, 162–163, 166–167
  Heschel, Abraham Joshua, 524–525
  Hillel, 330–331
  Hirsch, Samson Raphael, 190–191
  law, 104
  Levinas, Emmanuel, 526–528
  Maimonides, Moses, 492–495
  Mendelssohn, Moses, 175
  Plaskow, Judith, 533–535
  Rubenstein, Richard L., 519–520
  Spinoza, 170–171
  term, 317–318
  See also denominations; haftarah;
    Mishnah; mysticism; Oral Torah;
    Simhat Torah; Tanakh; prayer; worship
Torah scrolls, 6–7
  mantle for, 6–7
  scribes of, 6–7
  in synagogue, 310, 313, 314, 317–319
Torquemada, 120–121
Tosafot, 138
  Tosafists, 138–139
Twelve Tribes, 14–15

tzedakah, 134
  Purim and, 426

Umansky, Ellen, 532–533
Union of American Israel, 238
"Union of Israel", 166
Union of Orthodox Rabbis, 256
University for the Scientific Study of
    Judaism, 185
Vayikra. See Leviticus
Venice, Jews in, 150–151
Vespasian, 79–80, 89

Weizman, Chaim, 287
Wiesel, Elie, 535–536
Wise, Isaac Mayer, 223, 237–239
  See also Hebrew Union College
Wise, Stephen S., 230–232
women, 453–462
  feminist theology, 528–535
  mehitzah, 457–458
  organizations, 458
  religious duties, 455–457
    exclusion from, 457
  tradition and, 453–455
  See also Bible; worship
World Council of Synagogues, 252
World Jewry, xix–xx
  Israel and, 288–289
Worms, Germany, 126–128
worship, 362
  See also minyan; Pesah; prayer; Rosh
    Hashanah; Sabbath; Sukkot; Torah;
    Yom Kippur

Yahud. *See* Judaea
Yeshivah University, 256
yeshivot, 343
  Ashkenasic Jewry, 135
  Eastern Europe, 155
  Palestine and Babylonia, 93
  See also learning
Yiddish, 133
Yigdal (Maimonides), 118
Yishuv, 209, 211–213, 271–272, 281
  kibbutz, 211–212